Game Development with Godot 4 and C#

First Edition

Develop a dynamic 3D game while exploring a robust node system, level design, and animations

Kati Baker

<packt>

Game Development with Godot 4 and C#

First Edition

Portfolio Director: Rohit Rajkumar
Relationship Lead: Rohit Rajkumar
Project Manager: Sandip Tadge
Content Engineer: Shazeen Iqbal
Technical Editor: Tejas Mhasvekar
Copy Editor: Safis Editing
Indexer: Pratik Shirodkar
Proofreader: Shazeen Iqbal
Production Designer: Shantanu Zagade
Growth Lead: Namita Velgekar

First published: December 2025

Production reference: 1241225

Published by Packt Publishing Ltd.
Grosvenor House
11 St Paul's Square
Birmingham
B3 1RB, UK.

ISBN 978-1-80512-413-9

www.packtpub.com

I would like to dedicate this book to my wife and all who supported me in this process called writing.

– Kati Baker

Contributors

About the author

Kati Baker is a Staff Engineer who has been creating games since her first game jam in 2016. She is a programmer by trade and has spent part of her professional career in education, working as an Outreach Coordinator for NASA and a CS Innovator for 4-H. In both, she's worked with students to encourage learning in STEM, specifically computer science. In her spare time, she runs a monthly game jam, Godot Wild Jam, and completes her own personal projects. She has also given talks at leading conferences for her work with Godot. She is a big believer in continuing to learn, no matter what. Kati earned her Bachelors of Science in Computer Science from West Virginia University, and currently resides in West Virginia with her partner and plants.

I would like to thank my wife for continuing to nudge me in the direction I needed to get this book out the door. Huge thanks to my friends and colleagues for supporting me in this endeavor and occasionally asking me when it would be available for them. Here you are! The biggest thank you to every single person who has ever participated in the Godot Wild Jam. You're all Wildlings in my heart. Special thanks to Hayden Edwards and Shazeen Iqbal for their valuable edits. To Joanna of the Chickensoft community for valuable technical feedback. To Rohit Rajkumar, thank you for the kind words of encouragement on the final stretch when it felt impossible. To the entire Packt team for giving me this opportunity and continuing to believe in my ability to do this.

About the reviewer

Isaiah Jamiel is a software engineer and game developer based in Jakarta, Indonesia. He currently works as a .NET Software Engineer at Indocyber Global Teknologi, contributing to enterprise applications involving data integration, backend systems, and legacy application maintenance. Isaiah has prior experience as a full-stack developer and has led independent game development projects through NTC Studio, where he built games using Godot and C#. He holds a bachelor's degree in Cyber Security from Bina Nusantara University and has received recognition for his work in game development competitions.

Table of Contents

Chapter 3: Organizing and Setting Up a Project for a 3D Action Game 43

Part II: Creating a Simple 3D Action Game 63

Chapter 4: Creating Our Player Controller 65

Chapter 7: Adding Sound Effects and Music 217

Chapter 8: Adding Navigation and Pathfinding 243

Part III: Expanding Our 3D Action Game and Additional Resources 269

Chapter 9: Setting Up Lighting in Godot 271

Chapter 10: Understanding Accessibility and Additional Features 295

Chapter 13: Next Steps as a Godot Developer 367

Chapter 14: Unlock Your Exclusive Benefits 387

Appendix: Transitioning from Godot 3 to Godot 4 391

Preface

Godot is an open source game engine that enables developers to create interesting and unique projects, mainly video games. While Godot has a built-in scripting language called GDScript, C# has, over time, gained more support, especially in Godot 4.

Dedicated to Godot 4 and C#, this book guides you through creating a 3D project in Godot, using C# as the programming language from start to finish. In writing this book, I wanted to share my personal experience with Godot alongside my professional experience as a C# developer.

In this book, we will first discuss the relationship between the two and then spend time setting up our development environment. After that, we'll look at how best to organize our project to keep the assets and scripts as orderly as possible.

Once we have our development environment configured, we'll explore the various components to create a 3D action game. Some of those components will include a player controller, animations, user interface, sound effects, and pathfinding. Within each section, we'll discover more features built into Godot's engine and how best to leverage those features in our project.

As we wrap up a vertical slice of our 3D action game, we'll look at third-party plugins and applications that can improve our development life cycle. The last step for our project will be to export the game and publish it on the `itch.io` platform.

Finally, we will explore outside the game engine into the Godot community and see what other resources are available to Godot developers, such as C#-specific communities and other notable creators in the space.

Most of the features included in this book have been updated to Godot 4.4, and although the UI may change, the idea behind the usage can still be applied to future versions of Godot.

Who this book is for

This book is for developers and creators seeking more knowledge about the Godot Engine, specifically using Godot with C#. Experience with an object-oriented programming language is required to get the most out of this book.

What this book covers

Chapter 1, Introducing Godot 4, introduces the Godot Engine, including what makes it a viable game engine choice, and specific features that make it a worthwhile choice in game development projects.

Chapter 2, Understanding How C# Works in Godot, walks through the relationship between the Godot Engine and C#, as well as setting up a development environment to work fluidly between the two.

Chapter 3, Organizing and Setting Up a Project for a 3D Action Game, explores two different schools of thought when it comes to organizing a project for the rest of the book.

Chapter 4, Creating Our Player Controller, focuses on the player controller, creating animations, and keying controls to player actions.

Chapter 5, Creating Our Game World, illustrates the importance of level design, how to import a variety of assets, and how to add collision meshes to them for use in a level.

Chapter 6, Developing and Managing the User Interface, spends time creating a main menu to access the level and adding some simple animations to the UI.

Chapter 7, Adding Sound Effects and Music, explores sound buses and how to use them for either sound effects or music, and brings them together for UI, player actions, and level music.

Chapter 8, Adding Navigation and Pathfinding, implements navigation and pathfinding for a non-player character to autonomously move throughout the level.

Chapter 9, Setting Up Lighting in Godot, discusses lighting in a variety of ways, specifically for global illumination and interior lighting.

Chapter 10, Understanding Accessibility and Additional Features, reviews the project so far and highlights accessibility components, expanding the UI to accommodate a **Settings** screen.

Chapter 11, Exporting Your Game, walks through the process of exporting the project to multiple platforms and how it can be played by people outside the project.

Chapter 12, Contributing to Godot and Additional Resources, dives into how to contribute to the engine and provides feedback on issues while also highlighting third-party plugins to utilize in the project.

Chapter 13, Next Steps as a Godot Developer, explores the wider Godot community outside the engine, specifically C#-focused spaces.

Appendix: Transitioning from Godot 3 to Godot 4, provides insight on whether creators should upgrade to Godot 4, the benefits of doing so, and the process to upgrade.

To get the most out of this book

Prior programming knowledge is beneficial in getting the most out of this book. It's targeted at programmers with some experience but little to no Godot experience. No other technical set up is required as this book will walk you through everything you need.

To complete the exercises and examples provided in this book, you will need to download and install **Godot Engine 4.5.1**. You can download Godot Engine 4.5.1 (.NET version) from the official website at `https://godotengine.org/download/archive/4.5.1-stable/`.

Download the example code files

The code bundle for the book is hosted on GitHub at `https://github.com/PacktPublishing/Game-Development-with-Godot-4-and-C-Sharp`. We also have other code bundles from our rich catalog of books and videos available at `https://github.com/PacktPublishing`. Check them out!

Download the color images

We also provide a PDF file that has color images of the screenshots/diagrams used in this book. You can download it here: `https://packt.link/gbp/9781805124139`.

Conventions used

There are a few text conventions used throughout this book.

`CodeInText`: Indicates code words in text, database table names, folder names, filenames, file extensions, pathnames, dummy URLs, user input, and X (formerly Twitter) handles. For example: "Again, when `await` is read within an `async` method, it will not move on to the next line of code until the code to the right of the `await` word has finished executing."

A block of code is set as follows:

```
public void OnPlayClicked()
{
    GD.Print("Play button clicked");
    animPlayer.Play("MenuTransition");
    audioPlayer.Play();
```

```
    HideMenu();
}

public async void HideMenu()
{
    await Task.Delay(TimeSpan.FromSeconds(1));
    this.Visible = false;
}
```

Bold: Indicates a new term, an important word, or words that you see on the screen. For instance, words in menus or dialog boxes appear in the text like this. For example: "Enable the **Autoplay** checkbox and, most importantly, set the **Bus** property to **Music**."

> Warnings or important notes appear like this.

> Tips and tricks appear like this.

Get in touch

Feedback from our readers is always welcome.

General feedback: If you have questions about any aspect of this book or have any general feedback, please email us at `customercare@packt.com` and mention the book's title in the subject of your message.

Errata: Although we have taken every care to ensure the accuracy of our content, mistakes do happen. If you have found a mistake in this book, we would be grateful if you reported this to us. Please visit `http://www.packt.com/submit-errata`, click **Submit Errata**, and fill in the form.

Piracy: If you come across any illegal copies of our works in any form on the internet, we would be grateful if you would provide us with the location address or website name. Please contact us at `copyright@packt.com` with a link to the material.

If you are interested in becoming an author: If there is a topic that you have expertise in and you are interested in either writing or contributing to a book, please visit `http://authors.packt.com/`.

Subscribe to Game Dev Assembly Newsletter!

We are excited to introduce **Game Dev Assembly**, our brand-new newsletter dedicated to everything game development. Whether you're a programmer, designer, artist, animator, or studio lead, you'll get exclusive insights, industry trends, and expert tips to help you build better games and grow your skills. Sign up today and become part of a growing community of creators, innovators, and game changers.

`https://packt.link/gamedev-newsletter`

Scan the QR code to join instantly!

Share your thoughts

Once you've read *Game Development with Godot 4 and C#*, we'd love to hear your thoughts! Scan the QR code below to go straight to the Amazon review page for this book and share your feedback.

https://packt.link/r/1805124137

Your review is important to us and the tech community and will help us make sure we're delivering excellent quality content.

Free Benefits with Your Book

This book comes with free benefits to support your learning. Activate them now for instant access (see the "*How to Unlock*" section for instructions).

Here's a quick overview of what you can instantly unlock with your purchase:

PDF and ePub Copies

- Access a DRM-free PDF copy of this book to read anywhere, on any device.
- Use a DRM-free ePub version with your favorite e-reader.

Next-Gen Web-Based Reader

- **Multi-device progress sync**: Pick up where you left off, on any device.
- **Highlighting and notetaking**: Capture ideas and turn reading into lasting knowledge.
- **Bookmarking**: Save and revisit key sections whenever you need them.
- **Dark mode**: Reduce eye strain by switching to dark or sepia themes.

How to Unlock

UNLOCK NOW

Scan the QR code (or go to `packtpub.com/unlock`). Search for this book by name, confirm the edition, and then follow the steps on the page.

***Note:** Keep your invoice handy. Purchases made directly from Packt don't require one.*

Part 1

Understanding the Godot Engine and C#

In this first part of the book, you'll discover the Godot Engine, how it functions, and its relationship to the C# programming language. We'll explore creating a development environment, using Visual Studio Code, and create our own player controller with animations and controls. At the end of this part of the book, you'll have a solid foundation for how Godot operates and a rudimentary player controller. Lastly, you'll have a better understanding of the components needed for a clean project structure.

This part of the book includes the following chapters:

- *Chapter 1, Introducing Godot 4*
- *Chapter 2, Understanding How C# Works in Godot*
- *Chapter 3, Organizing and Setting Up a Project for a 3D Action Game*

Part 1

Understanding the Godot Engine and C#

1

Introducing Godot 4

Welcome to *Game Development with Godot and C#*, and thank you for taking this journey with me! You've probably picked up this book because you've heard about Godot and want to explore it as a viable game engine alternative. Or you've heard of Godot 4's latest release and want to know what all the hype is about. Or you've been using Godot and want to change how you use it. Or maybe you've never heard of Godot until now, but you know how C# works. No matter the reason, this book will teach you how to use C# in Godot and have fun while doing it.

We'll start this chapter by getting acquainted with the Godot Engine and setting up the tools we'll need for the exciting 3D action-adventure game we'll be making throughout the rest of the book. This chapter will serve as a foundation for getting comfortable in Godot and understanding in a broad sense what the engine is capable of feature-wise.

So, in this chapter, we will cover the following topics:

- What is the Godot Engine?
- How does the Godot Engine function?
- Navigating the Godot Engine

Technical requirements

All the code examples for the entire book can be found on GitHub here: `https://github.com/PacktPublishing/Game-Development-with-Godot-and-C-`.

Plus, to follow along with the book, you will need the following tools:

- The latest version of Godot (currently 4.5.1) installed
- The latest version of Microsoft's .NET SDK (currently .NET 8.0)
- An IDE (we will be using Visual Studio Code)
- C# extension as provided by Microsoft
- Knowing C# is not a prerequisite to utilizing this book, but knowing programming fundamentals and the **Object-Oriented Programming** (**OOP**) paradigm will be essential

Let's get those tools now.

Installing Godot 4

Download the Godot Engine, specifically Godot 4, by accessing this page: `https://godotengine.org/download`. The web page will auto-detect your operating system and present you with two download buttons – just **Godot Engine** and **Godot Engine - .NET**. We want the second option, which has C# support, so make sure to click that one.

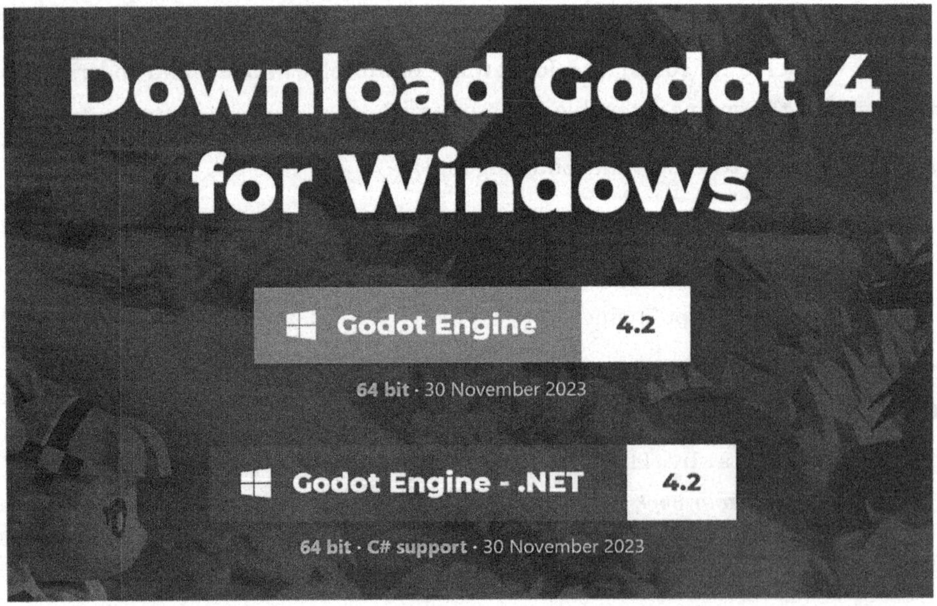

Figure 1.1: The download web page for Godot 4

After downloading the correct version of Godot, all that's left to do is extract the `.zip` file. Godot does not include an installation, so once the file is extracted, you can run it immediately with no additional setup.

Next, we will look at downloading the .NET SDK.

Downloading the .NET SDK

Alongside the .NET version of Godot, you also need to have Microsoft's .NET SDK. This will provide you with the **Microsoft Build Engine (MSBuild)** to compile the project we will build. MSBuild is what creates our `.csproj` file within our project and allows us to compile our code.

Download the latest stable version of Microsoft's .NET SDK from here: `https://dotnet.microsoft.com/en-us/download`.

Choosing an environment

While Godot has a built-in editor for writing scripts, it's best to download your own **integrated development environment** (**IDE**) or code editor when using C#. The biggest difference between an IDE and a code editor is that an IDE has more tools available for development, whereas a code editor is a text editor for code. For more information on supported IDEs and editors, visit `https://docs.godotengine.org/en/stable/engine_details/development/configuring_an_ide/index.html`.

For this book, I will be using Visual Studio Code (a code editor) and will walk you through how to set it up. You can download Visual Studio Code here: `https://code.visualstudio.com/`. Once installed and launched, you will need to configure it for use with Godot. Click on the **Extensions** button on the left-hand side (it's right below the **Debug** button that looks like a little bug with a play button). The button that has the blue two on it in *Figure 1.2* is the button to click.

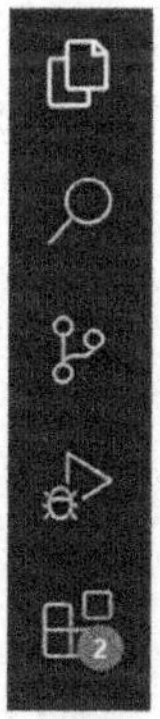

Figure 1.2: The toolbar on the left-hand side of Visual Studio Code

After opening the **Extensions** page, type `C#` in the search bar, and you should see a list of options come up. Select the one that says **C#**, making sure the creator is **Microsoft**, and click **Install**.

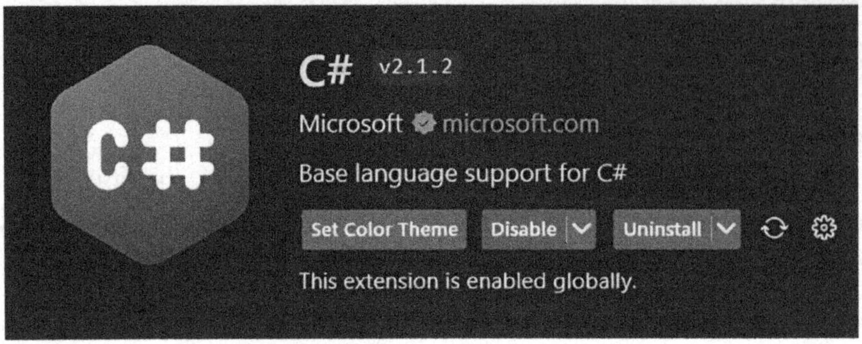

Figure 1.3: The C# extension page

> Note
>
> If you are using a different editor than Visual Studio Code, you can download the C# extension using this link: `https://marketplace.visualstudio.com/items?itemName=ms-dotnettools.csharp`.

With all the tools needed to begin programming in Godot, let's take some time to understand what the Godot Engine is and why it's useful.

What is the Godot Engine?

The **Godot Engine** is a robust game engine that's ideal for creating 2D and 3D games. It was created in 2007 by Juan Linietsky and Ariel Manzur; however, since its inception, many people have contributed to the engine, as you can see from the long, awesome list on the GitHub repository: `https://github.com/godotengine/godot/blob/master/AUTHORS.md`.

Since it is free and open source, it comes at no cost to you as a developer, and the source code is readily available to be modified or updated at any time. The license that Godot operates under is the MIT License, which is also commonly known as the Expat License; it puts development in the hands of developers and leaves it there.

In terms of function, Godot is flexible and easy to set up. You can download the engine on a USB drive and run it with no problem. If there's a feature you don't like, you can modify the source code yourself, or if there is a feature you like, you can continue building on it and open a pull request about it to the Godot community. If you like it, you may find yourself becoming a contributor to the engine too, which we'll discuss in *Chapter 12*.

The biggest drawback to this system, however, is that if a feature is not frequently used or kept up with development, it can be removed in a newer version. A good example of this is VisualScript, a visual scripting language for Godot, which was removed in Godot 4. The team has said that this may be reconsidered, but only as an extension, not a core feature of the engine. While this may seem like a negative, it can be a great boon in keeping the community engaged by providing valuable feedback on valued features.

Don't let that draw you away from Godot, though, as it has a myriad of powerful features that make it a versatile engine. The following are just a few of those key features and how they make Godot convenient to use:

- *Lightweight*: Downloading the Godot Engine is not only easy, but it's fast due to it being so small. The entire engine is barely over 100 MB, and as I said, it can fit on a USB drive.
- *Supports multiple languages*: Program in the integrated scripting language GDscript, use the recently added C# bindings, or any other number of programming languages supported by the community, such as Rust.
- *Git-friendly*: Godot uses a friendly and readable filesystem that makes it easy to create and maintain projects in places such as GitHub.

Overall, the Godot Engine is an excellent choice for both beginner and veteran developers. It's intuitive and easy to pick up, but due to its open development nature, features and upgrades are constantly being implemented to provide Godot depth and a wide array of capabilities that compete with other commercial engines.

With a better understanding of some of Godot's benefits, let's take a look at how it functions as a game engine.

How does the Godot Engine function?

What makes Godot unique is its **scene system** and **node structure**.

The scene system is the space where nodes are housed. Each scene is made up of nodes, and everything created in Godot is derived from the Node object. **Nodes** are the building blocks of our scenes and how objects are created in Godot.

The scene structure becomes a tree of nodes, as shown in *Figure 1.4*:

Figure 1.4: Scene hierarchy in the Godot Editor with an example node tree

For example, let's say we want to create a first-person character. It requires attributes such as a kinematic body, collision shapes, and cameras (if you don't know what these are, that's okay, we'll learn about these nodes in later chapters).

Each of these attributes would be a different node and, collectively, they would make a scene. In the previous figure, there are seven nodes in the current scene. Depending on the type of node that's present, there is a different icon next to the node's name. Let's break down each of these nodes, starting from the top and working our way to the innermost node:

- **Player**: The root of this scene tree, the **Player** scene, is the **Player** node, which has a running figure icon to indicate that it's a **CharacterBody3D** node.
- **CollisionShape3D**: This node provides a collision layer to our player object and is a child of the `Player` node.
- **Body**: The **Body** node is a **PackedScene** with nodes for the **Player** model attached to it, including all the pieces needed to animate it. This node has the symbol for a **Node3D** object (a red circle), but also notice the clapperboard icon to the right of the name of the node. This means this node is a **PackedScene** node, which means it's serialized. **Serialization** here means all the information relating to the scene has been converted from data types to bytes efficiently.
- **Camroot**, **h**, and **v**: These next three nodes are all **Node3D** objects and were created to control the position and movement of the **Camera** by script. There is a script attached to the **Camroot** node with a little scroll icon that's next to the node name. **Camroot** is the base of the camera; **h** and **v** represent horizontal and vertical movement, respectively.
- **Camera**: The innermost nested node is **Camera**, which has a camera icon next to it and allows us to create either a first- or third-person view of the player, depending on where we position the **Camera**.

Using the scene system allows developers to easily create prefabs out of nodes. There's no additional step to save this scene as a prefab; we can simply take **Player.tscn** with all these nodes on it and drag and drop it into another scene. This ability is the biggest distinction Godot has from other game engines, because it allows fast prototyping.

With the scene structure in *Figure 1.4*, we can see some important patterns that you may or may not be familiar with. Let's briefly cover them here:

- **OOP**: Another way to think about the scene system is in terms of **Object-Oriented Programming (OOP)**. When a system, or language, is OOP, it means that everything is derived from objects, and within those objects, you have your attributes and can modify them within the object. If you've used an OOP programming language before (such as C#), then transferring that knowledge to Godot will be very intuitive. We see this in the scene structure in *Figure 1.4* as well as the fact that everything in the scene derives from one object, a node.

- **Inheritance**: The other piece of Godot that goes together with the OOP paradigm is inheritance. **Inheritance** is just what it sounds like – an object inherits attributes from another object. Just like in our previous node tree, each node below another node inherits from its parent node.
- **Polymorphism**: Another important concept to know when using Godot is polymorphism. To understand how this works in Godot, let's consider a new scene that our player might pick up called Item. In the `Item` scene, we'll have a shape, collision, and the item model. If we wanted to have other item types have the same base properties, we could extend the `Item` scene to be used by any type of Item we wanted. While it may not be clear here, we will use this concept in *Chapter 5* when creating our world.
- **Composition**: The last idea we'll briefly discuss is composition, although it is not featured in *Figure 1.4*. This is something Godot does extremely well and should be used whenever possible. It goes hand in hand with an idea we'll discuss in *Chapter 3*, which is cohesion and coupling. Let's use an enemy as an example. Say we want our player to have Health and Armor. The Health would be its own scene, as would the Armor. These scenes would be named `HealthComponent` and `ArmorComponent`, respectively. Then, whenever we wanted to add either Health or Armor to an enemy, we could attach `HealthComponent` or `ArmorComponent` without needing to recreate everything. If this is still confusing to you, you can read more about it here: `https://docs.godotengine.org/en/stable/getting_started/introduction/godot_design_philosophy.html`.

Now that we've got a brief understanding of how the Godot Engine works, let's start navigating through it.

The next section will take some time to explain each component of the editor and their names. We'll also briefly discuss how each of those components is used in a project.

Navigating the Godot Engine

When you first launch the Godot Engine, you'll be greeted by the **Project Manager** screen, as shown in *Figure 1.5*:

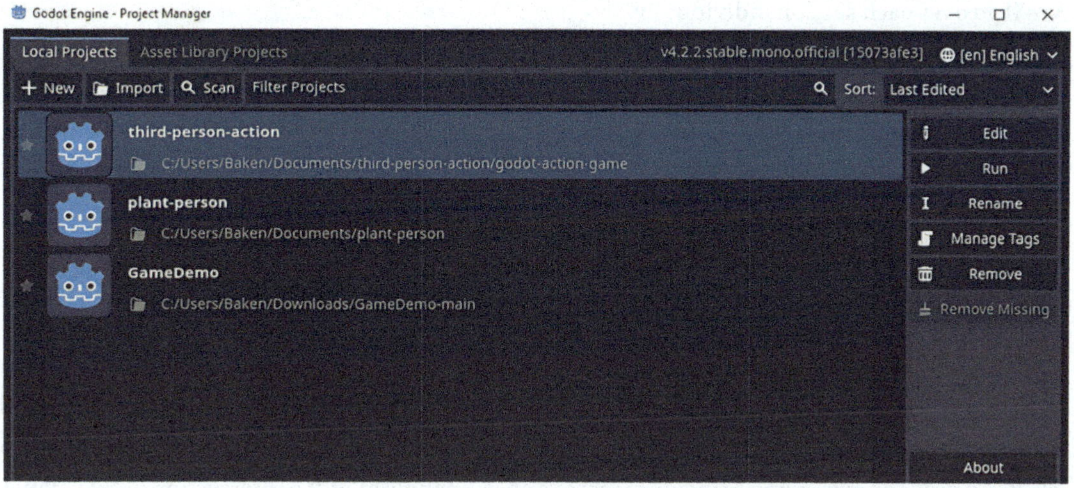

Figure 1.5: The Project List screen when launching Godot

Here, you can create, import, rename, remove, or delete projects. Click the **New** button and choose a name for the project. Godot will make sure you choose an empty folder, so all our project files will be housed in one location.

Once a project is created, Godot will take you to the editor screen. The default layout looks like this:

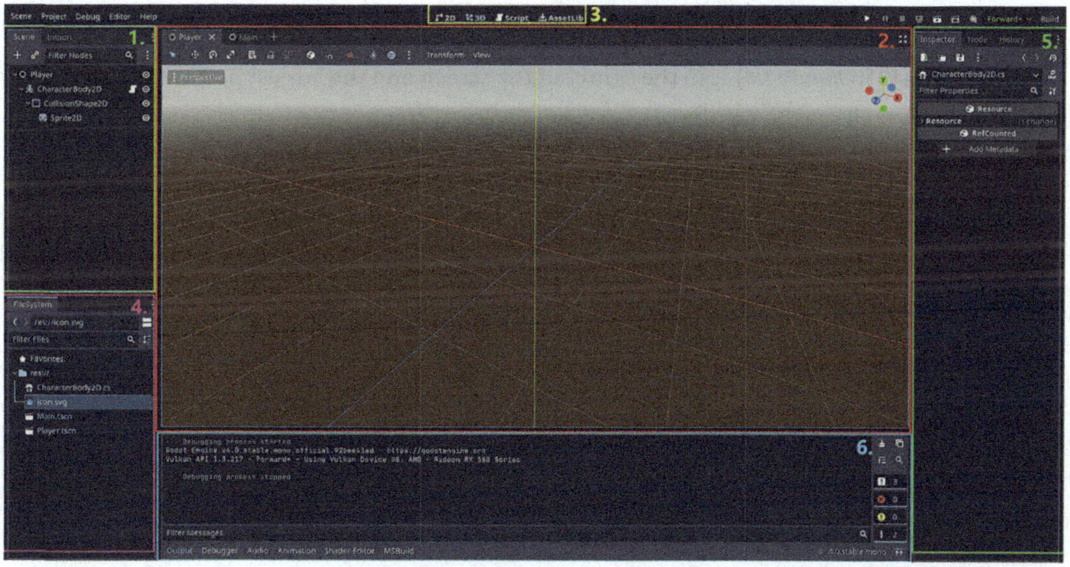

Figure 1.6: The Godot Editor in use

We'll go over each section individually.

Scene/Import docks

The **Scene/Import** dock (*1* in *Figure 1.6*) sits in the top-left corner of the engine, right below the menu bar. There you'll see two tabs – **Scene** and **Import**. We saw a close-up view of this dock in *Figure 1.4* when talking about Godot's node structure and scene system.

The default view of this dock is on the **Scene** tab, which shows the node structure of the current scene open in the Viewport. Selecting **2D** or **3D** from the screen buttons (3 in *Figure 1.6*) changes the views accordingly; as seen in *Figure 1.6*, the 3D view is selected.

Within the 3D view, you can select a specific axis to view objects on by clicking either the colored **X**, **Y**, or **Z** axes on the axis gizmo that lives in the top right corner of the Viewport. You can also click and drag the axis gizmo to view objects at a specific angle or at the intersection of two planes.

The second tab in this dock is the **Import** tab. As you might expect, it's related to examining the specific properties of resources. Resources are everything from 3D models to music to user interface images. Depending on the type of asset it is, there will be different properties to adjust and change as needed for your project. At the bottom of the **Import** tab, there is a **Reimport** button for when you've made changes to an asset and need to reimport it with different settings.

Viewport and screen buttons

The **Viewport** (*2* in *Figure 1.6*) is in the center of the screen and the largest part within the Editor. This is where you'll see the results of the scenes that you create.

At the top is a **screen navigator** (*3* in *Figure 1.6*) where you can toggle between the **2D**, **3D**, **Script**, and **Asset Library** screens. Clicking **Script** will show the scripts available in the opened scene, and clicking the **AssetLib** button will take you to Godot's Asset Library, where you can find useful third-party plugins or create your own to be added there!

FileSystem dock

The **FileSystem** dock (*4* in *Figure 1.6*) sits in the lower left-hand corner of the Viewport and represents the file structure of your project. Godot and its community don't have a recommended file structure when creating projects, mainly because there are no restrictions when structuring them, but they have some general information about how Godot interacts with the project structure. You can find more about it here: `https://docs.godotengine.org/en/latest/tutorials/best_practices/project_organization.html#organization`.

The example structure in *Figure 1.7* is a common one that's used in other game engines. While it's a viable format, we'll discuss other ways to structure your project in *Chapter 3*.

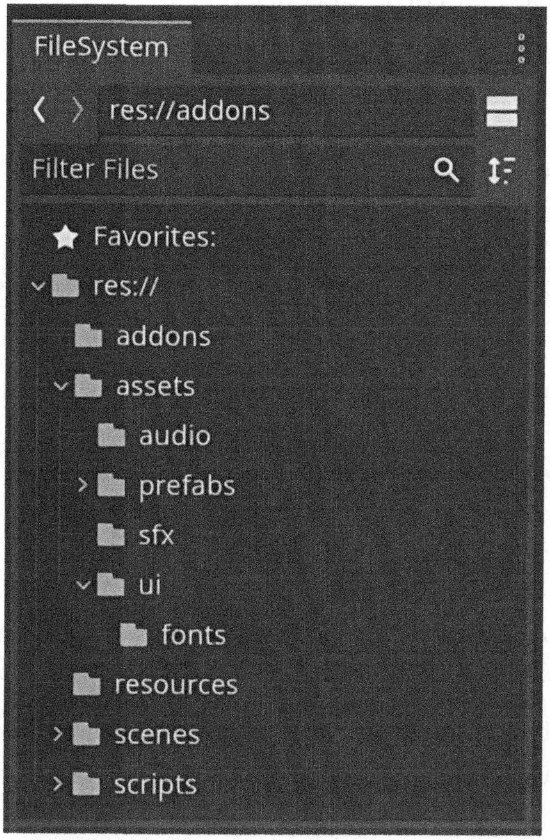

Figure 1.7: An overview of the file structure I use for my Godot projects and will use for this book's project

The only general rules when it comes to creating your file structure are as follows:

- Use *pascal_case* for folder names and filenames
- Use *SnakeCase* for nodes and scenes
- Include an `addons` folder for plugins and other third-party pieces

Though there is no standardized way to structure a project in Godot – it should be whatever works best for you – make sure to keep these rules in mind when creating your own file structure.

Inspector/Node/History dock

The **Inspector dock** (*5* in *Figure 1.6*) has three tabs:

- **Inspector**: By default, this is the visible tab. Here, you can see the details and properties of a selected node, including its scale, transform, and rotation. The information listed here will vary based on the type of node selected, but it will be an extremely useful space to reference as we work in Godot.
- **Node**: Much like the **Inspector**, this tab shows the signals you can implement based on the selected node, and provides a space to manage your groups. Signals and groups will be components we cover in *Chapter 4*.
- **History**: This tab is exactly what you'd expect it to be. It's a history of the actions you take in the project. You can limit the actions to be tracked by scene or globally. For example, if you moved an object in a scene, the **History** tab would add a log line. This would track the change much like you can do in a document. It's a convenient tool for understanding what actions you took during any given development session.

Bottom panel

The final panel we'll cover is the **bottom panel** (*6* in *Figure 1.6*). This panel has multiple buttons running along the bottom of it:

- **Output**: Provides a log of debug statements, errors, and warnings.
- **Debugger**: This is where you'll see more detailed error messages and can monitor resource usage.
- **Audio**: This is where you can add audio buses, apply audio effects, and augment the levels of each audio bus.
- **Animation**: The animation player allows you to preview animations, add bezier curves, and manage other animation components.
- **Shader Editor**: Here, you'll write your shaders. Godot uses a shader language very similar to GLSL, so if you are already familiar with it, it will be easy to transfer to Godot.
- **MSBuild**: This is the Microsoft Build Engine, and you can build your C# project from here. You can also see any warnings or errors when the MSBuild occurs.

With that, you have learned what the main components of the Godot Engine interface are and how they work together. While we didn't create anything within this project, this will be the project we use throughout the rest of the book.

Summary

In this chapter, you learned what the Godot Engine is and some of its history. You also learned about the different parts of the Godot Editor and how each of them functions individually. Now that you're familiar with the various pieces of the Godot Engine, we can look at how C# functions in Godot.

In the next chapter, we'll discuss how C# behaves in Godot, including some of the unique rules that we'll need to follow for the programming language. At the end of the chapter, we'll create a simple 2D script in C# to better understand the workflow of C# in Godot.

2

Understanding How C# Works in Godot

In this chapter, we will take a moment to discuss the interlinking of Godot's C# API and the C# language, as there are some important parts to be aware of when creating C# scripts that are unique to Godot, as there are with any C# bindings. We'll also configure Godot to improve our workflow, and then finish the chapter by creating our first C# script.

The goal of this chapter is to become comfortable with the process of creating C# scripts and attaching them to nodes, as well as understanding the relationship between the nodes and C# scripts. Understanding these components will be foundational for moving forward with more advanced topics as we progress through each chapter.

So, in this chapter, we will cover the following topics:

- Reviewing the changes to C# in Godot 4
- Setting up your C# environment
- Creating your first scenes and C# script

Technical requirements

For this chapter, the technical requirements will be the same as in *Chapter 1*.

All the code from this chapter is available in the GitHub repository here: `https://github.com/PacktPublishing/Game-Development-with-Godot-and-C-`.

Reviewing the changes to C# in Godot 4

Before jumping into the additional setup required for C#, we will cover some specific details about the relationship between C# and Godot 4. If you're new to Godot, these changes may not mean much now, but we'll highlight their benefits:

- C# support is now provided through the .NET SDK rather than the Mono SDK. This is beneficial for the following reasons:
  - There's only one framework to install to begin work in C#
  - Godot 4 uses the latest .NET SDK, allowing users to have greater access to C# features, such as providing access to class libraries and the C# compiler
  - As C# and the .NET SDK were both created and designed by Microsoft, this guarantees first-class support for its users.

  So, the migration from Mono to .NET is a huge upgrade that comes with Godot 4.
- Godot signals generate C# events, which we'll be discussing in more depth in *Chapter 4*. If you are a native C# user coming to Godot, then you'll probably be accustomed to creating events to handle input and data. This prior knowledge of events in C# makes using signals in Godot more intuitive as a C# developer.
- Now, many Godot API functions have been renamed to match .NET naming conventions. This means style guides for C# scripts in Godot are more aligned with the standard which uses PascalCase in their naming conventions for variables, functions, etc. within the programming language.

- More examples of C# scripts are being made available in the Godot documentation, as well as a page to highlight the differences between GDScript and C# in Godot, which means switching to C# in Godot will be easier than ever before.
- Since Godot moved to the .NET SDK, the official C# debugger is now available to Godot, which makes debugging easier and more developer-friendly.

For further details about the mentioned changes as well as additional ones, visit this page: `https://godotengine.org/article/whats-new-in-csharp-for-godot-4-0/`.

While this is a high-level overview of engine changes and may only intermittently impact us throughout the book, it's still good to be aware of, especially if you are coming from a previous version of Godot.

Now let's take some time to set up our C# environment with Godot.

Setting up your C# environment

In the previous chapter, we took the time to download the .NET version of Godot, install a code editor, and install the C# extension for our code editor to provide C# support. With our selected code editor (Visual Studio Code) installed, we need to configure Godot to recognize and open Visual Studio Code when editing C# scripts by default, rather than opening Godot's editor.

Configuring Godot for C#

To make sure the Godot editor is configured to open scripts with our IDE of choice by default, follow these steps:

1. Open the Godot project that we created in the first chapter.
2. Click the **Editor** button in the top-left menu bar. Then, click **Editor Settings**.
3. On the left of the **Editor Settings** page, scroll all the way down until you see **Dotnet**. Under this option, there should be two settings – **Editor** and **Build**. Click **Editor**.

4. In the **Editor** options, you should see an option called **External Editor**, set to its default setting of **Disabled**. Click the arrow next to the word **Disabled**, and you should be prompted with a drop-down menu of all the IDEs you can set to open when you edit C# scripts. If you followed the steps from the previous chapter's *Technical requirements* section, then you should see **Visual Studio Code**, or whatever IDE you've selected, in the drop-down.

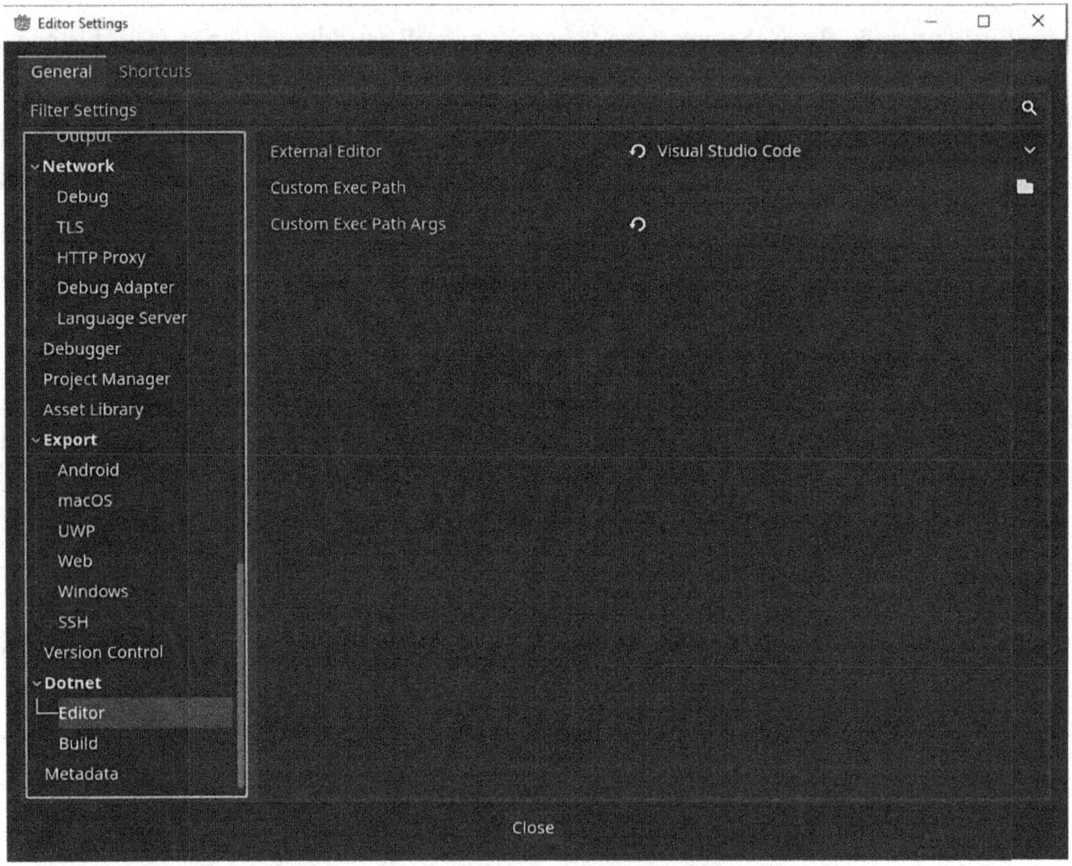

Figure 2.1: The Editor Settings screen with the Editor options selected

Once selected, Godot will now open C# scripts in the chosen IDE, which makes editing them super convenient. There's no need to restart the project or the engine to make these changes persist.

Configuring your IDE for Godot debugging

Now that Godot is aware of the IDE we're using, we can make sure our IDE knows what type of code to compile. Note the instructions in this section assume that you've followed the technical setup from the previous chapter and therefore have Visual Studio Code installed:

1. Open Visual Studio Code.
2. Click **File** in the top-left corner, select **Open Folder...**, then browse to the folder that holds our project (mine is normally located in the `Documents` folder). Then, click Select Folder on the project folder that you navigated to, not any of its sub-directories. This will add all the sub-directories and files to be opened in Visual Studio Code.
3. From the left-hand navigation toolbar, shown in *Figure 2.2*, click the run and debug icon (second from the bottom). This will open the debugging window.
4. From here, select the text that says **create a launch.json file**, as shown in *Figure 2.2*.

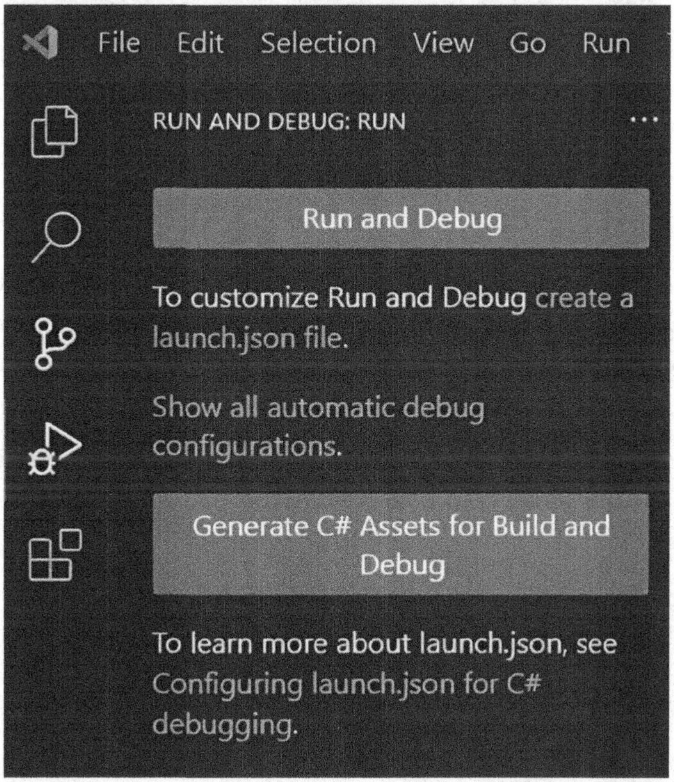

Figure 2.2: Creating our launch.json and task.json files in Visual Studio Code

After clicking this button, a new file should be created named `launch.json`. This will be in the `vscode` folder, which you can see on the left-hand side of Visual Studio Code next to our toolbar in *Figure 2.3*.

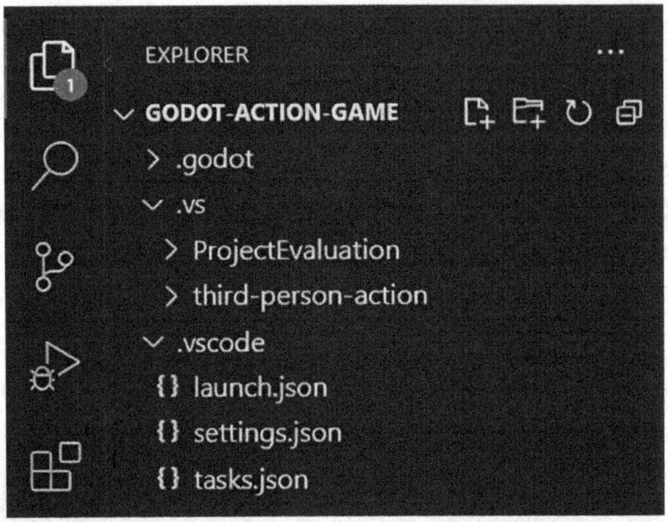

Figure 2.3: The newly created launch.json and tasks.json files in Visual Studio Code

> Note
>
> Visual Studio Code should automatically take you to the screen with the `launch.json` file present. If not, you can click the **Explorer** button from the Visual Studio Code toolbar (this is the first icon in the toolbar shown in *Figure 2.2*).

The `launch.json` file tells Visual Studio Code how it should handle our Godot project. If your `launch.json` file does not look like what is shown in the following code block, then replace the content with this code:

```
{
    "version": "0.2.0",
    "configurations": [

        {
            "name": "Godot Book",
            "type": "coreclr",
            "request": "launch",
```

```
            "preLaunchTask": "build",
            "program": "${env:GODOT4}",
            "args": [],
            "cwd": "${workspaceFolder}",
            "stopAtEntry": false,
        }
    ]
}
```

Let's break down what each component within it means:

- `version`: The version is arbitrary and only matters for internal use. The default is `0.2.0`, but you may set it to whatever you'd like.
- `configurations`: We can set up the `launch.json` file to launch our project in a variety of ways. For now, we'll only have one configuration, which will launch the main scene - any scene that is set as the main scene in the Project Settings of Godot - and attach a debugger. This allows us to set breakpoints and utilize other debugging tools in our C# code.

  Then, within the configurations array, we see a list of variables:

  - `name`: This is the name of the configuration and what will appear above the debugger when the run and debug button from the toolbar is selected. I've named mine `Godot Book`, as shown in *Figure 2.4*.

Figure 2.4: The name of the launch.json configuration above the debugger

  - `type`: This determines the debugger being used. We are using the `coreclr` .NET debugger.
  - `request`: The `request` property is either `launch` or `attach`. A `launch` configuration is more about starting our project in debug mode, whereas an `attach` configuration is about connecting Visual Studio Code's debugger to a process already running. We have it set to `launch`, since that's what we want to do with our project.
  - `preLaunchTask`: This calls the name of the listed task in the `tasks.json` file, which we'll be creating right after this. The name `build` corresponds to the `build` in the `tasks.json` file, which will build our project before launching it.

- `program`: This tells the debugger what program or file to execute with the debugger. There are two ways to fulfill this property:
    - The first, and probably best, way is by adding an environment variable called `GODOT4` to your system. Windows users should do the following:

    1. Click the **Windows** button and begin typing the word `environment`.
    2. Click the **Edit the System Environment Variables** option.
    3. From the first window that appears, click **Environment Variables**.
    4. From the second window that appears, **System variables**, click the **New** button.
    5. In the **Variable name** box, type `GODOT4`.
    6. Click **Browse File** and browse to the Godot executable. This is the same path that we can also copy and paste into the program property.
    7. Click **OK**. A machine reboot and/or a restart of Visual Studio Code and Godot may be required.

    - The second way, which can work in a pinch, is to copy the path to the executable. In this instance, we would want to copy the path to the Godot executable that we downloaded to run the engine. The reason the second way may not always be the best is when the executable is moved, the program property requires an updated path. Note that you will need to replace the backslash with forward slashes.
- `args` (short for arguments): This property is a list of arguments to pass into our program for debugging. You can find a list of available optional arguments here: `https://docs.godotengine.org/en/stable/tutorials/editor/command_line_tutorial.html#command-line-reference`.
- `cwd` (short for current working directory): This property tells Visual Studio Code where to find dependencies and other files.
- `stopAtEntry`: This property is either true or false and will stop the program if this configuration property is set to true.

> Note
>
> If you ever forget what each of these properties means, you can always refer to this list or hover over the property in your `launch.json` file, and Visual Studio Code will tell you. You can also find more in-depth information on Visual Studio Code's website here: `https://code.visualstudio.com/docs/editor/debugging#_launchjson-attributes`.

Now we'll take some time to create the `tasks.json` file. We mentioned this file when talking about the `preLaunchTask` property in the `launch.json` file. To get started, let's do the following:

1. Click the **Terminal** button in the top-left corner of Visual Studio Code.
2. Next, click the **Configure Tasks...** button at the bottom of the menu.
3. After that, we'll see a drop-down menu in the search bar in the top middle of the screen, as shown in *Figure 2.5*.

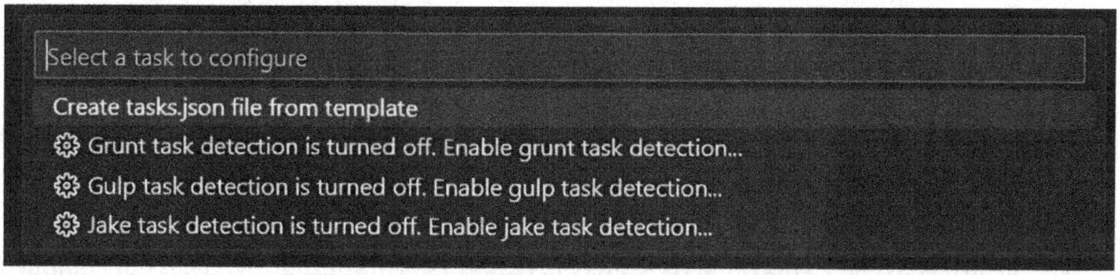

Figure 2.5: The drop-down menu after clicking Configure Tasks...

4. Click **Create tasks.json file from template**.
5. Here, we'll be given a list of templates to choose from. Choose **.NET**.

Afterward, a `tasks.json` file should be created and opened in your `.vscode` folder within your project. We don't need all of the code that's already in here. In fact, let's replace it with this code:

```
{
  "version": "2.0.0",
  "tasks": [
      {
```

```
            "label": "build",
            "command": "dotnet",
            "type": "shell",
            "args": [
                "build"
            ],
            "problemMatcher": "$msCompile"
        }
    ]
}
```

Much like the `launch.json` file, the `tasks.json` file is an array of tasks that will be executed at various times, depending on when we tell them to. Tasks are typically things such as testing, deployment, or, in our case, for building our project. Now that we have a `tasks.json` file, let's step through what each property means:

- `label`: This is the name of the task. Here, it's `build` (the same as in `preLaunchTask`). This is an arbitrary identifier, and you can rename it based on the purpose at hand.
- `command`: This is the name of the command to execute. We want to run .NET.
- `type`: This property determines the type of task, which can either be `shell` – referring to a shell command – or `process` – meaning a process to be executed. We have chosen `shell`.
- `args`: Again, this refers to the argument we're passing in to build the project.
- `problemMatcher`: This property scans the `tasks.json` file output (which is our compiled project) and makes sure that there are no errors. The `$msCompile` listed is the C# and Visual Basic compiler that we want.

With Visual Studio Code configured, we can begin to work in the engine and create our first scenes and C# script. This will be a beginner-level example of the engine and will include more engine navigation on top of the components listed.

Creating your first scenes and C# script

In this short example, we'll be creating two scenes – one is a **Player** scene and the other is our **World** scene where the player will reside. The player will be able to move left and right, jump, and dash.

So, with Godot set up, let's start by creating a simple script. In the **Scene** dock, you'll see an option to create your **Root** node. Here, we can see four options:

- **2D Scene**: This will create a scene with a generic 2D node as the root
- **3D Scene**: This will create a scene with a generic 3D node as the root
- **User Interface**: This will create a scene with a generic Control node as the root
- **Other Node**: This allows you to browse for a specific node to set as the root of the scene

At some point, we'll be creating all of these scenes, but for now, select **Other Node**.

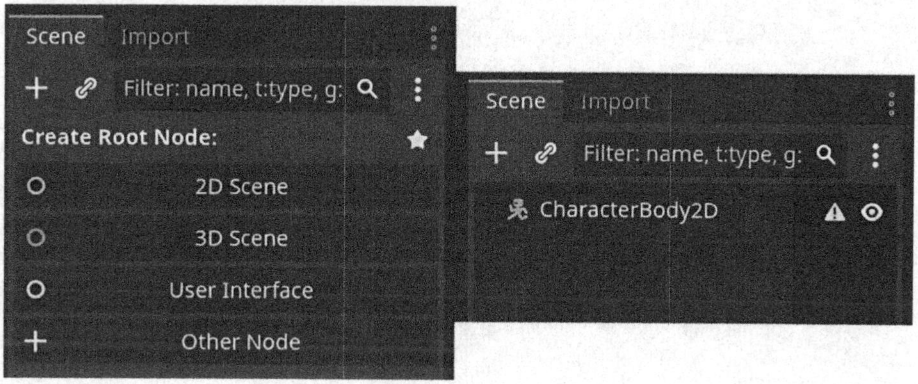

Figure 2.6: Godot's Scene dock

Now that our scene type is selected, we will start with creating the node structure for the **Player** scene, since it has multiple components. The **Player** scene is also going to be its own node in our **World** scene, so it's best if we create it first. Then, we can drop the **Player** scene into our **World** scene, which we'll create in *Chapter 4*.

Creating the Player node structure

After selecting **Other Node**, a new window will appear, as seen in *Figure 2.7*, giving us the option to select the node we want to create in the scene. This screen includes every type of built-in node that Godot provides.

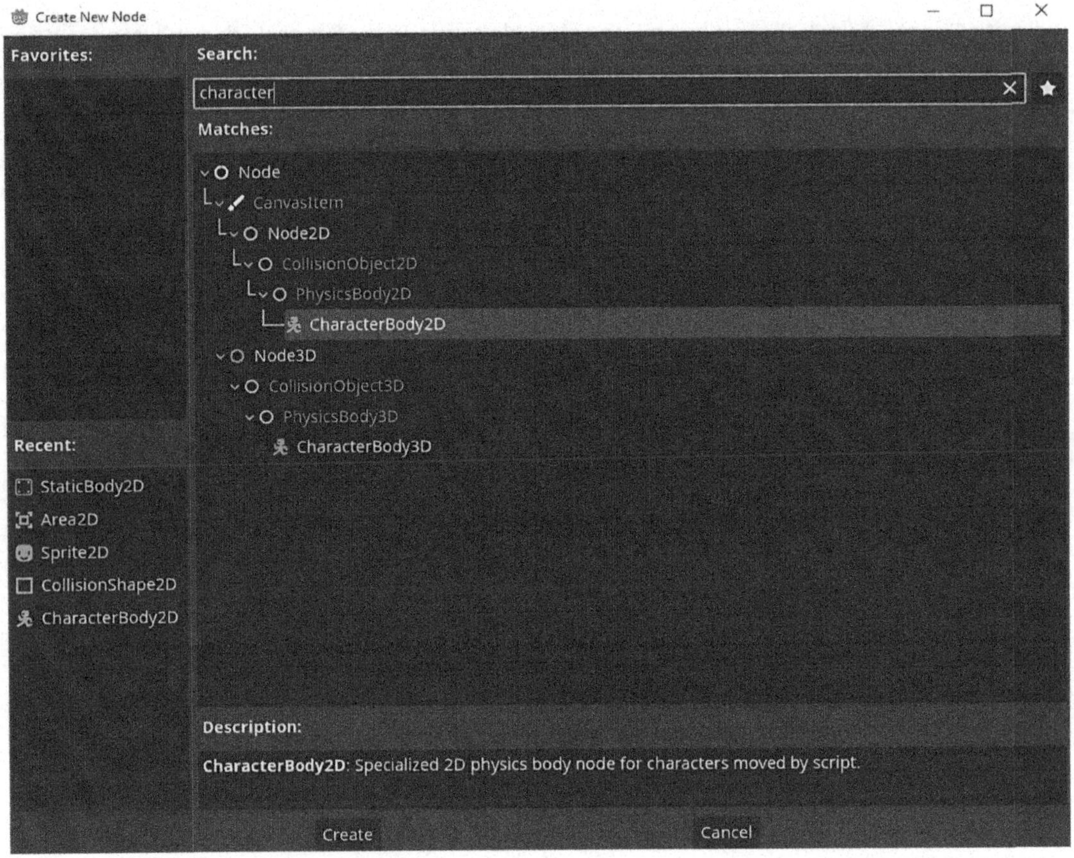

Figure 2.7: The Create New Node menu screen with search results on the word character

We need a node that can tell Godot that it is going to be a user-controlled type of node. So, in the search bar, type `character`. You will see the menu filter in real time. The two nodes that will be highlighted here are **CharacterBody2D** and **CharacterBody3D**. Since we are working in a 2D scene, we want to choose **CharacterBody2D**.

Select it and you will see a description of the node at the bottom – this is useful when you're not quite sure what node you want or need but have a general sense of its application. This node is a body that has no physics, which means that any collision detection we want to implement must be done in code.

Click **Create** and **CharacterBody2D** will be added to the **Scene** dock like so:

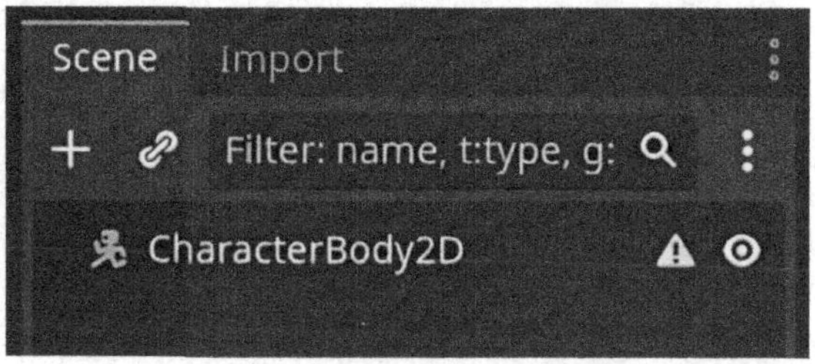

Figure 2.8: Player node structure so far

Now, a small caution symbol appears to the right of the **CharacterBody2D** node, as seen in *Figure 2.8*. Hover over it, and it will show a node warning saying that this node needs a shape. Without a shape, it cannot collide or interact with any other objects. Here are the steps to add a collision to our character:

1. Right-click **CharacterBody2D** (not **Node2D**). Then, from the drop-down menu, click **Add Child Node**.
2. Rather than searching for `character`, this time, search for `shape`. The immediate results will be **CollisionShape** and **ShapeCast** for both 2D and 3D, respectively.
3. Since we're in a 2D scene, select `CollisionShape2D`. This shape will allow us to provide collision bounds for our player's **CharacterBody2D** node.

Here, again, we see another caution symbol next to our newly added `CollisionShape2D` node. This time, it's a node configuration warning, telling us a shape must be provided. This may be confusing since we've added the correct node, but it's only telling us that we're missing something in regard to the node. To fix this, do the following:

1. Select the `CollisionShape2D` node and then look at the **Inspector** dock on the right-hand side. We can see a list of properties for `CollisionShape2D`, such as **Shape**, **Disabled**, and **One Way Collision**.

2. Notice that **Shape** says **<empty>**. This is what we need to provide to Godot so that the caution symbol will go away. Click the arrow to show a drop-down menu, as shown in *Figure 2.9*, and select **New RectangleShape2D**:

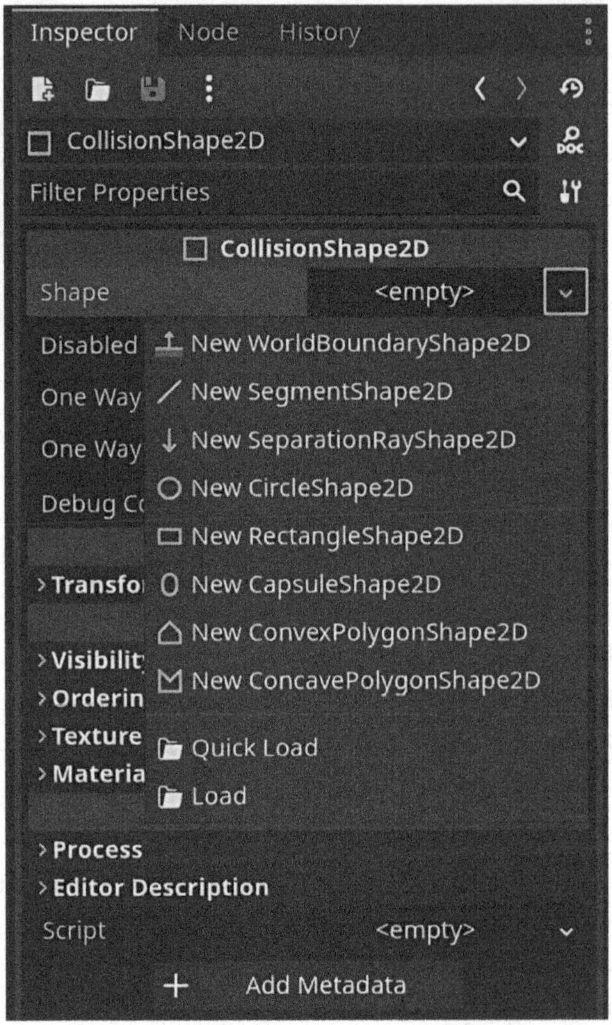

Figure 2.9: Selecting the shape for CollisionShape2D

After selecting this shape, you will see a small blue rectangle appear in the Viewport with nine dots around the edges with one in the center, as in *Figure 2.10*. You can use the scroll wheel on your mouse or click the plus sign on the zoom panel that's in the top-left corner of the Viewport. Once you are about 200% or so zoomed in, the blue rectangle (the collision shape that will be on our player) should be visible.

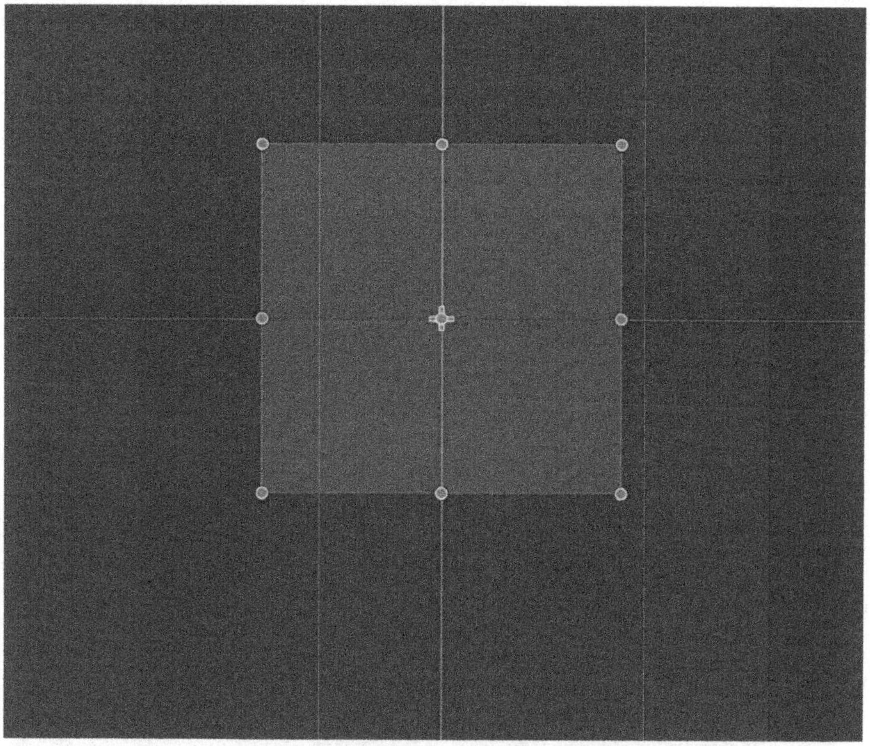

Figure 2.10: Collision shape sizing in the Viewport

Note

It's important to note that you should not resize the collision shape with the **Scale** property of the `CollisionShape2D` node in the inspector; rather, you should use the dots that are on the collision shape within the Viewport, or use the **Size** property.

Both options can be found under the **Transform** heading in the inspector, but be aware that **Scale** and **Size** are two different properties. The **Size** property is better to use here.

We have one more node to add and then the node structure of our **Player** scene is complete. So, right-click on our most recent node (the collision shape) and click **Add Child Node**, but this time we are looking for a `Sprite2D` node. If we click the `Sprite2D` node from the scene hierarchy and then look to the inspector, we'll see a **Texture** property. By default, it will say **<empty>**. Click the drop-down arrow next to **<empty>** and select **Load**. A new window should appear, and the only option available to us is an `icon.svg` file.

The result will look like a block version of the Godot Engine icon. It should appear in the Viewport after selecting it. Make sure the blue collision shape edges and the size of the icon match up – we want to be sure that the collision shape (the blue) lines up correctly with our sprite (the Godot icon block). Be sure to resize the icon sprite by using the small dots that are along the edges of the sprite, and the result will look like *Figure 2.11*:

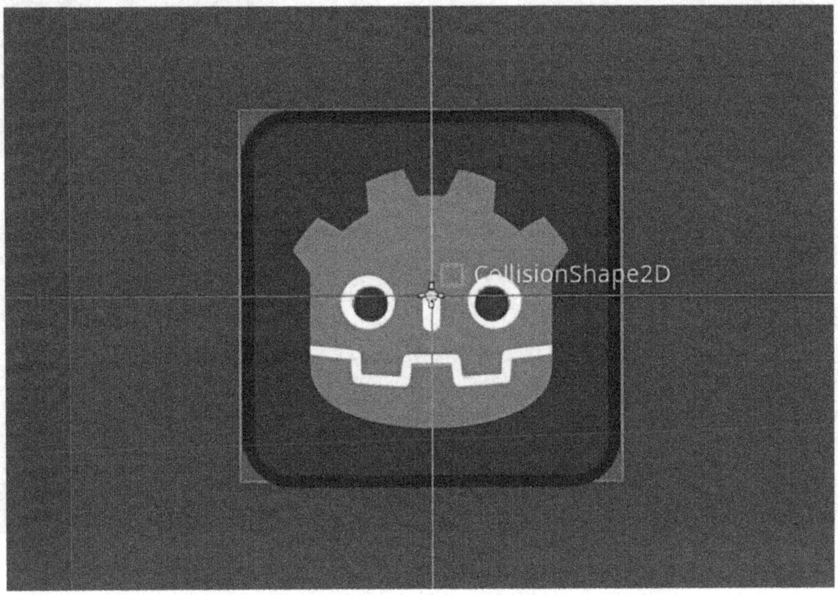

Figure 2.11: Our Sprite2D sitting on top of our CollisionShape in the Viewport

After that, our **Player** scene is complete, and the scene hierarchy should look like this:

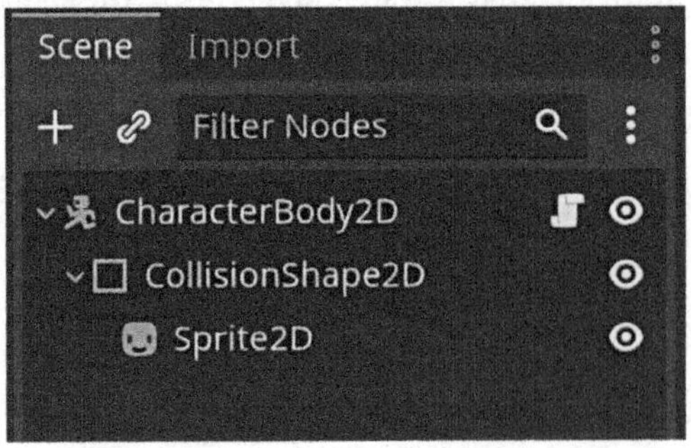

Figure 2.12: The Player scene hierarchy

Another viable option if you want to see the collision boundaries from `CollisionShape2D` on top of the sprite is swapping `Sprite2D` and `CollisionShape2D` around in the scene tree. This would set `Sprite2D` as the parent of `CollisionShape2D`.

Now, be sure to save the scene by going to **Scene** in the top-left corner, clicking **Save Scene As...**, and naming it `Player.tscn`.

> Note
>
> `.tscn` is a test scene file format that represents an individual scene in Godot. You can read more about it here: `https://docs.godotengine.org/en/stable/engine_details/file_formats/tscn.html`.

Adding a script to our Player Scene

With our final node added to the **Player** scene, we can now focus our attention on making our player move.

To start doing this, right-click on **CharacterBody2D** in the **Scene** dock, then click **Attach Script**. A window will pop up to give you some options before creating the script, as in *Figure 2.13*. The most important thing to select here is the language. When using the .NET version of Godot, you have the option of creating scripts in either GDScript or C#; in our case, set **Language** as **C#**.

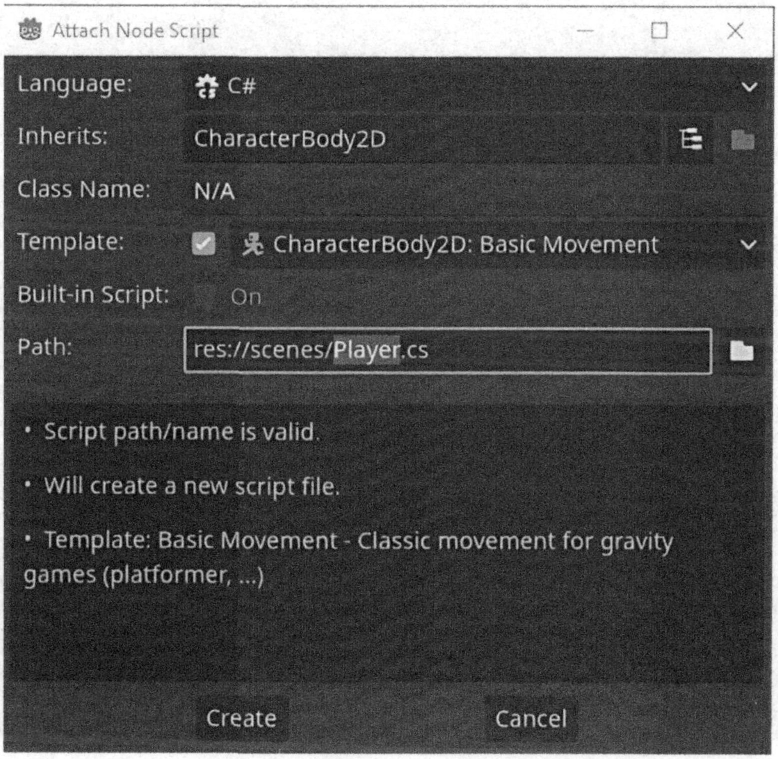

Figure 2.13: The Attach Node Script menu

A nice feature of Godot is that depending on the type of node we attach a script to, we have some options for templates. As you can see in *Figure 2.13*, for **Template**, we're going to be using the **Basic Movement** template that comes with the **CharacterBody2D** node. The script will appear in the Viewport, but if you configured your **Editor** settings as described at the beginning of this chapter, it should automatically open in the editor you chose. You can also double-click the script from the **FileSystem** dock and open it in an editor of your choosing.

Let's step through the script to understand how Godot interfaces with C#. For the next couple of paragraphs, I will be referencing *Figure 2.14*, which has the script that Godot automatically creates for the **CharacterBody2D** node:

```
public partial class Player : CharacterBody2D
{
    2 references
    public const float Speed = 300.0f;
    1 reference
    public const float JumpVelocity = -400.0f;

    // Get the gravity from the project settings to be synced with RigidBody nodes.
    5 references
    public float gravity = ProjectSettings.GetSetting("physics/2d/default_gravity").AsSingle();

    4 references
    public override void _PhysicsProcess(double delta)
    {
        Vector2 velocity = Velocity;

        // Add the gravity.
        if (!IsOnFloor())
            velocity.Y += gravity * (float)delta;

        // Handle Jump.
        if (Input.IsActionJustPressed("ui_accept") && IsOnFloor())
            velocity.Y = JumpVelocity;

        // Get the input direction and handle the movement/deceleration.
        // As good practice, you should replace UI actions with custom gameplay actions.
        Vector2 direction = Input.GetVector("ui_left", "ui_right", "ui_up", "ui_down");
        if (direction != Vector2.Zero)
        {
            velocity.X = direction.X * Speed;
        }
        else
        {
            velocity.X = Mathf.MoveToward(Velocity.X, 0, Speed);
        }

        Velocity = velocity;
        MoveAndSlide();
    }
}
```

Figure 2.14: The script Godot creates by default for CharacterBody2D nodes

Starting with line 5 in *Figure 2.14*, this is where we create our class with a couple of important details:

```
public partial class PlayerMovement : Godot.CharacterBody2D { //class info
}
```

First, the name of the class must match the name of the script; my script name in my FileSystem and on line 5 is `PlayerMovement`. After the class name, you'll see that the class extends a Godot class called `Godot.CharacterBody2D` – you must extend the node that the script is attached to. For example, if we had attached a script to our `Sprite2D` node instead, it would say `Godot.Sprite2D`.

> Note
>
> As of Godot 4.2, you no longer need to write `Godot` before the node you're extending, as it will automatically know that it should extend the class from Godot.

The next few lines declare constants for player movement, which creates things such as gravity and other static variables that will be repeatedly used throughout the project.

> Note
>
> Gravity is set up in Godot's **Project Settings**. You can change this by going to **Project | Project Settings | Physics | 2D** and changing the **Default Gravity** property listed there.

At line 13, we get to one of the main function calls in Godot, which is the `_PhysicsProcess` function. It looks like this:

```
public override void _PhysicsProcess(double delta) { }
```

This function happens at a fixed rate and maintains smooth physics for our game. Plus, it's called before each physics step, so it's perfect to use for our player when we need to process input actions that correlate to the physics step.

> Note
>
> A **physics step** is when all the calculations for physics in the game engine occur, such as movement and collisions. The default number of physics steps is 60 iterations per second by default and is different from the frame rate. You can read more about the physics engine in Godot here: `https://docs.godotengine.org/en/stable/tutorials/physics/physics_introduction.html`.

The parameter it takes is `delta`, which is the time that has elapsed in seconds between each process call. We'll be utilizing `delta` a lot to move various objects in our world, including our player. In fact, you should always include `delta` when making physics calls like this to objects.

Within our `_PhysicsProcess` function, we have two `if` statements (lines 18 and 22) that check whether the player is in the air. Let's break down what's happening in each of these `if` statements:

- The first `if` statement is as follows:

  ```
  if (!IsOnFloor())
  velocity.Y += gravity * (float)delta;
  ```

  Here, we're saying that if the player is in the air, then we need to add gravity to our player to put them back on the ground. The `IsOnFloor()` function is part of the `CharacterBody` classes. It returns `true` or `false` based on whether `CharacterBody` collided with another object in the current frame. In our case, we only want the code to execute if the function evaluates to be `false`.

  If `IsOnFloor()` evaluates to `false`, which means our player is not on the floor, then we're going to accelerate the player's movement on the *Y* axis only.

  Let's break down the main variables:

  - `velocity.Y`: This is the variable that makes our character move in the *y* direction, which is the *Y* component of velocity. Remember, our velocity variable is a `Vector3` and has a value for the *X* axis, *Y* axis, and *Z* axis.

  - `gravity`: This adds the **Gravity** value from Godot's **Project Settings** to `velocity.Y` (the default is `-9.8`, but this can be changed).
  - `delta`: This property is the time elapsed between frames. It's important to keep our physics in line with `delta` because with varying types of hardware, you still want your game to run smoothly regardless of someone else's frame rate. Here, the *Y* component of our velocity is then multiplied by `delta`. Each time this line executes, which is every time the `PhysicsProcess` function is called, we are changing the player's velocity over time. This is how the player falls slowly to the ground rather than making one immediate drop.

- The second `if` statement looks as follows:

  ```
  if (Input.IsActionJustPressed("ui_accept") && IsOnFloor())
  velocity.Y = JumpVelocity;
  ```

  If we're on the ground, which means `IsOnFloor()` evaluates to `true`, and we've hit the jump button, `Input.IsActionJustPressed("ui_accept")`, then we want to be propelled into the air. This function is one of many convenient collision-checking functions that we will use when creating our player controller later.

Let's continue to break down the input actions in this script.

On line 22, and again on line 27, we see references to `ui_accept`, `ui_left`, `ui_right`, `ui_up`, and `ui_down`. They can also be seen here:

```
Vector2 direction = Input.GetVector("ui_left", "ui_right", "ui_up", "ui_
down");
```

Let's break this line down from left to right. Here, we're declaring a `Vector2` variable called `direction`, and we're assigning it to be whatever the `GetVector` function returns. `GetVector` is a function from the `Input` class. The `Input` class takes in all the keyboard and mouse inputs and then processes them. `GetVector` specifically takes in string names mentioned in the code block, such as `ui_accept`, `ui_left`, `ui_right`, `ui_up`, and `ui_down`.

These strings are defined in Godot's input map. You can access the input map by going to **Project | Project Settings** and clicking the **Input Map** tab. By default, the input map does not show the built-in mapped commands. Toggle the **Show Built-in Actions** button, as seen in *Figure 2.15*, and you should see a list of input mappings.

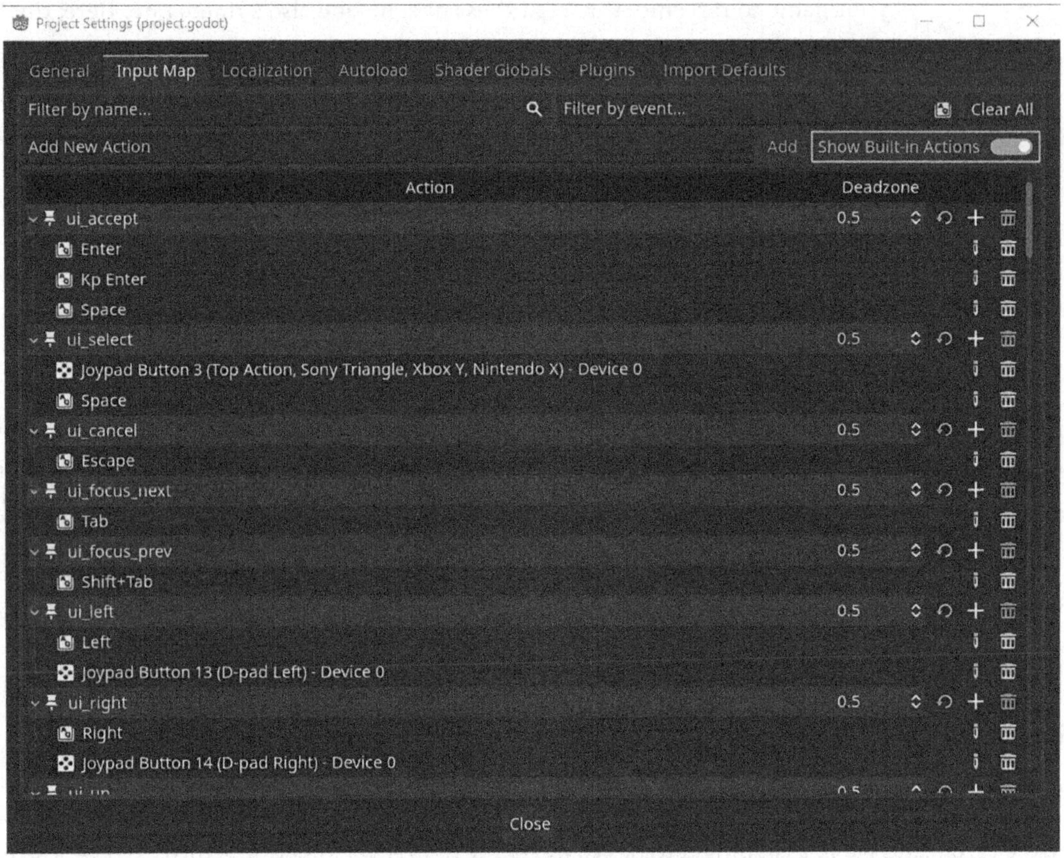

Figure 2.15: The input map from Project Settings

These input mappings can be removed or altered. You can also create new ones. Back in our script, we would check whether the player hit the *Shift* key by using the name running when we check for that player input in our script.

Back to *Figure 2.14*, the final line is a function called `MoveAndSlide`. This function call is almost always the last one when it comes to updating physics on a `CharacterBody`. What it does is tell Godot whether or not our `CharacterBody` has had any collisions of any kind, and then updates our velocity on that body.

Notice how in the template on line 37, the Godot template has set the `Velocity` to `velocity`. The lowercase version of `velocity` is just a placeholder variable, as declared on line 14. We update the `Velocity` property of `CharacterBody` after all other input has been registered, such as walking or jumping, before calling `MoveAndSlide`.

With the final line in the basic movement template reviewed, we can go back to Godot and start building our second scene, the **World** scene where our player will be housed.

Creating the World scene node structure

With our **Player** scene set up and script attached, we can focus on the **World** scene where our player will be placed. To start working in a new scene, click the + sign next to the name of the scene right above the Viewport. Once clicked, in the **Scene** dock, Godot will ask you whether this is a **2D**, **3D**, or **User Interface** scene – we will be selecting **2D**.

Since the script attached to our player allows them to jump, let's create a quick floor to test it. Add a child node and search for `StaticBody2D`. We want to use a static body here because it is a simple body that doesn't require constant physics updates.

Much like our player, the `StaticBody2D` node also needs a collision shape. Add `CollisionShape2D` as we did before and then another `Sprite2D` node. Then, for the `Sprite2D` node's **Texture** property, set the Godot icon and resize it to be stretched out like a thin floor.

Be sure to save the scene and name it `World`.

With both of our scenes set up, we can now add the **Player** scene to the **World** scene. Click and drag the `Player.tscn` file from the **FileSystem** dock and drop it into the **Scene** dock above. What we're doing here is nesting the **Player** scene within the **World** scene. If we look at *Figure 2.16*, we can see how **Player** is underneath the **World** node and has a variety of symbols next to it.

Figure 2.16: The World scene node structure

Let's review the symbols:

- The first one is a clapperboard. If we click it, it will open the **Player** scene. This is a quick and easy way to know when a scene has been nested inside another one.
- The script symbol means we have a script attached to this scene. This is referencing our `Player.cs` script that we created earlier.
- The eye icon next to all nodes means they are currently visible in the scene. If we want to toggle certain components to be visible or not, then we could click the eye. The selected component would be hidden from the Viewport and the open eye would change to a closed eye.

Make sure to place the player above the floor so that when gravity is applied to it, it will drop onto the solid surface below, as shown in *Figure 2.17*. You can hit *F5* or click the **Play** button, which sits right above the inspector.

Let's go ahead and do that now to test the player and make sure the logic of our player is working correctly.

Figure 2.17: Placing the player in our World scene above the floor

With our first project in Godot created and tested, we can move on to the project we'll be creating throughout the rest of the book. We'll be redoing most of these steps but using 3D nodes instead; this 2D example was introduced to get you familiar with navigating Godot's various docks and node system.

Summary

In this chapter, we finished setting up our environment by configuring Godot and selecting our external editor. We also discussed some C# changes that came with the release of Godot 4. This allowed us to create our first scene in Godot and get a bit more familiar with the node system. Alongside that, we created our first C# script and created a very rudimentary scene to test it out.

With the basics of how to create scenes and scripts, and combining them both, out of the way, in the next chapter, we will look at how to organize and structure our project.

3

Organizing and Setting Up a Project for a 3D Action Game

In this chapter, we'll be looking at how to structure our project, set up a GitHub repository to utilize version control for our project, and import the first set of assets we will need to get started creating our player controller, which we'll do in the next chapter.

When it comes to structuring projects in game development, there is no one right way to do it. Over time, you oftentimes develop a system that works well for you, or you adjust to what works best for the tool or system you're using at the time. With game development, there are two main schools of thought, structure by asset and structure by feature – we will consider each before deciding which works best for Godot. After that, we will save our work remotely in a GitHub repository to ensure we have a backup at the ready whenever needed, should something happen to our devices locally or we make changes that we would rather discard.

So, our goals for this chapter will be as follows:

- Structuring our project
- Setting up a GitHub repository
- Importing starter assets
- Pushing to GitHub
- Previewing the game

Technical requirements

For this chapter, the technical requirements will be the same as in *Chapter 1*.

All the code from this chapter will be available in the GitHub repository here: `https://github.com/PacktPublishing/Game-Development-with-Godot-and-C-`.

Structuring our project

When it comes to organizing a project, there are a multitude of ways to do it. Some developers keep things extremely organized and know where every asset is, while others have a fast and loose approach to project structure, which may work for them depending on the project size. Regardless of the system used, the important thing is to stay consistent with it.

In this section, we'll talk about two different approaches to structuring your project and which is preferred when it comes to development in Godot. However, before we get into the two schools of project structuring in game development, we should first discuss what coupling and cohesion are.

Each of these ideas focuses on the way in which our code base is written. Since we'll have multiple scripts throughout our project, it's important to decide early on how we're going to write our code. Of course, when it comes to theory, it can sometimes be difficult to apply, especially retroactively, but since we're creating this for educational purposes, we can practice implementing these ideas so that in future projects, they come more naturally.

Coupling and cohesion

If you've done software development before or are studying computer science in school, you may have heard the phrase "low coupling, high cohesion." The two terms have a direct correlation to each other. Let's explore how.

Coupling is the idea of how interdependent objects are to each other. We can also think of coupling as how many required connections one object has to another object, and how one object relates to other objects outside of it. For example, let's say we have a Player object and then a World object with all the data about the possible items the player can find. While it isn't impossible to manage, here are some reasons why designing an item system in the World object might be difficult for long-term development:

- It makes debugging and finding errors more difficult
- If we wanted any variance in our items, we wouldn't be able to have that variety unless we duplicated the same code in the World object, which makes the script cumbersome
- Reusing any items in other ways becomes challenging since they aren't their own objects

Ideally, we would want each item to inherit from an abstract item class that would trigger certain behaviors when the player triggers them.

Using the example we discussed, we can think of coupling as the line connecting Player and World in *Figure 3.1*:

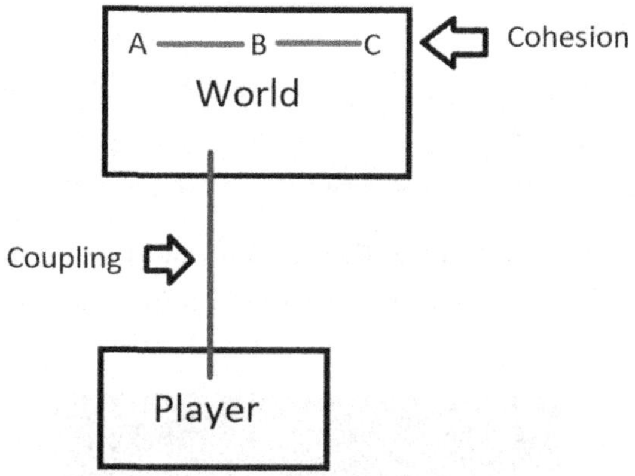

Figure 3.1: An example of cohesion versus coupling

Cohesion, on the other hand, is about what an object does. Whereas with coupling, we were looking at how an object functioned outside itself, here, we want to see all the relationships inside a specific object.

Going back to our example, the World script has all this information about the various Player items, but there isn't a need for the World to know the details of these items. The World is not impacted by what our Player has equipped. Also, if we wanted to create an additional item for our Player, we would have to change many parts of the World script, depending on how we implemented it, rather than adding/modifying a function call from an item class.

Going back to *Figure 3.1*, objects A, B, and C are considered cohesive as they are all the components within the World object, which could be generating items or spawning platforms. These components would be things the World needs and should know about versus putting items that appear in the World but function on the Player.

Ideally in development, we want high cohesion and low coupling. This means our objects are isolated among themselves and very rarely depend on other objects to function. This is super important, especially as we iterate on certain objects. When objects are decoupled, it's easy to modify them as it doesn't require changing a bunch of other unrelated objects. A great way to keep objects and scenes decoupled is through the usage of signals, which we'll talk about in a future chapter.

Knowing a little bit of this computer science theory will help us in the long run when it comes to a multitude of things, one of them being structuring our project. With an understanding between cohesion and coupling complete, let's turn our attention toward how we can utilize these ideas in structuring our project in a way that's easy and manageable.

Structure by asset

As the heading suggests, structuring your project by assets would mean that all the art is in one folder, all the music is in another, and so on and so forth. This is a very common project structure and may even be one you have used in the past with other game engines.

The benefit of structuring a project like in *Figure 3.2* is that it's easy to find a specific file, since you put everything into its own folder. Here, you can see how the **Player** scene and the Player script are split up:

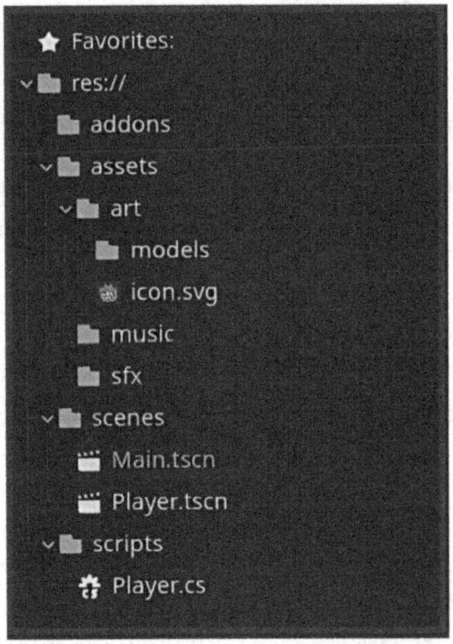

Figure 3.2: An example of structuring your Godot project by asset

A drawback, however, is when, say, you are working in the Player scene, which uses the Player script, but you also need to tweak the model or add a camera with its own script. Another drawback is that when you have many scripts and scenes present, it can be difficult to find the script you need to access. However, Godot has a very convenient feature that allows you to go directly into the script from the scene. When any scene is open, you can click the script icon for any object that has a script attached to it, as shown in *Figure 3.3*:

Figure 3.3: The script icon in the scene dock to directly access a script

Now, let's look at how we would structure our project by feature.

Structure by feature

Another way to consider organizing our project is by features. For example, this would mean that everything involving our player would be housed in one folder called `player`. This would include everything from the model to the script controlling the character, like in *Figure 3.4*:

Figure 3.4: An example of structuring your Godot project by feature

As well as a `player` folder, you can also see a `world` folder with the relevant world-related files inside.

Between structuring by assets and structuring by features, there is no right or wrong method – use what works best for you. However, let's look at what's best when working in Godot.

What's good for Godot?

With the way Godot is designed, many of the resources are contained within the scene itself, which means *it makes sense to group everything in a project by feature*. Going back to our Player example, we would create a folder called `player` and put the scene, art, scripts, and anything else relating to or called on by the player in there – essentially, what we have represented in *Figure 3.4*.

Of course, there are some components in our game that will not be impacted by either system. When we start designing systems in our game, we may want to reuse them in some places. So, two additional folders that will be beneficial in our structure will be the following:

- `lib` (for `libraries`, though some folks also call it a `utilities` folder): This is a place where we can reuse scripts or systems that show up in multiple scenes
- `addons`: For any third-party plugins or systems we may want or need

So, moving forward, we are going to be utilizing the structure-by-feature system. The reason we are doing this is because of how Godot packages scenes, and it means we'll have an easier time navigating to the various components in each of our scenes.

After deciding on how we want to structure our project, it's time to set up a GitHub repository to keep track of all the changes to our project.

Setting up a GitHub repository

Version control is an essential step in the software development life cycle. If you're unfamiliar with **version control** (also known as **source control**), it's the way in which we back up and maintain projects. It's not only for software projects but can be used for documentation as well.

For the purposes of this book, we will be using Git through GitHub – it's free, there's a lot of documentation for it, and it works super-well with Godot. Let's briefly break down the differences between Git and GitHub. Git is the distributed version control software that tracks changes between our files. GitHub, on the other hand, is a web-based Git repository. GitHub adds many graphical features when it comes to using Git and is where the Godot Engine code base is housed.

> Note
>
> Git is an open source licensed version control, while GitHub is maintained by Microsoft.

If you do not want to use GitHub or have a similar service that does the same thing, feel free to use that instead. Some GitHub alternatives include the following:

- *GitLab*: Very similar to GitHub in the services it provides.
- *Bit Bucket*: Used more for personal repositories. Created by Jira, the very popular ticket system used in development.
- *SourceForge*: An open source alternative to GitHub.
- *AWS CodeCommit*: An option that naturally has a lot of AWS integration.

Remember, all these alternatives use Git. If you don't want to use Git at all, some alternative version control software includes the following:

- *Mercurial*
- *Subversion*
- *Azure DevOps*

Finding the right version control for the project and workflow you're setting up is critical to the good management of a project, especially when you're working within a team. It's not unheard of for a team to switch version control systems, but it is a cumbersome undertaking that can be avoided with some forethought. Be sure to pick the one that best suits you and your team. For the purposes of this book and project, all the version control will utilize Git through GitHub.

Now that we know more about version control, let's get started in creating and setting up GitHub.

Creating a GitHub account

If you already have an existing GitHub account, feel free to jump to the *Importing starter assets* section, or, if you have an existing version control setup that you'd rather use, feel free to use that.

To create a GitHub account, first, you need to access the website at `https://github.com/`. Then, click the **Sign up** button that's in the top-right-hand corner, as pictured in *Figure 3.5*:

Figure 3.5: The Sign up button on the GitHub website

You should then see a screen that looks like *Figure 3.6*; each option will reveal itself on the screen as you progress through the form:

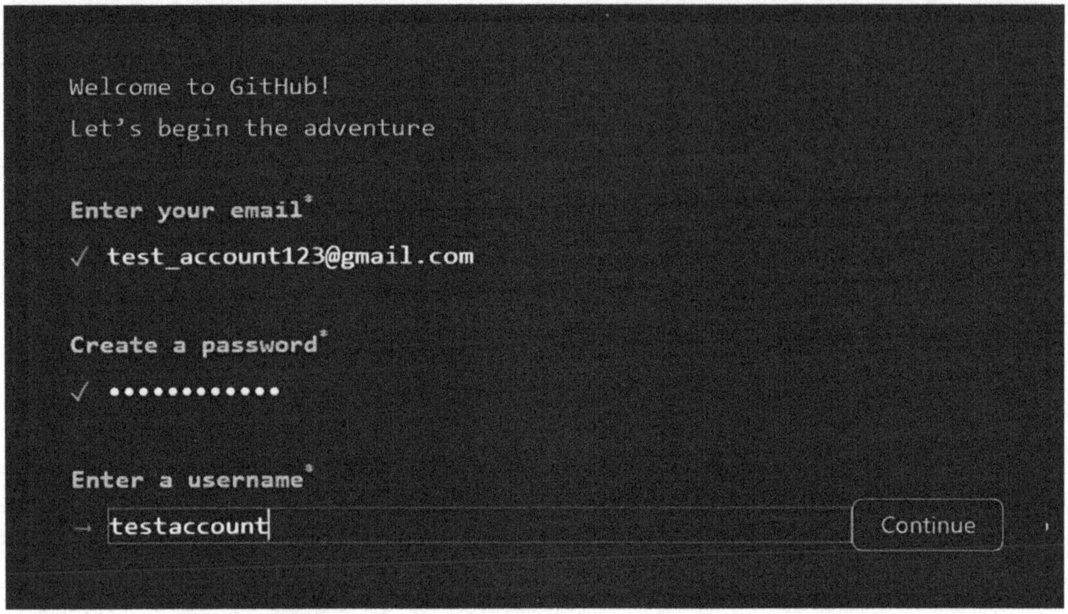

Figure 3.6: The Create Account form on GitHub

On this screen, enter your email address, and then create a GitHub password and username.

Once done, click the **Create Account** button that appears at the bottom of the form, and you'll be taken to a new screen that will require you to log in to your email and retrieve a code to validate your credentials.

The last step is just a short questionnaire from GitHub, asking about how you'll use this service. Feel free to click the **Skip Personalization** button that's at the bottom of the screen for this portion.

Once you have verified your account and successfully signed in, you'll be taken to the GitHub Dashboard, which should look something like *Figure 3.7*:

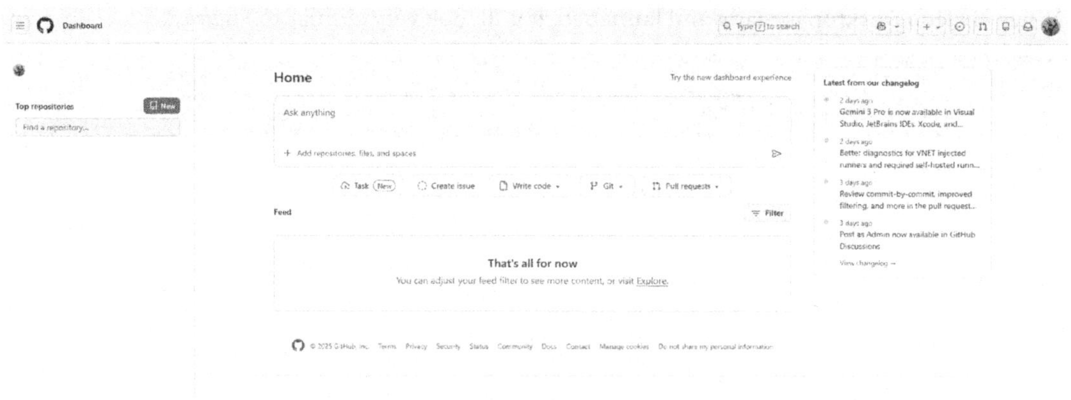

Figure 3.7: The GitHub Dashboard screen

This can, at first, be overwhelming and confusing to navigate. Thankfully, there is an application we'll install that will make interfacing with GitHub and its servers a lot easier.

Downloading GitHub Desktop

Now that we have created our GitHub account (or whichever version control system we're using), we are going to download GitHub Desktop, an application that allows us to clone repositories from GitHub and manage them in a local space on our machine. You can think of GitHub Desktop as a middleman between your local machine and the GitHub servers. Much like version control systems, there are multiple ways to access and manage a repository. This one is very user friendly and an excellent introduction to version control if you are unfamiliar with it.

To download the software, go to `https://desktop.github.com/`. From there, you should see a **Download for Windows** button (it may be something else, depending on the operating system you're using). Once downloaded, click the executable in your downloads folder and follow the steps to complete installation.

When GitHub Desktop is ready and launched, it will look very similar to *Figure 3.8*:

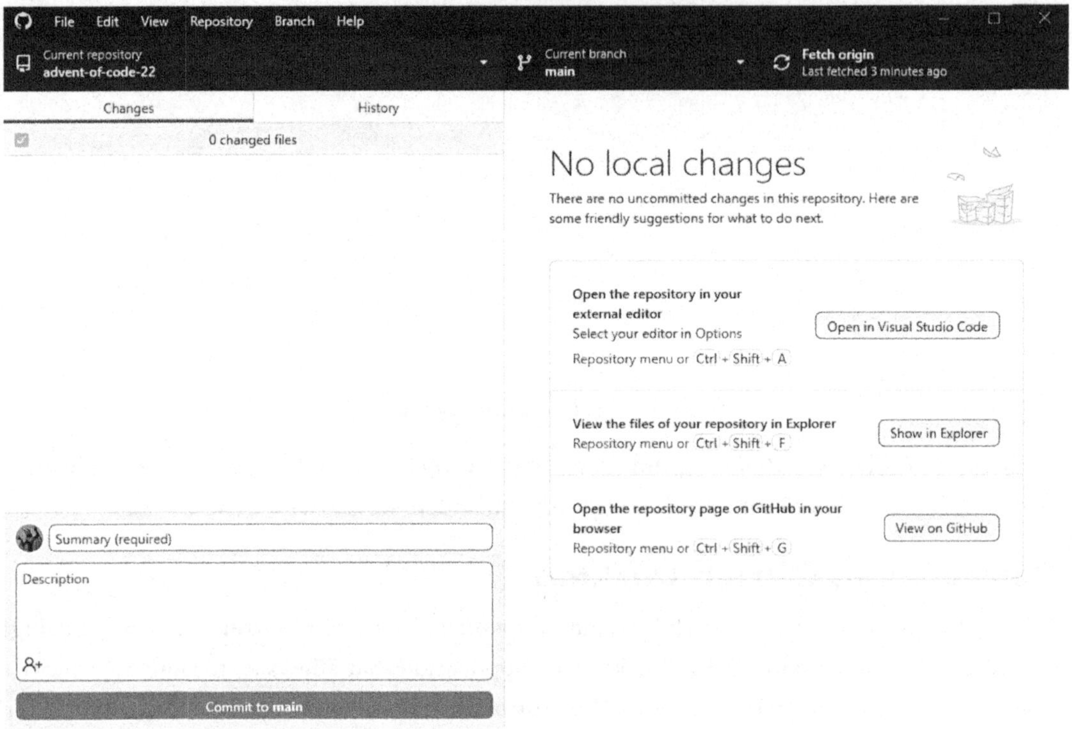

Figure 3.8: The main GitHub Desktop screen after installation

At this point, you aren't hooked into your GitHub account, so you have no repositories on your local machine yet. We'll be walking through how to do this next.

In GitHub Desktop, click the **File** button in the top-left corner, and then click **New Repository...**. This will make a new window pop up, such as that in *Figure 3.9*, asking you questions to provide information about the repository:

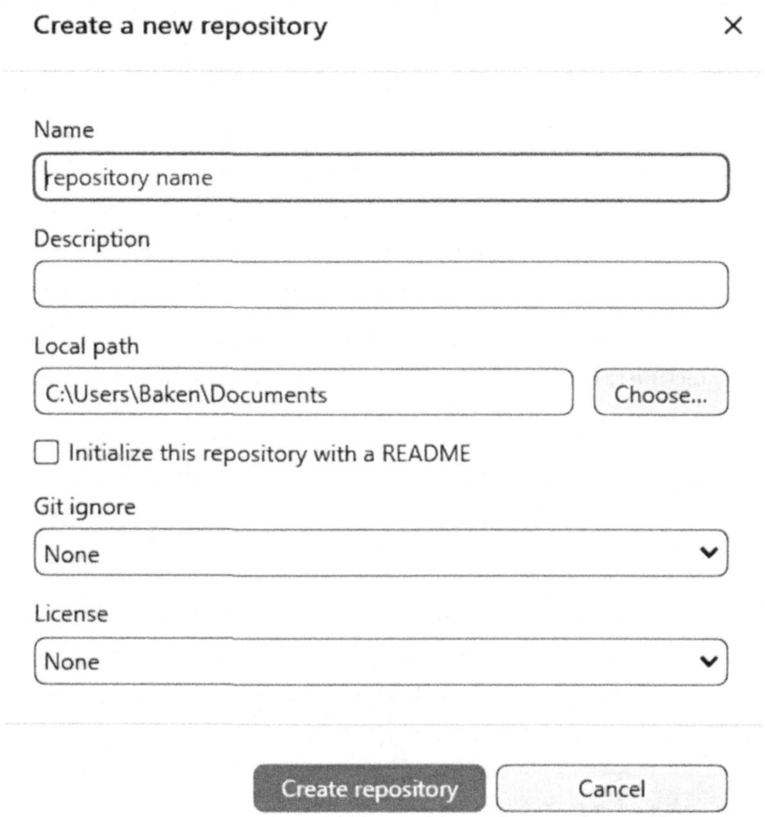

Figure 3.9: The pop-up form when creating a new repository in GitHub Desktop

The most important ones are the name and the path, but let's go through each one:

- **Name**: This is the name of the repository that you will see both on GitHub and in your File Explorer. Do not have any spaces in the name and make sure it's something you'll remember. I named mine `third-person-action-demo`.
- **Description**: The **Description** field is more of a note to yourself and anyone you'll be sharing the project with. It'll be on GitHub and let folks know the type of content that's in it.
- **Local path**: Just as the name indicates, this is where the local copy of the GitHub repository will be on your machine. I oftentimes select `Documents` and then a folder on my machine is created, using the repository name. So, the location of my project is `../Documents/third-person-action`.

- **Initialize this repository with a README**: This can be done if you want to add more information for others about how to use your project. This is important when sharing the project. If you don't create it now, you can create it later, so it's completely optional.
- **Git ignore**: One of the nice things that GitHub will do for us is ignore files we tell it to ignore, preventing machine-generated files from being pushed to our repository. Which files GitHub ignores will depend on the type of `.gitignore` file you create. If you click the **Git ignore** drop-down menu, there is an option for Godot. Feel free to select it, but since only one person will be working in this repository, it isn't completely necessary.
- **License**: This determines how others can use, credit, or change the work you've created. We'll be selecting the MIT license, which is also what the Godot Engine is under.

Now that we have our GitHub repository created locally, we can start adding assets to it that we'll be using for the project. These will give us something to push to GitHub later in the chapter.

Note

Alternatively, since we are using Visual Studio Code as our code editor, you can explore the option of **GitLens**, which is a VS Code extension. While we won't cover its setup here, you can learn more about it here: `https://marketplace.visualstudio.com/items?itemName=eamodio.gitlens`.

Importing starter assets

With our GitHub account and repository set up and our project decided, we can turn to downloading the first set of assets that we'll be using for the next chapter.

The following is a list of items we'll be downloading and importing into our project:

- A 3D model for our player from GDQuest
- Textures for our world from Kenney Assets

Let's look at how to import them.

Importing the character model

Since this book focuses on Godot and not 3D modeling, we will be utilizing a free pre-made model for our project. This rigged and animated model is provided by GDQuest and contributors. GDQuest is an excellent resource for tutorials on how to create games in Godot. The creator, Nathan, has been working hard to provide quality content to the Godot community for years in the form of YouTube tutorials and online courses. If you saw the blog post from Godot about version 4's release and watched the video, that was GDQuest!

To access the 3D character, go to the following GitHub repository: `https://github.com/GDQuest/godot-3d-mannequin/tree/master`.

In the folder structure listed in the repository on this web page, you'll see there is a folder called `godot-csharp`. This is what we'll be accessing once we download it.

Above the folder structure, there are buttons called **Go to file**, **Add file**, and **Code**, as shown in *Figure 3.10*:

Figure 3.10: The buttons available for accessing a repository on GitHub

Click the **Code** button, which will open a submenu with more options on how to copy the repository. We won't be cloning the repository, since we only need access to a few files. Instead, we can simply click the **Download ZIP** button, as seen in *Figure 3.11*:

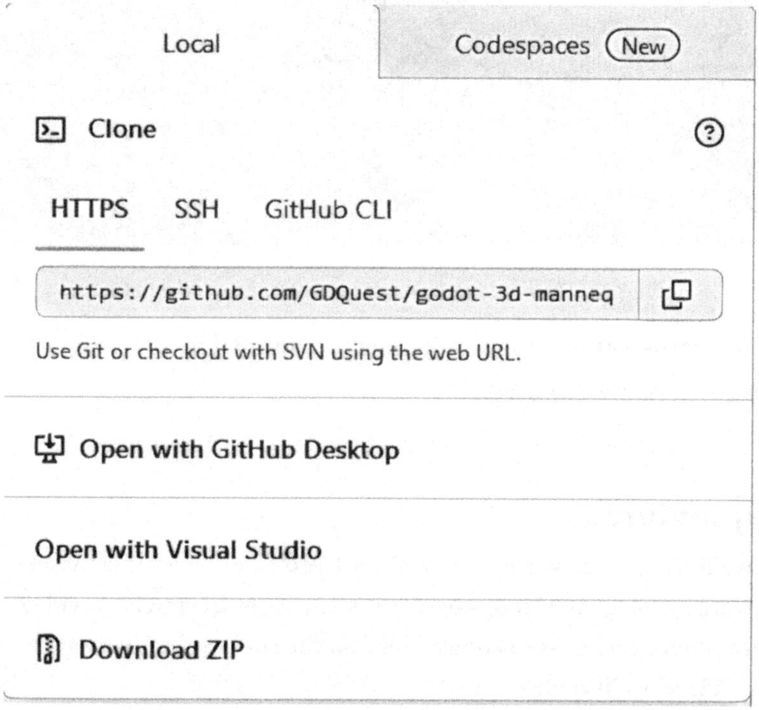

Figure 3.11: The submenu for downloading the GitHub repository files

Locate the zipped folder on your system and extract it. You should have an extracted folder called `godot-3d-mannequin-master`. We're going to navigate to the model by clicking into the following folders – so click `godot-csharp | assets | 3d | mannequiny`.

You will find some material files and a `.glb` file. The `.glb` file is the one we want. Click and drag it into our project by dropping it into the filesystem dock in Godot. There will be a pop-up that says it's importing the asset; once it's in your filesystem, double-click it to open it in Godot. A new window should appear, and you'll see a blue mannequin, as shown in *Figure 3.12*:

Figure 3.12: The mannequin asset correctly imported into Godot 4

Don't change any of the settings, as we only want to confirm that it was imported correctly; just exit out of this window and save your project.

Now we can move on to importing the textures used to paint the level we'll design.

Importing textures

The textures we'll use for designing our world are provided by Kenney Assets. This is a great resource when prototyping anything, whether it's 2D, 3D, or UI, and is provided entirely for free. While there are a lot of packages to choose from on the site, we will be using a texture package for the block-out level we'll create.

You can access the textures we'll be downloading at `https://www.kenney.nl/assets/prototype-textures`. Once downloaded, extract the file and drag the extracted folder into your Godot project, just like we did with our character model. I've renamed the `textures` folder to `env_textures` to stay organized. I also created a `player` folder and a `world` folder, which is what we'll need for the next couple of chapters. The filesystem structure can be viewed in *Figure 3.13*:

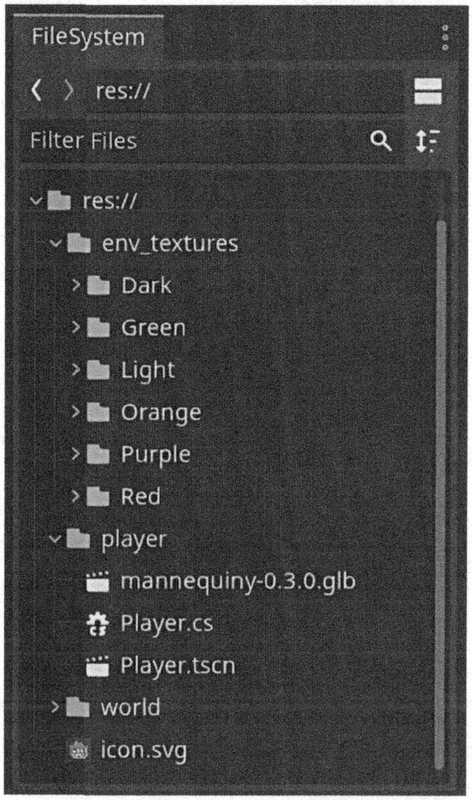

Figure 3.13: The current filesystem setup we have, structured by feature

We've now successfully imported our starter assets! With these couple of items in our project, we can start to build a player controller and a world for that player to live in. Before we do that, though, we need to push these changes to our GitHub repository to make sure we don't lose any progress, should something happen to our machine.

Pushing to GitHub

If you're familiar with the interface that is GitHub, feel free to skip to the next section of this chapter. Otherwise, let's get into how to manage our work in relation to GitHub.

At this point, we've created a repository through GitHub that's currently on our local machine. At the top of GitHub, there should be a black bar that says the current repository you're in, the branch you're on (**main** is always the first and default branch when creating a repository), and then the state the branch is in. You can see an example of this in *Figure 3.14*:

Figure 3.14: The top menu bar of GitHub Desktop

As we can see in *Figure 3.14*, the current state of the branch shows an arrow pointing upward that says **Publish repository**. This process is called **pushing** to a repository, meaning the repository can be stored on their servers. So, click the button and a confirmation menu will appear, as shown in *Figure 3.15*:

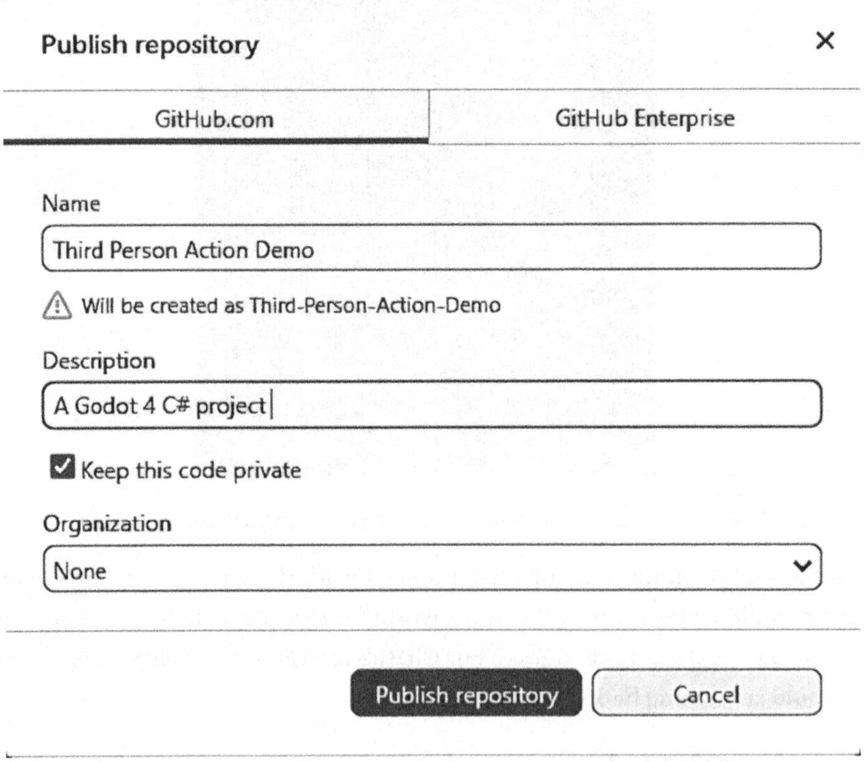

Figure 3.15: Confirmation menu when publishing a GitHub repository

The most important item in this confirmation menu is whether to keep the code private or not, but let's go ahead and break down what each of these options are:

- **Name**: The name of the repository that will be listed on GitHub's website and server. I've named it `Third Person Action Demo`.
- **Description**: A short blurb about the project. I've described it as `A Godot 4 C# project`.
- **Keep this code private**: This will determine whether the GitHub project is available to anyone, regardless of whether they have a GitHub account or not. The repository for this book is made public, but you can opt to keep yours private or not.
- **Organization**: These are groups on GitHub and multiple GitHub projects can be placed under them. As this is a singular project, it is not part of any organization.

We've already established a name and a description. Once we've decided on our privacy settings, we can click **Publish repository**. We've now successfully set up our GitHub repository on both our local machine and the GitHub servers!

For future GitHub usage, and whenever you're working in a team or on someone else's repository, the flow of GitHub is to almost always do these steps in the following order:

1. *Fetch*: This will download any changes or updates that have been made to your repository. This only really matters if more than one person is working in the same branch.
2. *Pull*: If there are any changes from someone else or if you switched machines, you can pull those changes from the repository down to your local machine.
3. *Commit*: After you fetch, you can commit any changes you've created. This is where you basically mark what files you want GitHub to save to its servers.
4. *Push*: Once committed, you push the changes to GitHub's servers and have successfully saved your work.

There are all kinds of other options with GitHub too – there's branching, forking, managing merge conflicts, and so on. While this may be overwhelming, we will only be working with the options just listed and will not be creating multiple branches. However, if you are familiar with version control and feel comfortable doing that, then of course feel free to. If you want to learn more about GitHub Desktop or troubleshoot an existing issue, check out the documentation for GitHub Desktop at `https://docs.github.com/en/desktop`.

Now, we'll take a moment to discuss the game we're going to create and the various systems we'll cover in Godot to make it.

Previewing the game

Currently, we have our project set up for version control and some of the assets we'll be using in the game. Now, let's talk about the game we'll be making in the rest of the book.

We'll be creating a 3D action-adventure game where the player will be able to run around the world, interacting with and collecting items. In the next two chapters, we'll be creating our player controller and designing our world. Yours won't look exactly like mine in *Figure 3.16*, but it will have the same player model that we downloaded and imported, as well as the same assets you see in the screenshot:

Figure 3.16: A screenshot of the game we're creating

Part 1 of the book is essentially the foundation, focusing primarily on the player. In *Part 2* of the book, we'll be covering UI and also looking at implementing audio, lighting, and pathfinding. Finally, we'll review our completed project and improve any components that we think need to be improved/reworked.

With the game completed at this point in the book, we'll spend the rest of it looking beyond our project. So, in *Part 3*, we'll look at how to export and publish our game to others so they can access it. We'll also discuss how to contribute to the Godot Engine directly as well as the documentation. Lastly, we'll explore additional resources so you can continue your Godot journey!

Then, we'll be at the end of our adventurous journey of creating a 3D action game in Godot using C#. While we won't cover every system in Godot, we will cover most of them. One of the best things about game development is that even though you'll be following a step-by-step guide throughout this book, your game, in the end, will be uniquely yours. So, let's get started and make a game in Godot!

Summary

This chapter was the final push in getting our environment and project set up before diving into Godot and C#. Here, we took the time to understand the best project structure based on what was good for Godot due to how it packages scenes and resources. Then, we imported the first couple of assets that we'll need to create a player controller. We discovered a couple of awesome communities that have a multitude of resources when it comes to creating projects in Godot. Finally, we set up a version control system to track and manage our project without the worry of losing it.

In the next chapter, we're going to work entirely in Godot and create our player controller. This will include setting up the node structure, creating and managing a camera on the player, and learning how to trigger various animations on our model. We'll end the chapter by extending the player controller to include some actions such as running and interacting with the world.

Part 2

Creating a Simple 3D Action Game

In this part of the book, we'll create a vertical slice of our 3D action game. We'll start by building out a 3D level and creating a world that feels lived in. Then, we'll build on top of this world, focusing on different areas. The first will be creating a main menu and providing a user interface for the player to navigate our world. After that, we'll add sound effects and music to add to the game's immersion. Lastly, we'll create a **non-playable character** (**NPC**) and provide it with pathfinding, making it move autonomously throughout our world. By the end of this part, you will have a vertical slice of a simple 3D action game with a deep understanding of Godot's theme editor, sound buses, and navigational agents.

This part of the book includes the following chapters:

- *Chapter 4, Creating Our Player Controller*
- *Chapter 5, Creating Our Game World*
- *Chapter 6, Developing and Managing the User Interface*
- *Chapter 7, Adding Sound Effects and Music*
- *Chapter 8, Adding Navigation and Pathfinding*

4

Creating Our Player Controller

In this chapter, we'll be looking at how to create a **player controller**. This is an object that lives in its own game scene and can be dropped into our game World (we'll design the game World later).

This chapter's goal will be to design the player controller in a manageable and easily extendable way. For example, we'll have the player able to walk, run, and jump, but if you wanted to add something such as a grappling hook or a double jump, you could do that with minimal work.

This chapter will be the foundation for how the player interacts with the world and will be pivotal in future chapters; not only is the world and level design important but how the player reacts to that world too.

Our goals for this chapter will be as follows:

- Creating our player's node structure
- Providing movement to our player
- Moving the camera
- Creating our animation tree
- Expanding our jumping animation
- Adding a run ability

Technical requirements

For this chapter, the technical requirements will be the same as in *Chapter 1*.

All the code from this chapter will be available in the GitHub repository here: `https://github.com/PacktPublishing/Game-Development-with-Godot-and-C-`.

Creating our player's node structure

In the last chapter, we downloaded and imported some of the assets we'll need with our project. One of those items was a rigged and animated character model from GDQuest. We will now take that model and expand its functionality to create a player that takes inputs and animations. To do that, we need to add specific nodes such as a camera, collisions, and a C# script.

Open Godot and select **Other Node**, which is in the **Scene** dock and below the 2D and 3D options. Much like we did in our 2D example in *Chapter 2*, we will be creating a character to interact with our world. So, search for **CharacterBody3D**, select it, and rename it to `Player`. Then, click and drag our open source character model, `mannequiny.glb`, from our **FileSystem** dock into our **Scene** dock.

With this step, we're nesting the mannequin model inside our **Player** scene. This means that the **mannequiny.glb** scene is packed into the **Player** scene. Packed scenes are serialized, isolated scenes that are written to file. They can be called through `ResourceLoader` and often sit inside other scenes. Let's look at an example.

When the scene for the **Player** model, **mannequiny.glb**, is initially added, it has a root node of **CharacterBody3D**, as shown in *Figure 4.1*. When it's added to the **World** scene, however, it's a single node with a clapperboard icon next to it. Being a single node in another scene, even though it has multiple child nodes, is what denotes it as a packed scene. This is something we will do repeatedly throughout the book, allowing us to have encapsulated objects that we can change with minimal rework.

However, we'll need to access some of these nodes, so go ahead and right-click the **mannequiny.glb** node that's in our **Scene** dock. Then, select **Editable Children**. This is the correct way to access any packed scene we have as it will keep a connection to the scene even after it's in another scene packed. We're doing this because we need access to things such as **AnimationPlayer**. Our screen should now look like *Figure 4.1*.

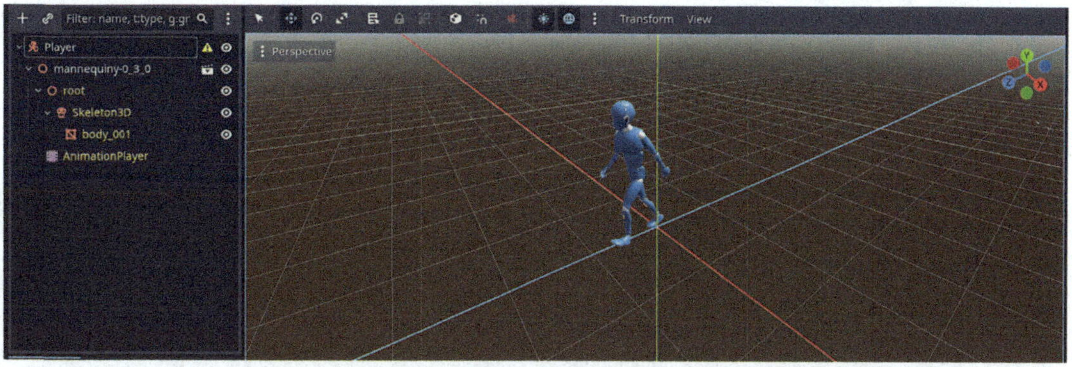

Figure 4.1: The Player scene in Godot after importing mannequiny

A close-up of the node structure can be seen in *Figure 4.2*.

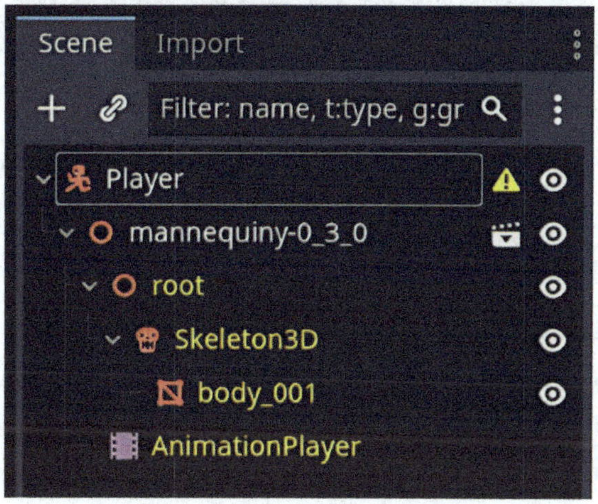

Figure 4.2: A close-up of the Player scene node structure up to this point

Notice how the nodes below **mannequiny-0_3_0** are gold now. This is because they are flagged as **Editable Children** in Godot. We do this so we only have to edit one instance of the **Player** model without needing to update every scene it's in. This concept may apply more to other packed scenes such as collectibles or something else that's easily repeated in the **World** scene. With the setting correctly applied, let's turn our attention to the **AnimationPlayer** we now have access to.

After adding the **Player** model, it will already be looping an animation. Before doing anything else, let's set the animation to **idle** as the default is set to **run**. Select **AnimationPlayer** from *Figure 4.2* and where the **Output** console is below the Viewport, there's a drop-down menu, as can be seen in *Figure 4.3*. Set this dropdown to **idle** for now.

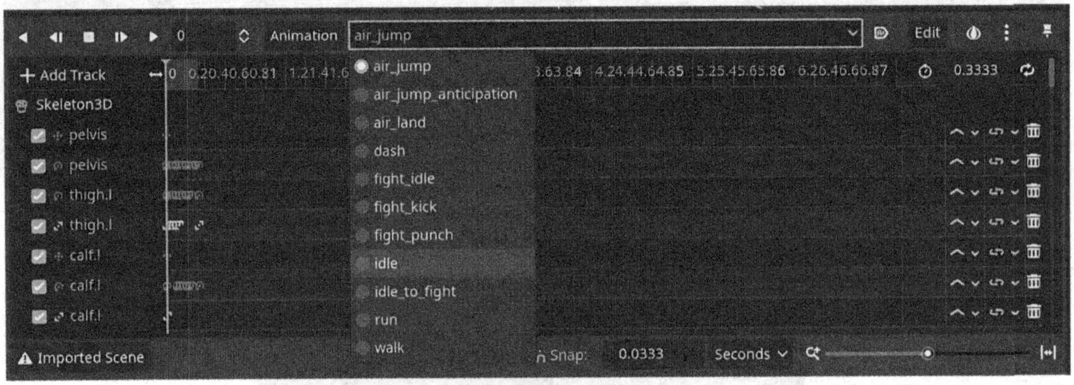

Figure 4.3: Setting the animation to idle for the player

Looking back at *Figure 4.2*, the **CharacterBody3D** that we renamed to **Player** should have a small caution triangle next to it, alerting us to the fact it has no collision currently.

To add a collision shape, follow these steps:

1. Right-click the **Player** node and select **Add Child Node**.
2. Find a **CollisionShape3D** (make sure it's for 3D and not 2D) and add it to our scene by making it a child of our root node, **Player**, which is the **CharacterBody3D** node.
3. Select **CollisionShape3D** to select the node. In the **Inspector** dock (right-hand side of the Viewport), there is an option for **Shape**. It currently says **empty**. Open the drop-down arrow next to the word **empty**, select **NewCapsuleShape**, and a capsule should appear on our character model in the Viewport.

The capsule is a bit larger than our model, which means when our player interacts with the World, they'll collide with objects sooner than we'd like. After selecting the **CollisionShape3D** node in the **Scene** dock, we can resize the capsule using the **Inspector** dock, setting the radius of the capsule to be a little smaller, so it hugs the model a bit better. The exact placement can be set by adjusting the **Height** and **Radius** values of the capsule and its **Position** values, as shown in *Figure 4.4*.

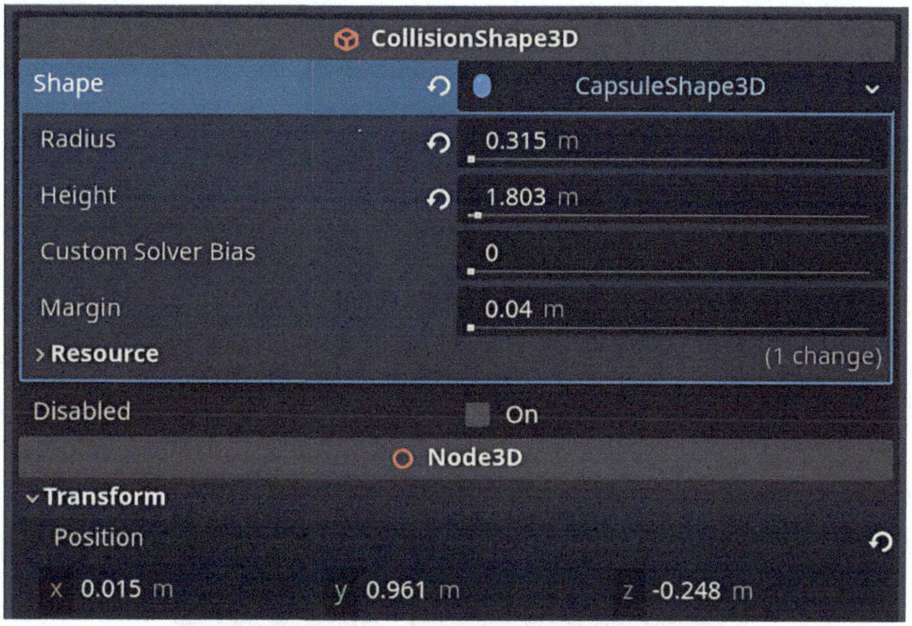

Figure 4.4: Settings for CollisionShape3D

After adjusting **CollisionShape3D**, as shown here, you can see the result in *Figure 4.5*:

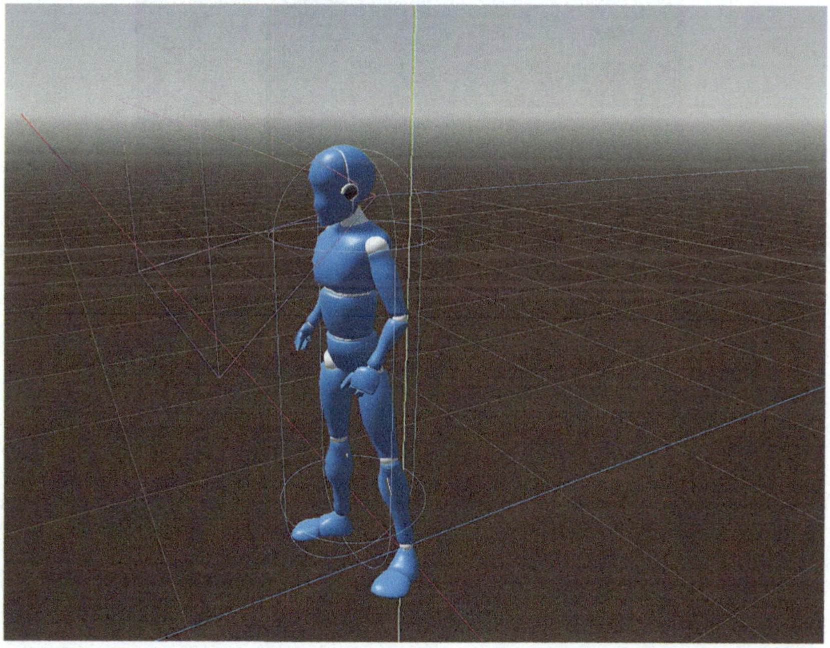

Figure 4.5: The Player model with a capsule collider around it

With our collision snuggly on our **Player** model, we can move on to the next part of setting up our **Player** scene. We'll be adding a camera to an empty **Node3D** to act as a camera mount along with a spring arm:

1. Right-click the **Player** node and select **Add Child Node**.
2. Find and select the **Node3D** node – this is a generic node that will act as a placeholder for our camera components.
3. Add a child node to our **Node3D** node, search for **SpringArm3D**, and select it.
4. Add a child node to our **SpringArm3D** node, search for **Camera3D**, and select it.
5. Select the **Node3D** node we created and rename it to `CameraPivot`.

Those were the final nodes to add to our **Player** scene. The node structure should now look exactly like *Figure 4.6*:

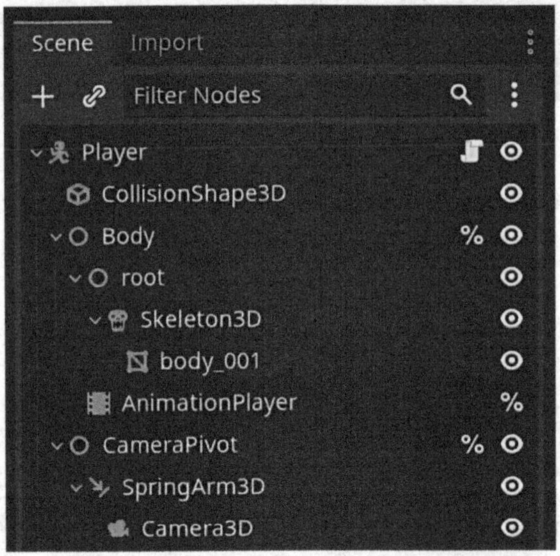

Figure 4.6: The Player node structure that's needed to get started

> Note
>
> I've gone ahead and renamed the **mannequiny-0_3_0** node to Body for the sake of clarity, which you can see in *Figure 4.6*.

With the **Player** nodes organized in the right hierarchy, we need to position some of these nodes in our Viewport in more functional places on our **Player** model. For example, the **Camera3D** and **SpringArm3D** nodes are, by default, not where we need them to be. Before doing that, however, let's take a moment to learn some nice tips and tricks for navigating the Viewport.

Navigating the Viewport

Since we will be moving in the 3D space of the Viewport quite a bit and working with various assets, let's talk briefly about how to maneuver around it. Each axis is a different color, and that color corresponds to one of the lines in the Viewport where our model is sitting. This makes it easier to know what axis we're working on or looking at. These are also represented back in *Figure 4.1*.

There are two ways to navigate space in the Viewport:

- Clicking the scroll wheel and rotating/panning with the mouse
- Right-clicking with the mouse and moving around using the *W*, *A*, *S*, and *D* keys

To speed up while using the right mouse click, you can also hold the left *Shift* key.

We can also augment how close or far away objects are by doing the following:

- Holding *Ctrl* and using *+* / *-*
- Pinching the mouse pad if you're on a laptop or using the scroll wheel
- Holding the right mouse button and moving the camera with *W*, *A*, *S*, and *D*

With a better grasp of how to navigate this space, let's finish setting up our player character's camera.

Configuring our camera

As mentioned, our **Camera3D** and **SpringArm3D** nodes are not placed in the most optimal places for our player. When we create them, they are generated in the scene at a default position based on their parent node position or at the origin of the scene, `(0,0,0)`. Let's fix that.

In the Viewport, click and drag the **CameraPivot** node – this will automatically move its children, **SpringArm3D** and **Camera3D** too – and position the camera to be directly behind the neck of the player, as shown in *Figure 4.7*. To do this, we'll need to rotate the camera on the *Y* axis to make sure it's facing the correct way, but we'll do that in our `Player.cs` script later. The Viewport, camera, and player should look like *Figure 4.7*.

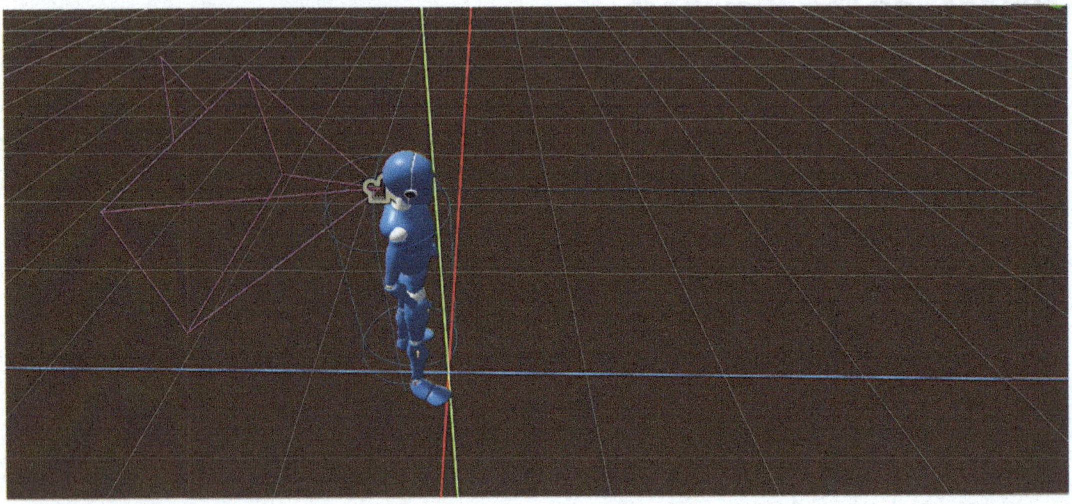

Figure 4.7: The camera positioning on the player's head

The purple-looking lines in *Figure 4.7* extending behind the **Player** model's face are the **Camera** node's viewable area, while a faint blue line above the grid (not the axis but further above) is the **SpringArm3D** node. It's extending out beyond the player's head. If we weren't changing the rotation of the camera angles in the script (and based on player input), we would want to change how this is set up. Instead, we'll move on to configuring our spring arm by looking at its properties.

With all nodes correctly positioned, let's make sure we have the properties of the **SpringArm3D** node correct. Highlight the node and look at the **Inspector** dock. Our **SpringArm3D** node has a default camera length of **1** meter. We want to set the **Length** option to be **3** meters instead. The way a **SpringArm** node works is that when the game starts, the **Camera** node will be pushed back along the length of the **SpringArm** node unless it collides with something, such as in *Figure 4.8*. When the player walks into the caves in our **World** scene and we rotate the camera, the camera is pushed closer to the player along the **SpringArm** node. This is why, sometimes when we rotate cameras in games, we get a close-up view of our character. You can see this effect in *Figure 4.8*, which is a sneak peek of the game World we'll be creating in the next chapter.

Figure 4.8: An example of our spring arm pushing the camera forward

The important part of a spring arm is that it allows the camera to move around collisions, so it can focus on the character as someone pans around without getting clipped out or blocked. Cameras are a crucial part of a third-person controller and require some unique conditions to be set, which we will look at when rotating our player and panning with the mouse.

> Note
>
> If you are unfamiliar with what a spring arm is and how it works in relation to cameras, you can read more about it here: `https://docs.godotengine.org/en/stable/tutorials/3d/spring_arm.html`.

And that's it for now! We'll be adding some more items to our player as we get deeper into development, but this is an excellent base to start with. Again, because our **Player** scene is encapsulated by itself, we can easily extend it to add more components. For example, we could create items that are their own packed scenes that are then added as children to our player.

Be sure to save the scene and name it `Player`. Then, go ahead and test it by clicking the **Play** button that's on a clapperboard in the top-right corner, as shown in *Figure 4.9*.

Figure 4.9: The Play button for running specific scenes highlighted

This **Play** button will run the currently open scene only, not the default one for the project. A new window should appear running the scene, and the player should float in the air. If there are no errors, then you're good to move on to the next step.

Next, we'll get our player moving and create a small test area for our movement to make sure our player is tuned and ready to go.

Providing movement to our player

As we saw in *Chapter 2*, providing base movement to a **CharacterBody** object is very easy. Godot provides a good foundation to start with in terms of scripting, so let's go ahead and create the movement script to get our model moving.

Attaching a script

To attach a script in our **Player** scene, follow these steps:

1. Right-click the **Player** node and click the **Attach Script** button.
2. Make sure the script is being created in C#, not GDscript.
3. Select the **Basic Movement** template from the **Template** dropdown. The template should be automatically selected in the **Template** box by default when attaching a script to a **CharacterBody** but confirm before moving forward.
4. Name the script `Player.cs`.
5. Click **Create** and the template script should open in the Godot editor.
6. Double-click the script from the **FileSystem** dock, and the script should open in the IDE you've configured in the **Editor** settings. Don't erase anything in the template as we'll be building off it in later sections – just simply save the scene.

It really is that easy! This script provides very limited movement in so much as we can only move left, right, forward, and backward, but it's a start, nonetheless. We'll be augmenting a lot of this boilerplate throughout the rest of the chapter. But next, we need a floor with collisions to test our movement.

Adding a test floor

To start adding a test floor, let's create a new scene by clicking the + sign next to the name of the **Player** scene, as shown in *Figure 4.10*:

Figure 4.10: The Player scene tab next to the button to create a new scene

In the Scene dock, we'll be prompted about what kind of scene we're creating – this will be a **3D** scene. Now, save the scene and name it `TestArea`.

Then, in the Viewport of the scene, you'll have some options for viewing the world. The main toolbar under the scene names are ways to interact with the Viewport. The other option right below that toolbar is our angle of view; this is a button that sits in the top left-hand corner of the Viewport. Click the **Perspective** button and make sure it's set to **Perspective**. You can see it in *Figure 4.11*.

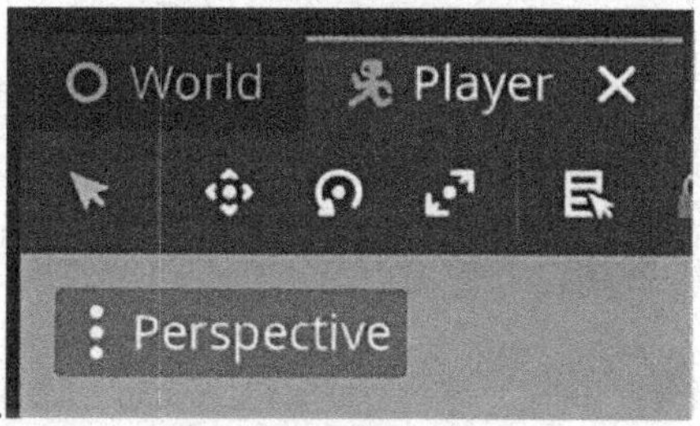

Figure 4.11: The Perspective button, sitting in the top-left corner of the Viewport

By being able to view a scene in a variety of ways, we can consider the flow of a scene and the way a player might move through it. We can also think about the way we shape the space around a player and what that communicates to them.

Now, when first designing a level, we do what's called **blocking out**. Most game engines have a way to quickly create prototypes with primitive shapes (e.g., boxes, cylinders, etc.). Godot has a convenient way to block out levels too. If you're unfamiliar with the term, when constructing a level, level designers often will gray-box or block out the level, so it can be tested for size, flow, and other metrics.

Note

If level design is an area of interest for you, I highly suggest participating in Blocktober, where designers create levels throughout October. You can read more about it here: `https://worldofleveldesign.com/categories/level_design_tutorials/guide-to-blocktober.php`.

To start blocking out an area to test our player movement, right-click **Node3D** in our newly created scene and add a **CSGBox3D** node. A white cube should appear at the origin of our scene. Change the size to be something like a floor in the **Inspector** dock – a small area of 25x1x25 should be fine.

Select the object (**CSGBox3D**) in the scene hierarchy. Then, in the **Inspector** dock, find the **Size** property. Change the size on the **x** axis to **25**, the **y** axis to **1**, and the **z** axis to **25**, as shown in *Figure 4.12*.

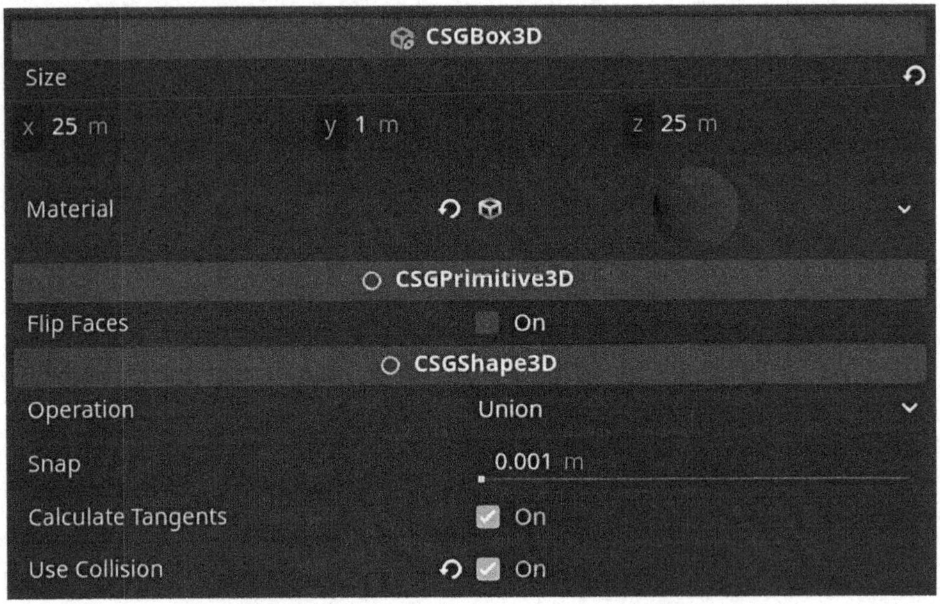

Figure 4.12: CSGBox3D properties for testing our player

By default, **CSGBox3D** nodes don't start with a collision on them, so be sure the **Use Collision** property is also selected, as shown in *Figure 4.12*.

The last thing we'll add is a texture to make it easier to have a contrast with our player against the floor we're creating. The textures we downloaded and imported into our project from Kenney Assets can be used to give the CSG boxes materials. To add a material, do the following:

1. Select the **CSGBox3D** node.
2. Find a texture in the filesystem to add to the node.
3. Click and drag the texture from the **FileSystem** dock into the empty material slot in the **Inspector** dock, as shown in *Figure 4.12*.
4. Make sure the **Use Collision** flag is checked **On** to ensure we don't fall through the floor!

The white block will now update with the texture of our choice. There are some material settings that can be changed around if desired, which you can find in the **Inspector** dock; these include the normal map for the material, shadows, UV maps, and more, though we won't worry about changing anything for the time being as this is only a testing space.

The last thing to do before running our testing scene is to drop our **Player** scene into it. We can do this by looking at our **FileSystem** dock and dragging **Player.tscn** into our **Scene** dock, as shown in *Figure 4.13*.

Figure 4.13: Adding the Player scene to our TestArea scene

Our testing area should look something like *Figure 4.14* where the player is sitting on top of a textured floor and using one of the textures from the asset we imported.

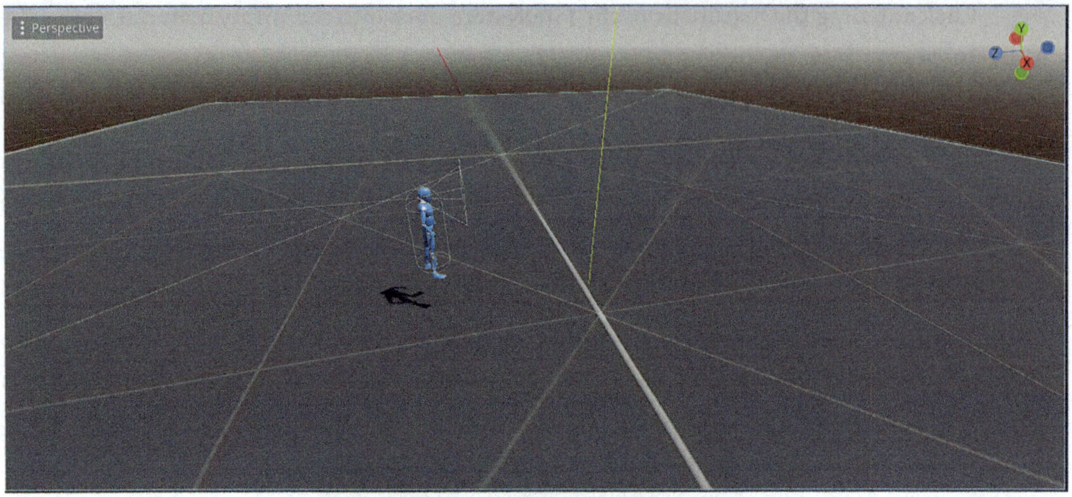

Figure 4.14: The testing area with a floor and our player

After running the game, we can see that our player moves, using the arrow keys by default, but our **Player** model doesn't turn and neither does our camera. Let's consider how best to pan around with the mouse, and then we'll look at augmenting our **Player** model to follow the direction we go.

Moving the camera

As mentioned earlier, the way a camera sits on a **Player** model is critical. Both first-person and third-person camera options provide different experiences for players. Specifically, a third-person camera offers a wider field of view. It can also provide unique narrative moments through the environment and by watching what happens to the player's body rather than feeling like it's being experienced firsthand. Using a third-person camera for our project is going to give us the opportunity to explore the camera and animation nodes in Godot, so let's get started.

Our first goal is to be able to look around. Right now, we can only see in one direction and on one axis. We need to add a couple of functions to our `Player.cs` script that we created in the last section. Open it up in the editor of your choice.

With the test area and `Player.cs` script created, we can start programming in C#! We'll first start by limiting the mouse cursor since we're creating a third-person player character.

Setting Mouse Mode

There are a lot of functions in Godot's API that allow us to customize the screen and mouse settings. **Mouse Mode** is one of those functions, which allows us to alter the way the cursor behaves in our game. We want the way the cursor behaves to be done before our player can move or do anything, so we will be creating a function called `_Ready` that will immediately be called by Godot on start.

The `_Ready()` function takes no parameters and is called when the object is created. It also runs only once, so it's a perfect space to initialize any settings or nodes that we may need access to later. To write the function, add the following lines above the `_PhysicsProcess` function:

```
public override void _Ready()
{
    // Access nodes we'll need from our scene here
    Input.MouseMode = Input.MouseModeEnum.Captured;
}
```

With this line of code in our function, we're telling Godot to capture the mouse. This locks its position in the center of the screen. We do this by accessing an enumerator in **Mouse Mode** called `Input.MouseModeEnum.Captured`.

Other available options for **Mouse Mode** include the following:

- `MouseMode.Enum.Visible`: Just as it sounds, it makes sure the cursor is seen on the screen.
- `MouseMode.Enum.Hidden`: This hides our cursors from the screen. You might think we want this option for our game, but we'll be tracking the mouse position in the next section.

The two listed options pertain to keeping the mouse in the window size of our game. This can be especially important when dealing with games that require a lot of mouse movement or rapid mouse clicks and time-sensitive games. You can read more about **Mouse Mode** here: `https://docs.godotengine.org/en/stable/classes/class_input.html#enum-input-mousemode`.

Now that the cursor is configured properly, we can look (pun intended) at how to move our camera with our mouse to look around our test area.

Panning with the mouse

With our mouse confined to the center of the screen, we can now add our second function, which will be the `_Input` function. We can place this right between our `_Ready` and `_PhysicsProcess` functions. So, first, declare the function, and then add an `if` statement for when the mouse moves. Our function should look like the following:

```
public override void _Input(InputEvent @event)
{
    if (@event is InputEventMouseMotion eventMouseMotion)
    {
    }
}
```

Next, we'll add the logic for rotating the camera in relation to the mouse, which will sit inside the preceding `if` statement. To do this, we need to access the camera to then rotate it:

1. Create a private `Node3D` variable called `cameraPivot` at the top of our script:

   ```
   private Node3D cameraPivot;
   ```

2. In the `_Ready` function, set our new variable to the `GetNode` function for accessing the node from the scene:

   ```
   cameraPivot = GetNode<Node3D>("CameraPivot");
   ```

With the `GetNode` function call, notice we that have to specify the type of node we are accessing. This is the string of characters in quotation marks. By doing this, we specify the node from our scene based on its hierarchy in the scene. If you're ever unsure what the path to a node is, you can always right-click the node from the **Scene** dock and select **Copy Node Path** to be sure.

> Note
>
> Rather than having long path names to manage, as well as not having to worry about the order of your nodes, you can right-click a node and select **Access as Unique Name**. A `%` symbol will appear next to the node, and you can access it the same way with the addition of the `%` symbol. So, instead of `CameraPivot` (as in the previous line of code), it would be `%CameraPivot`.

Also, notice we are accessing `Node3D`, which is the parent of `Camera3D`. We want to rotate both the camera and the spring arm together, which is why we placed them as children under `CameraPivot`. Any movement changes we make to `CameraPivot` will automatically be applied to `SpringArm3D` and `Camera3D`, since they are both children of the `CameraPivot` node. This allows us to only write the movement code once rather than twice.

Now, we're going to rotate the camera pivot one axis at a time. We'll first rotate it on the `Y` axis, using the `RotateY` function that's available on any `Node3D` object. So, in our `if` statement, type the following:

```
cameraPivot.RotateY(-eventMouseMotion.Relative.X);
```

Here, we're using the `eventMouseMotion` variable, which is our mouse position. Remember, since we're using the captured mode on `MouseMode`, we have to get the position by using the `Relative` function of `InputEventMouseMotion`. The final part of the code is accessing the axis, which is denoted with either `X`, `Y`, or `Z`. We want the `X` axis in this instance since, when we move the mouse left or right, we're rotating the camera horizontally on the `Y` axis.

Run the scene and see what you notice. The camera moves when we move the mouse, but it's sporadic and unwieldy to control. We can tweak the sensitivity of this by multiplying it by some factor called **mouse sensitivity**. Add a `private` variable to the top of our script like so:

```
private float cameraSensitivity_H = 0.05f;
```

We'll now multiply our mouse position with the horizontal sensitivity, so now our line in the `_Input` function should look like this:

```
cameraPivot.RotateY(-eventMouseMotion.Relative.X*CameraSensitivity_H);
```

Test the scene again, and if we move our mouse very slowly, we can see that it is working correctly.

However, something is still off. If we hover over `RotateY`, Intellisense should tell us the definition of it: **Rotates the local transformation around the Y axis by angle in radians.** This is important because we're not passing in radians at the moment to our `RotateY` function. We need something to convert our vectors (which are in degrees) into radians. Let's look at that next.

Creating a conversion function

Knowing math – specifically trigonometry, calculus, and linear algebra – is a boon when it comes to creating a 3D game. Even though the game engine does a lot of computational parts for us, we still need to know what mathematical functions to pull from the API, even if we don't know how to do them by hand. Having a math background can also help us understand issues that might occur when working in a 3D space.

If you're unfamiliar with any of the aforementioned math topics, I found Khan Academy's courses to be a good starting point (`https://www.khanacademy.org/math/`). For more advanced users, I found *Essential Mathematics for Games and Interactive Applications* by James M. Van Verth and Lars. M Bishop to be a great resource when it comes to math and game development.

In this section, we're going to use some trigonometry to get our player moving at a smooth and manageable pace. At the bottom of our script, we can add a short function called `ConvertDegreesToRadian` that takes in a `float` type and returns a `float` type:

```
public float ConvertDegreesToRadian(float num)
{
}
```

Rather than type Pi out, we can use the `Math` library that's part of the .NET framework (this is something that might take an adjustment, especially if you are coming from using GDscript). We'll multiply our mouse position vector by Pi and divide that by 180, like so:

```
num = num*((float)Math.PI/180);
```

In our final line, we'll return the variable we've manipulated (`num`):

```
return num;
```

So, our `ConvertDegreesToRadian` function should look like this:

```
public float ConvertDegreesToRadian(float num)
{
    return num * ((float)Math.PI / 180);
}
```

Now, go back and call the function. Put it into our `RotateY` function and be sure to capture both the mouse position and camera sensitivity. The line should now look like this:

```
cameraPivot.RotateY(ConvertDegreesToRadian(-eventMouseMotion.
Relative.X*cameraSensitivity_H));
```

Test the scene again. When we look left and right, it's a lot smoother and easier to control. It might even be a little too slow, depending on your machine settings.

Let's go ahead and exit out of this and repeat the previous steps for our player to look up and down.

We can add a separate mouse sensitivity variable to the top of our script and call it `cameraSensitivity_V`. Then, set it to the same value as `cameraSensitivity_H`. Both of these variables at the top of the script will look like this:

```
[Export(PropertyHint.Range,"0,0.5")]
private float CameraSensitivity_H = 0.05f;
[Export(PropertyHint.Range, "0,0.5")]
private float CameraSensitivity_V = 0.05f;
```

> Note
>
> Since we don't have a perfect number to use for the sensitivity, we can do something very convenient for ourselves. Godot allows us to export variables, which serializes them and makes them accessible in the editor. All you need to do is add the `[Export]` attribute above the variable. You can take it one step further and specify the type of variable. I've set mine to a range by doing `[Export(PropertyHint.Range,"0,0.5")]`, which gives me a slider in the editor.

Next, we'll add another line in our `if` statement that captures the mouse position, except this time, we'll be calling the `RotateX` function. It'll be the exact same line, but we want to be focusing on pivoting around the `X` axis rather than the `Y` axis as we just did. It will look like the following:

```
cameraPivot.RotateX(ConvertDegreesToRadian(-eventMouseMotion.
Relative.Y*CameraSensitivity_V));
```

Test it one more time, and we'll be able to move along both the `X` and `Y` axis. Yet when we do, we get some odd behavior. The camera tilts in a way that is outside of the range of what we want it to be. Let's see how to fix that.

Clamping the camera

To prevent our camera pivot from tilting in a wide variety of ways, we need to clamp our camera's rotation to a range that is manageable for both us and our player. Thankfully, the rotation component of `Node3D` has a `clamp` function. We'll need to give it a range that it can clamp to and from – essentially, the bounds we want to set.

Our `clamp` function takes in a `Vector3`, so we can define another variable at the top of our script. I called mine `maxSpringRotation`, and I found that `30` degrees felt fairly good in terms of movement (you can tweak these variables to what works best in your project). So, the variable declared should look like this:

```
private Vector3 maxSpringRotation = new Vector3(30,30,0);
```

Calling the `clamp` function will be done right after we rotate the pivot and inside our `if` statement within the `_Input` function. It will look like this:

```
cameraPivot.Rotation = cameraPivot.Rotation.Clamp(-maxSpringRotation,
maxSpringRotation);
```

With these two lines added, go ahead and test the scene and move the camera around in all directions.

Our camera is now smooth, but our player doesn't respond to our movement. Let's tie them together by moving the player with the camera and completing the camera portion of our player controller.

Moving the player with the camera

The final piece for making a relatively smooth camera that our player responds to is making the **Player** model turn, depending on our input. If we hit the left-moving key (currently the left arrow key), we want our **Player** model to face that direction. Since we're already rotating the camera based on input, let's have our **Player** model then follow our input commands to match with the camera.

To do this, the variables we need are as follows:

```
private Node3D body;
private Vector3 rotation;
```

Here, the body variable is going to be how we access our **Player** model in the scene tree, and the rotation variable is going to be a placeholder for the model's rotation.

Now, in the _Ready function, let's go ahead and get a reference to the **Player** model by doing the same thing we did for CameraPivot except, instead, we'll be doing it with the Body node. The line we'll be adding is the following:

```
body = GetNode<Node3D>("Body");
```

We also need to set our placeholder variable, rotation, to the body's rotation, so we can update it later. The rotation component of Node3D on a specific axis is a read-only variable, so we must update the entire rotation. Directly under the line we've just added, write the following:

```
rotation = body.Rotation;
```

Now, we can modify the model in a variety of ways, including rotation, transformation, and so on. We only want the player to move when we move in a specific direction, so we need to change the rotation in our _PhysicsProcess function when we're moving.

So, find the two lines of code where we update the X and Z components of velocity:

```
velocity.X = direction.X * speed;
velocity.Z = direction.Z * speed;
```

Then, after those lines, add a new line that involves some interpolation:

```
rotation.Y = Mathf.LerpAngle(rotation.Y, Mathf.Atan2(velocity.X,
velocity.Z), 0.15f)
```

With rotation.Y, we're rotating the **Player** model's body on the *Y* axis.

Let's use *Figure 4.15* to talk about what we're doing here in the code. If we run our game and move left and right, we're moving along the *X* axis. If we walk forward and back, we're walking along the *Z* axis; that's why we want to rotate along the *Y* axis, which is essentially looking straight up.

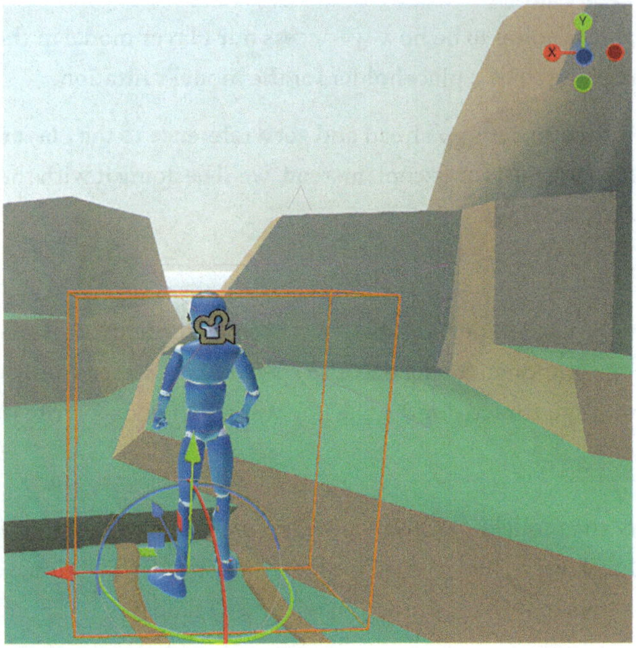

Figure 4.15: Our game in the editor, marked up with the X axis and the Y axis

Note

If you're unfamiliar with interpolation, be sure to read the Godot documentation, which gives a good overview of what interpolation is and how it works in Godot: `https://docs.godotengine.org/en/stable/tutorials/math/interpolation.html`.

So, in the code, we're setting the rotation equal to this `LerpAngle` function, which we're calling from the `Mathf` library that's part of the .NET framework. The word *lerp* is short for **linear interpolation** – a very general definition of linear interpolation is we are using math to smoothly move an object from point A to point B. Point A in our code is the current rotation we're sitting at on the *Y* axis (`rotation.Y`). Point B is the point that we're lerping to (`Mathf.Atan2(-velocity.x, -velocity.z)`).

As mentioned, we use all types of mathematical concepts to simulate the real world through pixels. The math function we're calling from `Mathf` is the inverse tangent, which takes our *Z* axis and our *X* axis and gives us an angle in response. If you've done trigonometry, the word *tangent* should sound familiar to you – it's one of the trigonometric functions defined as *tan = opposite/ adjacent* (the opposite is adjacent/opposite).

Let's use an example with our player, using *Figure 4.16*. Say we start turning to the right. To smoothly make that turn, we need the angle closest to our player. We're going to take the inverse tangent – adjacent over opposite. The line in our triangle that runs along the *X* axis is adjacent to us and labeled as such, as seen in *Figure 4.16*, and the line in our triangle that runs alongside the *Z* axis is opposite the angle we want to find, also seen in *Figure 4.16*.

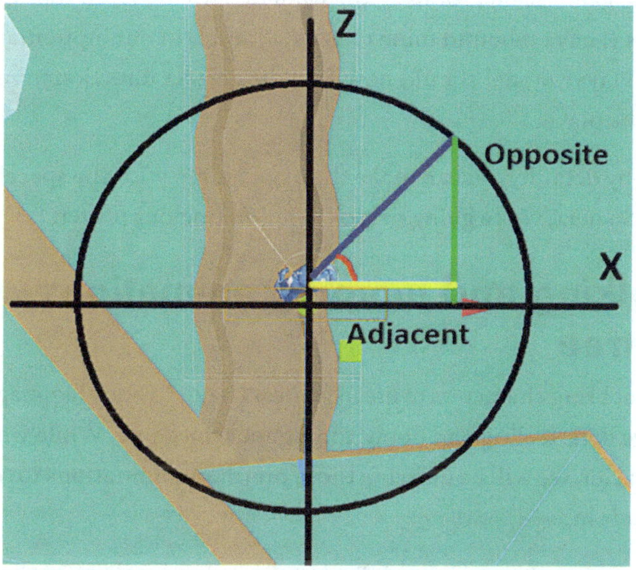

Figure 4.16: A visual representation of the Atan2 function

Remember, the *X* axis is how our player moves left and right, and the *Z* axis is how our player moves forward and back. That's why the `X` and `Z` components of `velocity` are what we give `Atan2` rather than the *Y* axis. The *Y* axis is for jumping only! The hypotenuse of our example is the radius of the triangle, which we aren't using in calculating the angle. The radius does extend from the origin, `(0,0)`, but I've moved it slightly for our example to better see the rest of the lines in the triangle.

Once we have our new rotation, we can set the **Player** model equal to that newly found rotation by writing the following:

```
body.Rotation = rotation;
```

Now, test our game scene and move in all four directions. It should work; however, if you test enough, you will see that we have one small bug. When you do a complete circle around the player and then walk forward, the player is going to move forward along the *Z* axis rather than reorient the forward direction based on where our camera is.

To fix this, we need to rotate the direction in relation to the rotation of the camera to make sure that wherever the camera is behind, then the front of that is our forward direction, even if it's not along the *Z* axis. We're just changing the relationship of what forward means to our model. After the line where the `direction` vector is defined, we can add this:

```
direction = direction.Rotated(Vector3.Up, cameraPivot.Rotation.Y);
```

Once more, test the game scene, rotating the camera, moving in all four directions, and using the movement keys (I have rebound mine to *W*, *A*, *S*, and *D* in our input map exactly like we did in *Chapter 2*). Our **Player** model should now face the correct direction in relation to where our camera is around the player.

Now, at this point, by default, you can make the player jump with the spacebar, yet we're still in a standing stance. So next, we're going to look at animating our player.

Adding walking and jumping animations with the animation tree

Animations are what bring characters to life in games. They add body language and communicate what characters are both feeling and doing throughout the game. While we won't be rigging or modeling our character, we will be utilizing those pre-made animations to trigger depending on the state our player is in.

Select the **mannequiny** (now named **Body**) scene and select **Make Local**. Select the **AnimationPlayer** node, and it will appear below the Viewport where the **Output/Debugger** dock is.

> Note
>
> The **Make Local** option tells Godot to give every instance of these nodes their own resource. This is useful when you have multiple enemies and want them to utilize resources that are unique to their instance.

It will look like *Figure 4.17*, though different animations may be pre-selected:

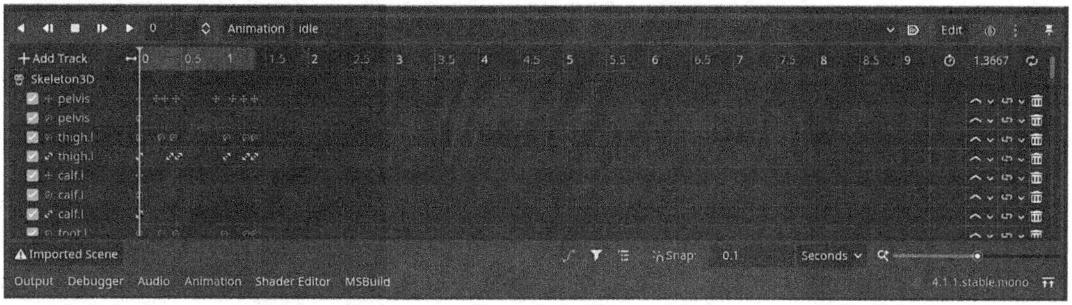

Figure 4.17: The idle animation track that appears when selecting AnimationPlayer

Next to the word **Animation**, there is a drop-down menu where you can select different animations, as seen in *Figure 4.18*

Figure 4.18: The drop-down menu of available animations

To see how the animation will look, select the **Play** button to the left of the **Animation** button (you can see it back in *Figure 4.17*).

We will implement most of the animations, but only a few now; we'll add the rest as we start building out our world and adding more interactable components. For now, let's start by getting a path to **AnimationPlayer**.

Before we do that, let's consider a couple of different ways we can implement our animations:

- **Manage everything in C# scripts:** We could have our animations triggered based on the input we're providing to our player, but this can become cumbersome and unwieldy as our player controller expands.
- **Use AnimationTree:** This is a state-based node for managing animations. While it can be confusing at first, the payoff for setting it up this way far outweighs any learning curve. Another benefit of using an **AnimationTree** node is we'll get smooth transitions between our animations and will be able to fine-tune many details when it comes to them. This is the option we'll be implementing.

To get started, let's right-click our root node in the scene (**Player**) and select **Add a Child Node**. Search for `AnimationTree` and select it. With the **AnimationTree** node added to the scene tree, we will be able to access it in our `Player.cs` script and trigger animations as needed.

> Note
>
> To toggle between multiple windows that are in the **Output/Debugger** dock, you can click the words along the bottom to switch views. For example, you can toggle easily between **Animations** and **AnimationTree.**

AnimationPlayer, which was showing our animations in the **Output/Debugger** dock, is now a blank space. We'll want access to it in our `Player.cs` script, so add an `AnimationTree` variable at the top for it like so:

```
private AnimationTree anim;
```

Just like with all the nodes we've been working with, we'll need to use the `GetNode` function to access the properties of that specific node. It will look like this:

```
anim = GetNode<AnimationTree>("AnimationTree");
```

Now we've got our `AnimationTree` node ready to be called in our script.

Next, we're going to step out of our script and work in the editor where the **Output/Debugger** dock is. As noted, **AnimationTree** had a blank space in its window – this is because we need to give it a tree root. If you look in the **Inspector** dock of **AnimationTree**, you'll see a **Tree Root** property that's empty. Click the drop-down menu and select **New AnimationNodeStateMachine**. There are a lot of options here, but we'll only be covering the **StateMachine** version.

Note

If you're interested in the different **AnimationNode** types, check out the Godot documentation on animation trees: `https://docs.godotengine.org/en/stable/tutorials/animation/animation_tree.html`.

Once selected, we'll have two nodes appear in the window below our Viewport – **Start** and **End**. Yet, our **AnimationTree** node has a warning sign next to the node, telling us that we need to have a reference to **AnimationPlayer**. There's a property in the **Inspector** dock called **Anim Player**, which appears when you have the **AnimationTree** node selected. We can click and drag **AnimationPlayer** into this slot or click the **Assign** button and select it from there.

With **AnimationPlayer** loaded into **AnimationTree** and a new **AnimationNodeStateMachine** created, we are almost ready to get into creating the different states we'll need for our player in **AnimationTree**. Before that, let's explore the navigation of **AnimationTree** as it can be confusing at first.

Navigating animation trees

As mentioned earlier, **AnimationTree** is state-based. When we loaded **AnimationPlayer** into **AnimationTree**, you can see two states appeared. One was **Start** and the other was **End**. Above this space, there are some controls to create more states, as seen in *Figure 4.19*.

Figure 4.19: Tools to create and connect states in AnimationTree

Here is a breakdown of what each button does listed from left to right:

- *Mouse Pointer*: Select and move nodes around
- *Plus sign*: Create a new node (you can also right-click in the empty space in **AnimationTree** to create a new node)
- *Connector*: This connects nodes and provides a smooth transition between animations
- *Trash can*: When a node or connection is selected, we click the trash can to remove it

With the tools of navigating **AnimationTree** nodes covered, we can get into creating one and setting up the animations we want our player to have based on what's been provided with our model.

Creating the AnimationTree node

Let's go ahead and add our **idle** animation to the state machine by right-clicking next to the **Start** block. Then, hover over **Add Animation** and click **idle**. We have this list of animations because we've tied **AnimationPlayer** to **AnimationTree**, and you can see this back in *Figure 4.18*. **AnimationTree** pulls the data necessary from **AnimationPlayer**, so we have access to everything from **idle** to **walk** and **run** and **jump**. If this was not the case, we couldn't access them in the state machine.

You should now see a node labeled as **idle** with a **Play** button inside it, just like the **Start** and **End** nodes. Click the connector button above **AnimationTree** and drag it from the **Start** node to the **idle** node, so it looks like *Figure 4.20*:

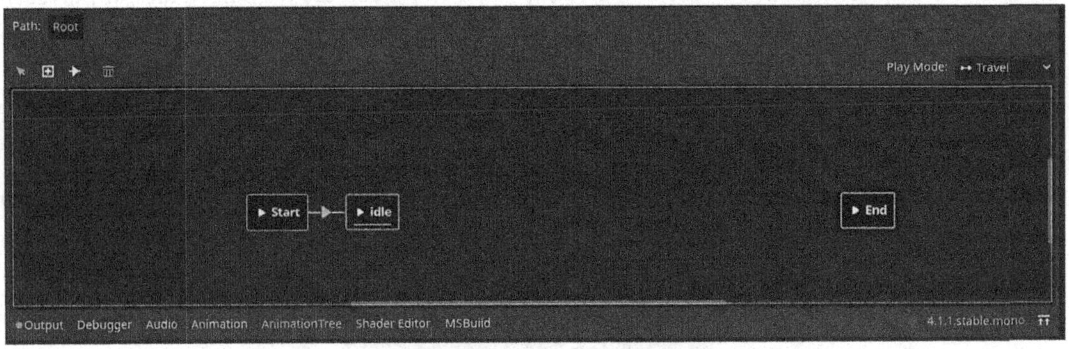

Figure 4.20: The current state of AnimationTree after adding the idle animation

If we click the small **Play** button that's on our **idle** node, nothing happens. This is because we don't have the **Active** property on **AnimationTree** set to **true**. So, select the **AnimationTree** node, and in the **Inspector** dock, click the checkmark next to the **Active** property (see *Figure 4.21*). The **Player** model should now be looping through the **idle** animation in the Viewport.

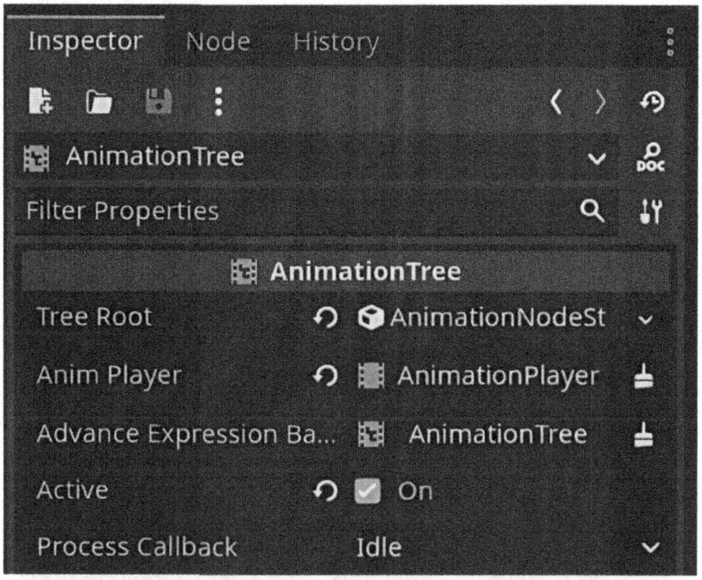

Figure 4.21: The AnimationTree node set to Active in the Inspector dock

Go ahead and test the scene and notice that our player has an idle animation no matter what our input is, but at its default, it is standing idle, which is correct. Let's move on to adding a walking animation.

Walking

Right-click in the state machine space again and add the **walk** animation. Select the connector button on the **AnimationTree** node and drag one from **idle** to **walk**. Now, our player is looping the **walk** animation.

At some point, we will want to stop moving and will need a way to return to our **idle** animation. Currently, our connectors between nodes are just one way, but if we add a second one going from **walk** to **idle**, then the **Player** model will start to flicker rapidly between the two animations. This is because we aren't setting any conditions on the animations for when they should play.

> Note
>
> If, when adding the **walk** node in **AnimationTree**, the animation only plays once, then you need to make sure the animation selected is set to **Looping** in **AnimationPlayer.** This can be found in the top-right corner of **AnimationPlayer**.

Conditions are how we connect the state machine in Godot to our `Player.cs` script in C#. The **Condition** property sits on the connectors, or transitions, of **AnimationTree**, so if we select our connector that goes from **idle** to **walk**, we'll have two lists of properties – **Switch** and **Advance**. Expand the **Advance** one, and you'll see **Mode**, **Condition**, and **Expression** listed.

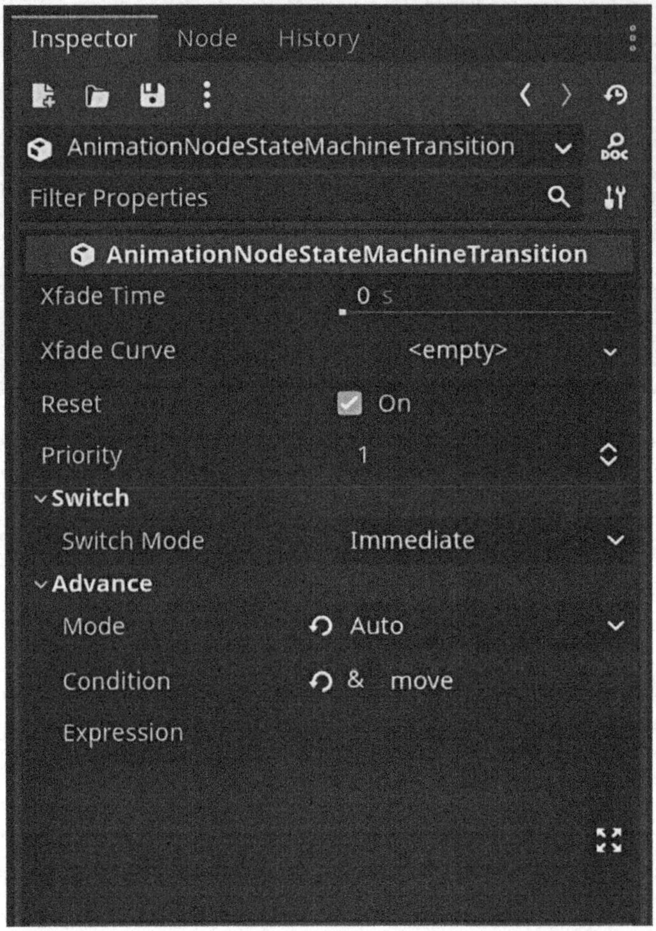

Figure 4.22: The Inspector dock when selecting a connector (animation transition) from AnimationTree

In *Figure 4.22*, we can see I've already added the word `move` to the **Condition** property.

Next, I'm going to select the other connector (the one going from **walk** and pointing toward **idle**) and add a condition called `idle`. Now, our **AnimationTree** node should look like *Figure 4.23*. Notice how when we have a connector piece selected, it highlights the connector with a blue outline.

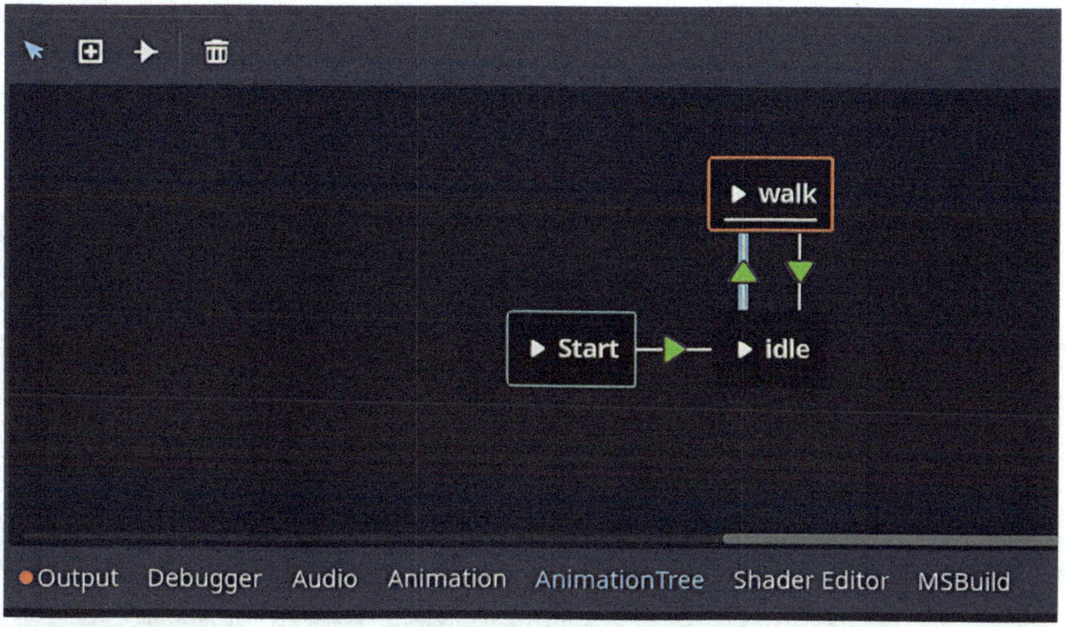

Figure 4.23: The current state of AnimationTree

Now that we have two animations in our state machine, let's look at how to call these in our `Player.cs` script. Currently, if we run our game, we still only run the **idle** animation. This is because it's our default animation state on start, and we aren't providing any logic to change between them.

Remember we already added the code for accessing **AnimationTree**. Now we need to use that variable and set the conditions for when to switch between animation states. We need to add the following line in our `_PhysicsProcess` function after our `inputDir` and direction variables have been set but before `MoveAndSlide` is called. I will be placing this line of code at the bottom right before `MoveAndSlide` as I feel it makes for cleaner code.

Here is the first line to add:

```
anim.Set("parameters/conditions/idle", (IsOnFloor() && inputDir ==
Vector2.Zero));
```

If you recall, `anim` is our variable for accessing **AnimationTree**. We're setting an animation with the `Set` function, using the path to the condition in our `idle` animation (`"parameters/conditions/idle"`), and then defining the conditions for when this animation should be set. When our player is idle, it's on the floor, and our direction is zero since we're not moving.

To get the path to the condition, we can select our **AnimationTree** node and hover over the condition we are seeking in the **Inspector** dock in *Figure 4.24*. In this figure, we hovered over the **Idle** condition and the path to it popped up. These conditions appear as we define them in our state machine, so if we removed one of them, they would no longer be listed here on our **AnimationTree** node.

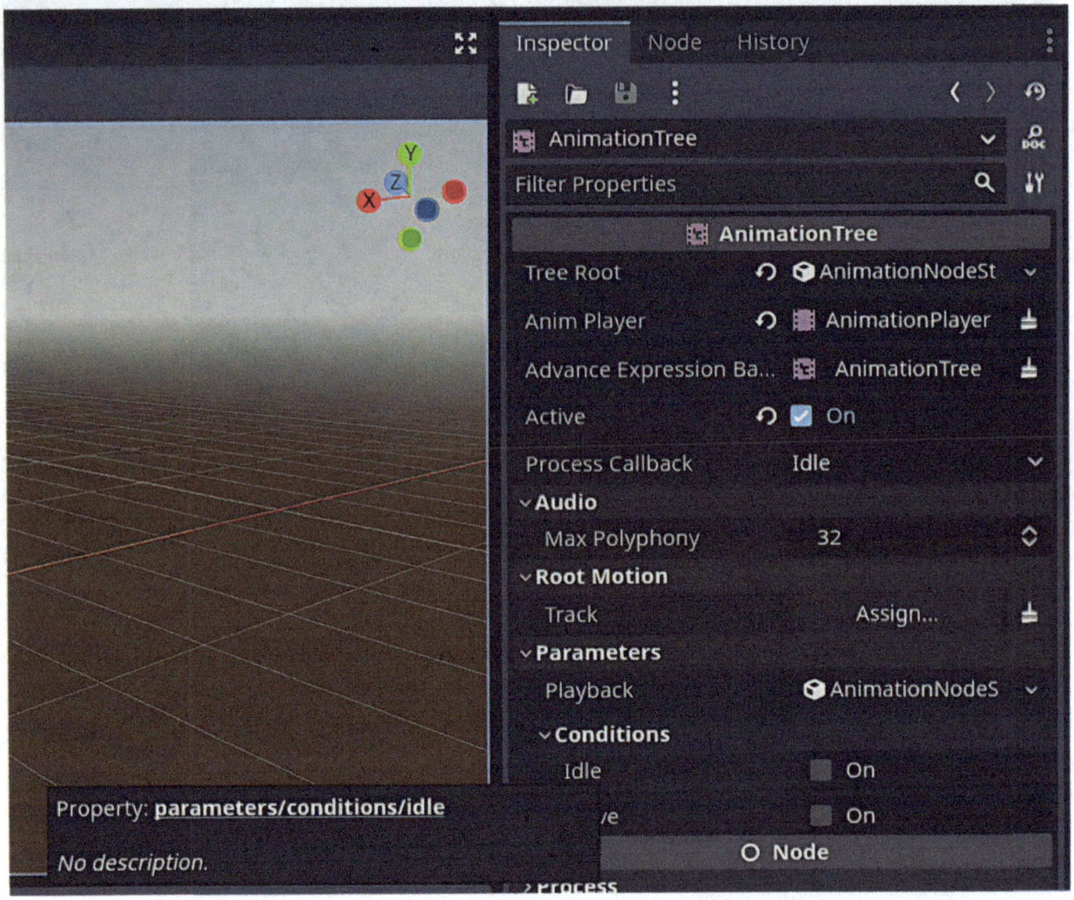

Figure 4.24: The Inspector dock when looking at AnimationTree and hovering over the Idle condition

Now we need to do the same thing, except utilize the `move` condition we set for the `walk` animation. This will be the second line of code added after the one we created for standing idle. It should look like this:

```
anim.Set("parameters/conditions/move", (IsOnFloor() && inputDir !=
Vector2.Zero));
```

Again, we're doing the same thing as we did before except our path is now for `move` and our conditions are slightly changed. When our **Player** model moves, it's on the floor but is moving, hence why we say `inputDir` is not equal to `Vector2.Zero` in the previous line of code.

Let's play our scene and test it out. The **Player** model should start in an **idle** position but as soon as we move in any of the input directions, the animation will switch to **walk**. We still don't have an animation for jumping, but we're going to add one now.

Jumping

Adding a jump is going to require more than one node because as our **Player** model jumps, there is an additional animation for landing the jump. Our **Player** model comes with some additional animations such as **air_jump_anticipation**. I challenge you to add this yourself once we've added the other two.

As we've done previously, we're going to make sure the *Mouse Pointer* tool in our **AnimationTree** node is selected, and we'll create a new animation and select **air_jump**. Next, we're going to drag a connector out from **idle** and connect it to **air_jump**. Unlike **walk** and **idle**, we want to make sure this animation is not looping. As a reminder, this is a setting in **AnimationPlayer** and can be toggled on/off when looking at a specific animation. Now, our state machine should look like *Figure 4.25*.

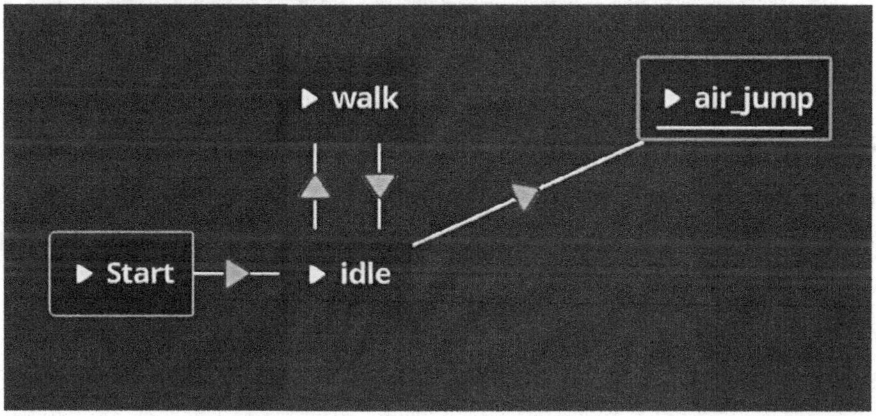

Figure 4.25: The AnimationTree state machine with the start of jump being added

Let's now add our second animation by creating a connector from **air_jump** and adding **air_land**. If we think about the steps that happen in a jump, we do the following:

1. Launch in the air (either while moving or standing still – ours will be stationary).
2. Then, gravity pushes us back down.

3. We land (sometimes in the same spot, sometimes elsewhere – ours will be in the same spot for now).

Thinking about the sequence of a jump, we know we need to draw a transition from **air_land** back to **idle**, since after we complete a jump cycle, we want to return to the state we were previously in. Yet, this will cause our model to flicker because we need two new conditions – we need one to track when we're in the air (we'll call this **falling**) and one for when we're done falling (**landing**).

Now we have a nice jump cycle that can be triggered only from the **idle** state, but we should be able to run and jump too. We'll add connectors from **walk** to **air_jump** just like we did from **idle** to **air_jump**, and then do the same from **air_land** to **walk**. If this is confusing, don't worry; you can reference *Figure 4.26* for clarity:

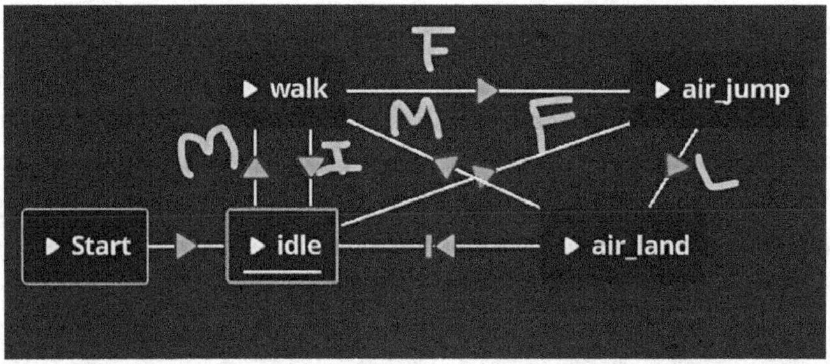

Figure 4.26: State machine transitions labeled with their conditions

For clarity, **M** is for **move, I** is for **idle, F** is for **falling**, and **L** is for **landing.**

Before we can test the scene, we need to be setting when these additional animations should trigger in our script, just like we did with both **idle** and **walk**. Back in our script and right after our previous lines of code, we can add these two lines:

```
anim.Set("parameters/conditions/falling", (!IsOnFloor()));
anim.Set("parameters/conditions/landing", (IsOnFloor()));
```

In the `falling` animation, we're calling it when we're not on the floor (i.e., not colliding with anything) and then we trigger `landing` when we collide with the ground. Now, we can test the game scene out and make sure that each of the animations are triggering when they're supposed to.

Once it's fully tested and working, give a celebratory hoorah to yourself! We're almost done with our animations. Yet, you'll notice that our player isn't able to walk and jump, so let's look at that briefly before adding the ability to run.

Expanding our jumping animation

Let's consider why our player isn't jumping and walking even though we're pressing the input key to move forward. If we look at the basic movement template we've used, specifically when our direction is not equal to zero and we're on the floor, there's something interesting happening in the `else` block. It's the following lines:

```
else
{
    velocity.X = Mathf.MoveToward(Velocity.X, 0, Speed);
    velocity.Z = Mathf.MoveToward(Velocity.Z, 0, Speed);
}
```

The `MoveToward` function takes our current velocity and slows us down until we reach our target value of zero, which is the second parameter in the `MoveToward` function. However, we only want to call these two lines of code if we aren't jumping.

A quick way to fix this is to add a Boolean for jumping. At the top of our script, create a `private` variable called `jumping`. The line will look like so:

```
private bool jumping = false;
```

We initially set it to `false` because, at the start, we are in an idle position that's grounded, therefore we aren't jumping. We'll use this variable to toggle between the type of physics we want to happen.

Within the `_PhysicsProcess` function, we're going to add an `if` statement for registering when the *jump* key is pressed. Now, in the `if` statement where our player pressed the *jump* key, we'll set `jumping` to `true` like so within the `_PhysicsProcess` function:

```
if (Input.IsActionJustPressed("ui_accept") && IsOnFloor())
{
    velocity.Y = JumpVelocity;
    jumping = true;
}
```

Currently, we still have the same issue as before – our velocity slows down to zero once we hit the floor, so we only jump straight in the air. Let's add an `if` statement around the lines where our velocity approaches zero:

```
if (jumping == false)
{
```

```
        velocity.X = Mathf.MoveToward(Velocity.X, 0, Speed);
        velocity.Z = Mathf.MoveToward(Velocity.Z, 0, Speed);
    }
```

Let's quickly test the scene out. We can move and we can jump. We can even move and jump together, beautifully flying through the air. But once we land, something odd happens – we don't stop moving! This is because we are not resetting the `jumping` Boolean to `false` so that we can gradually slow down to zero.

Luckily, this is an easy fix. We need one more `if` statement for when we touch the ground, using our `IsOnFloor` function again to tell Godot that we aren't jumping anymore. The `if` statement looks like this:

```
if (IsOnFloor())
{
    jumping = false;
}
```

This block of code can be placed anywhere in the `_PhysicsProcess` function. I have mine toward the top of the function after gravity is applied. Testing the scene again, we can confirm that running and jumping execute exactly how we want.

Our walking speed is fine, but most games provide the player with the opportunity to run, so let's consider how to implement that next.

Adding a run ability

The last section of this chapter includes adding a run ability for our player. This is logic that is not included in the basic movement template script we generated when creating our player; however, it is super easy to add!

We need to remove our `Speed` constant that is at the top of this script. After that, all we need are two additional constants called `runSpeed` and `walkSpeed` and then a variable for our current speed called `currSpeed`. Our two constants will look like the following lines at the top of our class:

```
public const float runSpeed = 8.0f;
public const float walkSpeed = 4.0f;
```

Alternatively, you could make them variables rather than constants and export them to the editor to tweak and change until you find a number that you like. I know that these numbers work well in this project for what we'll be creating, so I've made them constant.

Next, we will go ahead and create the variable for our current speed. We'll be using the constants to set our current speed, depending on our player input; this makes our code a little bit cleaner and prevents us from having to change too much of our code. Our variable will look like this:

```
private float currSpeed = walkSpeed;
```

By default, we want our player's movement to start at a walking pace, hence why we set it to `walkSpeed`.

With our constants and variables set up, let's look at utilizing them in our `_PhysicsProcess` function. Anywhere you see the word `Speed` for the constant we removed, be sure to change it to `currSpeed`, so that will be on the two lines where we set our `velocity` components here:

```
velocity.X = direction.X * currSpeed;
velocity.Z = direction.Z * currSpeed;
```

And then, once more, when we decelerate our player, we need to replace the previous `Speed` constant with our new `currSpeed` variable to the two lines of code that augment our velocity:

```
if (jumping == false)
{
    velocity.X = Mathf.MoveToward(Velocity.X, 0, currSpeed);
    velocity.Z = Mathf.MoveToward(Velocity.Z, 0, currSpeed);
}
```

With our new variables created and our current speed set up, we need to consider what key on our keyboard will trigger the run ability and tie our code to that input.

Mapping our run ability

When we went through our 2D example back in *Chapter 2*, we briefly covered the input map, but did not create our own key bindings. We'll go ahead and do that now for our running ability:

1. In the Godot Editor, click the **Project** button and access the **Project Settings** window. Then, select the second tab, called **Input Map**.
2. In the **Add New Action** box, type `run`, and click the **Add** button to the right of the **Add New Action** box.

The run command will now appear below in Input Map, as in *Figure 4.27*. Yet, it has no key bound to it to trigger it.

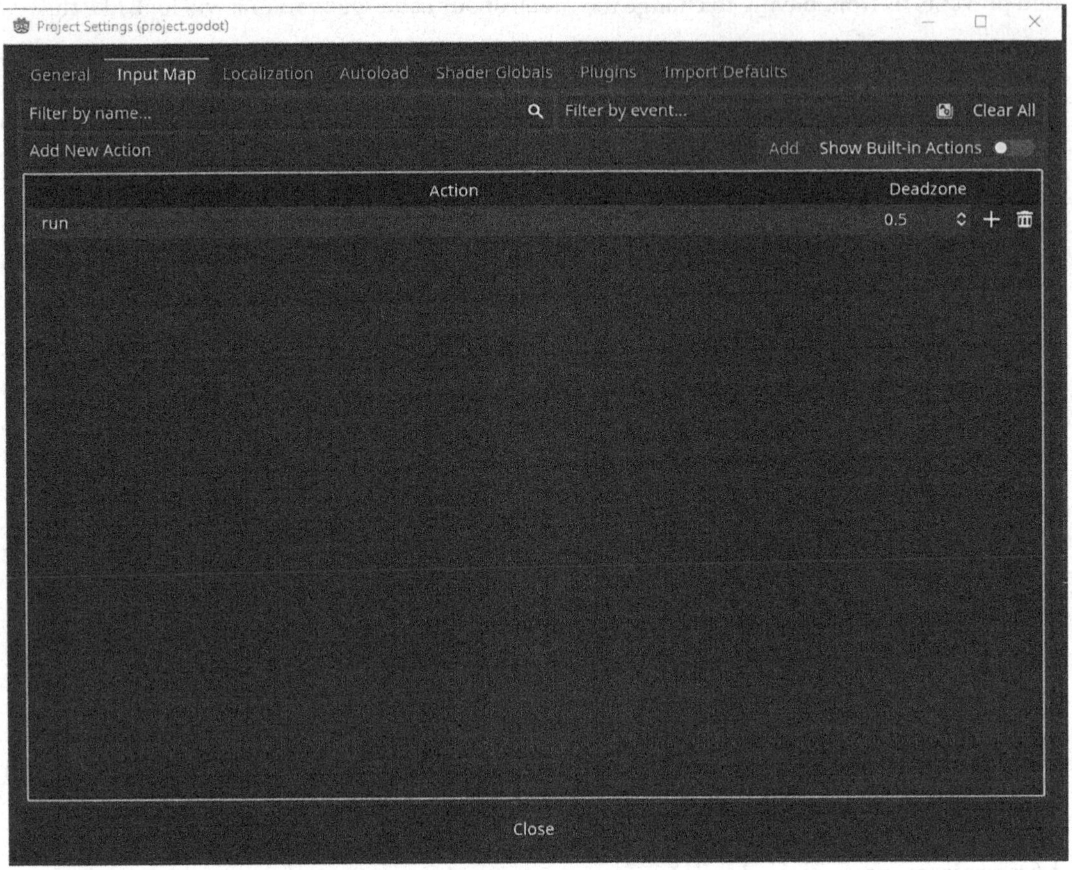

Figure 4.27: The Input Map screen with the run command created and not bound to a key

1. Click the + sign next to the line that says **run** and a new menu called **Event Configuration** will appear, as in *Figure 4.28*.

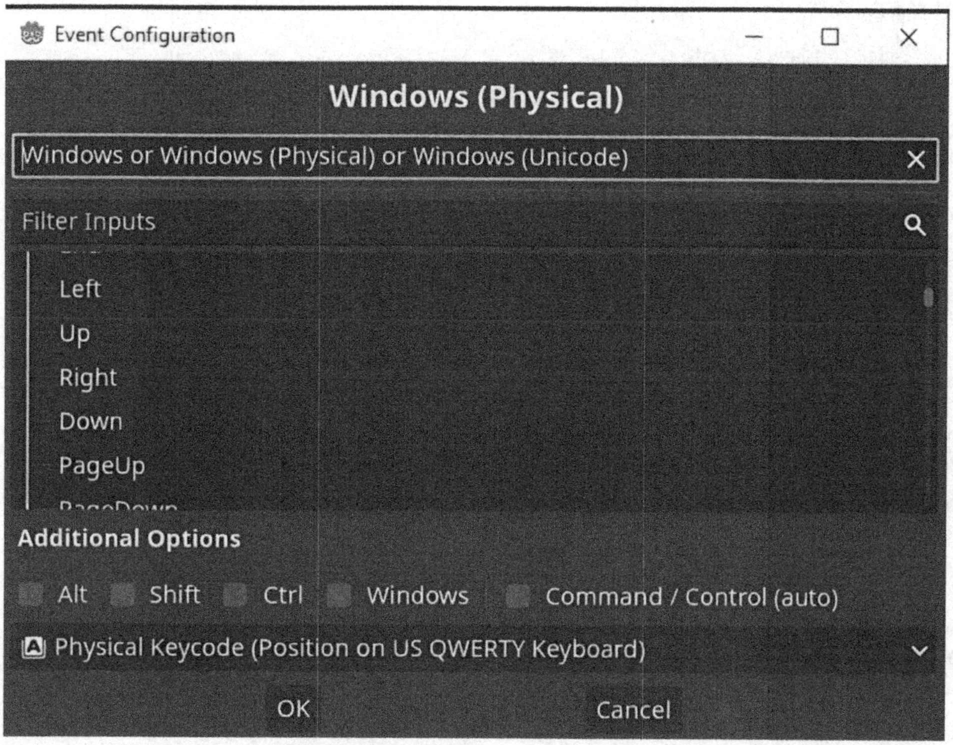

Figure 4.28: The Event Configuration screen to bind a specific key

2. With the mouse cursor in the box at the top, press the key to bind our **run** command to – I have chosen the left *Shift* key. Alternatively, you can scroll through the list and select a key.
3. Click **OK** once you have selected a key.

At the end of these steps, your **Project Settings** page should look like *Figure 4.29*.

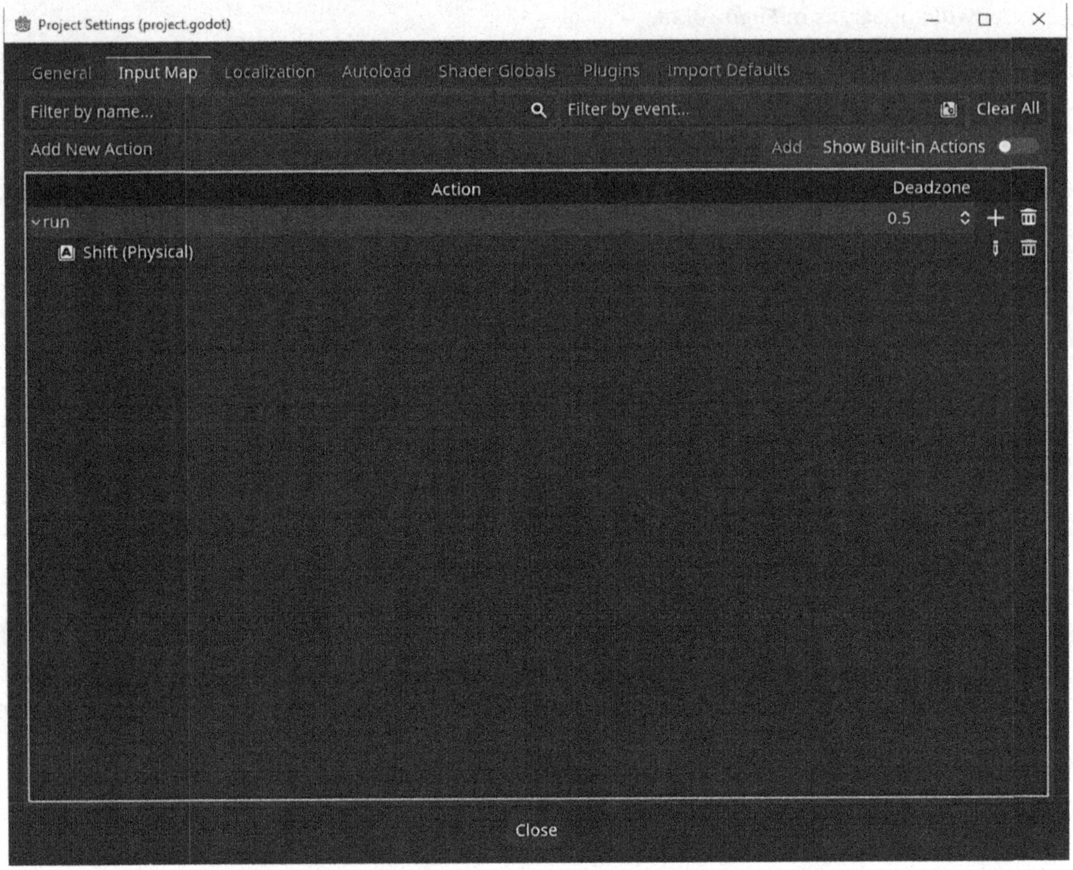

Figure 4.29: The run command bound to a specific key in the input map

Now, we can go back to our player script and utilize the input we've configured for **run** to trigger.

Registering run input

Stepping away from the **AnimationTree** node briefly, we should spend a moment programming the **run** animation into our **Player** model to make sure it triggers when it needs to. Back in our player script, we don't have to do anything else except add two `if` statements in our `_PhysicsProcess` function. I've placed mine after when we handle `jump`, but anywhere before our `inputDir` and direction variables is sufficient.

The first one we're going to add is making our player run when we press the key that we bound our **run** input to (this is *Shift*, unless you chose a different key). When we press the key, we want our `currSpeed` variable to be set to a new speed, `runSpeed`. We also need to make sure that when this key is pressed, we are on the ground and not airborne, so the code will look like this:

```
if (Input.IsActionPressed("run") && IsOnFloor())
{
    currSpeed = runSpeed;
}
```

Within the `IsActionPressed` function, we're using the string for the name of the command we created in *Figure 4.27*, which is `run`. Test the scene out and, while moving forward, press the *Shift* key. What happens when we stop? Our speed doesn't return to walking speed! This is where our second `if` statement comes in.

The `Input` class has a variety of functions available to us. So far, we've only been using `IsActionPressed` or `IsActionJustPressed`, but there's another function for when a key is released: `IsActionJustReleased`. This is the one we need because we want to stop running as soon as we stop holding the *Shift* key. So, immediately below our first `if` statement, add this:

```
if (Input.IsActionJustReleased("run") && IsOnFloor())
{
    currSpeed = walkSpeed;
}
```

Now, we're checking for when the key is pressed and released to know exactly when to switch between walking and running. The last thing, which you might have guessed already, is to add the running animation to our player.

Adding the running animation

We'll take a brief moment to extend our **AnimationTree** node by including the **run** animation. This will be quick and easy because almost all the conditions we need to enter and exit the running animation are already set up.

Let's open **AnimationTree** by going to our **Player** scene and selecting **AnimationTree**. We want to create a new animation block, which we can do by right-clicking in the **AnimationTree** space that's below the Viewport and hovering over **Add Animation**. From the list of available animations, go ahead and select the **run** one.

Note

Make sure that you're using the **Mouse Pointer** node tool that's at the top of the **AnimationTree** node from *Figure 4.19*.

Let's place our **run** block to the left of the walking animation, because we only want to trigger the running animation while we're already moving, which is how our player script is set up as well. Once completed, our **AnimationTree** node will look like *Figure 4.30*.

To get to that point, let's do the following:

1. Select the **Connect Nodes** tool from **AnimationTree** and draw a line from **walk** to **run**.
2. Set the condition to be running in this connection. To access that point again, click the connection on **AnimationTree**, and in the **Inspector** dock, expand the **Switch** property.
3. We also want a way to stop running, so draw a connection from **run** to **walk** and set its condition to **move**.
4. Finally, we may stop running and not return to walking. We could become idle, so we need to draw a connection from **run** to **idle**.
5. Set the condition for this connection to **idle**.

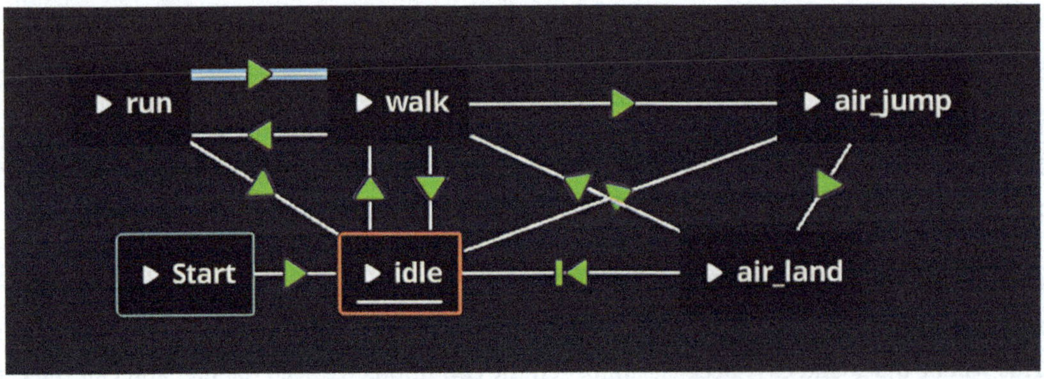

Figure 4.30: Our AnimationTree node with run added

Now, **AnimationTree** is configured properly, and we can switch back to our script to implement it in code just as we did the others. If we think about when we want the player to run, it'll be similar to the other animation-switching logic we've done already. We want the player to be on the floor, but we can no longer use our simple check for whether the player is moving because, if they're moving, there are two possibilities – they are either walking or running. We can, however, check whether our currSpeed variable is set to either walk or run. So, add the following line below all the code we've entered so far:

```
anim.Set("parameters/conditions/running", (IsOnFloor() && currSpeed ==
runSpeed));
```

Once you have done this, don't forget to set the options for running in the **Inspector** window, as shown in *Figure 4.31*. Make sure to expand the **Advance** option and set the following:

- **Mode: Auto**
- **Condition:** move

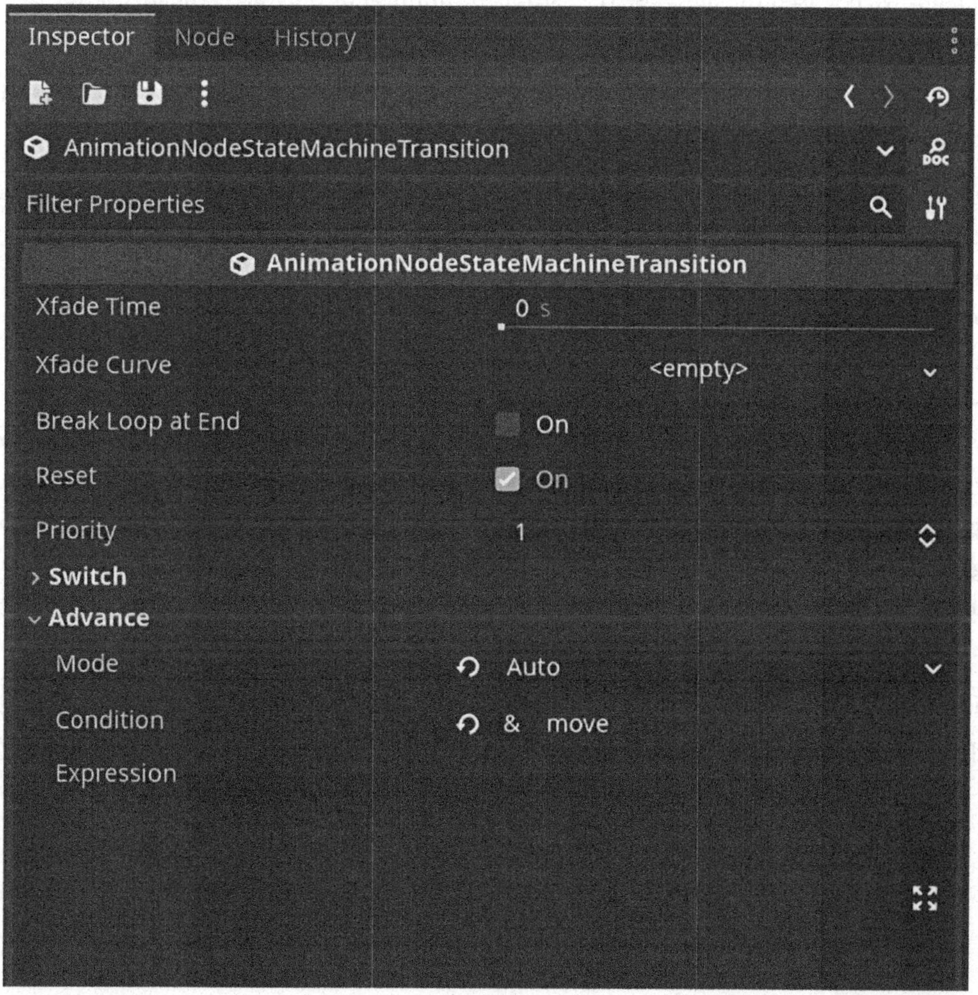

Figure 4.31: The Advance property group in the Inspector window of the run animation

As previously stated, we check whether we're on the floor and whether `currSpeed` is set to `runSpeed` (which is done when we hit our *Shift* key).

Before we test the scene out, we need to update our line for when to trigger the `walk` animation. The current line only checks whether we're on the floor and moving, which was fine before since moving meant we could only be walking:

```
anim.Set("parameters/conditions/move", (IsOnFloor() && inputDir !=
Vector2.Zero && currSpeed == walkSpeed));
```

Just like for running, we're checking to see whether `currSpeed` is set to `walkSpeed`, which would happen if we released the *Shift* key (i.e., stopped running) or only used the arrow key to move forward.

Even though our code is set up, we need to configure a few properties on the **run** node within **AnimationTree**.

With this logic added and **AnimationTree** set up, we can finally test our scene out. We should be able to walk, run, and jump effortlessly. You'll even notice that if you go to the edge of your test area and walk off it, the player will enter the **air_land** animation since they're falling, which is pretty neat.

Summary

We covered the fundamental components of creating a third-person player controller in Godot. This included camera movement and moving the player with the camera. We also discussed the importance of a strong mathematical foundation when it comes to 3D development. Then, we triggered animations such as walking and jumping, which were built into the character model, using a state machine to implement them in our game logic. Lastly, we added the ability to make the player run.

This is a great foundation for moving into the next chapter, which will focus on developing the world our player will live in by creating a level, collecting items, and having our player interact with the world around them. We will continue to extend the player controller as needed throughout the rest of the book, but for now, we will utilize what we have created here.

5

Creating Our Game World

Now that we have our player, we can turn our attention to creating the world our player will live in. In this chapter, we'll be downloading and importing more assets to design, decorate, and test our first level.

Once the level design is complete, we'll utilize shaders to simulate wind flowing through our trees. Then, we'll get back into C# and program spawning and collecting items around our world and conclude the chapter by discovering particle systems to create rain!

So, the chapter will cover the following topics:

- Importing world assets
- Adding collisions
- Designing our first level
- Creating movement with shaders
- Preparing game physics
- Creating and gathering collectibles
- Adding rain to our level

Technical requirements

For this chapter, the technical requirements are the same as in *Chapter 1*.

All the code from this chapter is available in the GitHub repository here: `https://github.com/PacktPublishing/Game-Development-with-Godot-and-C-`.

Importing World Assets

Much like we did when downloading and importing our textures, we are going to add a bunch more items to our project. The ones I'll be using are again from Kenney Assets, so let's get started:

1. To access Kenney Assets, visit `https://kenney.nl/assets/nature-kit`.
2. Click the **Download** button and unzip the files wherever you have downloaded them.
3. Then, click into the `Models` folder. We will only be grabbing a specific folder here, called `GLTF format`. Ideally, you'll want to have all your models be in the glTF 2.0 format as it's the format supported by Godot.

> Note
>
> Godot does not support the FBX format due to it being a proprietary format. There is a converter available if using FBX is the only option available. You can download the converter here: `https://godotengine.org/fbx-import/`.

4. Click and drag the `GLTF format` folder into our Godot project by dropping it into the **FileSystem** dock. A small window will appear in Godot, showing the import progress.

   Once this pop-up disappears, importing will be complete. We can see all the imported models in the **FileSystem** dock. You should notice that every object is a `.glb` file with a clapperboard icon next to it.

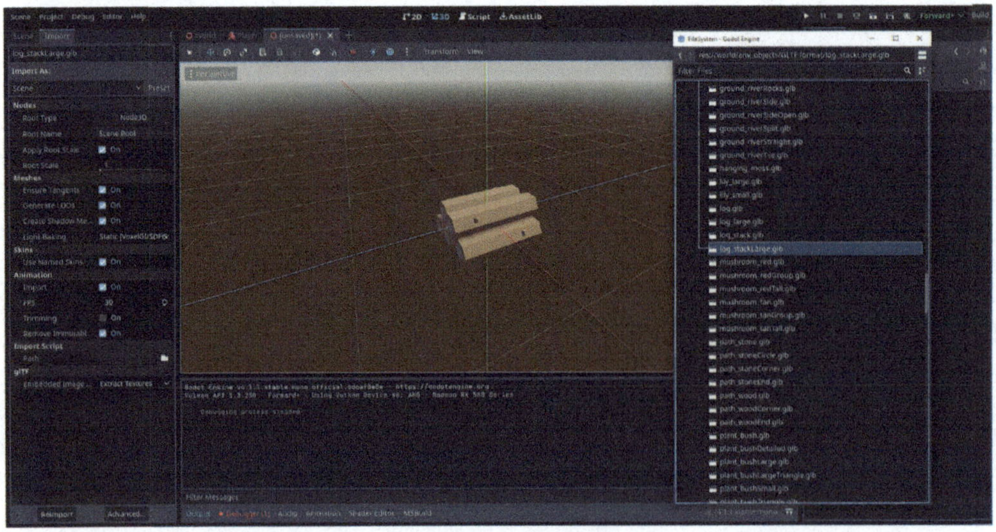

Figure 5.1: The Import tab of the Scene dock with a floating FileSystem dock

I like to make **FileSystem** a floating dock, so I can easily scroll through the various objects within a project. To do this, you can select the stacked three dots in the top-right corner of the **FileSystem** dock. When selected, a new menu will appear, as shown in *Figure 5.2*.

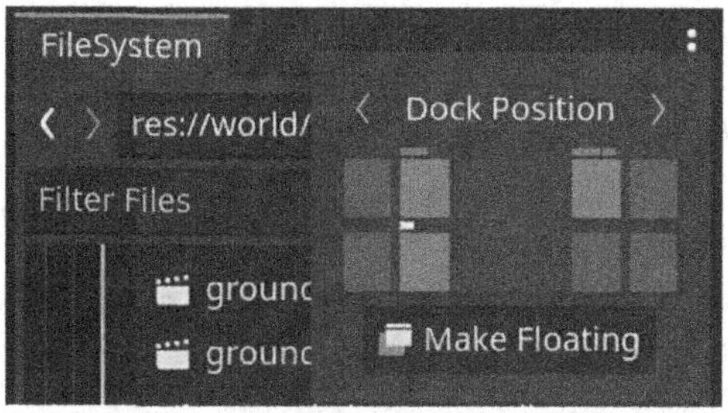

Figure 5.2: Making the FileSystem dock a floating dock

I want to view both the **FileSystem** dock and the **Import** tab, so I can see the details of the object I'm selecting from the **FileSystem** dock. To view the **Import** tab, click the **Import** tab on the **Scene** dock, at the top of *Figure 5.3*.

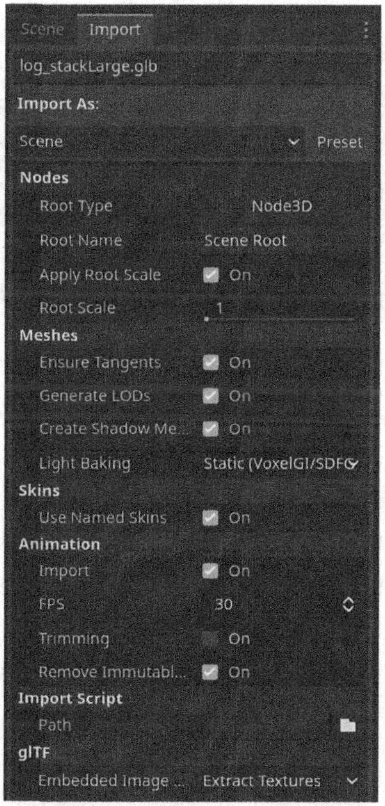

Figure 5.3: The Import tab of the Scene dock

With our floating dock on the right-hand side, we can see a list of our imported models, as well as the **Import** tab, as pictured in *Figure 5.4*. With this, we can select any object from the **FileSystem** dock, and its name will appear in the **Import** tab, where we can reimport it with some modified options (such as physics options).

Note

You can always search the name of a file if you aren't sure where it was imported to in your project. I've created a new folder in our `world` folder called `models` and have placed all the files from the `GLTF format` folder in there.

Now, let's create a new scene by clicking the + icon above the Viewport, then select **Node3D** from the **Scene** dock and drag one of our objects into the Viewport, as shown in *Figure 5.4*.

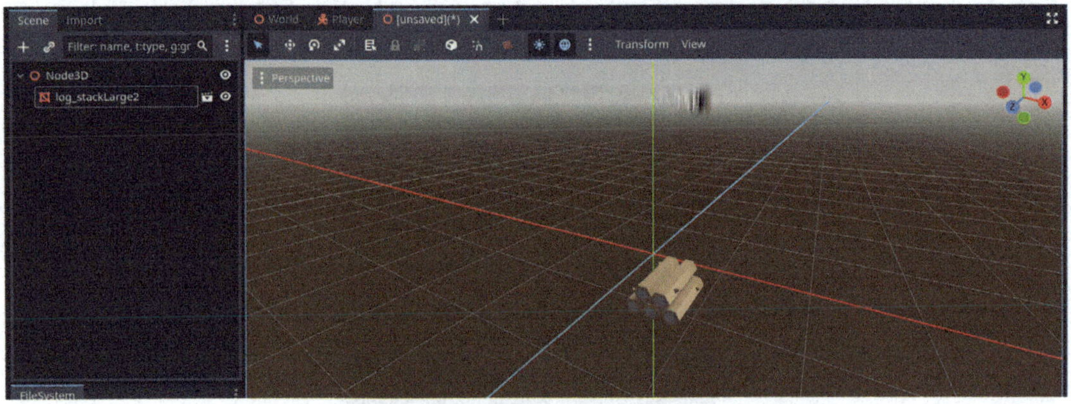

Figure 5.4: Dragging our imported model into a new scene

I've selected the **log_stackLarge2** one. Once the model is in the scene, notice that it is packed like our mannequin was. We can tell by the clapperboard icon next to the **log_stackLarge2** node in the **Scene** dock. Like in the previous chapter, we want to access and alter its nodes. To do this, let's make it accessible by right-clicking and selecting **Editable Children**. The object should now be expanded with a node structure like *Figure 5.5* in the **Scene** dock.

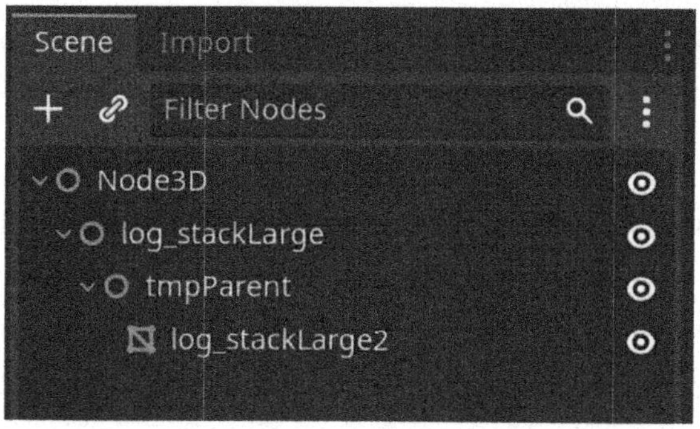

Figure 5.5: Node structure of imported assets once made local

Note

The reason Godot does not save over the original 3D model is to avoid making changes to that source file. This is one reason why we might have a large variety of import options when it comes to adding files.

In this node structure, everything except for the last node, **log_stackLarge2**, is a type of **Node3D**. Instead, the final node is a **MeshInstance3D** node. This is what we'll be attaching collisions to in the next section.

Adding collisions

Now that we have a set of items in our project, it's important to note that these are only models, meaning they don't have any collisions or functions added to them beyond looking nice. We must add collisions to the meshes provided so that our player won't run straight through them. There are a couple of different ways we can do this:

- The first is a method we used back in *Chapter 2*, where we attached a collision area and then manually changed its size
- The second method is having Godot create collisions for us

Let's briefly step through both methods as each is viable, depending on your workflow.

Manually adding collisions to imports

In the **Import** tab, make sure that **log_stackLarge2** is selected from the filesystem; you should see its name appear at the top of the **Import** tab.

We won't need to change any of the settings on this tab, but if you're interested in knowing what each does, you can read about them here: `https://docs.godotengine.org/en/stable/tutorials/assets_pipeline/import_process.html`.

Instead, we'll be clicking the **Advanced** button that's at the bottom of the **Import** dock. A new window will appear, called the **Advanced Import Settings** screen, where you should see the model with its node structure, as well as more options on the right-hand side, as pictured in *Figure 5.6*:

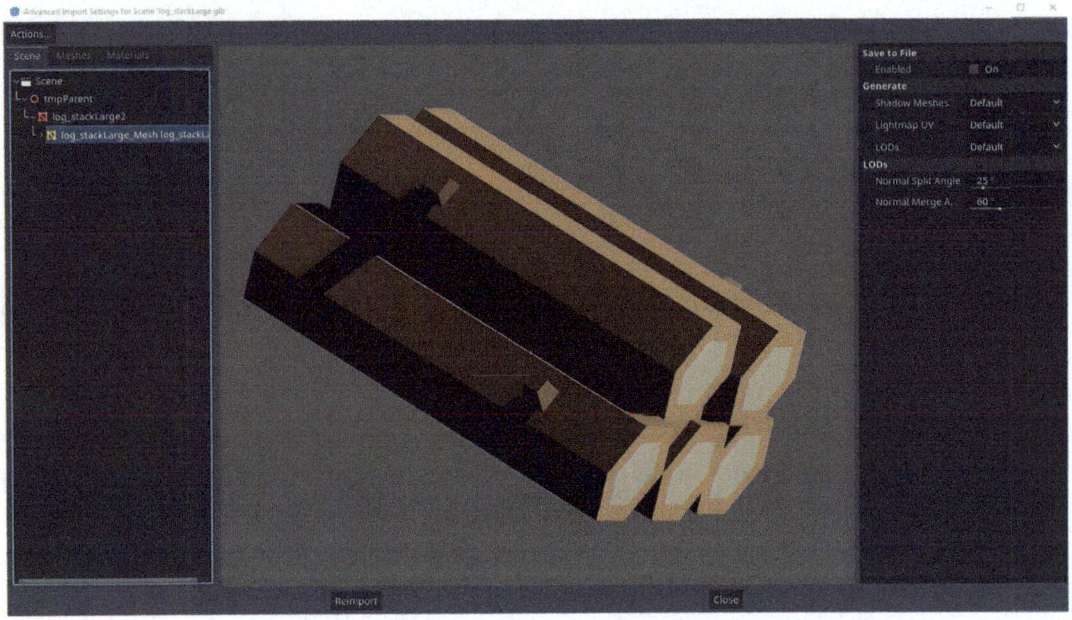

Figure 5.6: The Advanced Import Settings screen

On this new screen, you can fully rotate the model and examine it, as well as zoom in and out with the scroll wheel. This can help ensure that the model was imported correctly, especially if you are importing large scenes or objects such as buildings or vehicles.

We can also select each of the nodes in the scene, which will generate different options on the right-hand side. You'll notice that the yellow node with the **MeshInstance3D** icon can be expanded. If we expand that, you can see all the materials that are on this mesh, as in *Figure 5.7*. If you want to only see meshes or materials, you can use the tabs that are shown at the top of *Figure 5.7* too.

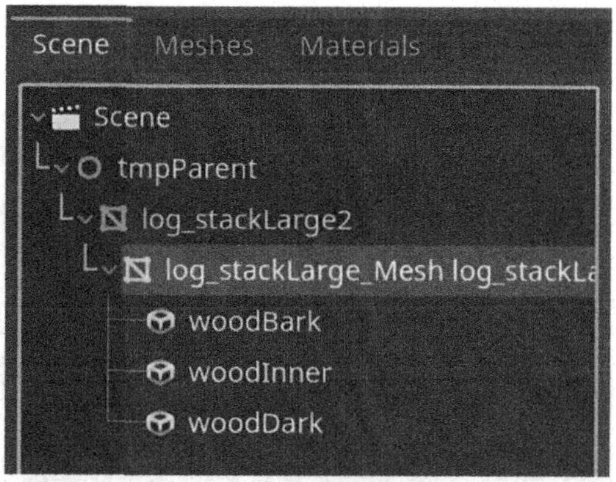

Figure 5.7: Expanded node structure on the Advanced Import Settings screen

Let's talk briefly about the nodes listed in *Figure 5.7* and why they're important when adding collisions, before moving forward. If we expand out the tree of nodes, we see the scene is composed in the following way:

- **Scene**: The root node of the tree.
- **tmpParent**: This is a **Node3D**-type node that is a placeholder for the object's resources.
- **log_stackLarge2**: This is a **MeshInstance3D** node, which means it includes the Mesh resource and surfaces of the object. When this node is selected, we can tell Godot what types of physics, if any, the object should have, as well as the occlusion settings.
- **log_stackLarge_Mesh log_stackLarge**: While this node has the same icon as the previous one, it provides properties based on shadows and UV mapping. This is the Mesh resource of the object that we mentioned earlier. A Mesh resource has all the array-based geometry for an object.
- **woodBark, woodInner,** and **woodDark**: All of these nodes are material resources and apply color and shading to an object. This includes how it responds to light.

Understanding how an object comes together in the engine is important when importing and adding collisions to it. If we select the **log_stackLarge2** node (which is a **MeshInstance3D** node, as denoted by the box icon with a line through it in *Figure 5.7*), the options on the right-hand side include one for **Physics**. If we click the checkmark and make sure **Physics** is enabled, then more options appear. We have some new headers here, specifically another one called **Physics**, as shown in *Figure 5.8*.

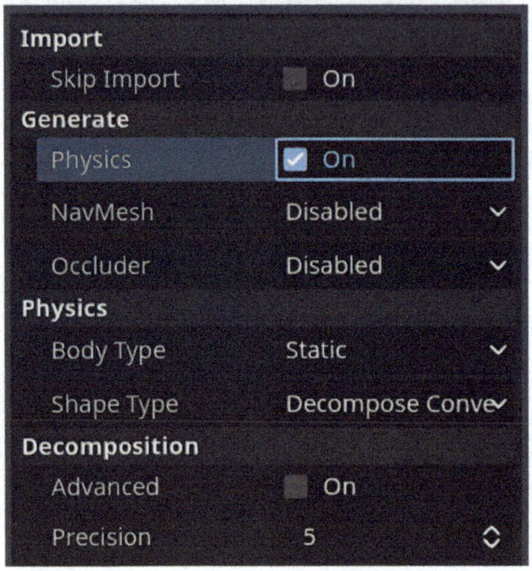

Figure 5.8: The Physics options on the Advanced Import Settings screen for meshes

You'll also notice that in the middle of the window, the model now has lines drawn across it, as in *Figure 5.9*. This is the collision shape Godot has generated for us for this mesh once we select for physics to be generated.

Figure 5.9: Our selected model with collision lines on it

When it comes to the type of physics an object will have, we have a few different options. The options under **Physics**, specifically **Body Type**, are as follows:

- **Static**: As stated, it will create a **StaticBody3D**. This is good for when we have pieces that won't move or be impacted by physics, but the player should still not go through them.
- **Dynamic**: This will generate a **RigidBody3D**. We would use these objects for things we want physics applied to, such as vehicles or objects that are unique in their shape.
- **Area**: Creates an **Area3D**, which is great for floors, walls, and other general large areas.

After **Body Type**, there is another field called **Shape Type**. This option gives us control over how many triangles should be drawn for the collision. Does it need to be highly detailed and precise when it comes to collision, or is it a lone stationary object that essentially acts like a wall? The answers to these types of questions will determine which option is applied. We will leave it be for now but will discuss collisions in more depth in the next section.

For now, let's go ahead and click the **Reimport** button. While it may look like nothing in our **FileSystem** dock has changed, we have applied the **Advanced Import Settings** settings, which include our newly generated collisions, to the model we're reimporting. So, let's click back to our **Scene** dock and make sure we're in our **World** scene. Then, if we drag our `log_stackLarge.glb` file from the **FileSystem** dock into our Viewport, we can test our newly applied collisions out.

With our object selected in the Viewport, we notice the arrows coming out from its origin in multiple colors. We can manipulate this object in three different ways: position, rotation, and scale. To select each of these modes, we can use the toolbar that's at the top of our Viewport. You can find the toolbar by referencing *Figure 5.10*:

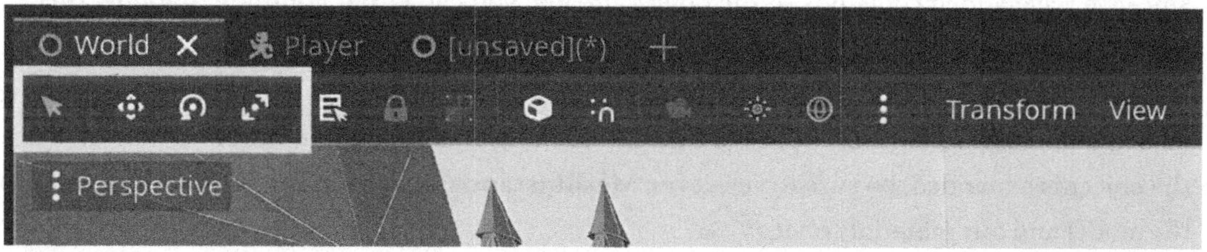

Figure 5.10: The toolbar at the top of the Viewport

Let's look at the modes in this order, starting with the cursor:

- **Select Mode**: Used to select an object you want to move in the Viewport. It is denoted with a colored arrow on each axis, as well as a colored ring on each axis.

- **Move Mode**: Used to move an object by clicking and dragging one of the colored arrows on the axis you want to move along.
- **Rotate Mode**: Used to rotate an object by clicking and dragging one of the circles on the axis you want to move along.
- **Scale Mode**: Used to scale an object up or down by dragging the square ends to scale the object on a specific axis.

Of course, we can manipulate all of these properties precisely from the **Inspector** dock of any selected object under the **Transform** property.

> Note
>
> To toggle between these modes quickly, you can hit the *W* key (position), the *E* key (rotation), or the *R* key (rotation) while focused on the Viewport with an object selected. The *Q* key will make them all available via the **Select** mode.

Once you have the object reasonably scaled in relation to the player, test the scene out. You'll notice that the player is unable to run through it; therefore, our reimport of the model with collisions was successful.

Now, let's go ahead and look at another way we could add collisions that might be useful in a different workflow.

Generating collisions after placement

Since we have added collisions to the object already, you can either continue to follow this example as is using the `log_stackLarge.glb` file or grab one of the other models and open it in a new scene. I'll be using the `statue_column.glb` file for the next example. If you're using a new object, remember to unpack the scene by right-clicking and selecting **Editable Children**. Once the object is expanded, be sure to select the **MeshInstance3D** node in the **Scene** tab which has the model and our materials on it.

Now, with the **MeshInstance3D** node selected, a new button will appear in the toolbar at the top of the Viewport. It'll say **Mesh**, with the icon for **MeshInstances** next to it. You can see it on the far-right side of *Figure 5.11*. This button only appears when you have a mesh selected.

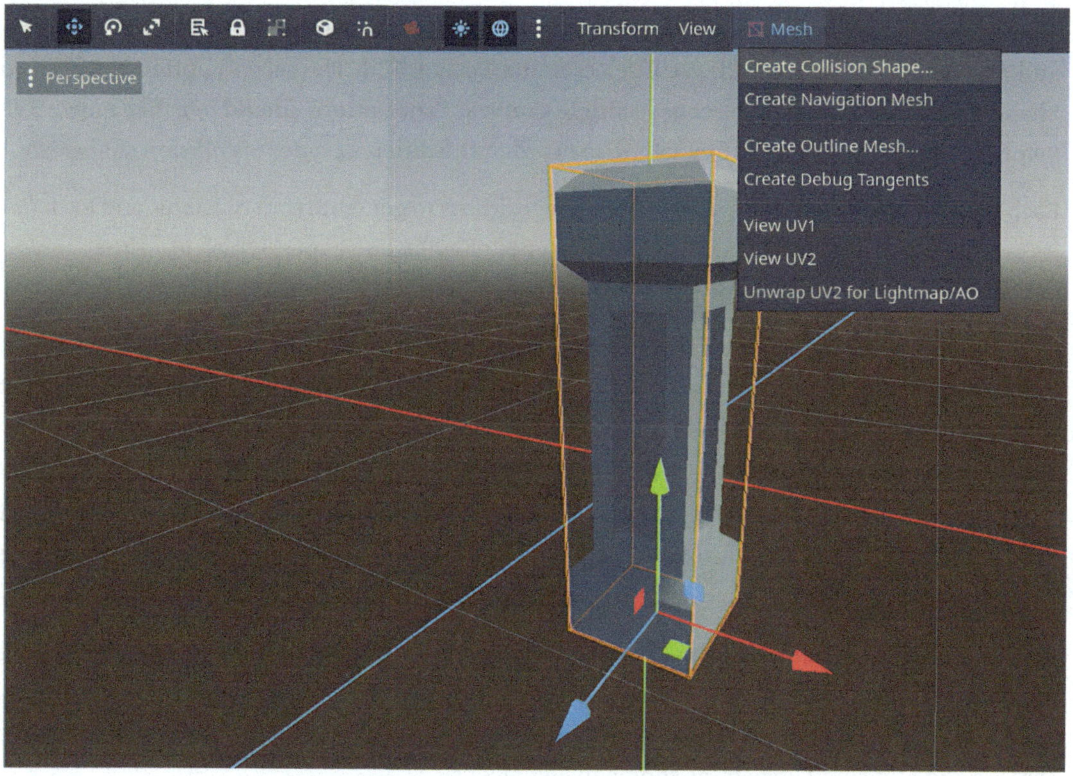

Figure 5.11: Viewport toolbar with the Mesh button available

Click the **Mesh** button and a dropdown will appear with options for creating different types of collisions. We're going to select **Create Collision Shape...** as adding collisions to the mesh is our plan. Once clicked, a new pop-up window will appear, as shown in *Figure 5.12*.

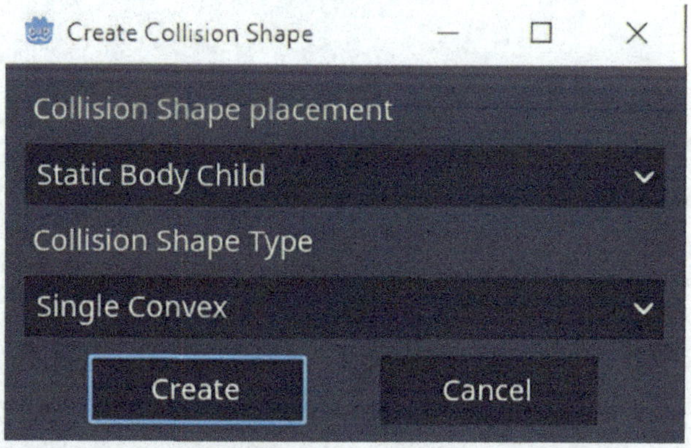

Figure 5.12: The Create Collision Shape pop-up window with options

The first option, **Collision Shape placement**, provides two choices from the drop-down menu: **Sibling** and **Static Body Child**. We'll select **Static Body Child**. The second option is **Collision Shape Type**, and we'll want to choose **Single Convex**. Your options should look like *Figure 5.12*. Before clicking the **Create** button, let's discuss what the different types of collision shapes are.

Each type of collision creation uses different algorithms to generate the collisions, and each has its own use case. Let's discuss the two main types of collision shapes, which are either convex or concave:

- **Convex collision shapes**: These are created using a mix of primitive shapes (box, sphere, cylinder, etc.) and concave shapes. They are good for solid objects and generally any object that is convex shaped.
- **Trimesh collision shapes**: These are also known as concave collision shapes and are good for any object. However, as the name implies, they use triangles to generate collision and can be quite resource-intensive, depending on the object. They do offer the most accurate collision, but the use case will vary from project to project.

Returning to generating collisions for our column statues example, we want to select something that is good for performance and simple for collision detection. Looking at our drop-down options, we're going to select **Create Single Convex Collision Sibling**. This option generates collisions that are good for small objects, as shown in *Figure 5.13*.

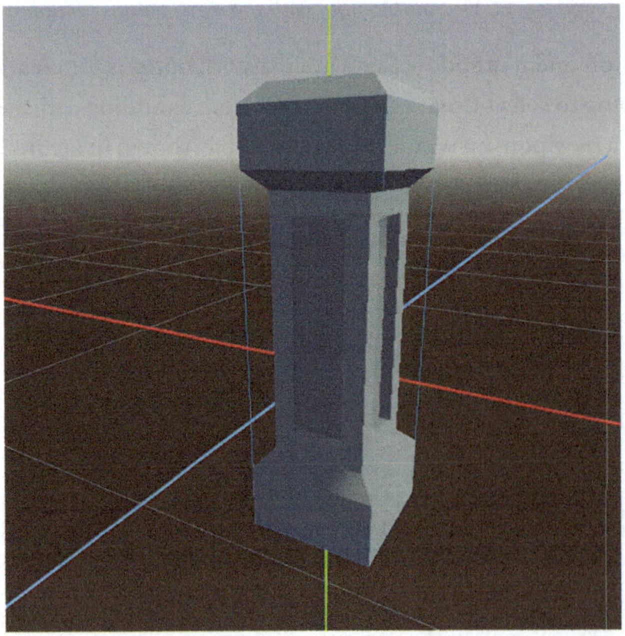

Figure 5.13: Collisions added to the statue_column model

The blue lines around the edge of the column are the collision shape that's been added. Rather than having to set it ourselves, Godot created it automatically based on the selections we made through the Mesh resource.

> Note
>
> There are a couple of different ways to generate collisions for our meshes, and it's important to understand the difference between both, especially when you're working in specific environments or need to target certain platforms. Being aware of the geometry that Godot will create and knowing the different types of collision will help you make better choices when determining assets in your game. If you'd like to read more about the different collision shapes, you can do so here: `https://docs.godotengine.org/en/stable/tutorials/physics/collision_shapes_3d.html`.

Now, you're going to start building the level and creating a space that's entirely your own. You will see screenshots of what I've created in the **World** scene, but I've provided no step-by-step process for how objects should be placed in your scene. This next section is a creative and rewarding part of game development, so take your time and enjoy it!

Designing our first level

After spending time in all the surrounding docks, we're going to work in the Viewport for a while as we add models and design our first level.

The test area that we used for trying out our player movement is somewhat unnecessary now. Let's keep it for future testing by right-clicking the **Node3D** that's labeled **Floor** and selecting **Save Branch as Scene**. This option will take the selected node and every child node under it and make a new scene of those nodes. Therefore, if we make our floor node the parent of a new scene, we get both the floor and the boxes we placed for testing in its own scene. Now, whenever we want to test some new object or mechanic, we can drop those objects in there and have a playable area to test in.

Go ahead and pick a model or a few to use for the ground. I am using the models from the Nature Kit packet provided by Kenney Assets (they are the same ones we imported at the start of the chapter); for the ground specifically, I am using models that are named in the format **bridge_objectName**. Drag the objects from your **FileSystem** dock to the Viewport. They should then appear in the scene tree. Using the models from the kit along with the ways of adding collisions that we've discussed, go ahead and place them in a way that you would enjoy as a player.

Figure 5.14: A cute campsite created, using Kenney Assets to design a level

At this point, you might notice that our level is a bit dark. We have no shadows or sky light. Before we add a node to represent our sun, let's create what's called a **WorldEnvironment** in Godot. This node makes many settings available to us, such as volumetric fog, shadows, and other rendering options to make our scene look sharper.

Right-click on our root node in the **Scene** dock (the one at the top of the list) and select **Add a Child**. Then, search for **WorldEnvironment** and add it to our scene. Our **WorldEnvironment** node has a warning on it in the **Scene** dock – hovering over it tells us it needs an **Environment** property. The warning is telling us that it can't work correctly without pointing to an environment resource, which we'll create next.

Now, if we look at our **Inspector** dock, we'll find that we have **Environment** and **Camera Attributes** properties available. From the **Inspector** dock, create a new environment by clicking the drop-down arrow next to the word **empty**, as seen in *Figure 5.15*. From the list, select **New Environment**.

Figure 5.15: Creating the Environment property

Once created, the environment will appear in the **Environment** property. Now, click **Environment** to access the options available in *Figure 5.12*. Many of the options listed deal with light and how components in the scene are rendered, and there are some fun options we'll look at, such as glow and volumetric fog.

Figure 5.16: Options available once the environment is created

For now, let's expand the **Background** setting and change **Mode** to **Sky**. The Viewport should immediately change in color tone, and a new property should appear directly below **Background** called **Sky**. Let's expand the **Sky** property and create a new **Sky** resource, as in *Figure 5.17*:

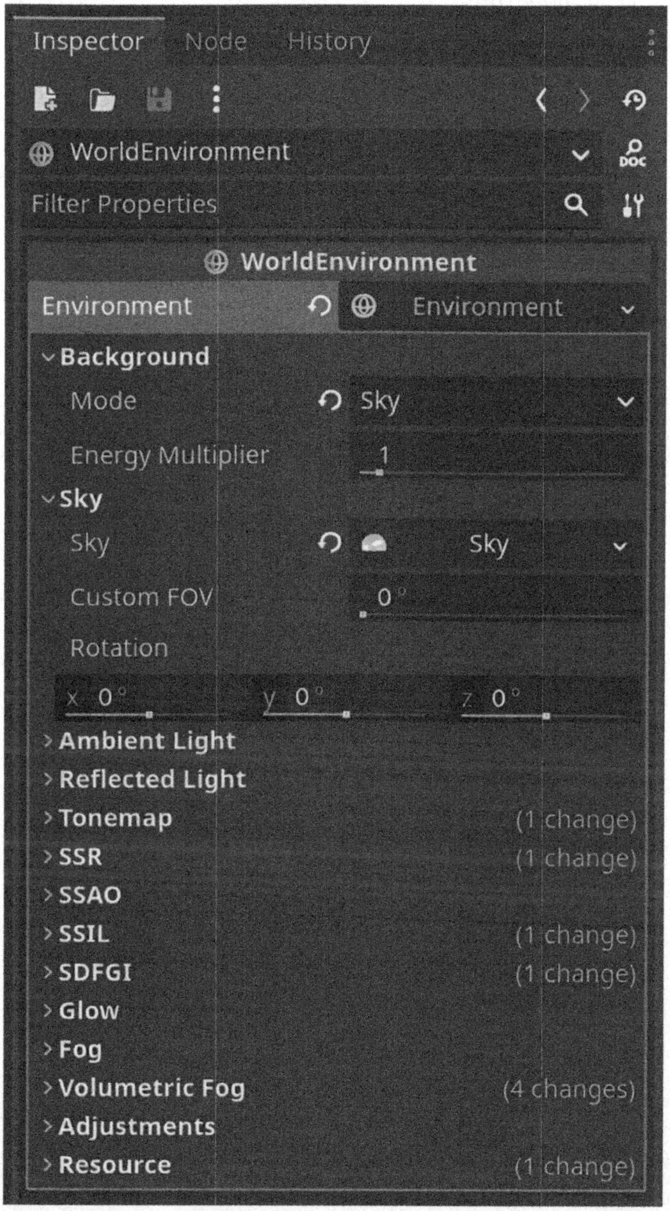

Figure 5.17: The WorldEnvironment node with a new Environment and Sky

Click into the **Sky** we've created and add a new **Sky Material**. Then, select **New ProceduralSky Material**. We can click further into this new material, changing the color of the sky and the horizon, as well as the ground and sun, as seen in *Figure 5.18*. Choose a color for the sky that you'll enjoy. I've gone for a classic sky blue.

Figure 5.18: Options available when creating a Sky Material

As seen in *Figure 5.18*, there are also options for augmenting the ground's color in the Viewport and the sun's angle. We won't be exploring any of these options but feel free to if you want a more specific skyline or sunrise/sunset.

That's it for our **Sky Material**. Let's minimize the **Sky** property and explore a couple of other environment variables we want enabled.

There are two properties we want to enable in our **WorldEnvironment**:

- The first is **SSIL** (which stands for **Screen-Space Indirect Lighting**), which provides indirect lighting and is often used in conjunction with other lighting sources. We will discuss lighting sources more in *Chapter 9*. For now, expand the **SSIL** field and enable it (we won't change any of the default settings).
- The second is **SDFGI** (which stands for **Signed Distance Field Global Illumination**), which provides semi-real-time global illumination. This pertains to global illumination in the scene; if you'd like to know more, you can read about it here: `https://docs.godotengine.org/en/stable/tutorials/3d/global_illumination/introduction_to_global_illumination.html#doc-introduction-to-global-illumination-comparison`. Expand the **SDFGI** property and enable it (again, don't change the default settings).

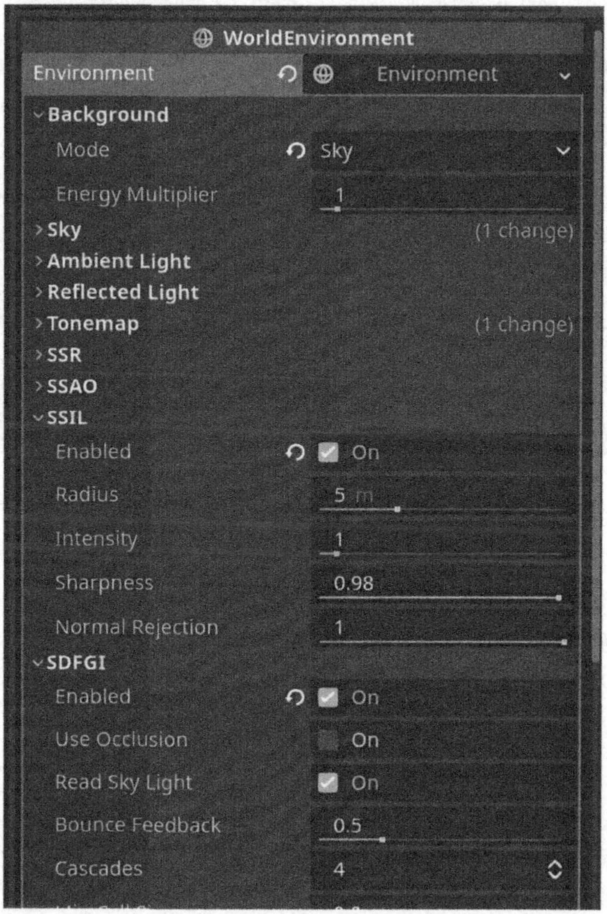

Figure 5.19: The SSIL and SDFGI properties for WorldEnvironment

The last setting we'll mention is **Volumetric Fog**, which is at the bottom of the **Environment** property list (see *Figure 5.20*). It's a new option in Godot and once enabled, you can see the entire level covered in a gray fog.

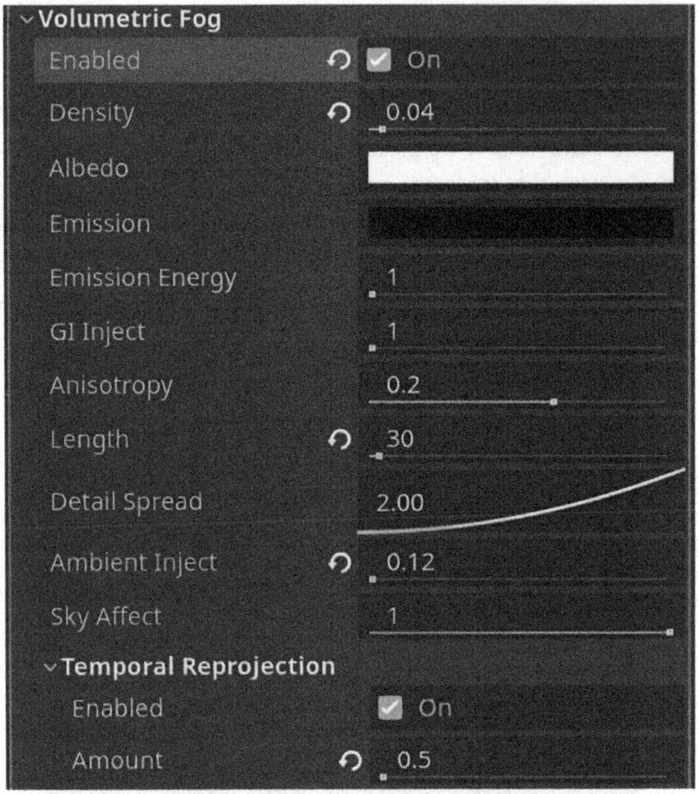

Figure 5.20: The Volumetric Fog property options in the WorldEnvironment

Density and **Length** are two important options here. **Density** refers to how much fog there is. I have set this to `0.04`. **Length** refers to the distance at which the fog is computed – the lower the value, the more detail you'll get (it's recommended to run it at a lower setting). I have mine set to `30`. You can see the result of these options in *Figure 5.21*:

Figure 5.21: The game with volumetric fog on

Note

If you just want to use **Volumetric Fog** nodes in specific areas and not the entire scene, you still need to enable the **Fog** property in the **Environment** list (as listed in *Figure 5.16*). However, set **Density** to `0` and configure the **Volumetric Fog** node separately in your scene.

Now, the creation of our WorldEnvironment is complete. So far, everything is static in our level, so let's shake things up and give them life by making our trees look like they're moving in the wind with shaders.

Creating movement with shaders

Shaders are an extremely powerful tool when it comes to creating games. They can set the mood in an environment sky, or they can generate heightmaps to make terrain. They can be applied to materials and surfaces to generate all kinds of behaviors to make our worlds and characters feel like they've come to life. We're going to use shaders on the tree model that's in our kit from Kenney Assets, specifically `tree_pineDefaultA2.tscn`. If you aren't super familiar with shaders, that's okay. This will be a very brief introduction to what they are, how they function, and how we can use them in Godot.

Within Godot, shaders use their own language that's separate from both GDScript and C#. This is known as a graphics programming language. One of the more common graphics programming languages is called **OpenGL Shading Language** (**GLSL**). However, Godot uses its own graphics programming language that's based on GLSL. With a separate language, there are, in fact, separate programs for creating shaders. These programs run on your GPU and can control both geometry and pixels.

The important thing to remember when creating shaders is that they are executed when rendering occurs. This means the way we approach creating functions for them is different than what we would create in C#. There are also some additional references in the *Further reading* section of this chapter that dive deeper into explaining how shaders function and their role within a game engine.

Shaders in Godot are made up of what are called **processor functions**, which are the main functions of the Godot shading language. The first is the `vertex()` function, and the second is the `fragment()` function. They can be defined as follows:

- `vertex()`: This function runs over all vertices in a mesh and can set their position
- `fragment()`: This function is run on every pixel on a mesh

If you want to learn more about the `vertex()` and `fragment()` functions, or processor functions within Godot, you can do so here: `https://docs.godotengine.org/en/stable/tutorials/shaders/introduction_to_shaders.html#`.

We'll be using the `vertex()` function to make our trees move back and forth as if swaying in the wind. To get started, open our `tree_pineDefaultA2.tscn` scene, then select **MeshInstance3D** from the Scene tree, which should be labeled **tree_pineDefaultA2** in the scene.

From the **Inspector** dock, we can see the mesh of the tree, as shown in *Figure 5.17*. Click the tiny tree image in the **Mesh** box:

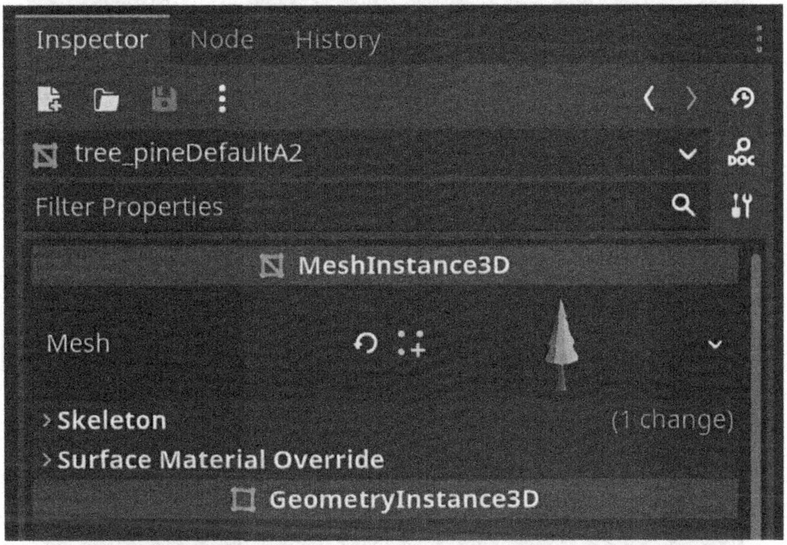

Figure 5.22: The mesh to click on when adding shaders to materials

Once expanded, we can see that there are two materials on this model. The first is under the **Surface 0** property. Expand this, and you'll see the green material that's for the leaves, called **leafsDark**. The second material is under **Surface 1**. Once expanded, you can see that this is the bark of the tree, and it's called **woodBarkDark**.

We will only be adding a shader to the **leafsDark**, or **Surface 0**, material, since we only want the tops of the trees to sway, not the trunk. You can see **Surface 0** in *Figure 5.23*. Click the small down arrow next to the green sphere (the **leafsDark** material) and you should see options for creating a new material or a new shader material. At the very bottom of this dropdown, there is a **Convert to ShaderMaterial** option. Click this and a new property, called **Shader**, will appear.

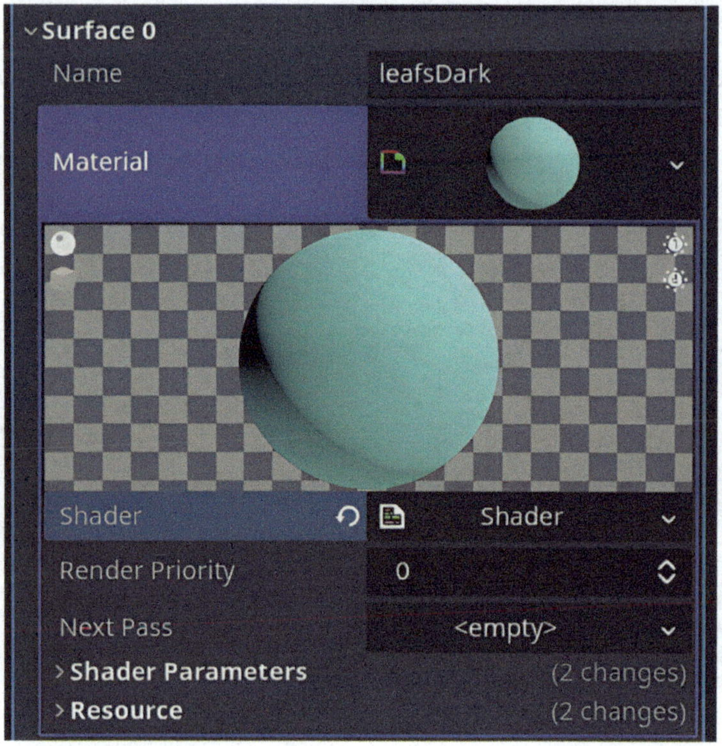

Figure 5.23: The material after converting it to a shader material

We now need to find the **Shader Editor** along the bottom of our **Output** dock, so we can write the code we need to augment the behavior of this material. You can see what the Shader Editor looks like with the shader we just created in *Figure 5.24*.

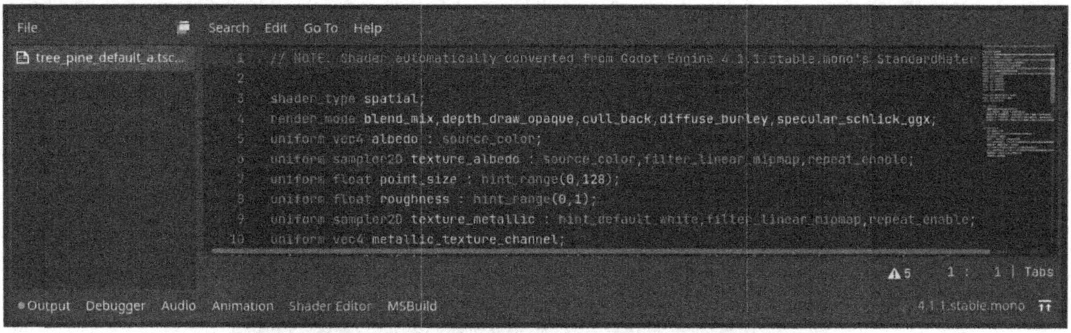

Figure 5.24: The Shader Editor in Godot

Converting the material into a shader material forced Godot to preserve all the current attributes of the material, such as its color and other behaviors, and generate the code for those same behaviors in the shader language. We'll briefly step through what some of these lines mean and then add our own `vertex()` function as mentioned before.

The first line we will look at in *Figure 5.20* is line 3:

```
shader_type spatial;
```

This code denotes that the shader will be on a 3D object. Here, `spatial` covers a wide variety of shader options, which, if you're interested, you can read more about here: `https://docs.godotengine.org/en/stable/tutorials/shaders/shader_reference/spatial_shader.html`. Other types of shaders in Godot are **CanvasItems**, **Particles**, **Sky**, and **Fog**.

The next line is `render_mode` – this tells Godot how to render the material. The previous URL details what each component of this line entails, but we will not need to change it.

After that, there are a bunch of lines with the `uniform` keyword. This is how we create variables in the shader language. They can be nearly any data type, and once declared in the shader script, they're available as one of the shader parameters in the **Inspector** dock. For example, look at line 5, which says the following:

```
uniform vec4 albedo : source_color;
```

Then, click into our **Inspector** dock for the mesh and look at the shader parameters of the **leafsDark** material (see *Figure 5.25*), and we can see that we can augment the values of these parameters in the **Inspector** dock. These parameters are exported from the Shader Editor. This makes it very easy to access other variables, such as noise textures to utilize in our shader programs.

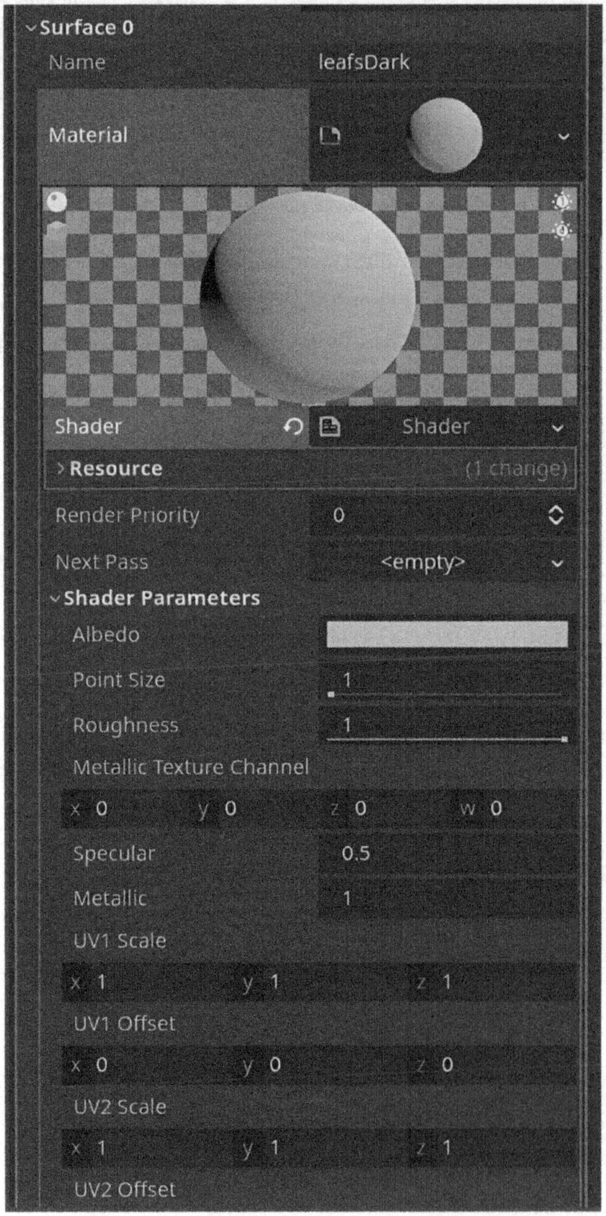

Figure 5.25: The shader parameters available on the leafsDark material

Back to the code, let's scroll down until we're at the line that looks as follows:

```
uniform vec3 uv2_offset;
```

Underneath this, we're going to add our own variables. We want to make it look like our trees are swaying in the wind, so we'll create a `wind_strength` variable by typing the following:

```
uniform float wind_strength = 0.02;
```

We've set this variable to something arbitrary (`0.02`), but you'll see that once we save it, we'll be able to adjust it from the **Inspector** dock. So, click **File** | **Save File** and then look in our **Inspector** dock, under **Shader Parameters**, for **Wind Strength**, as seen in *Figure 5.26*:

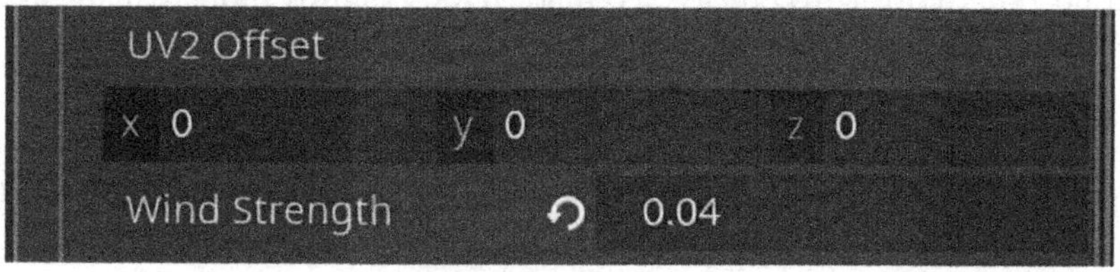

Figure 5.26: The Wind Strength variable in the Inspector dock

This is cool, because we can pass many properties to our shader, since `uniform` takes almost any data type. Now, we can create our `vertex()` function. Declaring it will look like this:

```
void vertex() {}
```

The `vertex()` function doesn't have a return type, so it's set to `void`. It also does not take any parameters – remember, the shader is running in a loop over the material, so when we make a change to any of the vertices, it will change constantly throughout.

Within our `vertex()` function, let's go ahead and add the following line:

```
VERTEX.x += sin(VERTEX.x + TIME) * wind_strength;
```

Here, we're accessing the x channel, the *X* axis, of the `VERTEX` variable, and adding those variables to a sine function (written in code as `sin`) that takes in the VERTEX variable and TIME. Adding `TIME` here makes the tree appear animated. We complete the statement by then multiplying everything by our `wind_strength`.

Our tree should now appear to move ever so slightly on the *X* axis in the Viewport. This is a great opportunity to test out what different shader functions and variables will do to our material. For example, if we take out `wind_strength`, the tree will move very far left and right in the movement of the `sin` function. This is one of the fun things about shaders – with each line of code we write, we can see in real time how it will impact our objects.

If you played around with the code, make sure you've reset your shader code to match the previous line of code I provided before continuing. Now, we can also go to our **Inspector** dock and update `wind_strength` to see how smaller or larger numbers impact the animation. Try it out now!

Once you're done tweaking `wind_strength`, we're also going to change how the *Z* axis behaves for `VERTEX`. It will add a bit more depth and give our tree a fuller body sway. Our line of code will look like this:

```
VERTEX.z += cos(VERTEX.z + TIME) * wind_strength;
```

This is essentially the same line as before, except we're focusing on the `z` channel. Using the cosine function here (written in code as `cos`) made it look slightly more realistic as it now sways in our artificial wind. You can try it out with a sine function and see whether you like that better. It's up to you.

Be sure to save the shader file and the **Tree** scene. Then, go back to our **World** scene and place some trees in it if you haven't already. If you already have some trees in there, they should automatically update and be swaying in the Viewport. Test out the scene with your player and see whether you like the results. You can always come back and add more to the shader if you like.

This was just a brief dive into the topic of shaders; there's a lot more you can discover with them. Now, we're going to shift our focus and look at how to set up and maintain different collision layers, as well as preparing our player for some in-game physics.

Preparing game physics

Tracking physics can get complicated fast. Rather than keeping tabs on every single item in an environment, we can set up something called collision layers and masks.

First, let's better define what each of these are:

- **Collision layers**: These are used to tell objects what layer they live on.
- **Masks**: These are listeners. They are scanned by other objects to determine collision.

For example, let's say we have two objects, Object A and Object B. Object A lives on Layer 1, and Object B lives on Layer 2. If Object A has a mask for Layer 2, then Object A can collide with Object B.

Both layers and masks are denoted by a range of numbers. For any object that has collision (such as a **MeshInstance3D**, aka the **StaticBody3D** from our mushroom item), we can augment the layers and masks. You can see how they look in *Figure 5.27* under the **Inspector** dock of the selected collision object. By default, each layer and mask are set to 1; as all objects are on Layer 1 and scanning for Layer 1, everything can collide with everything.

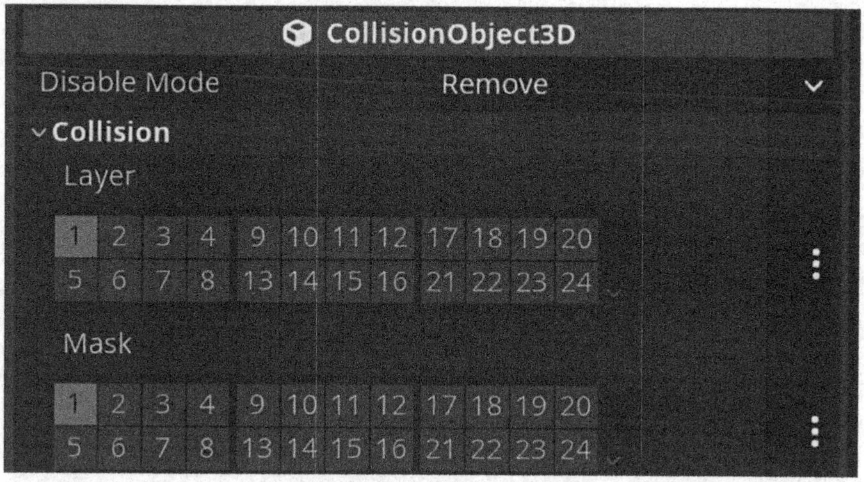

Figure 5.27: The view for collision layers and masks from the Inspector dock

We're going to set up three layers: the first one will be for our player, the second one will be for our collectible items, and the third will be for the world. This will allow us to keep track of what our player is colliding with and what the autonomous objects we create throughout the book are running into as well.

To create our layers, we can click the three vertical dots to the right of the **Layer** box shown in *Figure 5.27*. It will give the **Edit Layer Names** option. Click it, and it will open a new window that's part of **Project Settings**. For the first three layers, add the player, collectible, and world in the following order, as seen in *Figure 5.28*.

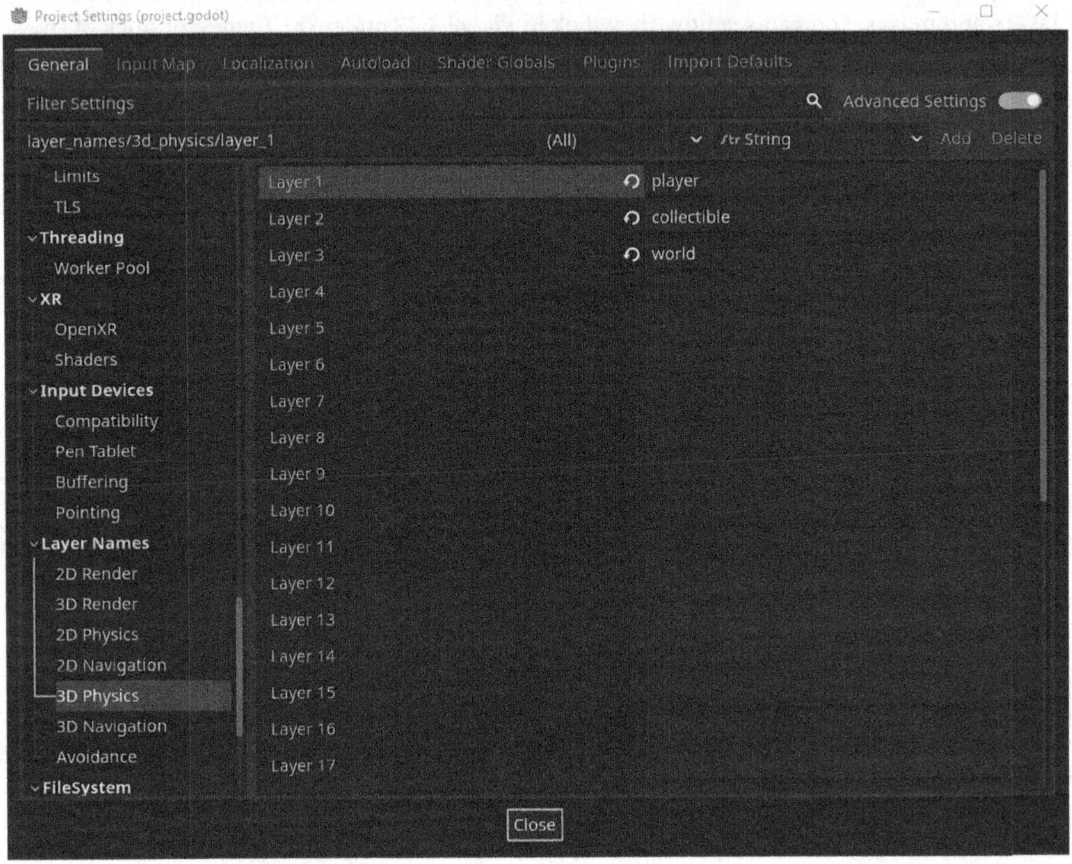

Figure 5.28: Creating the layer names for our collision layers and masks

> **Note**
>
> Notice that within **Project Settings**, we're in the **Layer Names** section, and specifically under **3D Physics**, not **3D Render**, which also has a list of layer names.

Once that's done, click the **Close** button.

Now, let's set the layers and masks for some objects we've already created. For anything we've placed in the world so far, we want to make sure that the **StaticBody3D** nodes placed to provide collisions are set to Layer 3, which is the **World** layer. Rather than remembering that Layer 3 is the world one, you can click the three vertical dots next to the **Collision** property (just like we did when editing the layer names), and you'll see that our three layers are checkbox options. Select **world** for all ground pieces, trees, and so on, as shown in *Figure 5.29*:

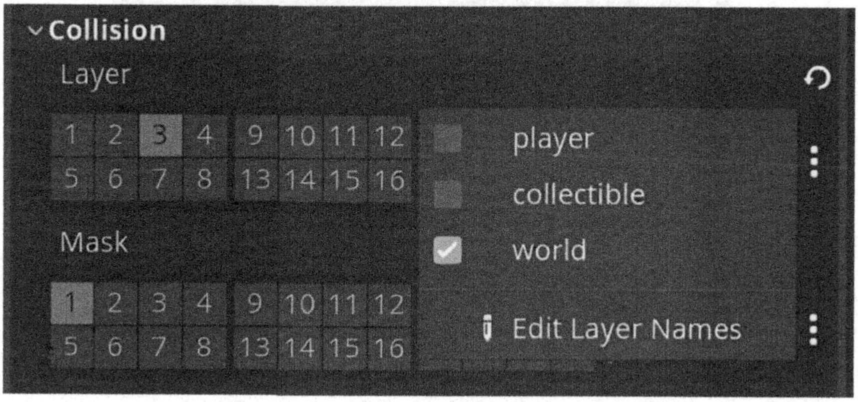

Figure 5.29: Adding an object to the world layer via the Inspector dock

As you probably guessed, we're going to switch to creating a new scene, a mushroom item, that our player will be able to pick. We'll be utilizing masks later in the chapter, but for now, having the layer set up and understanding the difference between the two is sufficient.

Creating and gathering collectibles

With our world feeling more alive and cozier by the minute, let's add some simple mechanics that our player can perform, such as picking up items. To set this up, we'll take a mushroom model we've imported, add collisions to it, set its layers and mask values, and then write a script to tell the mushroom when it's collided with the player.

Setting up our model

To get started, let's pick a model to serve as our collectible item. I've decided that our character will be foraging through this cute forest area and will be collecting mushrooms.

Create a new 3D scene and drag one of the mushrooms into the Viewport. I've selected the **mushroom_red.glb** model. Once it's in the scene, right-click the node and select **Make Local**. Then, from the **Scene** tab shown in *Figure 5.30*, right-click the **mushroom_red** node and select **Save Branch as Scene**.

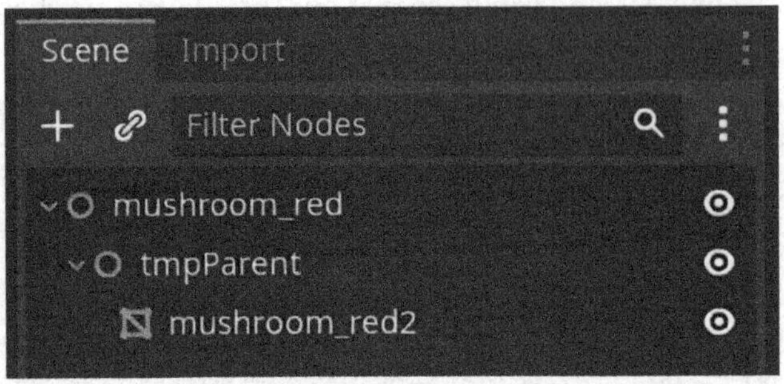

Figure 5.30: The node structure of our mushroom item

When you click on the **mushroom_red** node, the properties shown in *Figure 5.31* will appear in the **Inspector** dock. Personally, I felt the mushroom was too tiny in relation to our player and the rest of the world, so under **Transform**, I set the **Scale** property to 3 on every axis.

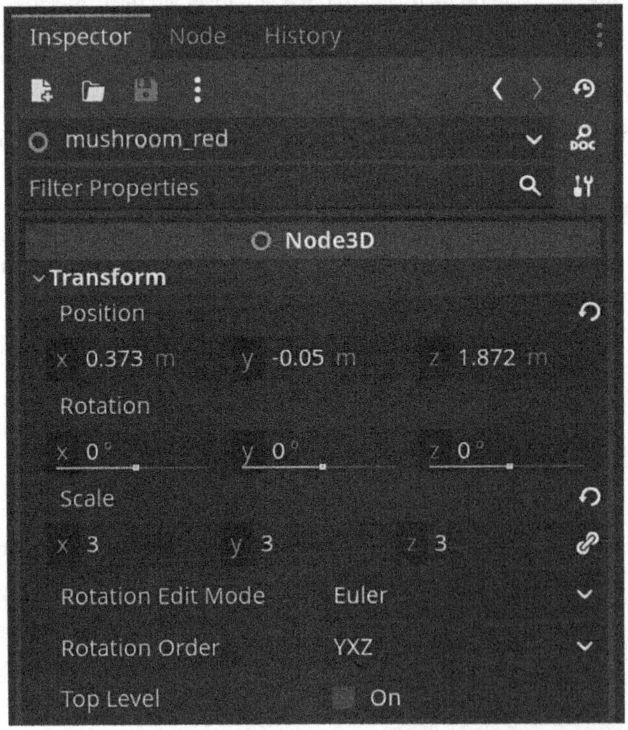

Figure 5.31: The Transform property of the mushroom_red node

We now need two more nodes before this node structure is complete – a physics body and a collision body. So, right-click our **mushroom_red2** node, which is also the **MeshInstance3D** here, and add a new node of type **StaticBody3D**. Remember, **StaticBody3D** is our physics body here.

In previous chapters, we would have added **CollisionShape3D** manually, but let's use the way we learned at the beginning of this chapter. Select the **mushroom_red2** node, click the **Mesh** button that's at the top of the Viewport toolbar, and select **Create Single Convex Collision Sibling**. A new node will appear in the scene tree called **CollisionShape3D**, and you should see collision lines on the mushroom model in the Viewport. It should look like *Figure 5.32*.

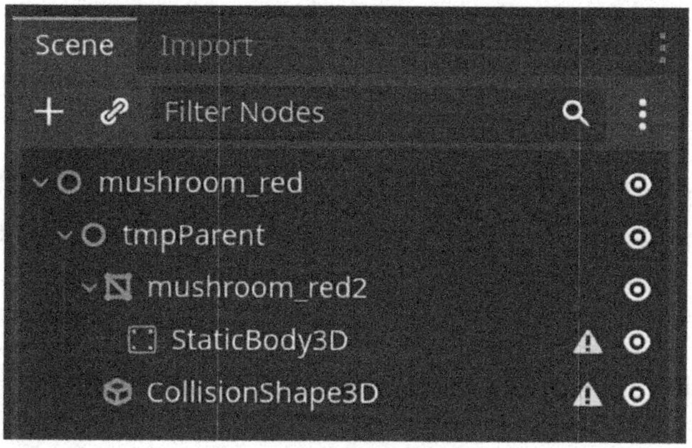

Figure 5.32: The current node structure of our mushroom item

We have two warnings on both **StaticBody3D** and **CollisionShape3D**. This is due to the ordering of our nodes in the scene; the two aren't aware of each other. To fix this, we need to make **CollisionShape3D** a child of **StaticBody3D**. So, reorganize the scene tree to look like *Figure 5.29*, and the warnings will go away:

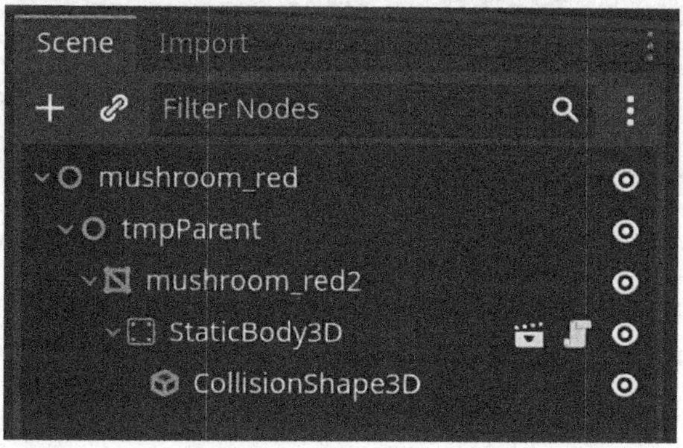

Figure 5.33: The complete node structure for the mushroom item up to this point

As we discussed in the previous section about the importance of collision layers, we need to set the layer for our mushroom item. Let's do the following:

1. Select **StaticBody3D**.
2. In the **Inspector** dock, under the **Collision** property, let's set the **Collision** layer to be on Layer 2, which is, if you recall, what we set our collectibles to be back in *Figure 5.34*.
3. While in the **Inspector** dock, we also want to deselect Layer 1 collision and remove it from the mushroom object, since they aren't our player. Remember, Layer 1 is for our player's collisions only.

   Remember, our player is on Layer 1, and we want our player and our collectibles to be on separate layers; our player has no awareness of Layer 1 (there are no other players), so our collisions wouldn't work if we left the collision layers in their default state.

4. Now, look at the **Mask** layers. The mask settings for our item should be Layer 1 only. Mask settings are used for objects to listen to other objects. Our player is on Layer 1, and our mushroom is listening to Layer 1, so the mushroom will know when the player collides with it.

See *Figure 5.34* for the collision layer and mask settings for a visual guide on what to set for layers and masks.

Figure 5.34: The collision layer and mask for our mushroom item

With the collision configured for our mushroom item, we can turn our attention to adding a script to add functionality to it.

Adding a script to the mushroom object

Just like we did with the player, when we completed our node structure, we went ahead and created a script to attach it. However, we won't be attaching the script to the root node of our **mushroom_red** scene. Instead, we'll be attaching a script to **StaticBody3D**. There are two specific reasons why we're attaching it to our collision node. The first one is that we want to trigger functions when our player collides with this object. The second is we want to reuse this **StaticBody3D** in other objects we may deem as collectibles.

Reusing one singular component leads to the idea of **composition**, which is largely what Godot's node system is. Composition is having one component serve its most singular function, which makes it reusable and easily extendable. We'll apply this idea later when we create a different type of collectible, but for now, mentally bookmark the idea.

Back to attaching scripts to our mushroom item, start by right-clicking **StaticBody3D** and selecting **Attach Script**. We'll get the following pop-up menu to create a new script, shown in *Figure 5.35*. At this point, it should already be set to C#, since we've already created a script in the project.

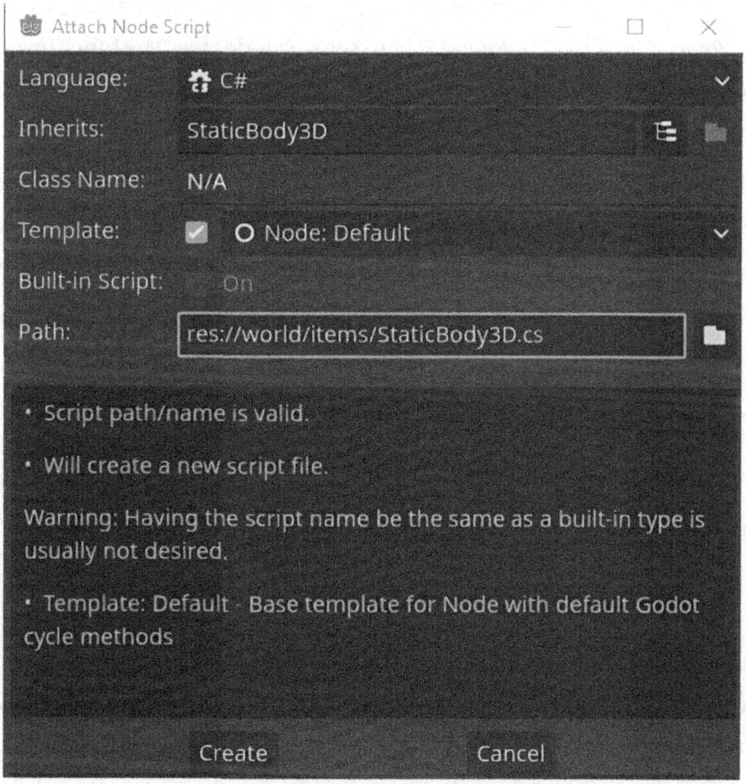

Figure 5.35: The pop-up menu for attaching a script

Rename the script `CollectibleTrigger`. Our plan is to have this script fire after our player collides with the mushroom object in the world and then we can do whatever we want with it, such as increment how many mushrooms we have, give us points, or heal us – it's totally up to us! Now, click **Create**.

As before, we'll see our default functions of `_Ready` and `_Process` when we create the C# script (which we utilized in *Chapter 4* when creating our player script). However, here we will be creating new functions. Instead, we're going to create a function that will delete the mushroom item and call `PickUp`, which we'll trigger when our player collides with the mushroom (more on this in the next section). We only need to put one line in the function, so `PickUp` will look like this:

```
public void PickUp()
{
    this.GetParent().QueueFree();
}
```

The function we created, `PickUp`, will utilize some built-in Godot functions, such as `GetParent` and `QueueFree`. The `GetParent` function gets the parent node, which will be the **Node3D** named `mushroom_red`. You can look back at *Figure 5.29* to see the node tree. The function called `QueueFree` prepares a node for deletion at the end of the frame and deletes all its child nodes, which is what we want to happen when we collide with it.

In the game, the mushroom will disappear. By disappear, I mean that it will be removed from the **World** level visually, and it will also be removed from the scene tree hierarchy. When we test our game, be sure to look at the scene tree and notice if it's removed. When the game stops running, they will return as `QueueFree` is triggered only during runtime.

> Note
>
> We must call `GetParent` before calling `QueueFree`, because remember this script is not on the root node of our scene. If we only called `QueueFree`, we would delete the collision and not everything else. `GetParent` accesses the parent node of our **StaticBody3D**, which is the **MeshInstance3D**, and promptly removes it.

With the node structure complete and our collectible scripted, let's spend a moment getting our player script ready for registering collisions and discerning whether our player is touching the ground, a mushroom, or any other object we place in our scene.

Checking player collisions

Our player is going to be running into all types of objects, and sometimes we're going to want to know which type of object that is, so we can perform some specific function in our game. For example, we want to know when our player is touching the ground, so it doesn't fall through it, but we don't necessarily need to know what every object on the ground is. In the case of our collectible item, we want to know when the player collides with it, which we're able to do by getting a list of all current collisions per frame from our player.

To do this, we're going to switch from the Editor back into our player script from the previous chapter. Here, we're going to create a new function that checks whether we've run into an item. We'll place this after the conversion function we created that allowed us to convert degrees to radians. The function name and parameters look like this:

```
public void CheckForCollectibleCollision()
{
}
```

> Note
>
> For me, I'd rather have slightly longer function names that tell me exactly what they do, rather than having to guess it. I'm also a big fan of the summary comment that can be created when writing C# – to create a summary function, type three forward slashes (///) above the function, and it should auto-create it.

Of course, our Player could hit multiple objects at once before **MoveAndSlide** is called again. Remember, **MoveAndSlide** is called in our Player script to process physics and is a built-in Godot function from the **CharacterBody** node. For reference, we created a 2D version of this in *Chapter 2* and our 3D version is in *Chapter 4*.

To find out what is colliding with our player, we'll use a function called `GetSlideCollisionCount` to tell us what the number of contacts with the player is. So, inside our new function, we'll create a loop to iterate through those collision contacts:

```
for(int index=0; index < GetSlideCollisionCount(); index++){}
```

At each iteration of our loop through these collisions, we're going to get more information about those collisions, specifically what type they are. What we're going to do is create a collision variable that is going to hold the collision that we want more information about at each iteration of the loop, like so:

```
KinematicCollision3D collision = GetSlideCollision(index);
```

`GetSlideCollision` is what will tell us more information about the type of collision our player has hit. Now, we'll add an `if` statement to check whether what we collide with is in a type of `CollectibleTrigger` that we created earlier. The `if` statement will look like this:

```
if (collision.GetCollider() is CollectibleTrigger collectible)
{
    GD.Print("Collided with collectible");
}
```

Once we have our collision object, we check the collider on it and see whether it's of the `CollectibleTrigger` type with the C# `is` keyword. I've added a `print` statement that will output on the Godot console to say whether we've collided with the collectible. Our complete function should now look like this:

```
public void CheckForCollectibleCollision()
{
    for (int index = 0; index < GetSlideCollisionCount(); index++)
    {
        if (collision.GetCollider() is CollectibleTrigger collectible)
        {
            GD.Print("Collided with collectible");
        }
    }
}
```

Next, drag the `mushroom_red.tscn` scene from **FileSystem** into the Viewport and place it within the player's walking area. Now, let's test it out and see what happens. We should get a line of text in the **Output** console that looks like *Figure 5.36* when our player collides with the mushroom.

Figure 5.36: The Output console when the player successfully collides with our mushroom

Yay! We're correctly detecting collisions with our player on our mushroom item. Next, we need the player to pick up the mushroom and not just run face-first into it.

Picking up our mushroom item is super easy, since we've already laid all the groundwork for it in our `CollectibleTrigger` script. Remember the `PickUp` function we programmed in there? Now, we have a place to call it. Inside this `if` statement we just wrote, we're going to write the following:

```
collectible.PickUp();
```

With this line, we are referencing an object that has the `CollectibleTrigger` type script on it; then, we're using that object, `collectible`, to call the `PickUp` function, which is inside the `CollectibleTrigger` script. Essentially, we only want the mushroom to disappear from our world if the player collides with the mushroom's collider. Once that happens, delete the mushroom from our world.

Now, save the script and test the scene out. When our player walks into a mushroom, the mushroom should disappear, and we should still have our `print` statement in the **Output** dock. This is great and all, but we're probably going to want more than one collectible on our level. How can we do that? We'll use the idea of composition as mentioned earlier to achieve it.

Creating multiple collectibles

Cool, so we have a mushroom item that our player can pick up, but we are probably going to want more than one to pick up throughout our level. Let's take a moment to make that happen.

In our **mushroom_red.tscn** scene, we have a **StaticBody3D** for collision, and it has a script we attached to it in a previous section to delete it from our scene tree when the player collides with it. Rather than manually replicating this node and attaching the script to any object we want to make an item, we can save this **StaticBody3D** as its own scene. By doing this, we're using composition and saving ourselves redundant work.

To do this, let's right-click on our **StaticBody3D** node from the **mushroom_red.tscn** node structure and select **Save Branch as Scene**. A prompt will appear to ask you what name to give this scene. I have named mine `PickupComponent`. This will create a new scene with **StaticBody3D** and **CollisionShape3D**.

A clapperboard icon appears next to **StaticBody3D** in our mushroom scene, as shown on the left-hand side of *Figure 5.37*. If we click the clapperboard icon, it will open the newly created scene, as shown on the right-hand side of *Figure 5.37*. We can delete the **CollisionShape3D** node here and have a single node of the **StaticBody3D** type with our `CollectibleTrigger` script attached.

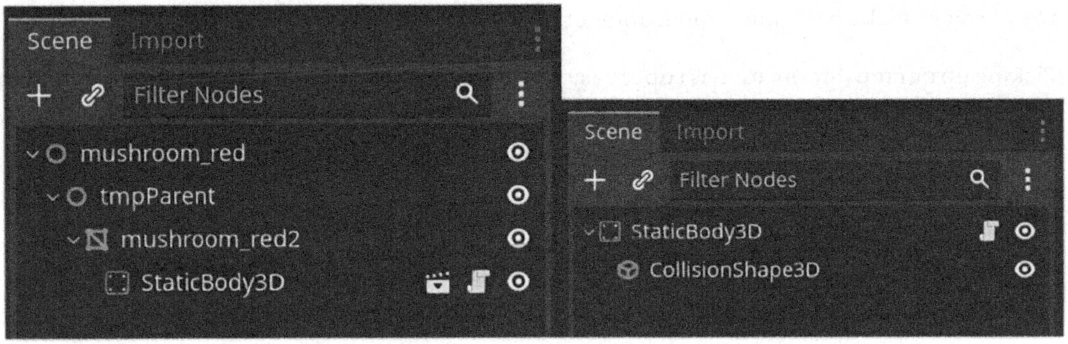

Figure 5.37: mushroom_red.tscn with a packed scene (left) and the packed scene expanded (right)

Now, save this scene and test the scene again to make sure we didn't break anything (we always want to check this anytime we make significant changes to our project).

With our functionality preserved, let's grab another mushroom model. I'm selecting the `mushroom_tanGroup.glb` one. We'll create a new scene and drag the model into our scene tree. Now we need to expand this model to access the mesh. To do that, click the clapperboard icon next to the node, and a popup as in *Figure 5.38* will appear. We want to click **New Inherited**, which will create a new scene with that model's nodes in it.

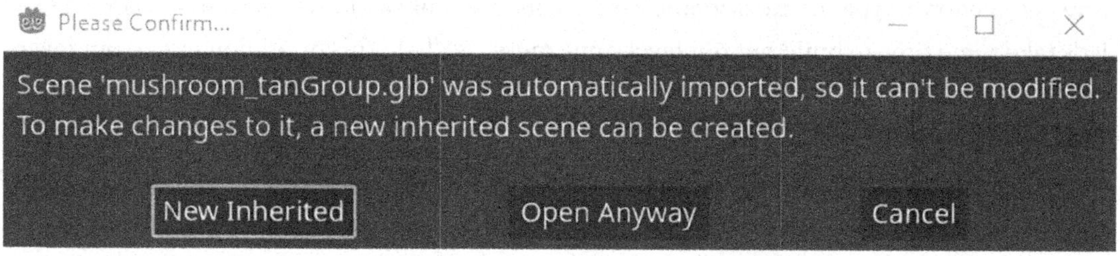

Figure 5.38: The popup for creating a new scene from imported models

Once we've clicked this button, a new scene with the mesh will be created – name it something you'll remember; I'm leaving it as **mushroom_tanGroup.tscn**.

Let's click the mesh and add some collisions just as we did for **mushroom_red.tscn**. This will require selecting the mesh, clicking the **Mesh** button above the Viewport, and selecting **Create Single Convex Collision Sibling**. Now, previously, we would have created a new node to add our **StaticBody3D** here, but we already have one created with the script we need. Instead, we'll drag our `PickupComponent.tscn` from **FileSystem** onto the Viewport. Once it's in the Viewport, it will be added to the scene; make sure to parent the nodes correctly as in *Figure 5.39*:

Figure 5.39: The complete node structure for our second mushroom item

Save the scene, and let's place it in our world with the other mushroom. I've placed them under a **Node3D** that I've renamed `Collectibles` to keep them together. Be sure to place this second mushroom in a scene that's within the walking path of the player and test it out. We should be able to successfully walk into both mushrooms and have them disappear. We should also now see two `print` statements in the **Output** dock that say **Collided with collectible** from our **print** statement in the script.

Now, we have two types of mushrooms we can collect in our world. With these systems in place, let's take some time to build out our level some more. We'll do this by adding rain to our level.

Adding rain to our level

Currently, we have a sun and the beginnings of a cozy area for our player to explore in. Let's add some more atmospheric effects by creating rain and adding some fog to the level to change the ambiance of the game. We'll be adding rain by creating a particle system. This is a common use case for particle systems, but don't let that suggest that that's all they're used for. Particles can be used for simulating fire, explosions, space debris, air bubbles, weather patterns, and more.

In our **World** scene, click on the plus sign above our **Scene** dock, as seen in *Figure 5.40*. This will add a node as a child of our root node, which is exactly what we want.

Figure 5.40: The plus sign to add child nodes of the root node in a scene

We are looking for 3D particles, specifically the **GPUParticles3D** node. You may have noticed, when searching for the **GPUParticles3D** node, that there were also **CPUParticles3D** nodes. While these are both viable options, the GPU version allows for more customization when it comes to creating particles and therefore is the preferred one in this instance.

Select the **GPUParticles3D** node type and a box will appear in the Viewport at the origin with gold lines. In the center of it, there will be a white cloud icon, as pictured in *Figure 5.41*. The gold lines indicate the bounds of where the particles will be generated.

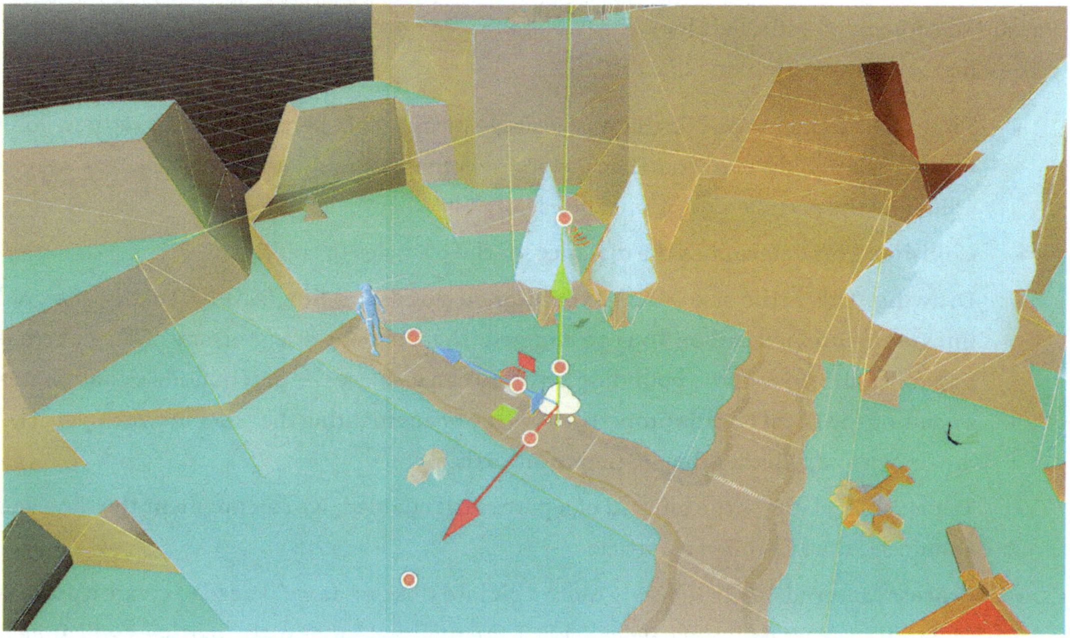

Figure 5.41: The GPUParticles3D node in our levels

When you select the **GPUParticles3D** node in the scene dock, you will see a lot of options for configuring them. The three properties that are active by default are as follows:

- **Emitting**: This is a checkbox that, when selected, ensures the particles are active and seen in the Viewport.
- **Amount**: This is the number of particles that will be generated in each frame. To start, let's set **Amount** to something much larger than **8**, such as `500`. You can increase it further, depending on the type of storm you're going for; maybe it's a light drizzle, and there aren't that many drops, or maybe it's a downpour, and there are thousands. It's up to you!
- **Sub Emitter**: This is when we want to utilize another particle or VFX effect to trigger as particles are being spawned. It allows us to have another particle or VFX nested into an existing one. This is very useful when it comes to VFX work.

Beyond the default options, let's look at a few of the other properties to make sure our particles come a little bit closer to looking like rain:

- **Time**: This property details the way a single particle will behave. We can set how long the particle should exist in the scene and whether it should emit only once, as well as adjusting the particle's positional behavior.
- **Collision**: This determines the distance for the particles to collide.
- **Drawing**: This is the size of the **Axis-Aligned Bounding Box** (**AABB**), that is, the gold lines we mentioned earlier. You can augment them here by dragging any of the dots that appear on the sides of the bounding box. You can also use the parent node's coordinates by setting the **Local Coords** property to be true or augmenting the order in which particles are drawn and whether they're tied to any axis.
- **Trails**: This relates to the tail end of a particle. If enabled, we can augment the time you should see the tail end of a particle.
- **Process Material**: We'll be diving quite a bit into this one as we'll need to create a process material to generate our particles. This is the material for how the particles will appear in the game, such as the shape, size, and color. Once a process material is created, we can augment the way it is generated in the AABB through gravity, color, direction, and more.
- **Draw Passes**: Here, we determine the mesh(es) to generate and can change their size and shape as well as the material. We'll also be spending more time in this section on making our particles appear more rain-like.

With all of these properties available to us, there's a lot of customization when it comes to creating particles. Whether we're making something that's for a campfire or rain or a cool special effect when a player casts a magic spell, the ideas are endless and up to the developer.

Now, as mentioned, we're going to spend most of our time on the **Process Material** and **Draw Passes** properties. So, let's go ahead and expand the **Draw Passes** section; we're diving into this property first so we can see how the particles behave as we update them.

In the expanded **Draw Passes** area, we can see **Pass 1**. Click on the drop-down arrow next to it and create a **New RibbonTrailMesh**. We should now see a square strip, running the length of our **GPUParticles3D** box. It will look something like *Figure 5.42*.

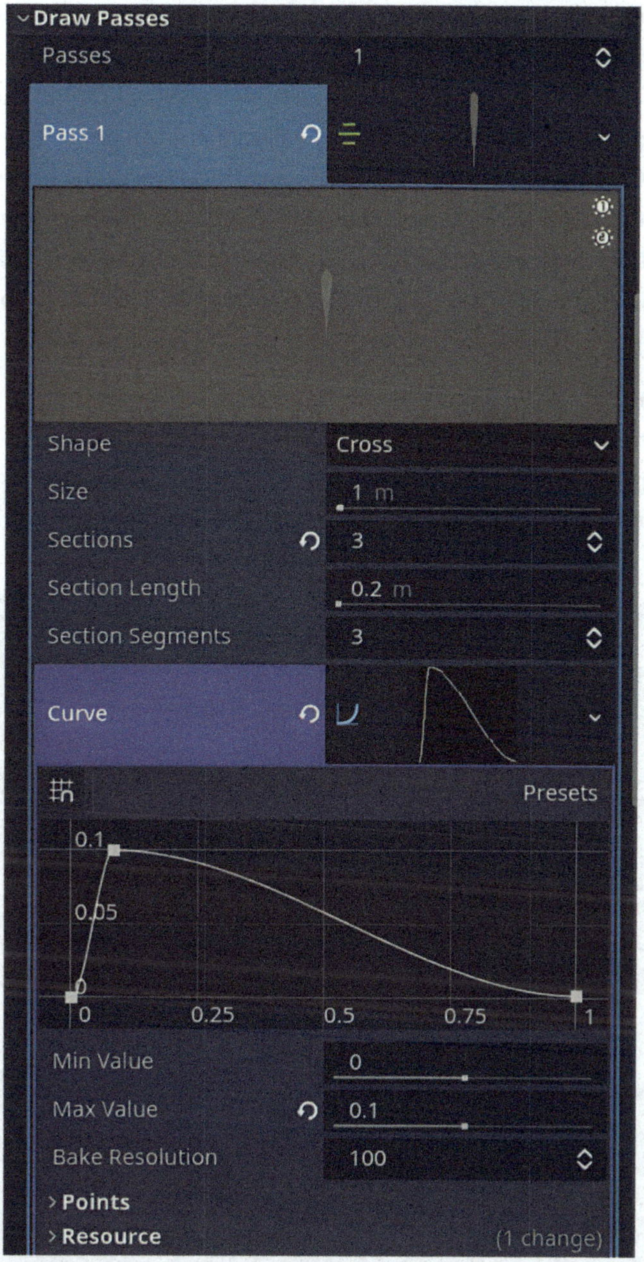

Figure 5.42: The Draw Passes options for particles

Let's reduce **Section Length** to `0.02` to shorten the ribbon mesh and make it look more like falling raindrops. We can also reduce the number of sections on the mesh – by default, it's set to **5**, but I have set mine to 3.

The last setting we'll change here is creating a curve to shape our ribbon mesh into more of a raindrop. Currently, we still have blocky squares for particles, so we will create a curve to better shape it. To create the curve, or shape, for our mesh, we need to click into the empty box next to the **Curve** property and create a new curve. As we augment the properties in the Draw Passes property in the next paragraph, Godot will auto create the graph of the curve for us. A graph will appear below the **Curve** property, as seen in *Figure 5.42*. If we set **Max Value**, it will be easier to create our points along the curve, so set this to `0.1`. As you can see in *Figure 5.42*, I have three points along my curve. I start at **0** and then go up to **0.1**; then, I end up back at **0**. You can add points by clicking on the graph, starting from the first point at 0, and following along the curve you create.

With our particle more clearly defined as a raindrop, we can go ahead and create the material that will generate the particles and determine their collective behavior. To do so, now expand the **Process Material** property in the **Inspector** dock. The only option is to click the empty box and create a new material for the particles. So, select **New ParticleProcessMaterial**. Then, when you click on the newly created material, you'll get options that look like *Figure 5.43*.

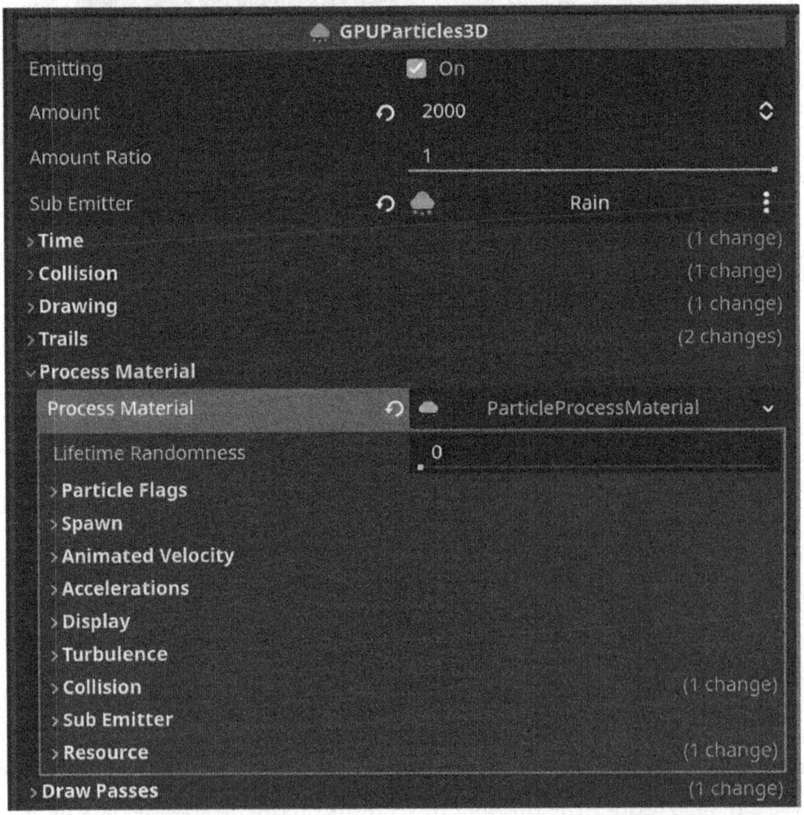

Figure 5.43: The options available for a process material

Expand the **Spawn** property and select **Box** next to the **Emission Shape** property. Currently, the **Box** property is set to **Point** by default, but this means all our particles would spawn in the same spot in our AABB, which we don't want to happen. We want them to spawn throughout the box space, so make sure **Box** is selected in the dropdown, as shown in *Figure 5.44*.

Below the **Emission Shape** property is another property called **Emission Box Extents**, as shown in *Figure 5.40*. Here, we want the particles to cover the entire level and sit slightly above the level. I've set mine to be **X: 50, Y: 10**, and **Z: 50**. Depending on how you built your level, your box extents may be set to different points (if you're covering your sky, it will be fine).

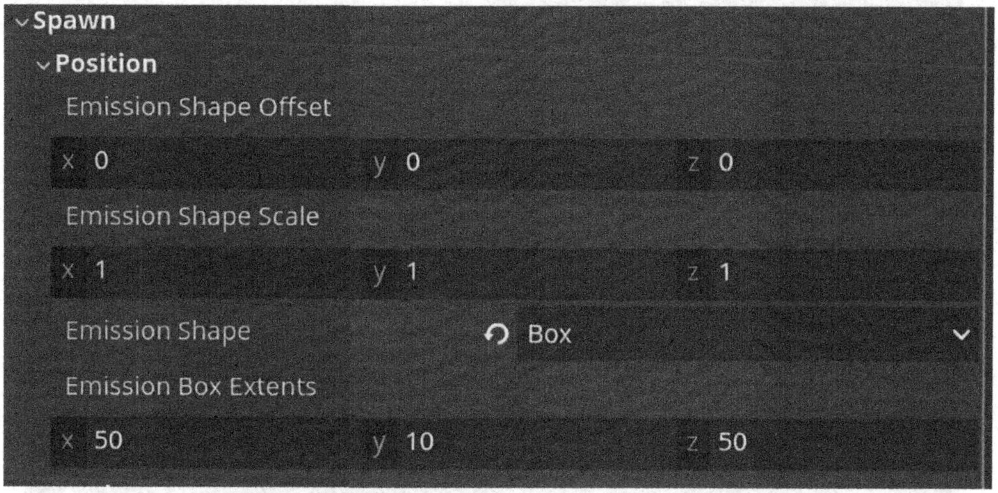

Figure 5.44: Setting the position and shape of our particles

You may have noticed that the direction our raindrops are flying in the box extents is not right. By default, they are zipping across our level sideways. Under the **Direction** property, we want to set **Y** to `-1`, so our raindrops appear to be falling. We can also set **X** to `1`, which makes our rain come across tilted as if a strong wind were pushing it that way. With **X** and **Y** configured, we may want to strengthen one of these axes. I changed **Y** to `-3` to make the slant in the particle slightly less dramatic. There's no need to set **Z** to anything here, but you can if you want to make your rain look like it's been pushed back by the wind.

So far, we've set **Emission Shape** and **Direction**. Now, we'll look at setting various velocities. Before doing that, do note that the **Gravity** property, by default, is set to `-9.8` on the **Y** axis. Now, expand the **Initial Velocity** property and you'll see options for **Velocity Min** and **Velocity Max** inside it. The higher the velocity set for the particles, the more of a torrential downpour it will appear to be in your game. I've set my **Velocity Min** to `100`, and my **Velocity Max** to `150`, but feel free to tweak these numbers to your liking.

There are two more properties left for us to modify, and those are **Color** and **Collision**. Both will be quick adjustments, and then our rain will be complete! Inside the **Process Material** properties, let's expand **Display**. There is a property there called **Color**. Click the color box and set its hex code to **#D5E6F2**, as shown in *Figure 5.45*.

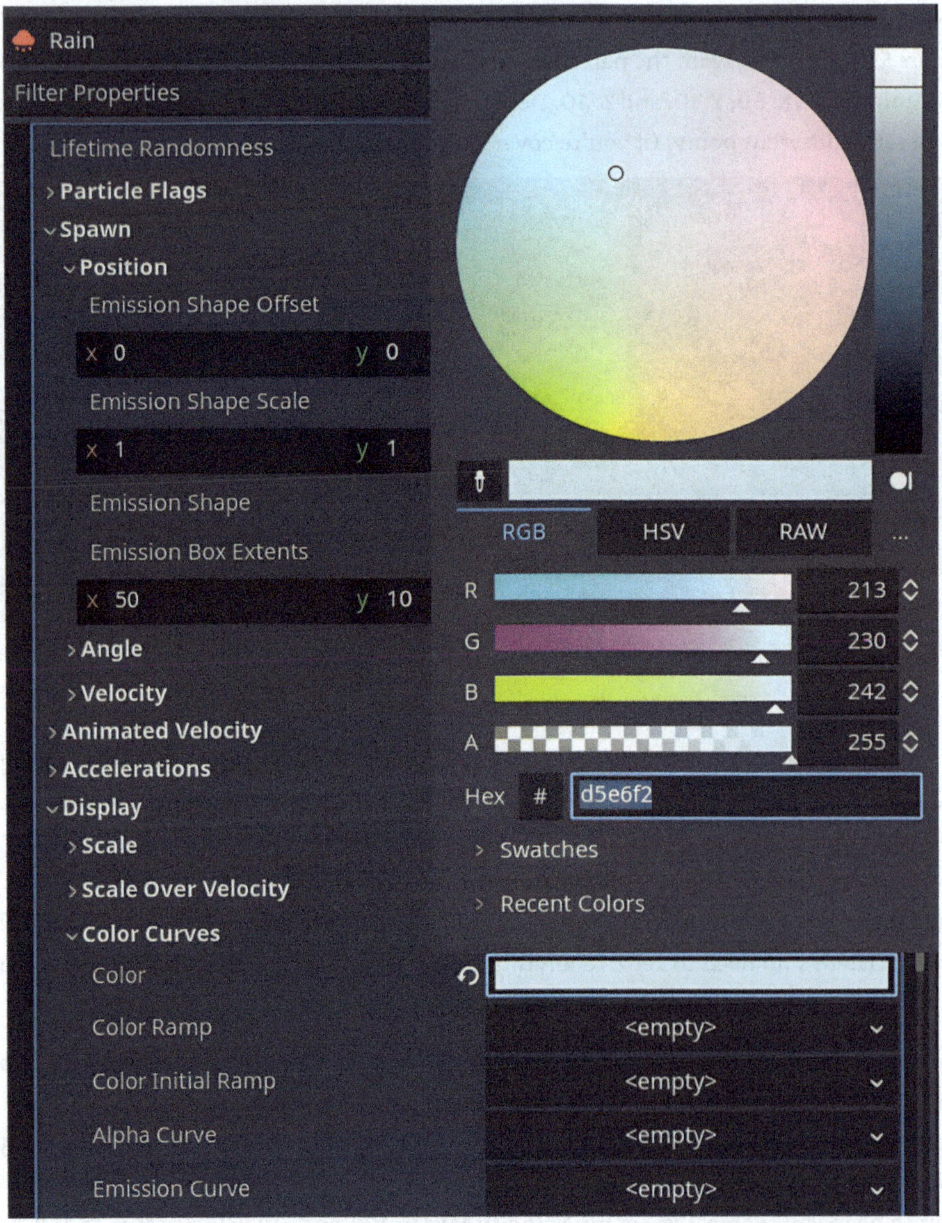

Figure 5.45: The Display properties for our process material

Once that's set, we can collapse the **Display** options. The last process material property we'll look at is **Collision**. Expand it and look for the property named **Mode**. We'll set it to **Hide on Contact**. This means when the particles collide with an object in our **World** scene, they'll disappear. You can see how this looks in *Figure 5.46*.

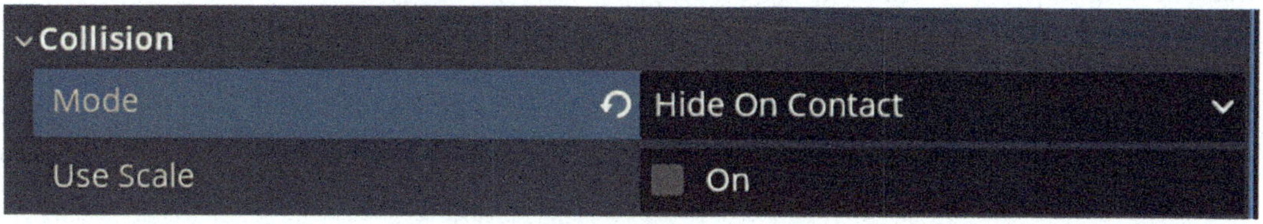

Figure 5.46: Collison properties for rain particles

Once both the **Color** and **Collision** properties have been set, we can look back at how the rain is behaving in our **World** scene.

Figure 5.47: The rain effect completed and existing in our world alongside fog

Our **World** scene is feeling more and more alive with all the dynamic elements we're adding. We spent some time building a level and adding items and effects for our player to interact with, which will give them more immersion as they explore the space we've created.

Summary

This chapter covered a wide variety of topics that all related to how the player interacts with our world. We started by importing our assets and discussed two methods of adding collisions. We started designing our level and spent time with shaders, leveraging their use to simulate wind blowing through our world.

After such a long chapter on the 3D aspects and lighting, we will turn our attention to the UI. We'll look at using Godot's UI theme editor to create a cohesive style that's easy to implement. After that, we'll create a main menu, add animations to our menu, and look at how to create a settings page with volume sliders for music and SFX.

Further reading

- *The Book of Shaders*: `https://thebookofshaders.com/`
- *Godot Shaders*: `https://godotshaders.com/`

6

Developing and Managing the User Interface

Our world is coming to life, and our player can explore and react to that world. Now, we need to provide feedback to the player about what they can interact with, collect, and use. The most common way this is conveyed is through **user interfaces (UIs)**. This is everything from the main menu to start the game, all the way to menu screens for selling items at a shop. Anything that's interfaced in a 2D capacity is part of the UI.

In this chapter, we'll be creating our main menu where you'll start the game. To create the main menu, we'll utilize a variety of **control nodes** such as panels and buttons. We'll also add functionality to the **Play**, **Settings**, and **Quit** options, and when the player selects the **Play** button, we'll create a short animation. After this, we will create a **Settings** menu that includes two volume sliders and a **Close** button.

Our goals for this chapter will be the following:

- Introducing control nodes
- Creating a UI theme
- Adding a main menu
- Designing a **Settings** screen
- Adding a **Close** button

Technical requirements

For this chapter, the technical requirements will be the same as in *Chapter 1*.

All the code from this chapter will be available in the GitHub repository:

`https://github.com/PacktPublishing/Game-Development-with-Godot-and-C-.`

Introducing control nodes

When we first opened Godot and were asked what type of scene we wanted, we were presented with three options – **2D Scene**, **3D Scene**, and **User Interface** – as shown in *Figure 6.1*:

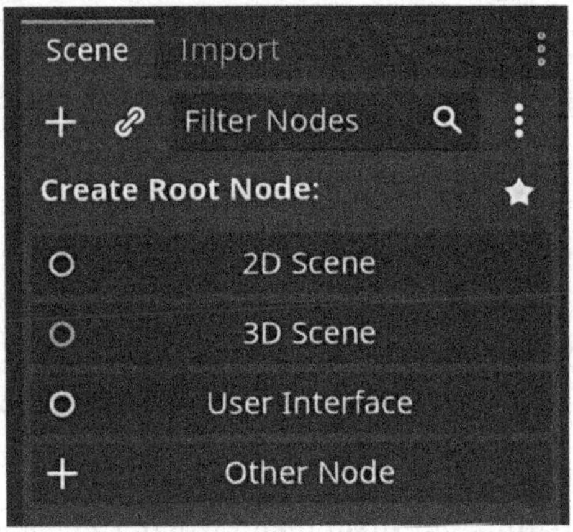

Figure 6.1: The Scene dock options when creating a new scene

So far, we've dealt with the **2D Scene** and **3D Scene** options. Now, we're going to explore the **User Interface** nodes. Below that, there is another option called **Other Node**, which allows you to select a more specific node that belongs to one of the three existing node types. Instead, we're going to explore the realm of creating a seamless UI.

So, let's create a new scene by clicking the **+** sign above the Viewport, as we did in previous chapters. Then, from the **Scene** dock, click the **User Interface** option for our scene type. The root node of this UI scene will be a control node. The Viewport will change to a 2D view and will look like *Figure 6.2*:

Figure 6.2: The Viewport after creating a UI scene

Notice the origin sits in the top-left corner of the screen. This will become an important detail to note when anchoring our UI elements as we design additional UI elements that cover the screen (such as the main menu and pause screen).

With this 2D view set, let's add some more control nodes to get familiar with how they function. **Control nodes** are 2D nodes that are used to create rich and responsive UIs. Everything from buttons and sliders to containers is included in control nodes. Let's walk through creating our first control node:

1. Right-click the existing control node, or click the + sign above the dock, and add a child node.

   All the UI nodes are control nodes and so have a green color (matching the **User Interface** icon color back in *Figure 6.1*). We can see a list of them if we expand the **Control** nodes out, as seen in *Figure 6.3*.

2. Select **Label** from this list and add it as a child node. Labels are control nodes that focus on providing text to our UI:

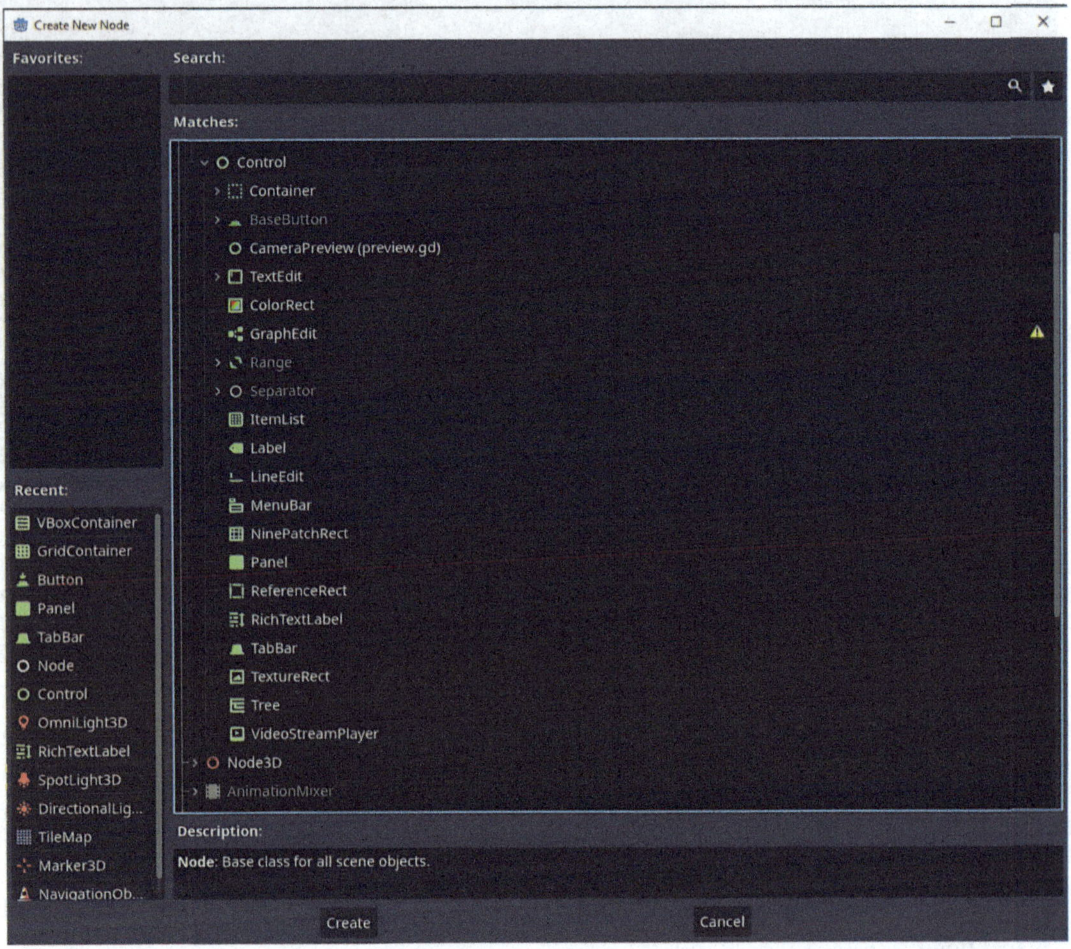

Figure 6.3: The selection of control nodes available

Once we've added it, the Viewport will create an empty box with green points on each corner, as seen in *Figure 6.4*:

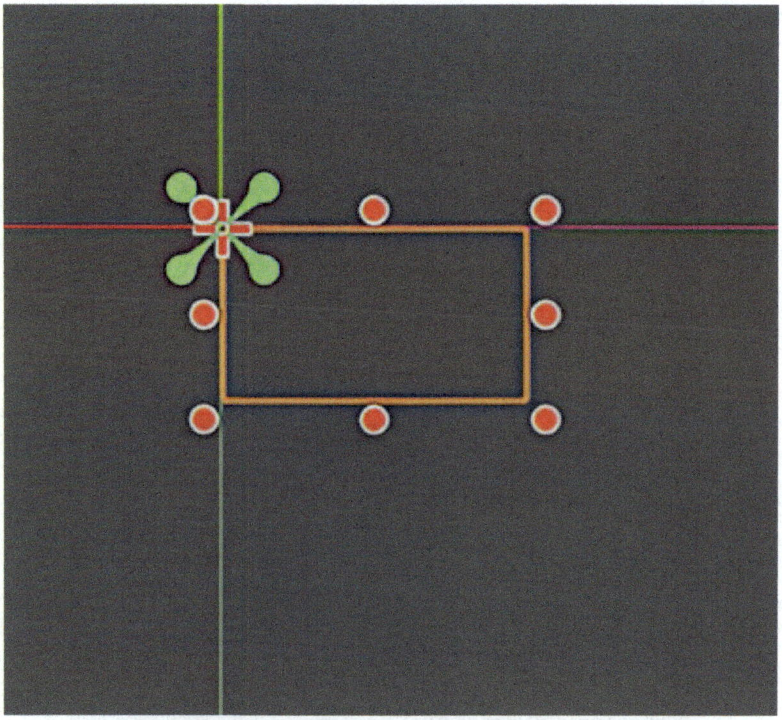

Figure 6.4: The Viewport with a label created and the anchor points sitting at the origin

The green points are the anchors for our label. **Anchors** are used to preset the way UIs will appear regardless of the platform or device they're on. They're an essential part of a UI, especially when you're launching a game on multiple platforms. The **Label** node has four anchor points, which again are represented by the four green pins that, by default, appear at the origin. Wherever we position the label, we'll want to set the anchors accordingly. Typically, the pins will be around the node, but they can be placed anywhere. Just remember – the UI will scale according to its anchors. We'll discuss this more later as we further develop our UI.

The eight dots around the edge are the **bounds** of the **Label** node. We can resize the label to be bigger or smaller by dragging any of the eight dots, and we can also move the label by clicking and dragging inside the bounds.

Currently, the label is blank because we haven't put any text in it. Select the **Label** node in the **Scene** dock, and in the **Inspector**, we can explore the **Label** properties. The first property listed is the **Text** property. By default, it is empty. Go ahead and type the word `Test` in it, as seen in *Figure 6.5*:

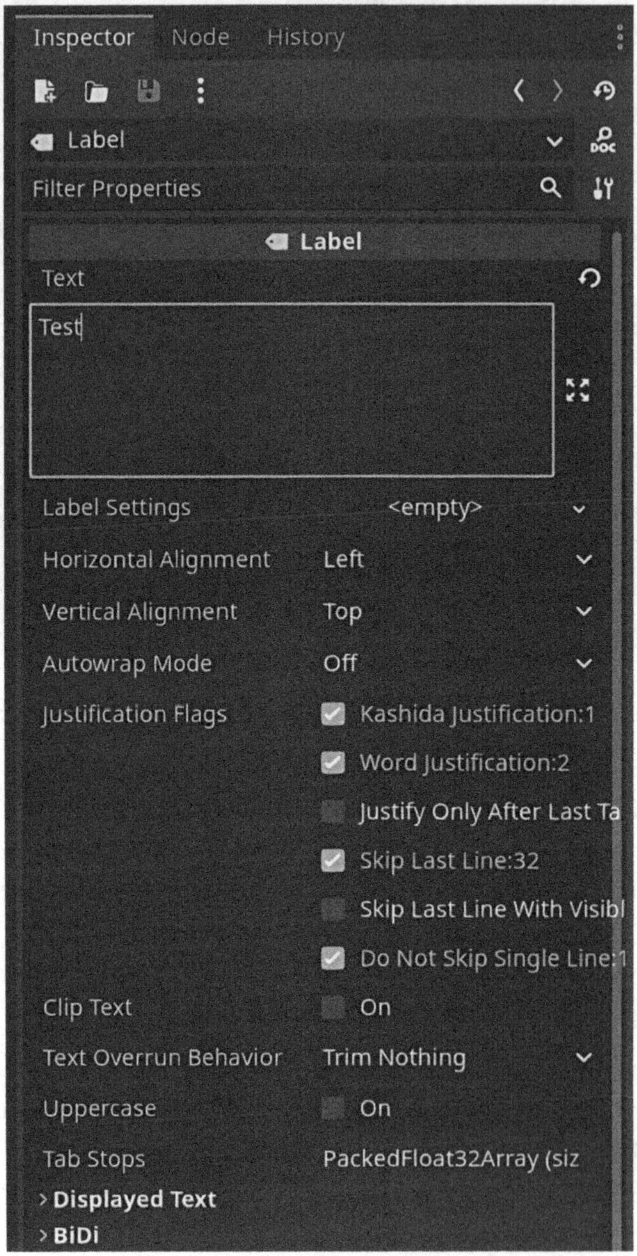

Figure 6.5: The default label properties with the word "Test" written

Below the **Text** property, there is a **Label Settings** property. Click the down arrow next to the empty box and select **New LabelSettings**. This will give us options we need to augment how the text is displayed, as in *Figure 6.6*:

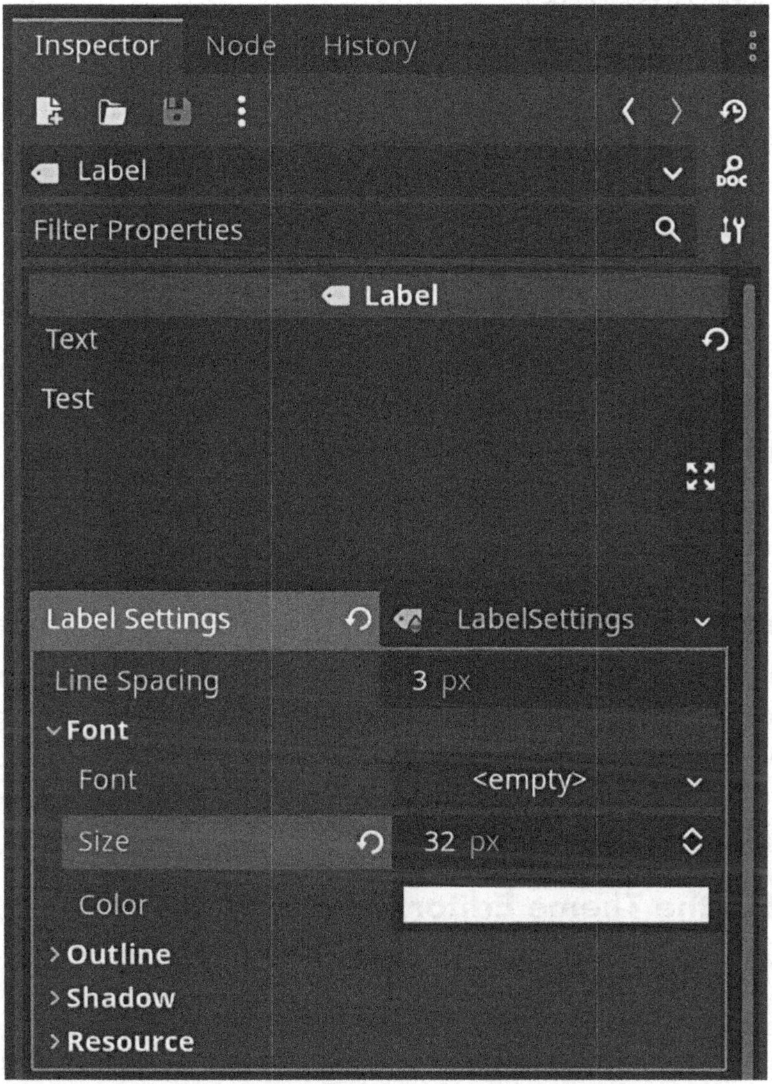

Figure 6.6: The Label properties with label settings added

If we expand the **Font** option after creating our label settings, we can set the font's size. The default size is set to 16, but that is quite small and may be hard to read, so we will change it to 32 pixels instead. In the Viewport, you should see the word **Test** automatically update in real time, with the result shown in *Figure 6.7*:

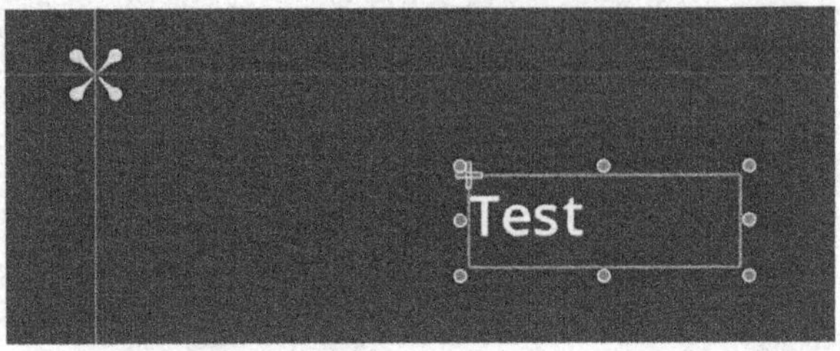

Figure 6.7: Adding text to our label, with a size of 32 pixels

While we only covered the details of one control node, the important thing to remember is how to anchor them. We'll cover other types of control nodes throughout the chapter, and while the properties of them may change, the general overall structure will not.

Now that we have a better understanding of how control nodes operate, let's apply what we know to create a theme for all our control nodes.

Creating a UI theme

With an understanding of what control nodes are, we can start looking at creating a theme for some of the menus we'll be designing. A **UI theme** is the idea that we can design and create the way a specific control node behaves and then all other control nodes of that same type will also behave the same way. It's easier to understand through an example, so let's create a new theme and jump right in.

Navigating the Theme Editor

From our practice scene, we can do the following:

1. Select the root **Control** node from the **Scene** dock.
2. Then, look at the **Inspector** dock of the selected node. Here, we have a list of properties that we can augment.
3. Expand the **Theme** property out, and you'll notice it's currently empty. As we've done with previous properties, click the drop-down arrow next to the empty box and select **New Theme**.

By clicking **New Theme**, we are creating a **Theme** resource. This will look like *Figure 6.8*:

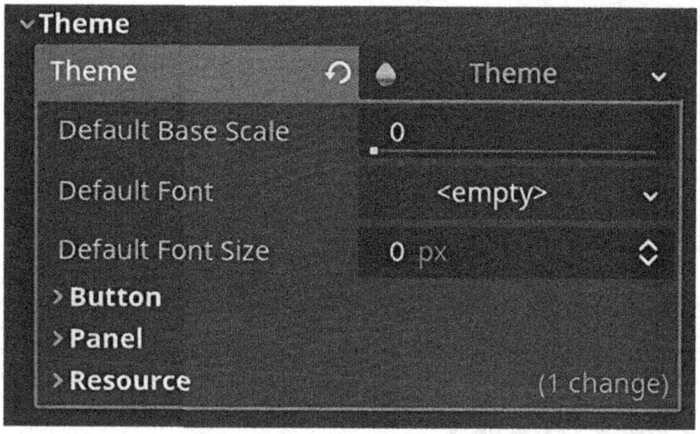

Figure 6.8: Creating a new theme on a control node

Once created, a new panel called the **Theme Editor** will appear on the **Output** dock, as in *Figure 6.9*. You may also notice we have some additional properties available now that we've created a theme in the **Inspector** (we will explore more of these shortly):

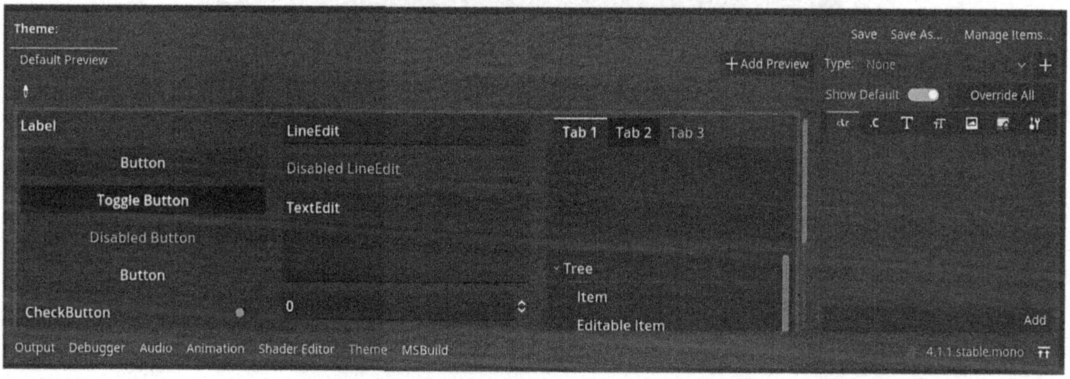

Figure 6.9: The Theme Editor on the Output dock

As you can see in *Figure 6.9*, the bulk of the options are under the **Default Preview** tab. The huge benefit to this is that once we style a control node, we can see how it will look in **Preview** mode under this tab. All you need to do is hover or click, depending on the state of the control node, on the control node you want to preview in the **Default Preview** tab. For example, if we want to see how a **Button** control node will react, we can click or hover over **Button** in this **Default Preview** tab to see how it behaves depending on those states. This makes it super easy to style the UI without needing to create and place it in your scene.

On the right-hand side of the Theme Editor, you can see a variety of buttons, tabs, and toggles. We can customize each of these UI types here, and when we do, every time we call a node of that type (when the **Theme** resource is applied to the scene), it will be styled in the same way we styled it in this theme. Do note that the UI type selected on the right-hand side will determine what properties are generated to customize and change on the right-hand side of the Theme Editor.

Note

If the Theme Editor disappears for any reason, navigate back to the node where you created the **Theme** resource and click on it. The Theme Editor should reappear then.

Creating our first UI type

To better understand how to navigate the Theme Editor, let's create and style a **Play** button. To start augmenting the button object, click the + sign in the top-right corner of the Theme Editor as seen in *Figure 6.10*, right next to the **Type** drop-down menu:

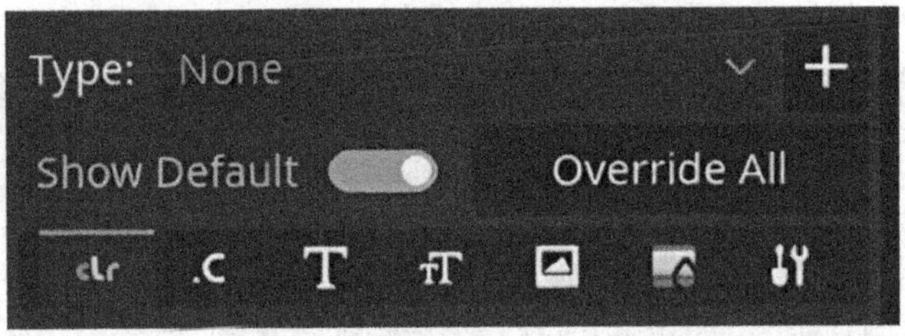

Figure 6.10: The Type selection within the Theme Editor

Once you click the + sign, a new window will appear, as in *Figure 6.11*:

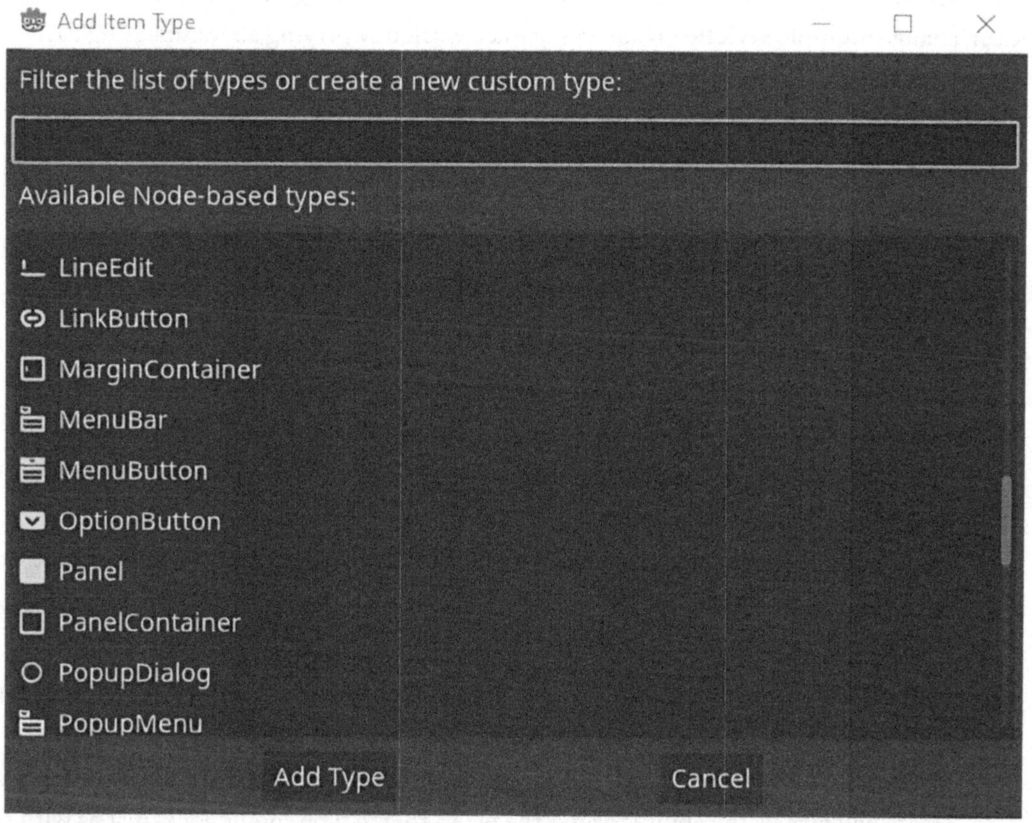

Figure 6.11: The Add Item Type window in the Theme Editor

Next, search for the word `button` and select **Add Type**. Now, the **Button** type should be the selected UI object in the **Type** dropdown of the Theme Editor.

Back in *Figure 6.10*, below the **Type** dropdown, there are two options:

- The first is **Show Default** – with it toggled on, you'll see all the various states the type can be changed to. Make sure **Show Default** is toggled on.
- The second is the **Override All** button – this is to override the style of a UI type that's not the base version of the control node type. We will leave it as is for now.

After these two options, we have the property tabs as seen in *Figure 6.12*. These are the tabs to style each theme type we've added to the Theme Editor. This is a great panel to access because we can change multiple **StyleBox** resources at once without worrying about updating each one:

Figure 6.12: The property tabs for theme types

These small symbols pack a lot of information, so let's break down what's inside each one:

- **Color**: This allows you to change both the font and icon color of a theme type, specifically in various states such as **hover**, **click**, or **disabled**, to name a few.
- **Constants**: These are specific parameters that should apply to all theme types, such as the outline size or the height separation. These values will vary based on the theme type selected.
- **Font**: This is simply the place to upload font files to use when creating text for a theme type.
- **Font Size**: This property allows you to adjust the font size for all versions of a specific theme type.
- **Icons**: Here, we can add multiple icons and create textures to overlay with a theme type. Adding iconography is a very useful way to communicate what an item or menu does.
- **StyleBoxes**: This is the tab we'll primarily be working on. Each **StyleBox** resource we create will give us the ability to alter the way a theme type should look. Just as with the **Color** property, we can augment the way a theme type appears depending on the state it's in (**pressed**, **hover**, **focus**, and so on).
- **Custom Settings**: This is for creating theme-type variations. For example, say we created and styled some buttons – though they have the same shape and design, they may differ in color, fonts, and type. We could create a type of variation that builds on top of the original **Button** theme type we created, then we can alter it as needed.

While we won't use all the property tabs listed in the Theme Editor, it's good to know how to navigate this space, especially since there's a lot of customization available.

With the **Button** object set to the selected type, select the **StyleBoxes** property tab. Here, we can see more options, as shown in *Figure 6.13*:

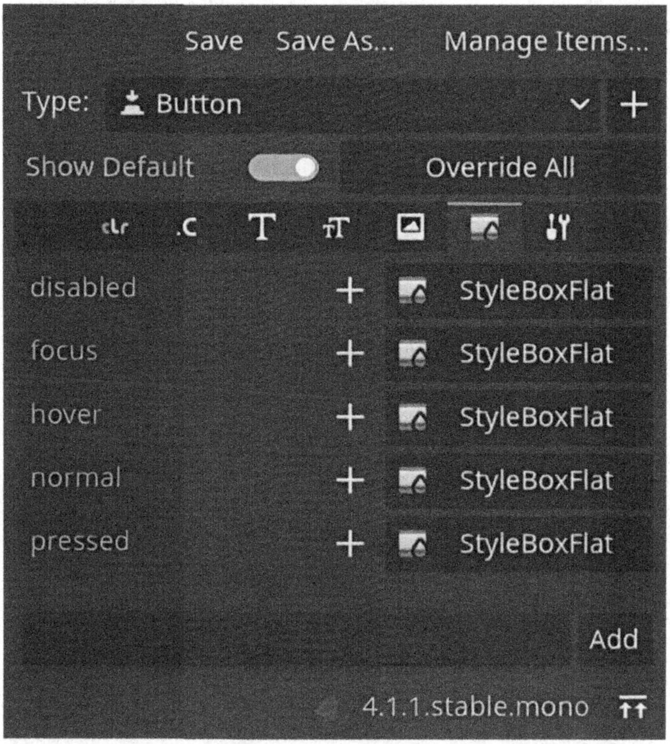

Figure 6.13: The styling options for the selected UI object in the Theme Editor

On the left-hand side of *Figure 6.13*, we can see a list of the different states a button can be in. Across from that, each button state has a **StyleBoxFlat** component with a + sign next to it. This means we can style the button to look different, depending on the current state the button is in. Let's go ahead and change the style of the button for its **normal** (aka default) state.

Click the + sign for the **normal** state, and it will add an empty box, as in *Figure 6.14*:

Figure 6.14: Creating a new button state

When you click the dropdown, a variety of options will appear:

- **StyleBoxEmpty**: An empty **StyleBox** resource that does not display anything.
- **StyleBoxTexture**: Adds a texture to the **StyleBox** resource and alters how a UI object looks.
- **StyleBoxFlat**: Customizes the way the UI looks by manipulating various properties (for example, **Color**, **Font**, and so on) and does not require a texture.

- **StyleBoxLine**: Displays a single line often used to add textured or colored separators to demarcate the UI. They can also be used in sliders and for framing different pieces of the UI.

For our purposes, we're going to select **StyleBoxFlat** since we have no textures to include in the UI. However, we can still achieve a very customized look, leveraging the properties provided by Godot.

Once the **StyleBoxFlat** option is selected, it will replace the empty drop-down box. Then click the **StyleBoxFlat** resource, and the Theme Editor will disappear, providing a new window in the **Inspector** dock, as in *Figure 6.15*:

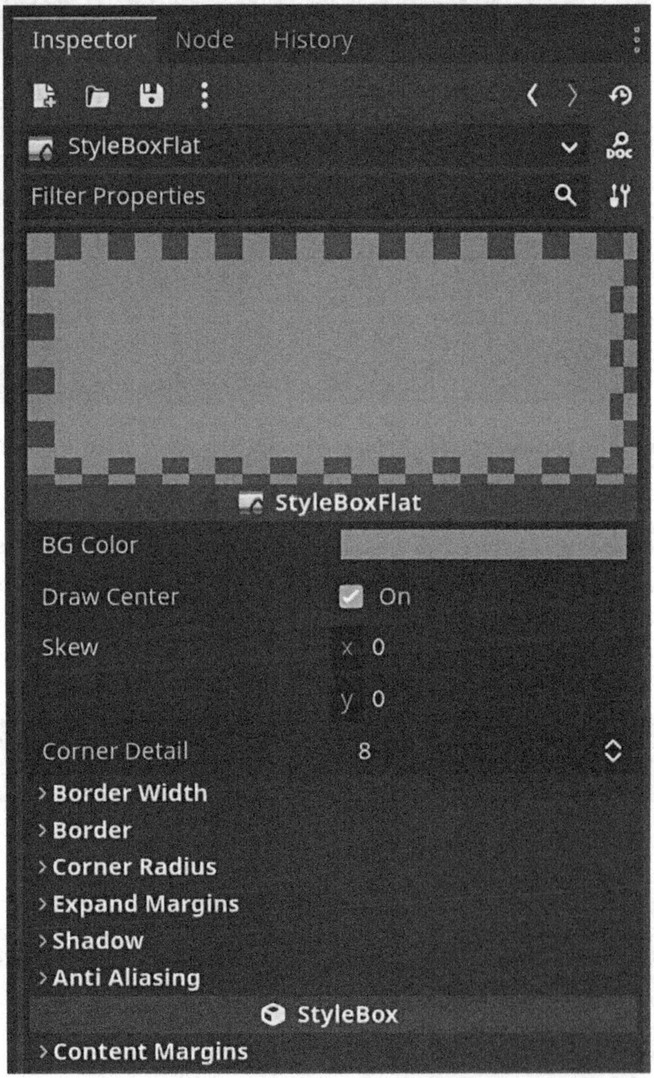

Figure 6.15: The StyleBoxFlat properties in the Inspector

The grayed-out image in *Figure 6.15* is the current preview of the style for the button state. As we change the nested properties, the box will update in real time, so we can see if the style changes are what we want to use for our game. Let's go through each property and make the following changes:

- **Border Width**: Here, we'll set all the edges (**Left**, **Top**, **Right**, and **Bottom**) to 3 pixels. You'll see the edge of the button padded by a gray and white color in the **Inspector** dock right above the **BG Color** property, as seen in *Figure 6.15*.
- **Border**: There are only two options here:
    - **Color**: Currently, this is set to gray and white, which we're seeing now. Select the colored bar and set it to something that contrasts with the current button's color. I've chosen a dark blue that you can create using the `#163660` hex code.
    - **Blend**: This is a toggle for blending the border color into the button color. It's up to you whether to leave this enabled or not, depending on the colors you've chosen. I've checked it for our project.
- **Corner Radius**: This property rounds the corners of our button. We can round only the top left and right corners of the button to give it a softer look. We can also round either corner or all of them. I am going to round them all by setting each corner to **5** pixels.
- **Expand Margins**: This pads the margins of the button out. We can make the button much bigger than the text, if needed, or design it to hold a sprite instead. I'm only padding the left and right margins to 3 pixels.
- **Shadow**: This setting provides the ability to create shadows around the UI object and is broken into three options:
    - **Color**: This sets the color of the shadow around the button. You can play around and see if there's a color you like, but I will be leaving this in its default state.
    - **Size**: The size of the shadow, which I've set to 2 pixels.
    - **Offset**: The offset is where the shadow sits around the button. Say you want the button to look like it has some depth; you could set the shadow to be offset on the *X*-axis and the *Y*-axis. I've set both to be 2 pixels on mine.

With these properties set, our button is styled within our **Theme** resource for the **normal** state. The other button states' changes are not. You can see the way it's styled in *Figure 6.16*:

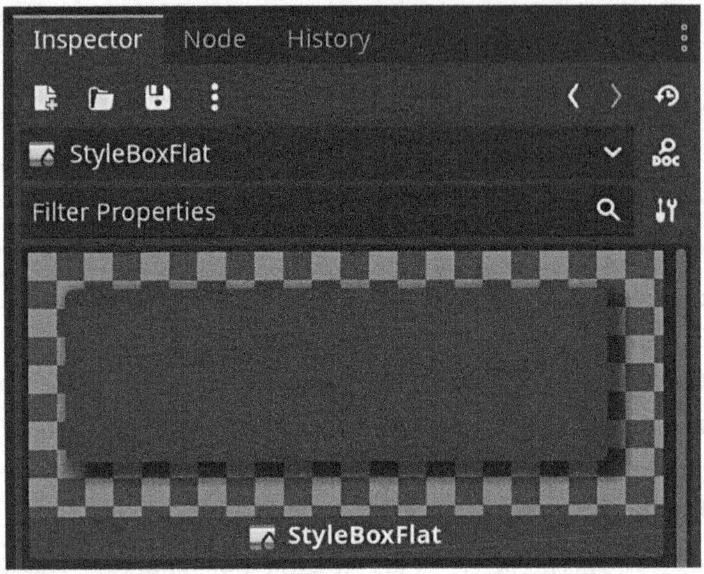

Figure 6.16: StyleBoxFlat after adjusting our settings

Now, let's get back to the Theme Editor. Notice, we're not on our Theme Editor when we're inside the **StyleBoxes** tab. In fact, we're manipulating the properties of **StyleBox** resources within the **Inspector** dock. Now, instead of clicking the root control node of the scene and finding the **Theme** resource attached to it, we can simply click the small back arrow near the top-right of the **Inspector** dock, as seen in *Figure 6.17*:

Figure 6.17: The back arrow at the top of the Inspector dock

Now, if we look back at our Theme Editor, you'll notice that the **Button** UI type isn't the only item that looks different. You can scroll down or expand the Theme Editor by dragging the top edge into the Viewport, as I've done in *Figure 6.18*:

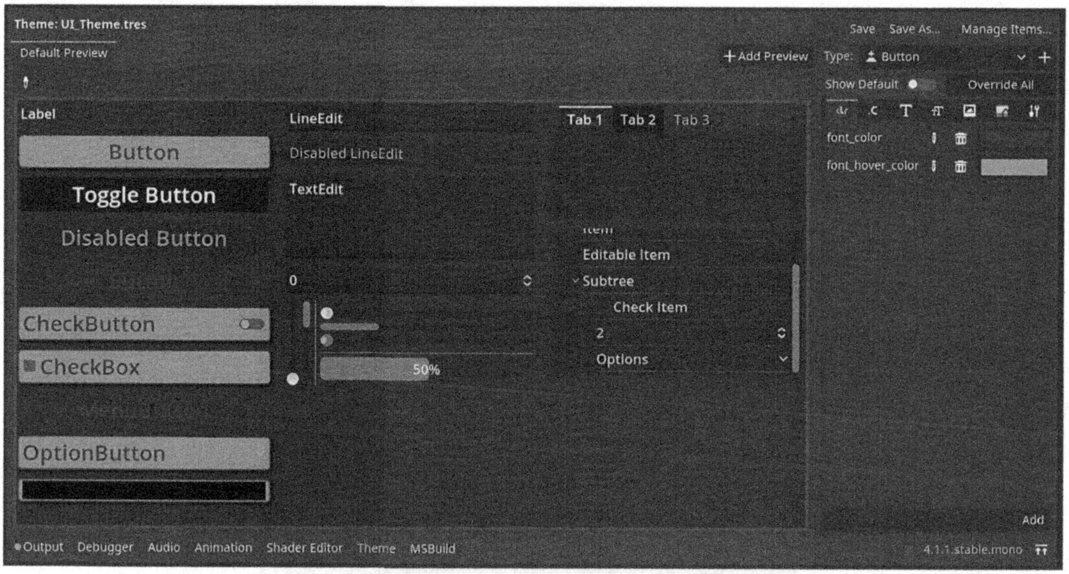

Figure 6.18: The Theme Editor after the Button UI type has been styled

Here, you'll see that every other **Button** type is styled to our **Button** type. This is because UI types such as **CheckButton** and **CheckBox** all derive from **Button**. This is where we can start to leverage the Theme Editor. Rather than recreating what we did with the **normal** state of our **Button** type, we can reuse that base for other types of buttons, such as checkboxes and check button toggles. While we won't do it here, it's good to keep it in mind as we style various control nodes since they can impact each other indirectly.

With our **Button** theme created, let's add some **Button** nodes to the scene and test them out. To do so, click the + sign under the **Scene** dock, as shown in *Figure 6.19*:

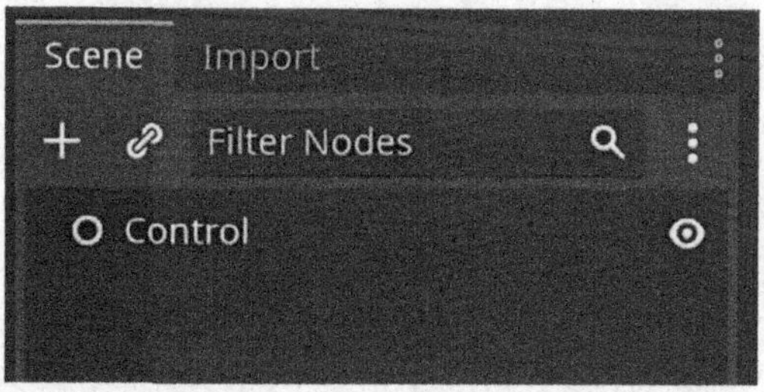

Figure 6.19: The + sign for adding nodes to a scene in the Scene dock

The button will appear in the origin of our Viewport. It will look like a tiny blur, as seen in *Figure 6.20*, since we have no text inside it, though the blue and black blur means our theme has been applied:

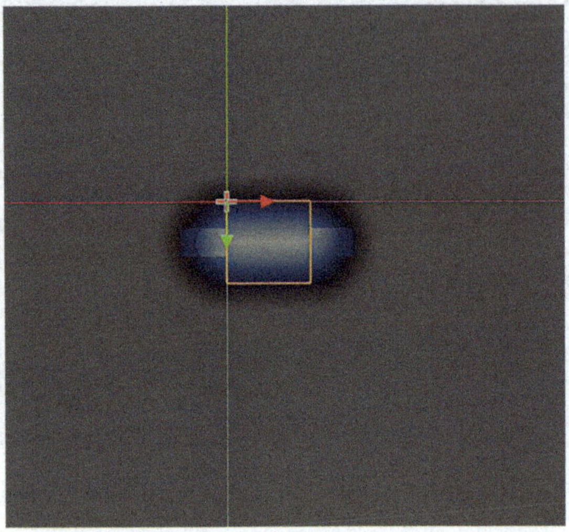

Figure 6.20: A newly created button with our theme

Now, select the **Button** node from the Viewport, look for the **Text** property in the **Inspector** dock, and type the word `Play`. Once the text is added, the button begins expanding. You can see how it has the exact configurations that we created in the Theme Editor. *Figure 6.21* shows the result:

Figure 6.21: Adding text to create our Play button

Repeat this process to create two more buttons – **Quit** and **Settings**. Be sure to move them out of the way of each other, using the Viewport tools we covered in *Chapter 4*.

Sweet – we've now created a theme for a button and easily created the beginnings of a main menu. I've stacked all my buttons vertically, as in *Figure 6.22*:

Figure 6.22: The main menu buttons themed by the Theme Editor

At this point, it's worth noting the light blue lines that can be seen in *Figure 6.22*. These are the screen edges of your game. If we create any UIs outside of these blue lines, then we will not see them when we run our game.

Let's now move on to how to utilize the **Theme** resource we created.

Reusing our saved theme

Now that we've become a little bit more familiar with the Theme Editor, we can go ahead and work on creating a **Theme** resource to reuse throughout our game:

1. We can save the scene as `ThemeTesting.tscn`. We can then reuse the `ThemeTesting.tscn` scene for previewing how UI components will interact, as well as configuring them in our editor in an isolated space that won't interfere with other scenes.

2. Before closing the scene, be sure to select the topmost root node that has our **Theme** resource in the **Theme** property.
3. Then, in the **Inspector** dock, you'll see a list of properties. One of them will be a **Theme** property, as shown in *Figure 6.23*.
4. Click the small drop-down arrow next to the **Theme** resource, select **Save As...**, and name it `UI_Theme.tres`. This allows us to load this theme into other scenes:

Figure 6.23: The Theme property on our control node

Save this in a location that makes sense. I've created a new folder called `user_interface` where I've placed our testing scene as well as the **Theme** resource. You can see the project structure breakdown for what we have up to this point in *Figure 6.24*:

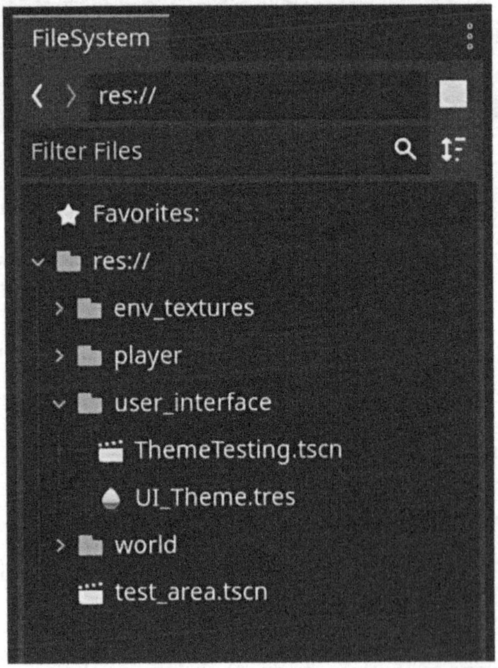

Figure 6.24: The organization of the project and adding a place for the UI

Now, the **Theme** property should look like *Figure 6.25*:

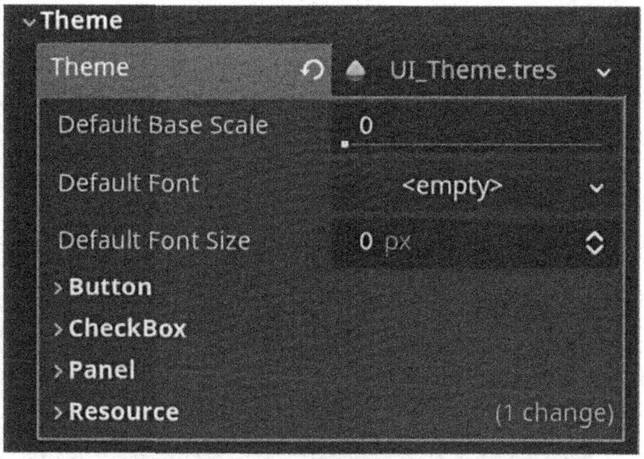

Figure 6.25: The Theme property after saving our Theme resource

Notice the additional properties within this **Theme** property, such as **Button**, **CheckBox**, and **Panel**. The **CheckBox** and **Panel** properties are not covered in this chapter but are added here to show that once configured in the Theme Editor, they are added as an item type to create in the **Inspector** dock. From here, we can adjust the property values of specific theme item types added to our **Theme** resource. This can sometimes be more convenient than digging into the Theme Editor and navigating to the property tabs we covered earlier.

We now have a saved **Theme** resource in our project. This means we are able to customize the look of any control node we want in our project and reuse it throughout.

With that, let's close this scene and move on to creating our main menu scene.

Adding a main menu

Understanding the Theme Editor and creating a **Theme** resource makes us fully equipped to start creating our main menu scene. This scene will be the first piece of the UI the player sees. Get started by creating a new scene and selecting a **User Interface** node for the root of the scene, as done in the previous section. Then, follow the next steps:

1. With a new UI scene and a root control node, rename the node to something more memorable, such as **MainMenu**. It's always important to name nodes what they are so that it's easy to debug and navigate a scene.

2. Next, find the **Theme** property in the **Inspector**, select the drop-down arrow as shown in *Figure 6.26*, and then select **Load**:

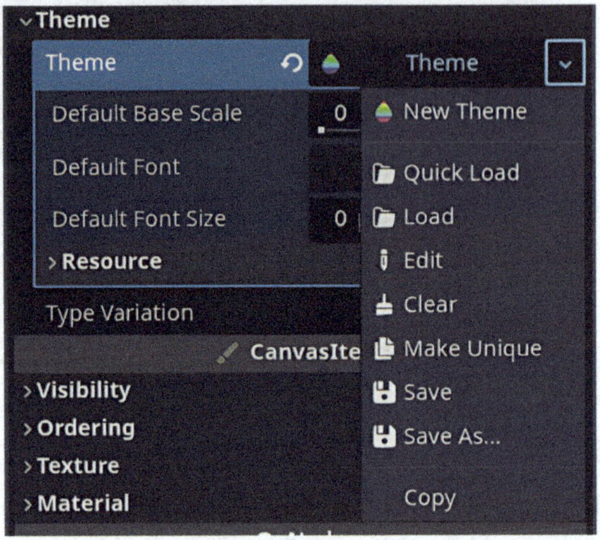

Figure 6.26: Loading a Theme resource into a new scene

3. Navigate to where we saved the `UI_Theme.tres` resource and select it. This will open the Theme Editor and allow us to customize more control nodes.
4. Click the + sign in the **Scene** dock and search for the **Panel** node. Once added, you'll see a small opaque square appear at the origin of the Viewport, as in *Figure 6.27*:

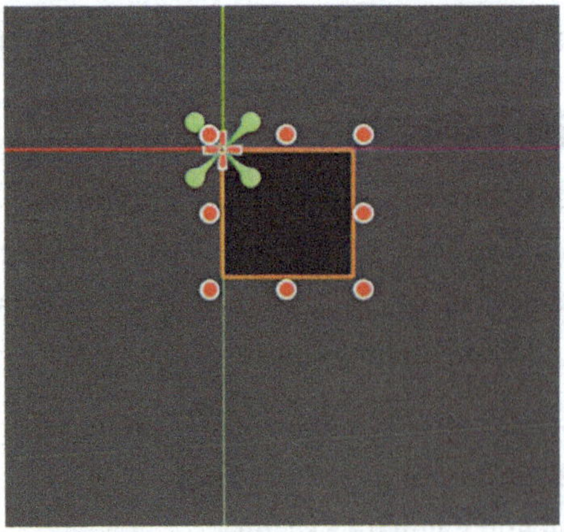

Figure 6.27: A panel added to our MainMenu scene

5. Expand the **Panel** node by using the eight dots on its edges so that it looks like *Figure 6.28*:

Figure 6.28: The Panel node expanded with its position and size included

For the exact position and size, you can see the values of the **Panel** node on the right-hand side of the screen, as in *Figure 6.29*:

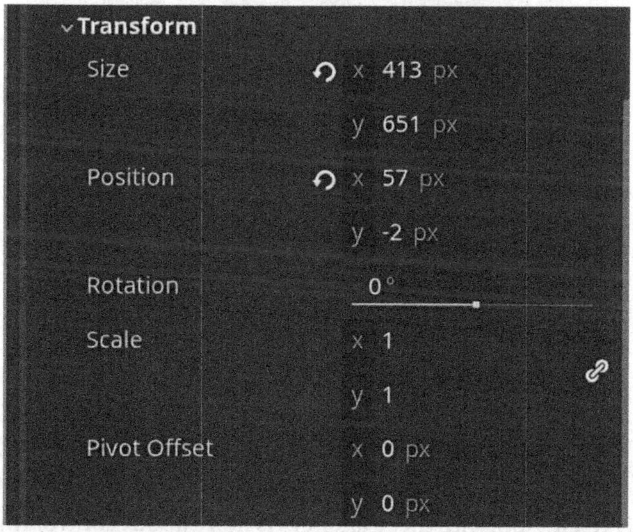

Figure 6.29: The exact size and position of the Panel node

This **Panel** node is going to serve as the background for our main menu text and set of buttons. Even though we didn't customize the **Panel** node, we can always navigate back to the Theme Editor and customize it afterward to something that aligns better with the vision of our game. Again, the Theme Editor is awesome for prototyping and keeping a cohesive theme throughout your project.

Once our **Panel** node is properly sized and positioned, we're going to anchor it to the size of our Viewport. While we could design all our UI to be set for one resolution, we'll utilize anchors in Godot to allow our UI to adjust with any given resolution. To do this, drag each corner of the anchors until they look like *Figure 6.30*:

Figure 6.30: The panel with anchors on each of the corners

This means when we resize the game window, the panel will resize appropriately because it's anchored to the screen in some way. It's different from setting the **Transform** property, which sizes the **Panel** node itself. Applying these anchors is more about controlling the behavior of the UI, regardless of the platform we're on.

Now that we have our **Panel** node properly placed in the scene and anchored, we're going to add a container.

Adding our buttons

With our **Theme** resource loaded, we can go ahead and add our buttons. We'll use another control node, **VBoxContainer**, to hold all our buttons.

A **container** is a nice way to auto-size and space multiple UI objects. Think of an inventory system where each item is in its own cell and evenly spaced out. Or think about a row of buttons along the top of your screen. For our purposes, we're going to use a container to hold all our buttons in the main menu. The one we're about to use, **VBoxContainer**, has a *V* in front of it to denote that it holds objects vertically. There is also one for holding objects horizontally, denoted by an *H*:

> Note
>
> Godot has many types of containers, and while we won't go over all of them, I recommend reading this page to better understand the different types available: `https://docs.godotengine.org/en/stable/tutorials/ui/gui_containers.html`.

1. Add a **VBoxContainer** node by selecting the + sign in the **Scene** dock. Make sure it's parented under the **Panel** node.
2. With our **VBoxContainer** node selected, set the **Transform** property in the **Inspector** dock to what's configured in *Figure 6.31*:

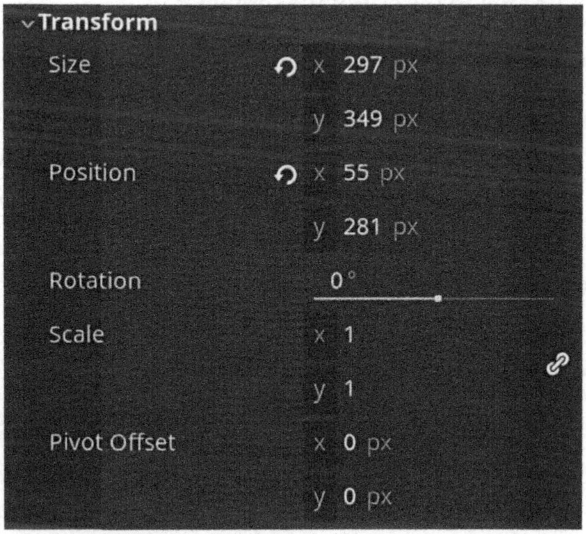

Figure 6.31: The Transform property set for the VBoxContainer node

The **VBoxContainer** node should now be placed within our **Panel** node. Next, we're going to anchor the container within the **Panel** node. Rather than dragging the anchor points, we can select the container node and set an anchor preset.

3. Above the Viewport, click the **Anchor Preset** icon (which looks like a green circle with two lines through it), panel, as seen in *Figure 6.32*, will open:

Figure 6.32: Anchor preset options for control nodes

4. Select the button at the bottom that says **Set to Current Ratio**, which will place green anchor points around the size of the container.

With our container anchored, let's start adding buttons to it by taking the following steps:

1. Add a **Button** node to the scene by clicking the + sign as usual. Again, we want to make sure this new **Button** node is parented within our **VBoxContainer** node. You can reparent the node by clicking and dragging it in the **Scene** dock so that it's under the **VBoxContainer** node.
2. Next, rename the **Button** node to **Play**.
3. After renaming the node in the **Scene** dock, let's also add text to the **Button** node. Navigate to the **Text** property in the **Inspector** dock.
4. Type the word `Play` in the **Text** property of the **Button** node, as we did earlier in this chapter.

Our node tree in the **Scene** dock should look like *Figure 6.33*:

Figure 6.33: The node tree in the Scene dock as of now

> Note
>
> If no node is selected in the **Scene** dock when adding a new node, the new node will be parented under the root node.

Now, we want to duplicate the **Play** button three more times – either right-click the **Play** node and select **Duplicate** or select the node and use the *Ctrl* + *D* shortcut. Rename the three new buttons as **Settings**, **Credits**, and **Quit**. You should also rename the **Text** property to the name of each node. Our node tree should look like *Figure 6.34*:

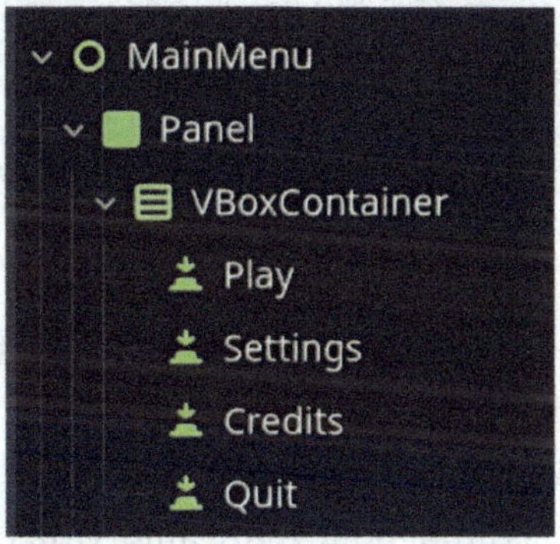

Figure 6.34: The node tree after duplicating our Play button

And our Viewport should look like *Figure 6.35*:

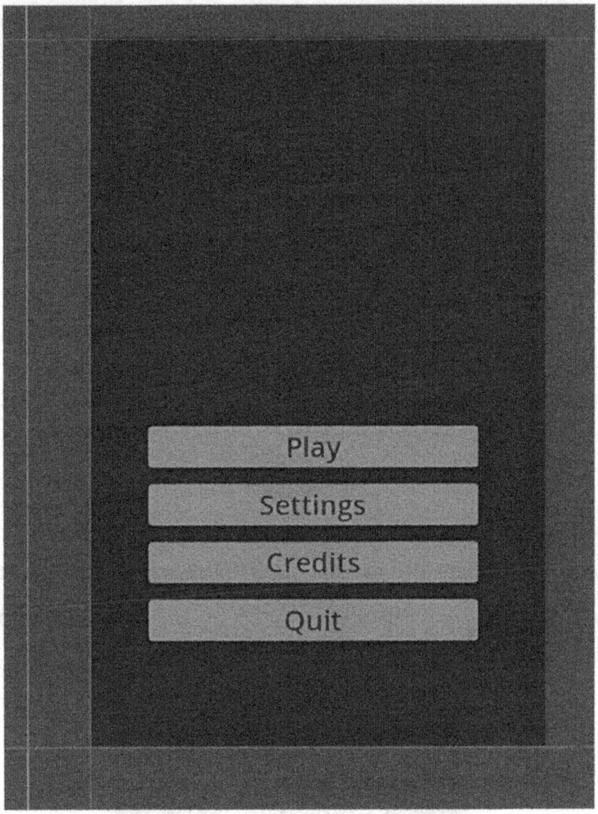

Figure 6.35: Our main menu after adding all our buttons

Notice that since our root node, **MainMenu**, has the **Theme** resource attached to it, every child node, such as the buttons, is themed the way we designed it in the Theme Editor. However, the **Panel** node is not, because we did not design it in the Theme Editor. You could go back and design it if you plan to use many panels throughout your game. Otherwise, designing it once does not necessitate adding it to the **Theme** resource.

Now, save this scene as `MainMenu.tscn`. Having created our main menu, we are presented with a couple of options of where to place it. We could keep it isolated and load other scenes as needed, depending on the button the player clicks. Another option that has become very popular is to embed the main menu on top of the world in some way. The latter route is a more interesting one both aesthetically and coding-wise, so we're going to implement it next.

Embedding our main menu

To start embedding our main menu, let's do the following:

1. Open our `World.tscn` scene.
2. Click the + sign from the **Scene** dock and add a **Camera** node. This camera is only going to be active while we're on the main menu.
3. Rename this node to **MenuCamera**. This camera should not be nested under any other node but rather a direct child of our root node, **World**.
4. In our level, we will position the **Camera** node somewhere high in the sky, providing a bird's eye view of the world and showcasing our level.

Showcasing our level provides a great opportunity to invite our players into the world, especially when the main menu will be the first screen they see. Then, for the UI, we'll have the main menu sit on top of the view of our level. This will provide an active and alive world rather than a static background for our main menu. If you are struggling to picture what this will look like, you can jump ahead to *Figure 6.39* to see it in action.

First, we need to position the **Camera** node. Here's how we can do that:

1. Select the **Camera** node in the **Scene** dock and then in the **Inspector** dock, set the **Position** and **Rotation** properties to be that of *Figure 6.36*.
2. Be sure to select the **Camera Preview** button in the top-left corner of the Viewport to determine whether you like its location:

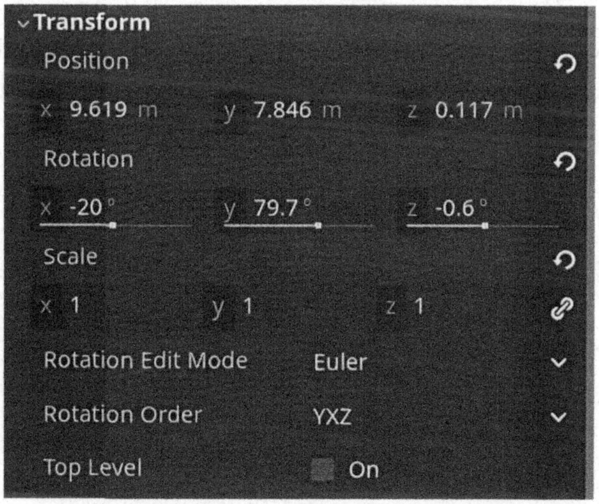

Figure 6.36: The Transform property of MenuCamera

Once our **MenuCamera** node is positioned, we want to set it to be the **Current** camera. To do this, we'll take the following steps:

1. Select the **MenuCamera** node.
2. Navigate to the properties in the **Inspector** dock for the **MenuCamera** node.
3. Select the checkbox next to **Current**.

We are now done setting up the **MenuCamera** node and will move on to adding our **MainMenu** scene to our **World** scene.

Drag the `MainMenu.tscn` scene file from the **FileSystem** dock into the **Scene** dock. An alternative to dragging the scene from one dock to another is clicking the **Instantiating Child Scene** icon, which appears as a chain link icon, as shown in *Figure 6.37*:

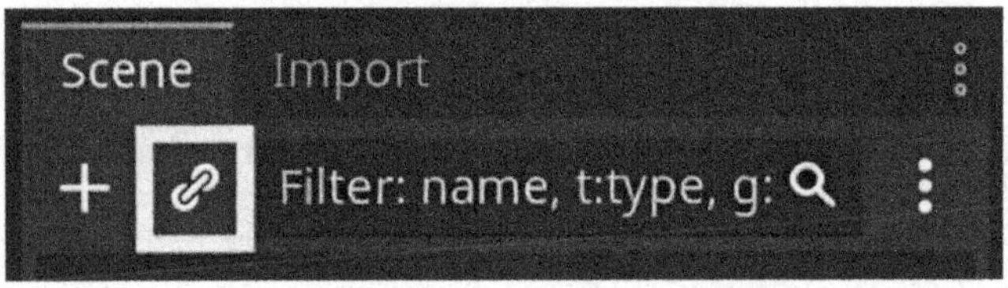

Figure 6.37: The chain icon for instantiating scenes

Once the **Instantiating Child Scene** button is clicked, it will provide a pop-up menu with all the scenes created in your project. Click the `user_interface/MainMenu.tscn` one, and it will be added as a child node. We did something like this with our **Player** scene in *Chapter 5* when we added our **Player** scene to our **World** one; here we're doing the same thing except with our UI.

The last thing to do in our node tree is to drag the **MainMenu** node under the new **MenuCamera** node, as in *Figure 6.38*. We do this to manage the scene a little bit better, keeping related nodes with each other:

Figure 6.38: The World node tree after adding our main menu

It's also fine if the **MainMenu** scene is only a child of the **World** node. Alternatively, we could instantiate and add the scene from a script, which we'll do later regarding our **Settings** page.

Note

Notice the highlighted icons next to **Player** and **MainMenu** in *Figure 6.38*. This quickly shows that these are instantiated scenes nested in our **World** scene. We can also refer to them as nested scenes.

Now, save the scene and run the game. You should see a screen like *Figure 6.39*:

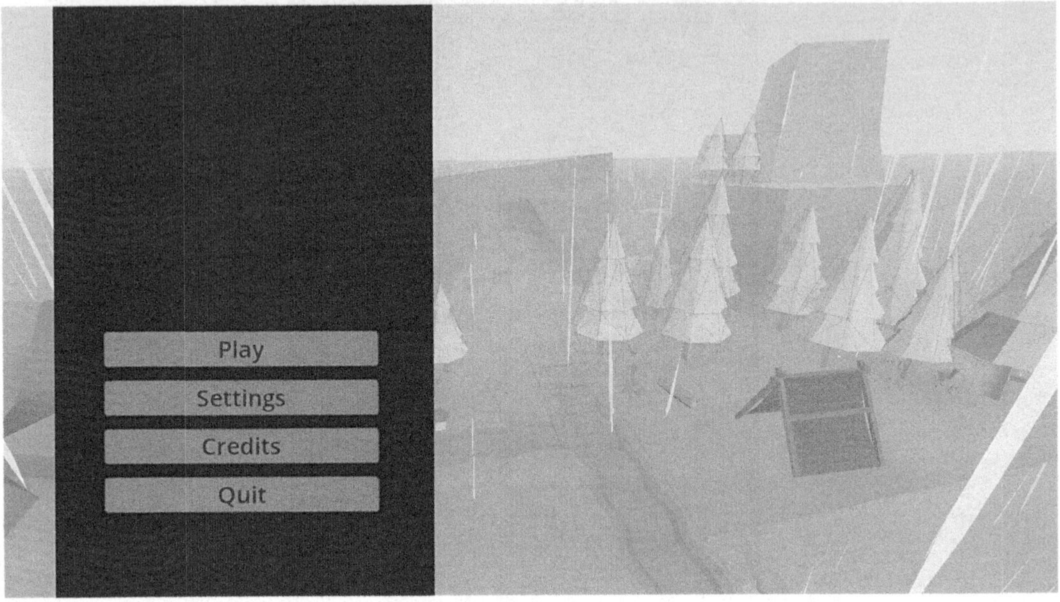

Figure 6.39: The main menu embedded in the World scene

At this point, our menu has no functionality whatsoever. We can click and hover over the buttons all we like, but they don't do anything yet. So, let's go back into the editor to make our menu buttons do what they say they are supposed to.

Connecting menu buttons

Before we get started hooking the menu buttons up, we need a script attached to the root node of our scene. To attach a script, do the following:

1. Right-click the root node, **MainMenu**, in the **Scene** dock.
2. Next, click the **Attach Script** button. A new pop-up window will appear.
3. In this new window, be sure to name the script `MainMenu.cs`.
4. Click the **Create** button from the pop-up window.

Of the four buttons we've created, the simplest one to set up is **Quit**. So, switch to our `MainMenu.tscn` scene and select the **Quit** node. Then, with this node highlighted, click the **Node** tab that's along the top of the **Inspector** dock, as shown in *Figure 6.40*:

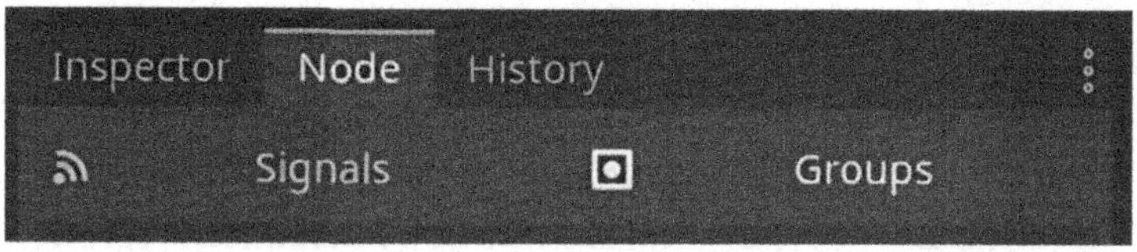

Figure 6.40: The Node tab for the Quit node

This **Node** dock is how we can access the signals of a specific node. We did it once before when creating our items in *Chapter 5*. For our button, there is a list of signals that we can connect to, depending on the state of our button. Double-click the first signal, `button_down()`, and a new window will appear, as in *Figure 6.41*. We're selecting `button_down()` because we want to quit the game once this button is clicked:

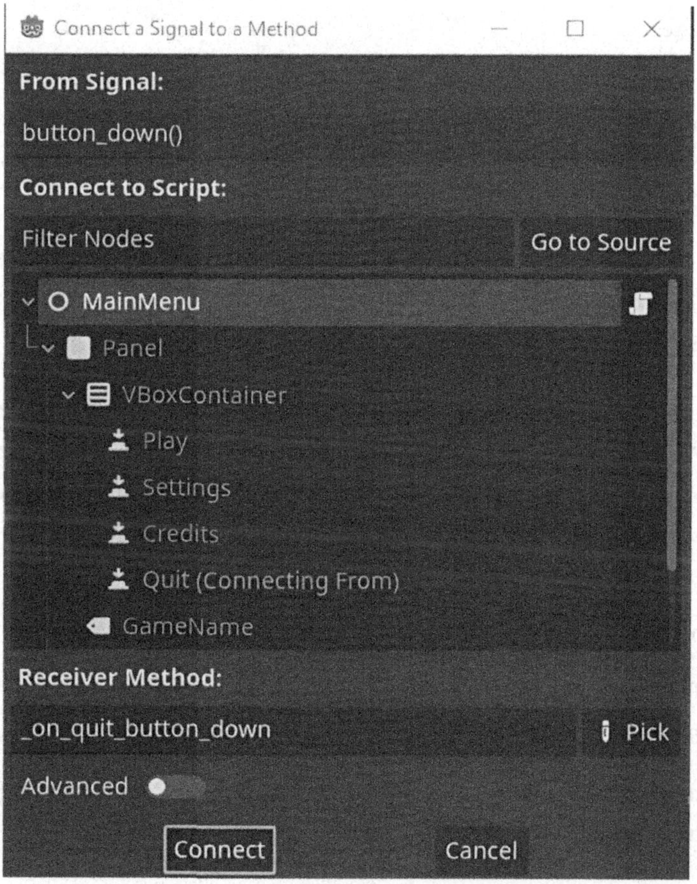

Figure 6.41: Connecting a signal to our Quit button

It's important to note that we're able to connect to this signal because we already have a script created to do so. If there was no script in this scene, we would need to create one to add the signal. The reason for this is because of the **Receiver Method** portion of this window. This is the name of the function that will run once the signal is emitted. By default, the receiver method is going to be added to our `MainMenu.cs` file.

Now, Godot automatically generates a name for the function, which is why it says `_on_quit_button_down` in *Figure 6.41*. Instead, rename it to `ExitGame()`.

Then, click the **Connect** button. You will be taken to the script in Visual Studio Code (or whatever IDE you have configured for Godot), and you can see the newly created function.

> Note
>
> If we already created a function in any script and are connecting it to a signal, we could select the **Pick** button that's next to the receiver method function name and search for the function. This is useful when we have multiple scripts in a scene with multiple functions and need to find a specific one.

In this new function, we'll add one line of code:

```
GetTree().Quit();
```

The `GetTree()` function will get the active scene tree – this is `World.tscn` since `MainMenu.tscn` is nested inside **World**. Meanwhile, `Quit()` is a built-in Godot function that quits the application. Save the scene, and you'll notice that you can't test it out. We have no cursor because of how we set up our player controller. Don't worry – we'll fix this in the next section.

For now, repeat that process for both the **Play** and **Settings** buttons. We'll create two receiver methods, one for each button respectively, and name them the following:

- For the **Play** button, name it `OnPlayClicked()`
- For the **Settings** button, name it `OnSettingsClicked()`

Now that part of our main menu is functional, we're going to look at adding an animation to provide a transition to the menu and then connect that to our **Play** button.

Adding a transition animation to the menu

Before we dive into the code, let's walk through what we're about to do. When we click the **Play** button, we want the menu to slide out from the screen and then switch our view and control to our **Player** node. A few things we'll need to account for, though, will include the following:

- Making sure we lock the **Player** node when we're on the main menu and then unlock it when we leave it
- Toggling which camera is the **Current** camera
- Updating the way the mouse appears in the game because currently, it's not visible

To get started, open the `World.cs` script file to add the transition we need.

> Note
>
> With the Godot editor configured to Visual Studio Code, you can simply click the scroll icon next to the **World** node to open a script.

We'll first need to provide a reference to the new camera node we created (**MenuCamera**). Inside the script, add the following variable to our `World` class:

```
private Camera3D menuCamera;
```

The `menuCamera` variable will control the view of the game world that the player will see when starting the game. Something to be aware of is that we can only have one camera set to the **Current** camera of any given scene. We'll use this knowledge to toggle between the menu camera and the one that is sitting on our player.

With our newly created variable, assign it to a node in the `_Ready()` function. Anywhere after the class declaration but before any function definitions is a valid space. It will look like this:

```
menuCamera = GetNode<Camera3D>("MenuCamera");
```

Next, still in the `_Ready()` function, add an `if` statement to check if our `menuCamera` variable is the current one by writing this:

```
if(menuCamera.Current) { }
```

Within this `if` statement, write two lines of code. The first is the following:

```
Input.MouseMode = Input.MouseModeEnum.Visible;
```

This changes the way the mouse operates in the game. In *Chapter 4*, for our player controller, we used the `Input` class to hide the cursor and make the cursor be the center of the screen. We're just reversing that here by making it visible so that we can interact with the UI.

The second line we'll write is the following:

```
player.ProcessMode = ProcessModeEnum.Disabled;
```

The `ProcessMode` property exists on every node object and determines how nodes are processed in a scene tree. There is a short list of options that we can access to alter how a node is processed. You can find them here: `https://docs.godotengine.org/en/stable/tutorials/scripting/pausing_games.html#process-modes`.

By default, all nodes have their `ProcessMode` property set to `Inherit`. However, you can see in the second line of code we added that we're setting the player's `ProcessMode` property to be `Disabled`. This means that the **Player** node and all its children (the entire nested scene) will not process or run. We want the **Player** node to behave like this only while we're on the main menu; otherwise, you could run around the world as the player while still sitting on the start screen.

At this point, save this script and test the game. You should be able to move your mouse around the main menu and click **Quit** to exit the game. Nice!

Now, back in the editor, open our `MainMenu.tscn` scene. Then, click the + sign and add an **AnimationPlayer** node. We saw this node briefly when we were animating our **Player** node; however, we focused more on the **AnimationTree** node than we did the **AnimationPlayer** node. Here, we're going to use the **AnimationPlayer** node and add keyframes to animate our menu off the screen.

Once the **AnimationPlayer** node is added, an **Animation** panel should replace the **Output** panel, as in *Figure 6.42*:

Figure 6.42: The AnimationPlayer node in Godot

In the top-left corner of *Figure 6.42*, you'll see buttons for playing animations, stepping through keyframes, and stopping animations. We can use these controls to test how our animation looks in the Viewport, which we'll do in a moment. For now, next to these playback controls, click the **Animation** button. This will open a dropdown to create a new animation, which you can see in *Figure 6.43*:

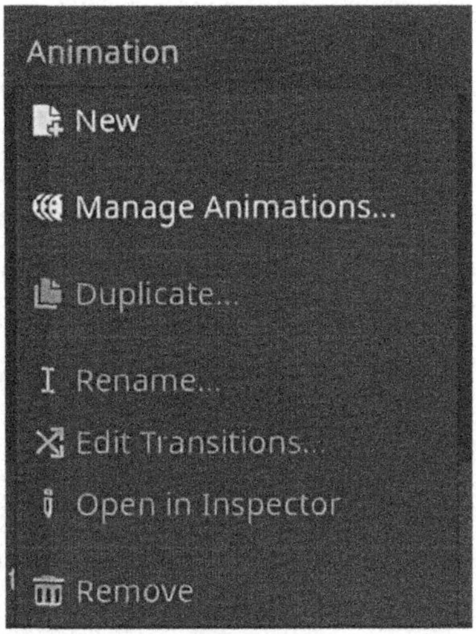

Figure 6.43: Creating a new animation in the AnimationPlayer node

Select **New** and a pop-up window will appear, asking us to name the new animation. Name it **MenuTransition** and select **OK**:

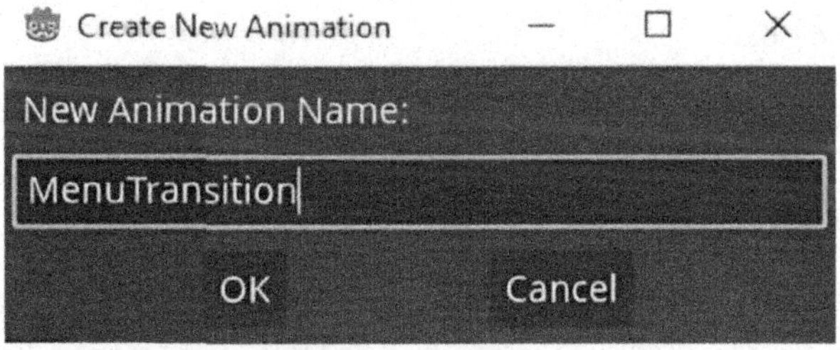

Figure 6.44: Naming a new animation for the AnimationPlayer node

After naming the animation, you'll see that a timeline has been added right below the playback and animation select controls, as shown in *Figure 6.45*:

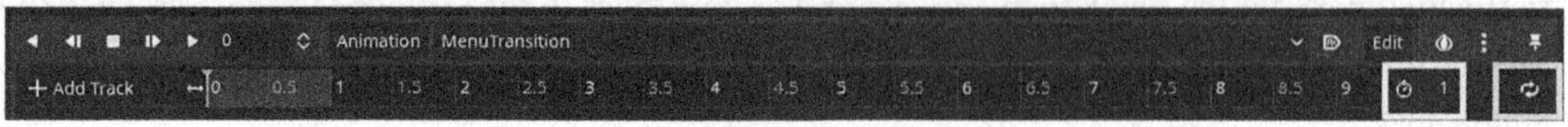

Figure 6.45: The timeline for the AnimationPlayer node

There are a couple of things to point out on this timeline. They are the following:

- We can add tracks to the **AnimationPlayer** node by clicking the **+ Add Track** button.
- On the other end of the timeline after the set of seconds markers, there's a stopwatch icon with a **1**. This is the default length of the **MenuTransition** animation. You can also tell the length of an animation by seeing the light gray coloring that covers the timeline from 0 to 1.
- Right at the end of the timeline is a looping symbol. If you click it, it will cycle between three different types of looping:
    - **Default**: By default, looping is turned off. The first click turns looping on.
    - **Reverse Looping**: The second makes the animation loop from beginning to end and then runs the animation backward, from end to beginning.
    - **Forward Looping**: The last option is forward looping, which starts from the beginning of the animation on every loop.

One last thing to notice about the **AnimationPlayer** node is that with the **Animation** panel open, you can look at any property in the **Inspector** dock and notice a small key icon next to it now, as highlighted in *Figure 6.46*:

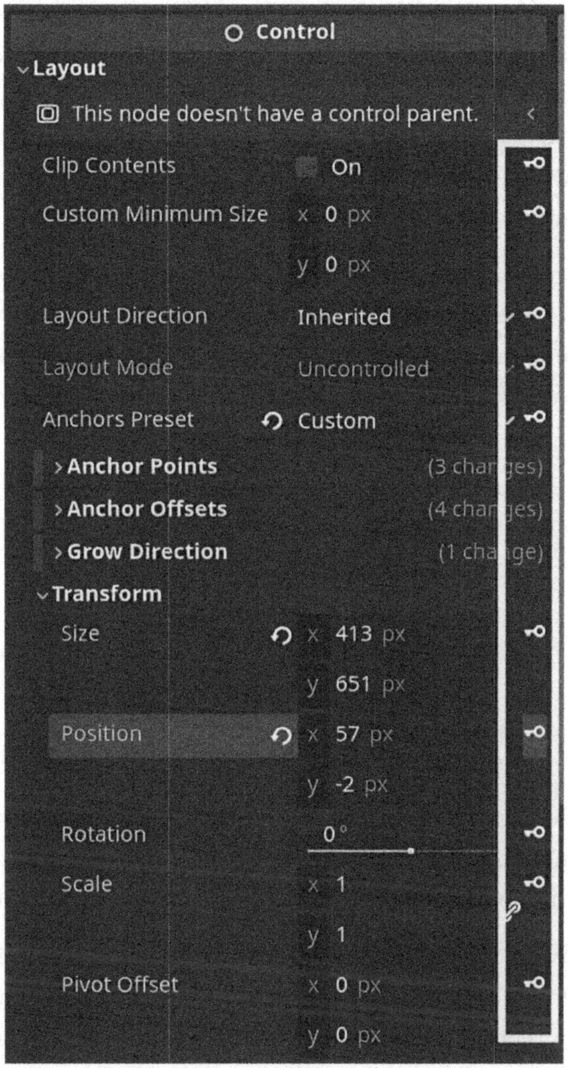

Figure 6.46: The Panel node's properties with the Animation panel open

The keyframe icons next to each of the properties do not alter the properties on the nodes. Instead, it takes the current state of that property and adds it to our **AnimationPlayer** node. Go ahead and change the length of the animation from **1** to **0.5**. The animation we're creating is going to be a quick one. Next, we're going to click the key icon that's next to **Position**, which is the property whose name is selected in gray in *Figure 6.46*.

After clicking the key icon, a new pop-up window will appear, asking you to create the new keyed frame and add the **Position** property to the animation track. By adding the **Position** property as a keyframe to the **AnimationPlayer** node, we are not setting the **Position** property of any specific node. Rather, we are taking the current **Position** property and adding it as an animation track. The pop-up window we see after clicking the keyframe icon is asking us to confirm that we do want to add the **Position** property as an animation track.

Now, click the **Create** button, and two things should appear on the **Animation** panel, as shown in *Figure 6.47*. The first is the node that's added to the track (in our case, **Panel**) and the second is the properties of that node that have been added as keyframes (in our case, **Position**). By default, the **visible** property is added, but we can always uncheck it to disable it on the animation track:

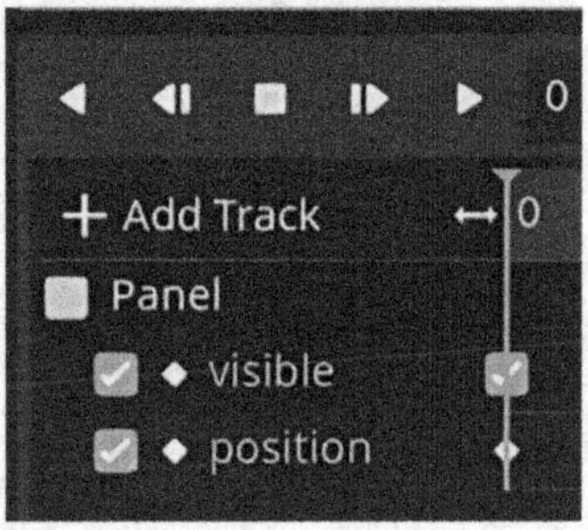

Figure 6.47: The Panel node on the animation track

In *Figure 6.47*, we can see some checkmarks. The two checkmarks on the left mean the properties are active on the animation track. The third checkmark at the start of the animation timeline determines whether this node is seen or not. We want it to be left like this.

The last thing to be aware of is a blue line that runs from the top of the **Animation** panel and through the properties we've added to the animation. This determines what point of the timeline we're looking at. You can click and drag this to move along the length of the animation, or you can use the box next to the playback controls. Set the number in the box next to the playback controls to `0.5` (visible in *Figure 6.48*) so that now, the blue line should be at the end of the animation.

Now, in the Viewport or via the **Transform** property, we're going to move our **Panel** node off screen. Moving something off screen means moving it outside of the blue lines as shown in *Figure 6.22*. Once we've moved it, we want to key the current location into the end of our animation. I'm moving mine down, so the animation will have the **Panel** node slide down and out of view, but you can move yours in any direction you'd like.

The **Transform** values for the **Panel** node are **64** for **X** and **692** for **Y**. After setting these values, select the **AnimationPlayer** node by clicking the **Animation** button at the bottom of the **Output** panel (you can see it highlighted in *Figure 6.48*).

At this point, the **Inspector** dock should still show the properties of the **Panel** node, and with our **AnimationPlayer** node, open, the key icons should now be visible next to those properties, just like in *Figure 6.46*. Click the key icon next to the **Position** property again, and a diamond should show up on the animation timeline at the **0.5** marker for the new position.

Our **Animation** panel should look like *Figure 6.48*:

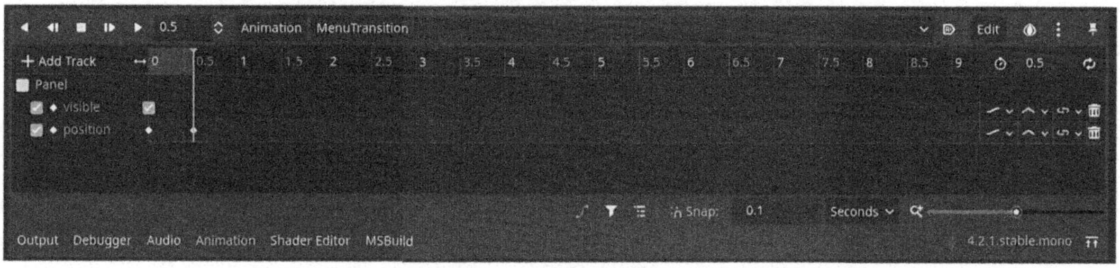

Figure 6.48: The MenuTransition animation complete

After setting the keyframe, move the blue bar back to the beginning of the timeline and select the **Play** button. You should see the **Panel** node and all its children move in the Viewport.

Awesome – we have an animation for our menu. Now, we need to go back into our `MainMenu.cs` file and trigger the animation once we click the **Play** button from the menu.

Note

If you don't remove the scene like we do later in this chapter, you will want to disable the buttons, especially if they are tied to any keyboard input, as they may still trigger.

Adding an `AnimationPlayer` class to our script is very easy. We'll declare a `private` variable at the top of our class like this:

```
private AnimationPlayer animPlayer;
```

Then, in our `_Ready()` function, assign the `private` variable to the node in our scene like this:

```
animPlayer = GetNode<AnimationPlayer>("AnimationPlayer");
```

The last line of code to add is in our `OnPlayClicked()` function. It will call the `Play` function from the `AnimationPlayer` class, and once we provide the name of the animation, that's the one it will run:

```
animPlayer.Play("MenuTransition");
```

Now, save the script and run the game. When we click the **Play** button, we should see the menu transition off screen. Of course, now we just sit in a bird's eye view of our game world, because we haven't toggled back to our **Player** camera and allowed for the **Player** node to be processed. To do so, we need to add code to both our `MainMenu.cs` file and our `World.cs` file.

In our `MainMenu` script, we're going to add two lines of code. The first will be inside our `OnPlayClicked()` function after the animation plays:

```
World root = GetOwner<World>();
```

Here, we're creating a `World` variable and calling it `root`. We're using a built-in Godot function called `GetOwner()` that will get the owner of this node. Remember – our `MainMenu` scene is nested in the `World` scene, so its parent, or owner, is **World**.

The next line will be the following:

```
root.PlayerStart();
```

What we're doing here is we're taking our `World` variable, `root`, and calling a function from the `World.cs` file. We haven't created this function yet, but we're about to, so let's save this script and switch to `World.cs`. It may throw an error because it can't find `PlayerStart`, but don't worry – we're going to go create it now.

Underneath our `_Process()` function, we'll create a new function called `PlayerStart` like so:

```
public void PlayerStart() { }
```

Now, inside the body of this function, we're going to reverse the logic we had in `_Ready()`. First, we want to make sure our **Player** node is processing which means it can receive both input and physics. To do that, we'll write the following:

```
player.ProcessMode = ProcessModeEnum.Always;
```

Again, we're referencing a pre-existing list of options on how the **Player** node should be processed.

The next line will be changing the mouse input:

```
Input.MouseMode = Input.MouseModeEnum.Captured;
```

With `MouseMode` set to `Captured`, you shouldn't see the cursor at all after clicking the **Play** button.

Save this script and test the game out! You should be able to click the **Play** button, watch a short animation of the menu, then switch to your **Player** view and play the game as we've created so far.

At this point, two out of four of our menu buttons – **Play** and **Quit** – are functional. We're now going to turn our attention to creating a **Settings** page and connecting our menu button to it.

Designing a Settings screen

With a functional main menu screen and two working buttons, we're now going to set up the **Settings** screen and connect its button to this new UI.

Create a new scene by clicking the + sign above the Viewport, and in the **Scene** dock, select **User Interface**. We are once again presented with a 2D view of a blank scene. Double-click the node and rename it to **Settings**. What we will create here are two volume sliders – one for music and one for sound effects – and a **Close** button to return us to the main menu. Of course, we can add many other things here such as UI or video settings, but this chapter will not cover those topics.

Another thing we need to do is ensure our **Theme** resource is applied to all children nodes in this scene. This means when we start to add objects such as buttons, they'll already be designed in the way we want or need. So, add the `UI_Theme.tres` resource into the **Theme** property of our newly created UI node. We're going to be expanding on the **Theme** resource in this section as we add our volume sliders. We'll circle back to the Theme Editor and volume sliders after making our settings look a bit nicer.

Next, we will frame the **Settings** page with its own background as we want it to open on top of the main menu. We can do this by adding a **ColorRect** node. Click the + sign, and once the **ColorRect** node has been selected, it will appear in our Viewport, white by default. If we select the **ColorRect** node and then look in the **Inspector**, we can see its first property is **Color**. Go ahead and choose a color that will contrast well with black – I chose a light blue (the hex color for it is `#ABD4F6`).

With a color selected, we also need to resize the **ColorRect** node to fill the screen. The only property I've changed is **Size**, which you can find under the **Transform** property when the **ColorRect** node is selected (see *Figure 6.49*):

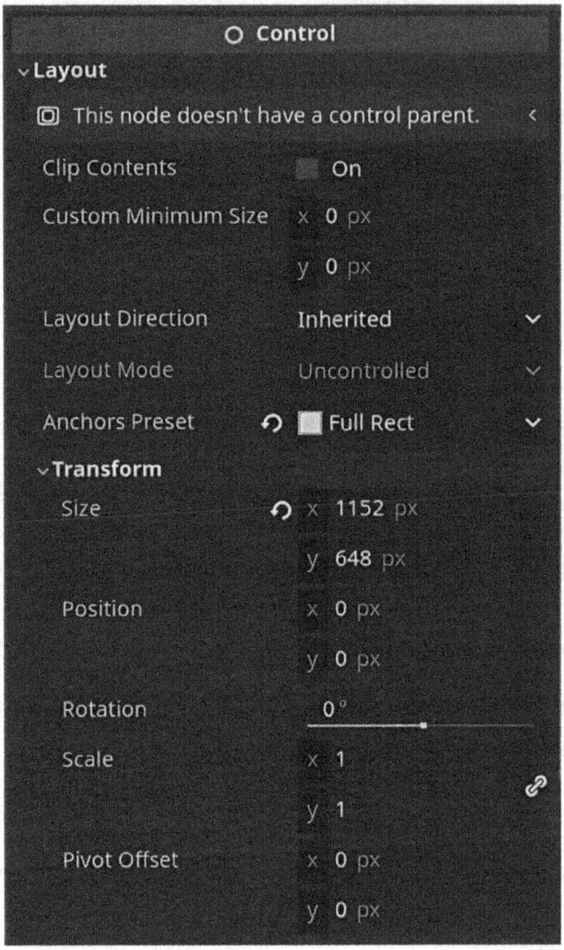

Figure 6.49: The Layout and Transform properties of our Settings node

The only other thing to do is to set our anchors for this node. Go ahead and click the anchor button at the top (if you forget where this is, refer to *Figure 6.32*), then click the **Set to Current Ratio** button.

Now, click the + sign yet again and add a **Label** node. This node will be for labeling the page we're on, so rename it to **Title**. Then, with the new node selected, update the **Text** property by entering the word `Settings`. Then, find the **Font Size** property and bump it up to something such as `75` pixels, as seen in *Figure 6.50*. You can also add custom fonts in the property just above this one if you would like. I am leaving mine to Godot's default font:

Figure 6.50: The Font Sizes settings on our Label node

Next, let's update the **Transform** property by adjusting the **Size** and **Position** values of this label. For the **Transform** property, set the following options:

- **Size**: **x**: `384 px`, **y**: `103 px`
- **Position**: **x**: `362 px`, **y**: `55 px`

> Note
>
> The **px** unit listed stands for **pixels.**

Now, we can move on to adding, then designing, our volume sliders.

Adding our volume sliders

As you may have noticed, Godot's built-in suite of UI nodes offers a lot of usability and flexibility. We're going to add some sliders to add to our `Settings.tscn` scene.

When we click the + sign on the **Scene** dock this time, search for the **HSlider** node (the *H* in the name stands for horizontal) and rename it to **MusicSlider**. This node needs to be parented below the **Settings** panel we created earlier. Now, position the slider in our scene. We want **HSlider** to be centered and under our title for the screen. The position and size are as follows:

- **Size**: **x**: `482 px`, **y**: `113 px`
- **Position**: **x**: `454 px`, **y**: `257 px`

Next to the slider, we want to add a **Label** node so that the player knows what the slider changes. Rather than adding a new **Label** node, we can select the existing **Label** node that we named **Settings** in our scene and duplicate it. You can duplicate it using the same methods mentioned while working with the **Play** node earlier.

Once duplicated, rename the node to **MusicLabel** and move it to the following position: **x**: `104 px`, **y**: `254 px`. Then, select the anchor button and set the **MusicLabel** node's anchors by clicking **Set to Current Ratio** from the anchor options above the Viewport (as shown back in *Figure 6.32*).

Now, we're going to duplicate multiple nodes at once to create our sound effect slider alongside its title. Click the **MusicLabel** node, hold the left *Shift* key down, and click the **MusicSlider** node. We should have two nodes selected now, as shown in *Figure 6.51*:

Figure 6.51: Selecting multiple nodes in a scene

> Note
>
> The selection keyboard shortcut may differ depending on your operating system; however, this is the command on Windows 10.

With these two nodes highlighted, you can use the *Ctrl* + *D* duplication shortcut to duplicate both nodes at once. When we do this, the duplicated nodes will be copied in the scene tree based on where their parents were. Therefore, our duplicated **Slider** and **Label** nodes will be parented under the **ColorRect** node.

After duplicating the **MusicSlider** and **MusicLabel** nodes, we should see **MusicSlider2** and **MusicLabel2** in the scene tree. Rename these to **SFXSlider** and **SFXLabel**, respectively.

Then, reposition **SFXSlider** to **x**: `454 px` and **y**: `400 px` and reposition **SFXLabel** to **x**: `104 px` and **y**: `400 px`. Our **Settings** screen should now look like *Figure 6.52*:

Figure 6.52: The Settings screen after adding our labels and sliders

The **Label** nodes we added contrast nicely with the background we chose, but the default colors of the sliders do not. We can quickly fix this by going back into our **Theme** resource.

Designing our volume sliders

We'll add a theme type for the **HSlider** node and configure it accordingly. To get back to our **Theme** resource, select the **Settings** control node – also the root node of the scene – and the Theme Editor panel should pop up in the bottom panel automatically (since we already have our **Theme** resource on the **Theme** property of this node).

With our Theme Editor open again, click the + sign next to the currently selected theme type. You can see this option in *Figure 6.53* where the **Button** theme type is my currently selected type:

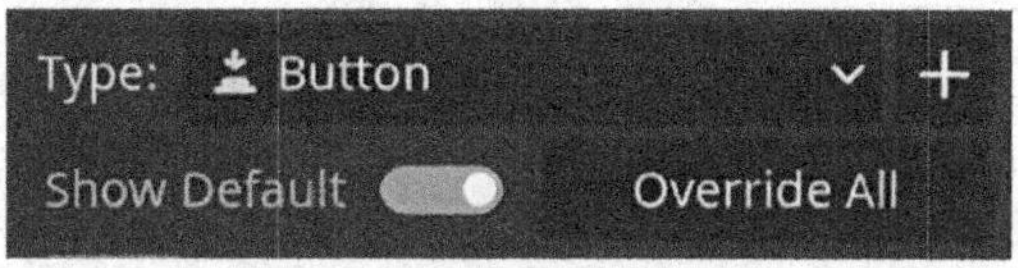

Figure 6.53: Creating a new theme-type resource

A new menu will appear. Search for the **HSlider** node, click **Add Type**, and the **HSlider** node should now be the selected type, as seen in *Figure 6.54*. This is an excellent way of highlighting how you can change and adjust different UIs as needed on the fly via the Theme Editor:

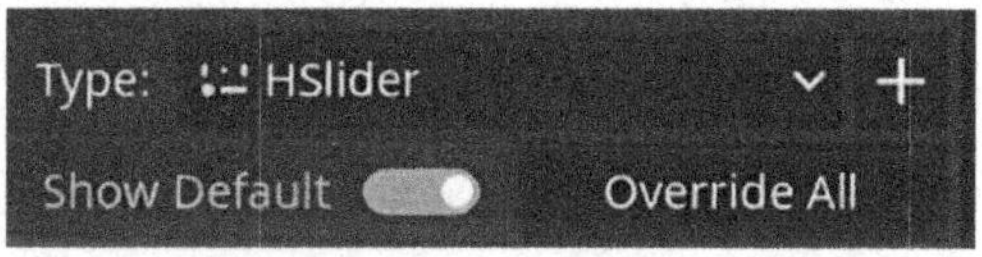

Figure 6.54: The HSlider theme type selected

Next, we're going to add and customize `grabber_area`, `grabber_area_highlight`, and the `slider` components of our **HSlider** theme type. First, we'll create **StyleBox** resources for the `grabber_area` and `grabber_area_highlight` components. Then, we'll look at the `slider` component, which will be a **StyleBoxLine** resource.

For our `grabber_area` component, click the rainbow-colored property tab, as shown in *Figure 6.55*, and create a new **StyleBoxFlat** resource for both the `grabber_area` and `grabber_area_highlight` components by selecting the + sign next to the **StyleBox** resource:

Figure 6.55: Adding a StyleBox resource to the HSlider theme type

With the two **StyleBoxFlat** resources created for the `grabber_area` and `grabber_area_highlight` components, let's create a **StyleBoxLine** resource that we need for the slider. Click the arrow next to the default **StyleBoxFlat** option for the slider and select the **StyleBoxLine** option. Then, click the + sign next to the **StyleBoxLine** option. You can see the three **StyleBox** resources created in *Figure 6.56*:

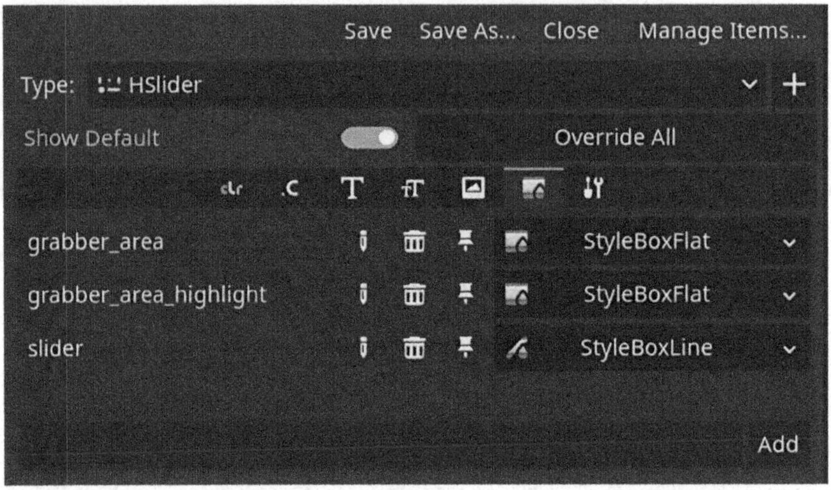

Figure 6.56: The StyleBox resources for our HSlider theme type

> Note
>
> *Figure 6.56* looks wider than the default version in Godot because you can resize and adjust the layout of the Theme Editor by dragging one of the edges. Otherwise, it can be difficult to read what you're configuring.

With our **StyleBoxFlat** resources created, we will set a color on each one and configure them in a way that fits our current background and setup.

For the **StyleBoxFlat** resource for which we created a `grabber_area` component, we're going to change the first listed property, **BG Color**, to the following hexadecimal color: `#003E65`. You can see where to type the hexadecimal number for the color in *Figure 6.57*. You can also select a color by dragging the pointer in the color circle or setting the **red, green, or blue** (**RGB**) settings. The **A** below the RGB settings is for **Alpha**, which determines how transparent the item is. Leave this set to 255:

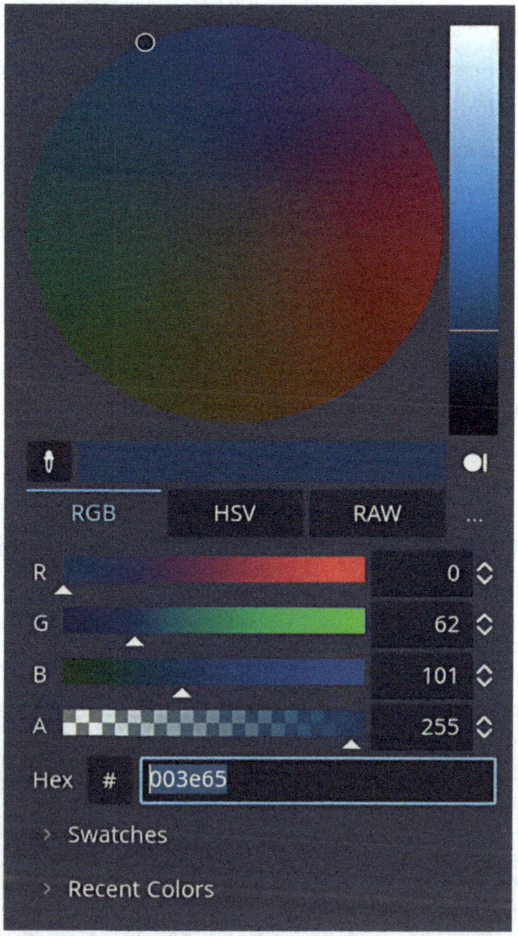

Figure 6.57: The color options for the BG Color property

After that, we're going to round the corners of the slider to something softer by expanding the **Corner Radius** property and setting **Top Left**, **Top Right**, **Bottom Right**, and **Bottom Left** to `10` pixels.

Moving on, for the **StyleBoxFlat** resource created for the `grabber_area_highlight` component, we'll change the **BG Color** property to the following hexadecimal color: `#CB8B59`. We'll also change the **Corner Radius** property to `10` pixels for each of the corners.

At this point, you should start to see the sliders change in the `Settings.tscn` scene.

The last **StyleBox** resource to adjust is the **StyleBoxLine** resource on our `slider` component. This **StyleBox** resource is significantly different from our flat **StyleBox** resources. The **StyleBox** line has a much smaller selection of properties to adjust. We'll change the **Color** property to match that of the `grabber_area` component. Then, change the **Grow Begin** and **Grow End** sizing to `-10` pixels. Once you set this property, you should see rounded corners. Then, change the **Thickness** property to 12 pixels. This will match in sizing with the custom slider image we're about to add.

For the custom slider image, we'll be downloading an excellent UI pack from Kenney Assets, which you can find here: `https://kenney.nl/assets/ui-pack` (the default one is rather small and opaque). Click the **Download** button, extract the zipped folder, and then select one of the circular images to drag and drop into the **FileSystem** dock. I chose the `red_circle.png` file. Be sure to place the image in the correct folder within your project – the `user_interface` one.

With the image in our project, we can return to the Theme Editor. Click the image icon shown in *Figure 6.58*. You should see the default image that's our current slider there. Click the + sign next to the row for the `grabber` state and browse to your circular image that we just imported from the Kenney UI asset pack. Repeat this process for the other states that the grabber will be in, such as `grabber_disabled` and `grabber_highlight`, until it looks like *Figure 6.58*:

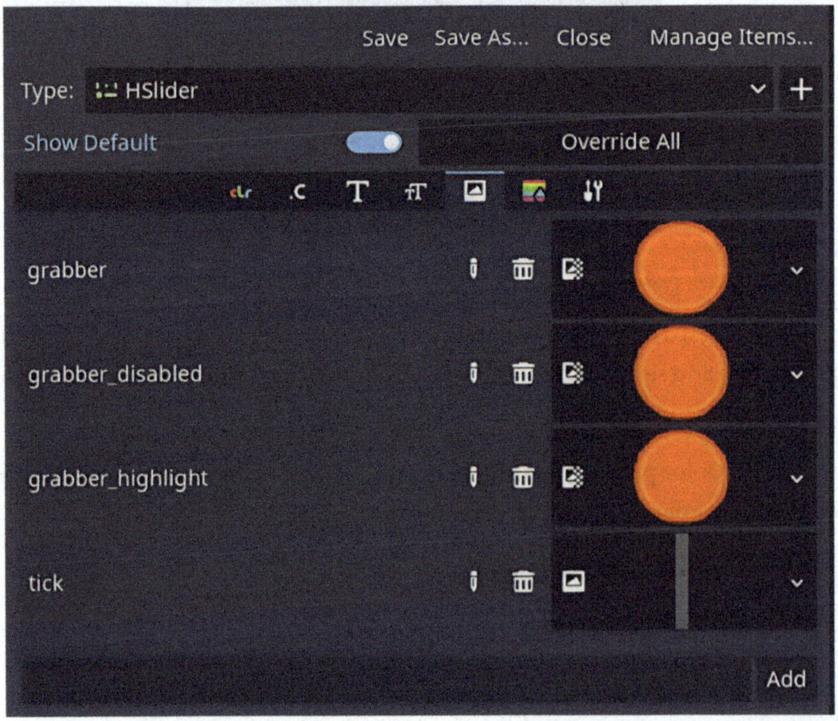

Figure 6.58: The images for the grabber on the slider

Save the scene. Now, to complete our **Settings** scene, the last component to add to this scene is the navigation for how to get from the main menu to the **Settings** screen and back.

Navigation on the Settings screen

To start adding navigation to the **Settings** screen, let's connect a signal to the **Settings** button, much like we did with the **Play** and **Quit** buttons.

To do this, click the **Node** tab at the top of the **Inspector**, open the `MainMenu.cs` file, and double-click the `button_down()` signal to add a function to it. A pop-up window will appear, asking for the function name. In the **Receiver Method** box, put the name `OnSettingsClicked`. Then, click the **Connect** button, which will open the `MainMenu.cs` file as it's the only script in the scene; otherwise, you'd have to select the script you'd want the function to be tied to.

> Note
>
> When adding a function name to the Receiver Method box, you do not include the parentheses that come after the function name.

When the script opens, it may or may not have automatically added the function name we just created. If not, we'll do it underneath the `ExitGame` function, like so:

```
public void OnClickedSettings() { }
```

Within that function, we'll create a `Node` variable called `settingsScene` – this is because we're going to add the `Settings.tscn` scene to our `MainMenu.tscn` scene via a script rather than dragging it into the scene node as we did with `MainMenu.tscn` in the `World.tscn` scene.

We'll write the following line within our `OnClickedSettings()` function now:

```
Node settingsScene =
```

I've left the equals operator as we will assign this new variable to Godot's `ResourceLoader` class. This class has a `Load()` function that allows us to load packed scenes from code and instantiates various scenes as we need them. Some common examples of this are when enemies are spawned in or a player fires a bullet. You can read more about the `ResourceLoader` class here: `https://docs.godotengine.org/en/stable/classes/class_resourceloader.html`.

For now, we'll assign our `settingsScene` variable with the following:

```
ResourceLoader.Load<PackedScene>("res://user_interface/Settings.tscn").
Instantiate();
```

First, we access the `ResourceLoader` class and then use the dot operator to call the `Load` function within it. We then pass in the path to our scene and instantiate it. This will cache the scene, or resource, and allow us to access it at later points throughout the game. Be aware that if the path changes, you will need to update this line of code with the correct one.

Even though we have instantiated the node, we don't have it added to the scene. We need to call one more function to make this happen:

```
AddChild(settingsScene);
```

Here, we call the `AddChild()` function, which takes the packed scene that we've instantiated and adds it as a child to the node that the script is on. In this case, the script is on the root node, so it will be added as a child to the **MainMenu** scene, which is what we want.

Save the script and test the scene out. You should be able to launch the game, click the **Settings** button, and then access your **Settings** screen. You may notice we still have a couple of issues, though. For one, we have no way to navigate back to the main menu screen. Let's look at adding a **Close** button to return to the main menu.

Adding a Close button

Adding a **Close** button is super easy thanks to our Theme Editor. In our `Settings.tscn` scene, click the + sign at the top of the **Scene** dock and add a new **Button** node. Make sure it's parented under the **ColorRect** node by dragging it underneath it.

Since we already themed our **Button** type, this new button will look like our main menu buttons by default. The reason is that we have the **Theme** resource (`UI_Theme.tres`) that we created and placed on our root node (**Settings**), which means any children that have a theme type will apply it. This is convenient because we must only add our **Theme** resource to the scene once.

Now, rename this new **Button** node to **CloseButton**. With the **CloseButton** node selected, let's look at the properties in the **Inspector** dock and update them. Scroll down to the **Layout** property and expand it to find the **Transform** property. Then, position it using the following values:

- **Size**: **x**: `70 px`, **y**: `77 px`
- **Position**: **x**: `996 px`, **y**: `55 px`

Moving on, in the **Text** property, we can put an uppercase **X** inside it (this being the symbol of a **Close** button). However, rather than using text, we could also use an icon from the Kenney UI pack. We can add the icon to our project and then upload it to the **Icon** property. Then, we would enable the **Flat** property, which is a quick way to disable the decorative customization we did with the **Button** theme type. Then, we would align it to be centered by selecting **Center** in the **Icon Alignment** dropdown. Finally, we'd enable the **Expand Icon** property to fill the size of the **Button** node we created, since the default size of the asset we downloaded is a little too small. You can see the settings for using an icon in *Figure 6.59*:

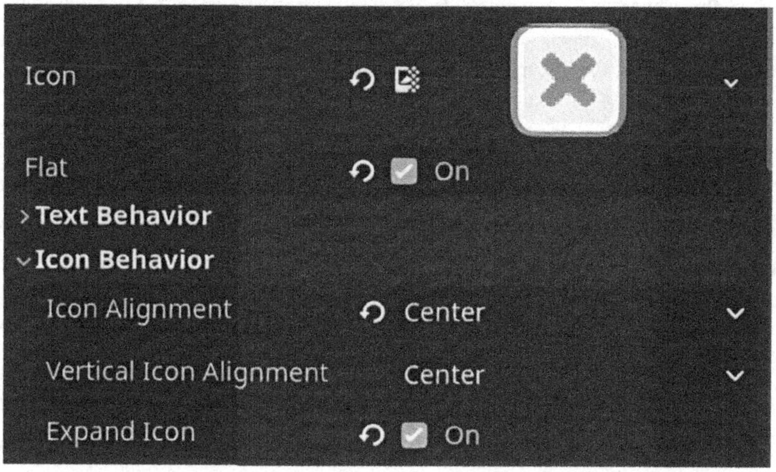

Figure 6.59: The Button properties to be set for using a .png file

Since the icon is being expanded, it may look a bit pixelated, but you can design or find images that will fit the specific size and resolution that you need for your project when using images for the UI. For this reason, I have chosen to utilize the **X** icon as text to showcase the customization we created for the **Button** node in the Theme Editor.

> Note
>
> If you add the icon rather than use the text, notice that only some of the **Button**-type properties from our **Theme** resource will be applied. For example, the way the button grows on highlighting will stay, but the color feedback will not.

With our **Close** button designed and placed, let's look at hooking it up to be a functional button. Keeping the **CloseButton** node highlighted, click the **Node** tab in the **Inspector** dock to get the list of available Godot signals. Once again, select `button_down()`. Once we've clicked **Connect**, a new popup appears where we must name the function we want to be tied to this signal in the **Receiver Method** box. Write `OnSettingsClose` and click the **Connect** button at the bottom of this popup.

Now, save the scene and open our `Settings.cs` file. In the class under our `_Ready()` and `_Process()` functions, let's declare a new function:

```
public void OnSettingsClose() { }
```

Then, within this function, we'll write a single line, like so:

```
this.QueueFree();
```

The `QueueFree()` is a method from the **Node** object in Godot that deletes whatever node called the method at the end of the frame. This line of code is saying to take this object, which is the root node, **Settings**, and destroy it.

The reason we can remove it this way from our scene is because, if you recall, we added the entire `Settings.tscn` scene as a child of our `MainMenu.tscn` scene. So, when we delete the settings scene, it will take us back to the main menu scene, which is what we want. We're basically instantiating and deleting the settings scene as needed rather than having it constantly exist somewhere in the project. This keeps our scenes clean and independent of each other.

Save the scene and test out the **Settings** screen. It should look something like *Figure 6.60* unless you used the Kenney UI icon instead of the **Theme** resource for the **CloseButton** node:

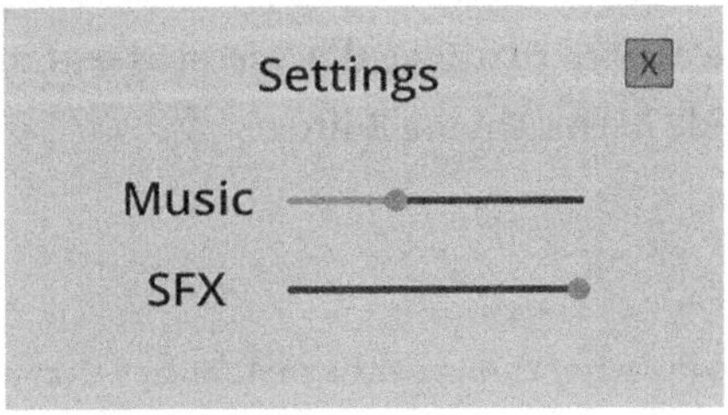

Figure 6.60: Our Settings screen after setting up the nodes and theming

You should also be able to move the slides, but right now, they don't do anything. Don't worry – we'll get to that in the next chapter.

Summary

This chapter was all about the user experience and creating a well-designed UI to make the experience a good one.

We successfully added a UI for our game to allow our player to start and exit the game. The first component we built was the main menu, which allowed us to navigate to various other UI screens, such as the settings and the credits. Within the **Settings** menu, we included a volume slider. Through all this, we discussed control nodes and how they function in Godot.

With the addition of a UI, we can now turn our attention to more specific areas within Godot, such as audio, pathfinding, lighting, and more.

7

Adding Sound Effects and Music

So far, we have a player, a world, and the beginning of a UI for our users to interact with. Now, we're going to make our game come alive with audio.

Both music and sound effects play a crucial role in games. Music can set the tone of an environment, let you know when you're in danger, or shift the narrative in a specific direction. Sound effects can have a similar result – adding footsteps when your player moves, providing button feedback when you hover or click on a piece of UI, or adding sounds when your player moves through the world (e.g., climbing through a window, scaring birds, or hearing a gunshot). The immersion that audio adds is a big one, and it's not an area to be overlooked.

In this chapter, we'll be covering audio, specifically adding music and sound effects to our game. We'll be exploring the specific nodes Godot has for audio, as well as understanding the audio bus system in Godot. After that, we'll dive right into adding sound effects to our main menu. Then, we'll add music to our world, and through code, we'll trigger each track to play depending on the input of our player. Finally, we'll take our audio knowledge and apply it to creating volume sliders in the settings menu we created in the previous chapter.

So, in this chapter, we will cover the following topics:

- Understanding Godot's audio nodes
- Working with audio buses
- Adding sound effects to the UI

- Adding music to our scenes
- Making our settings page functional

Technical requirements

For this chapter, the technical requirements will be the same as in *Chapter 1*.

All the code from this chapter will be available in the GitHub repository here: `https://github.com/PacktPublishing/Game-Development-with-Godot-and-C-`.

Understanding Godot's audio nodes

Godot's audio engine is a very easy one to pick up. More specifically, Godot 4 brought a lot of much-needed upgrades to the audio engine, such as polyphony support, an audio stream importer window, and a text-to-speech function. We'll get into more of these new features in later sections and chapters, but for now, let's discuss the audio nodes that Godot provides. You can see the audio nodes available in *Figure 7.1*:

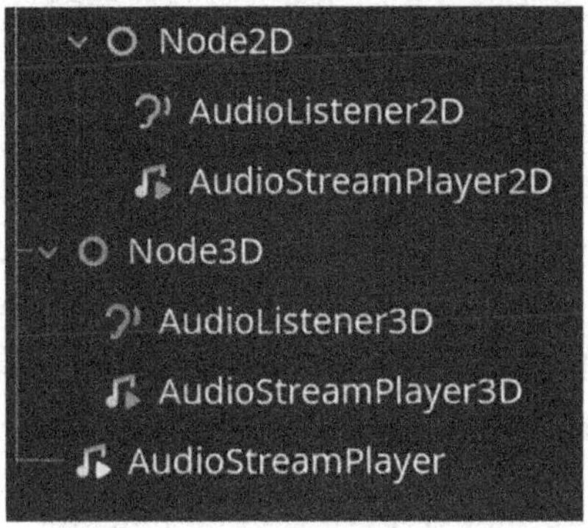

Figure 7.1: The available audio nodes in Godot

As you can see, we have positional audio nodes that are for either 2D or 3D audio:

- **AudioStreamPlayer2D**: This allows for audio to be attenuated with distance to the player. An example of this could be UI-based and depending on whether it's on the left or right side of the screen, it will determine whether the audio comes out of the left or the right speaker more. By default, it's heard from the screen center.

- **AudioStreamPlayer3D**: Much like the 2D version, this node also allows for audio to be attenuated with distance to the player except it's in a 3D space rather than a 2D one. For example, if you had a fountain in your town square, the sound of running water could be heard. The distance from the fountain would change when using one of the positional nodes.

Plus, there is a default **AudioStreamPlayer** when the location of sound does not matter, which is what we'll be using throughout the chapter.

Here, it is also worth noting the **AudioListener** nodes, which focus on where audio is heard in the game. These could be used when the player is having a dream sequence or a telepathic conversation, or maybe when another character is whispering in one ear – in that case, you could shift where the sound is coming from. You can do this using the 2D and 3D AudioListeners:

- **AudioListener2D**: When there is no AudioListener2D node, the default listener is set to the center of the screen. Beyond the four corners of the screen or the sides of the screen, there is nowhere else for the AudioListener2D to be positioned.
- **AudioListener3D**: When there is no AudioListener3D node, the default is from the Camera3D node. A 3D listener can be placed anywhere in the level, allowing objects to listen and trigger based on sound.

> Note
>
> In Godot, much like **Camera**, there can only ever be one active **AudioListener**.

That's it as far as audio nodes go. Of course, within each of these nodes, there are a lot of properties and options that we will be navigating throughout the chapter as we add sound effects and music to different components of our game. We will only be using the AudioStreamPlayer nodes, but it's good to have an overview of how the other audio nodes in Godot behave.

Next, we'll be looking at the audio bus in Godot and how to set it up to better control the volume of both sound effects and music.

Working with audio buses

An **audio bus** is a type of audio track that provides a single entry point for multiple audio tracks. You can find the audio bus in Godot by clicking **Audio** on the bottom of the **Output** panel (this is in the exact same space that we found the theme editor in the previous chapter).

Once selected, a new panel will appear that looks like *Figure 7.2*. This will have the default audio bus layout for Godot.

Figure 7.2: The audio bus layout panel in Godot

We can use the bus to adjust the volume and apply various effects to audio tracks as they come through the bus. For example, we will have a bus for sound effects, which means channeling their audio to that bus if they are tagged as a sound effect. What this means is every time a button is clicked, or a collectible item is picked up, the audio track of each of those actions will be set to play through the sound effect bus.

The Master audio bus

Even though we'll have multiple audio tracks, all of them will funnel into our sound effect audio bus. The sound effect bus will then funnel into the **Master** bus. Any audio bus we create will still be channeled through the **Master** audio bus. You can see this in *Figure 7.2* with a close-up of it in *Figure 7.3*:

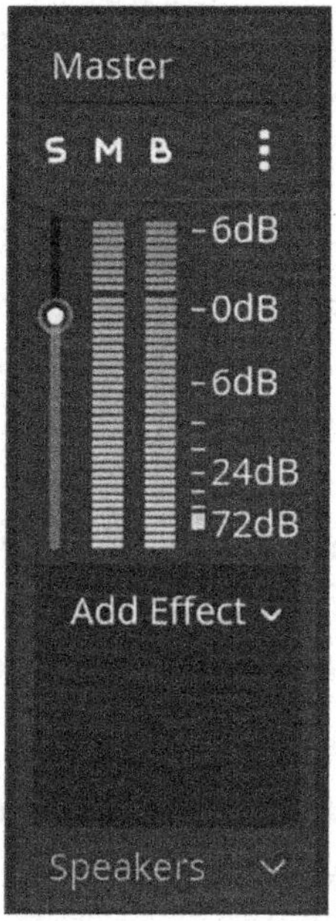

Figure 7.3: The Master bus in the default layout bus in Godot

Each bus is broken up in the following ways:

- **Bus name**: Here, the audio bus's name is **Master.**
- **Solo, mute, and bypass**: The letters **S**, **M**, and **B** underneath the bus name are audio effects that can be set for the bus. *Solo* means only the bus in solo mode will play, *mute* will silence the bus, and *bypass* will set the bus to bypass any audio effects.
- **Volume unit (VU) meter**: This tracks the volume of the specific audio bus. At its default, it's set to `0`, but it can be adjusted to set a default volume for all audio that's channeled through it.
- **Listed audio effects**: This small container in the audio bus has a dropdown called **Add Effect**. When clicked, you can add audio effects that are built into Godot. For a full list of effects and what they do, see the documentation: `https://docs.godotengine.org/en/stable/tutorials/audio/audio_effects.html#doc-audio-effects`.
- **Audio bus output**: The last dropdown (currently **Speakers** is selected in *Figure 7.3*) is where the bus will be routed to. In the **Master** bus, this is grayed out as it cannot be routed to any other buses, but when we add additional buses, we can select which bus they feed to.

Understanding the properties of an audio bus is important for the role they play on the audio bus. Looking back at *Figure 7.2*, notice the buttons in the top-right corner. Here, we can load the default bus layout (what you see now), save our current bus layout, and create a new layout. The audio bus layout is a resource that holds the **Master** audio bus and any additional audio buses we create.

From the buttons in the top-right corner, we can also add new audio (i.e., a new channel for audio to go through). We will do this now.

Adding audio buses

You can think of audio buses like lanes on a highway. Both the sound effects and **Music** audio buses that we're about to create represent their own lane – they're both going in the same direction (into the **Master** audio bus) but different cars (audio tracks) drive in separate lanes.

Now, we're going to add two buses, one for sound effects and one for music. Go ahead and select **Add Bus**. A new audio bus will automatically appear next to the currently listed ones. Let's change the new bus's name to `Music`, as I have in *Figure 7.4*:

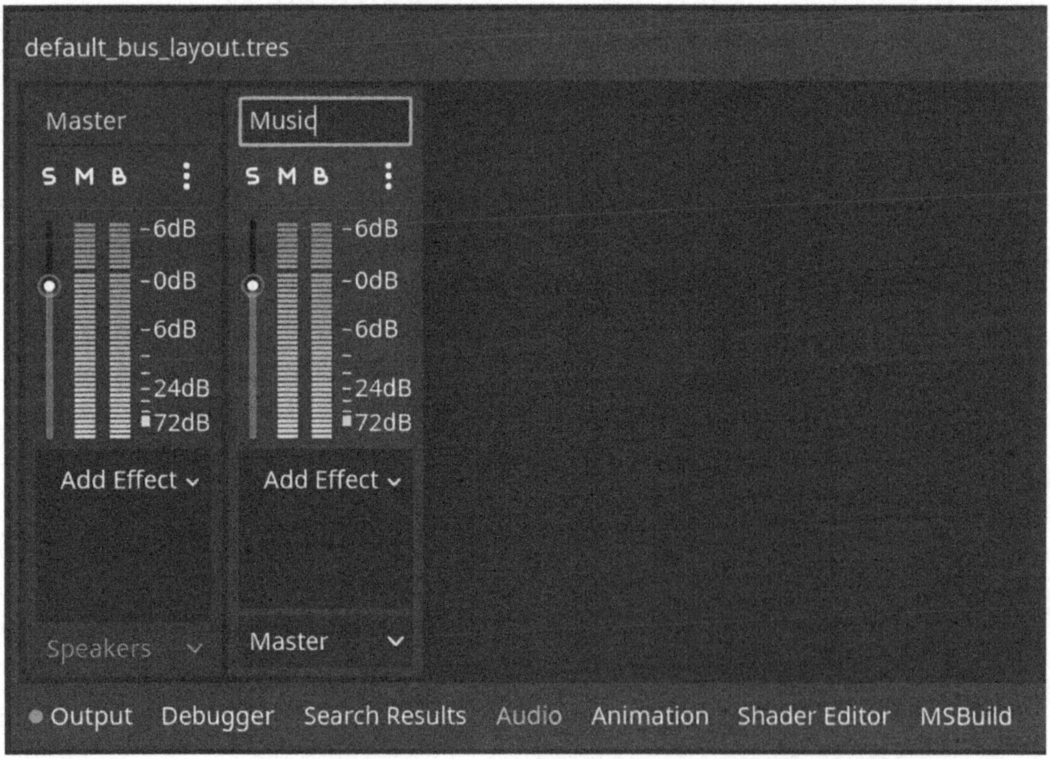

Figure 7.4: Adding a new bus and changing its name to Music

By now, we have two audio buses set up. We have the **Master** audio bus, which is there by default, and we have the newly added **Music** audio bus. Now, we'll repeat the steps we took but name the third audio bus `SFX` (for sound effects). That's it!

Implementing audio effects

There's one more important piece of information about audio buses that we'll cover before adding our first audio track. If we continue to look at the **Audio** panel, we can see that below the volume settings for each audio bus, there's a drop-down option to add an audio effect, as shown in *Figure 7.5*:

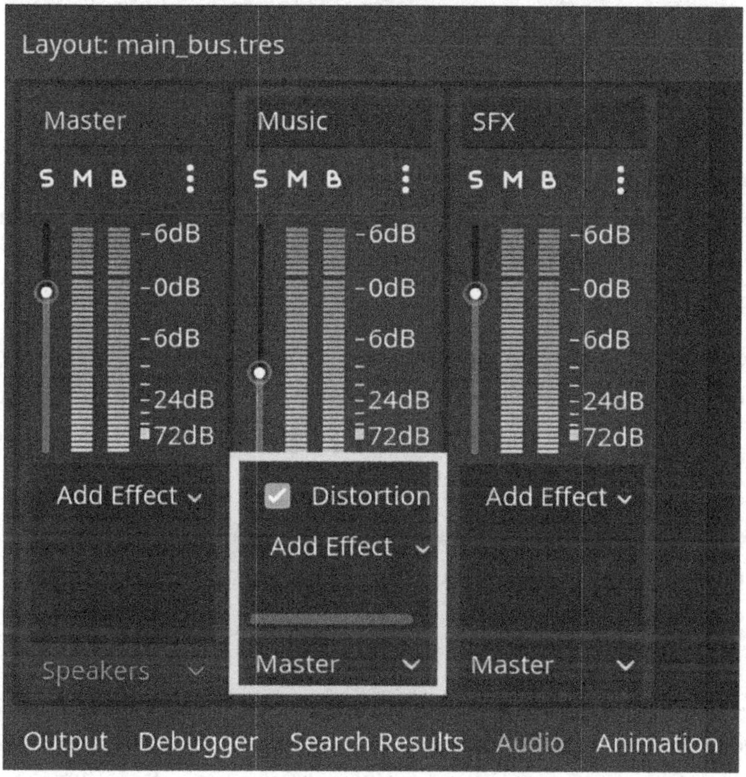

Figure 7.5: Adding an audio effect to a specific bus

Clicking into the dropdown gives a long list of audio effects, such as distortion, amplification, and reverberation, that we can add to the **Music** audio bus. In *Figure 7.5*, I've added the **Distortion** effect. Once added, the audio effect will be selected under the audio bus it was added to.

Clicking the word **Distortion** provides us with a set of properties we can change in the **Inspector** dock, as shown in *Figure 7.6*.

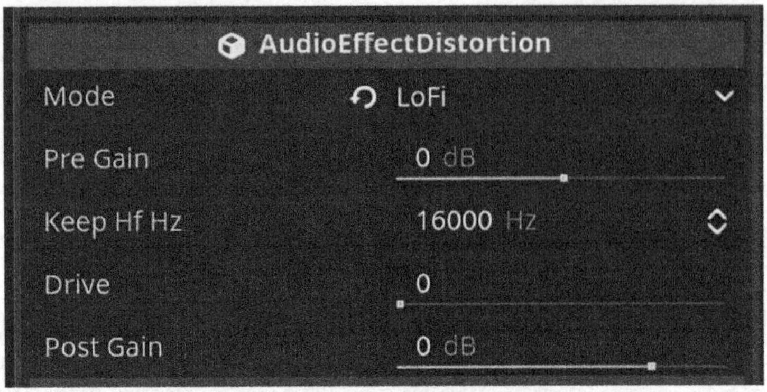

Figure 7.6: The properties of the Distortion audio effect

Each effect has its own set of properties. Here, **Distortion** has one called **Mode**, as shown in *Figure 7.6*. The **Mode** property gives you the option of the type of distortion you want. For example, I've selected the **LoFi** option. The other properties listed relate to how the volume is manipulated before, during, and after the effect is active.

Once the effect is added, you can toggle it on and off and hear the difference when we test our game. This will be once our audio tracks are added, which come later in this chapter. For a detailed view of the audio effects available, you can look here: `https://docs.godotengine.org/en/stable/tutorials/audio/audio_effects.html`.

Now that we know how to create audio buses and add audio effects to them, let's look at how we can add specific audio tracks to our scenes.

Adding sound effects to the UI

Adding sound effects to the UI we designed is going to make interacting with our game feel more alive. What we're going to do is add an audio file to our main menu and then trigger audio to play when we click any of our main menu buttons (**Play**, **Settings**, **Credit**, and **Quit**).

Setting up the AudioStreamPlayer node

Start by opening the `MainMenu.tscn` scene and adding a new node by clicking the + sign in the **Scene** dock – we'll add an **AudioStreamPlayer** node (since the audio from this node will be on the main menu scene, the position of it does not matter, which is why we're not using AudioStreamPlayer2D or AudioStreamPlayer3D). Rename this node in the scene to `MainMenuTransition`.

Now, we need to either create or find sound effects to add to the game. You can use the sound effects provided in the GitHub repository of this book (`MainMenuTransition.wav`), or you can create your own. I created mine by using ChipTone, a free browser tool that's available on `itch.io` (`https://sfbgames.itch.io/chiptone`).

> Note
>
> If you are finding or creating your own sound effects, make sure that the audio file is either a `.wav`, `.ogg`, or `.mp3` file, as those are the only three formats that Godot accepts. There are advantages and disadvantages to using each format. You can read more about that here: `https://docs.godotengine.org/en/stable/tutorials/assets_pipeline/importing_audio_samples.html`.

Once you have an audio file, click and drag it into our FileSystem dock within Godot. I've added mine to the `user_interface` folder as it will be used in the MainMenu scene. Once imported, go rename it to `MainMenuTransition`, as I have done in *Figure 7.7*:

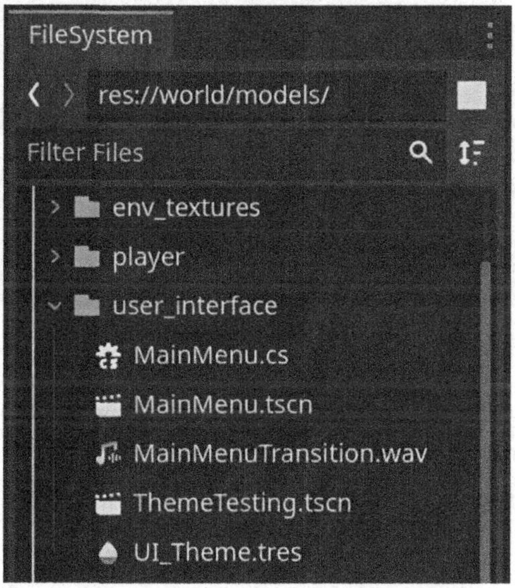

Figure 7.7: Importing audio tracks into Godot

With our audio node created and our audio file imported, select the **MainMenuTransition** node in our scene dock to see its properties in the **Inspector** doc. They are also shown in *Figure 7.8*:

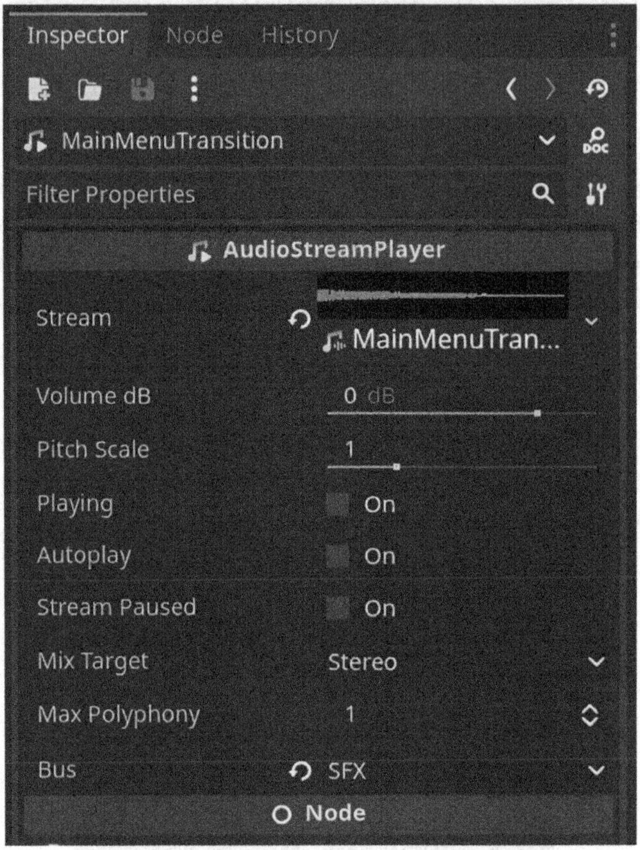

Figure 7.8: The AudioStreamPlayer node properties

As we step through each property on this node, please note we will only be changing the **Stream** and **Bus** properties. All others will remain at their default levels. However, it's still important to understand how each property impacts the node and project overall, so we will be reviewing each of them here:

- **Stream**: This is where we will load our audio track. You can browse for the audio file by clicking the drop-down arrow and selecting **Load**, or you can click and drag your audio file to the **Stream** property. Either way, load the selected SFX audio file into the **Stream** property.

- **Volume dB**: This is the volume of the chosen track. It can override what the default bus value is.
- **Pitch Scale**: This uses the audio file's sample rate as a multiplier to determine the pitch and tempo of the audio file.
- **Playing**: When this property is checked, then the audio file is playing.
- **Autoplay**: When this property is checked, the audio file will play as soon as it's loaded onto the scene.
- **Stream Paused**: This property will pause the audio file when set to true. Set it to false to continue playing.
- **Mix Target**: This property determines the channels the audio will be played through. It's useful to adjust when players have a surround-sound center or are using headphones versus speakers.
- **Max Polyphony**: This property allows multiple sounds to be played at the same time. Once the maximum number of polyphony sounds is passed, the older sounds will cut off.
- **Bus**: This property has access to the list of audio buses we created in **AudioBusLayout**. Set this property to **SFX**.

To reiterate, we are only changing the **Stream** and **Bus** properties here. Now, if we hit the play button to run our game, we still would have no audio. This is because we haven't written any code to tell this audio track to play. To fix this, let's dive into our `MainMenu.cs` file.

Coding our sound effects

To code our sound effects, first, we'll get a reference to our audio node by adding this variable to the top of our `MainMenu.cs` script:

```
private AudioStreamPlayer audioPlayer;
```

Next, in our `_Ready()` function, we'll assign the new variable to a reference of our audio node:

```
audioPlayer = GetNode<AudioStreamPlayer>("MainMenuTransition");
```

Be sure that the text in quotes is set to `MainMenuTransition` here because it needs to match the name of the node in your scene dock.

In *Chapter 6*, we created a signal called `OnPlayClicked()` in `MainMenu.cs` that would hide our main menu and change the player view. Within that function, we're going to add this line of code right before our `this.Visible = false` line:

```
audioPlayer.Play();
```

This line accesses the `Play` function within the `AudioStreamPlayer` class in Godot and will start the audio track that's loaded into the node's **Stream** property.

Now save the script and run your game. When you click play, notice something happens here – the UI animation for the main menu that we added in the previous chapter doesn't play. However, the audio plays, and the main menu disappears like it's supposed to.

What's happening here is that as soon as we call `Play` on our animation, we also immediately call `Play` on the audio, and then force the main menu to be hidden. The animation needs to finish before we call `this.Visible = false`, otherwise, it gets skipped.

To force our program to wait until the animation is done, we're going to utilize some features of C# and the .NET library. Within any programming language, there is something called **keywords** – these are reserved words that can't be variables or function names as they have a specific function within the language. As C# has expanded and been further built open, more keywords have been added. These are called **contextual keywords** because they are additional keywords that were not part of the original set of keywords when C# was created. The ones we'll be using are the `async` and `await` ones. This will bring asynchronous programming into our project.

> Note
>
> If you are unfamiliar with what asynchronous programming is, you can read more about it here: `https://learn.microsoft.com/en-us/dotnet/csharp/asynchronous-programming/`.

Alongside the two new keywords mentioned, we'll be utilizing the `System.Threading.Tasks` library for access to the `Task` functions (again, these are all part of.NET Framework). Tasks allow for asynchronous programming in C# through the usage of the `async` and `await` keywords. To add this library, go to the top of our `MainMenu.cs` file and add the following code under the `using System;` line:

```
using System.Threading.Tasks;
```

Next, create our asynchronous method and call it `HideMenu()`:

```
public async void HideMenu() { }
```

This means that when this function is called, like when our play button is clicked, it will run everything inside the function until it hits the word `await`. Once there, it will suspend execution until whatever is after `await` is completed.

Inside this function, we want to create a `Task` that will wait until the animation is over. Essentially, we're using `Task` to create a time delay and using the `async` method to wait until *X* amount of time has passed before executing the rest of `UI` logic/changes in our main menu transition. To do this, write the following line:

```
await Task.Delay(TimeSpan.FromSeconds(1));
```

Again, when `await` is read within an `async` method, it will not move on to the next line of code until the code to the right of the `await` word has finished executing. More specifically, the `Task` we created calls a `Delay` method from its library of functions. Within our call on `Delay`, we'll use the `TimeSpan` object and access its method called `FromSeconds`. We pass in the number `1` to the `FromSeconds` method, which takes `double` – this is a type of data structure for numbers in programming, specifically floating-point numbers, such as `3.33` or `5.99`. We could put any number we wanted in here, but we are specifically choosing `1`. We do this because we know the main menu animation is no longer than one second. Therefore, the animation is guaranteed to be completed before executing the rest of the `async` method.

Now, we'll move the `this.Visible = false` line underneath our `await` line, so it should be completely removed from the `OnPlayClicked()` function. Instead, we'll add a call to our `async` function by typing `HideMenu()` after playing both our animation and audio players. The two functions should look like this:

```
public void OnPlayClicked()
{
    GD.Print("Play button clicked");
    animPlayer.Play("MenuTransition");
    audioPlayer.Play();
    HideMenu();
}

public async void HideMenu()
{
    await Task.Delay(TimeSpan.FromSeconds(1));
    this.Visible = false;
}
```

> Note
>
> Alternatively, we don't have to use `Task`. I wanted to use them here to highlight how to utilize C# vast set of libraries. Yet, we can leverage Godot's signals system by creating a signal timer in code and writing: `await ToSignal(GetTree().CreateTimer(1f), SceneTreeTimer.SignalName.Timeout);`.

Regardless of the method, let's test the game again and see what happens. Once we click play, the menu should slide to the bottom of the screen all while playing its sound effect. Then, our camera should change to our player, and we should be able to play.

Now that we have sound effects triggering when the player interacts with the main menu, let's turn our attention toward adding music to our world.

Adding music to our scenes

Music can help bring a game environment to life and set the tone as a player navigates that space. Here, we're going to spend some time adding and triggering music to play in our world after leaving our main menu.

First, find a suitable song for your game. There are many sites out there that provide free tracks such as Kevin MacLeod's website (`https://incompetech.com/`). Just remember to thoroughly review the license, make sure you credit the work properly, and that it is a Godot-compatible format. Or, if you are a composer, you can create one yourself!

I'm going to be using `Midnight Tale.wav` by Kevin MacLeod (which you can find in the GitHub repository; see the *Technical requirements* section). This track sounds very much like you're in a tavern or wandering through some woods. Whether you are using the same track or a different one, download and import it by dragging the file into the **FileSystem** dock. I've placed mine in the `World` folder, as shown in *Figure 7.9*:

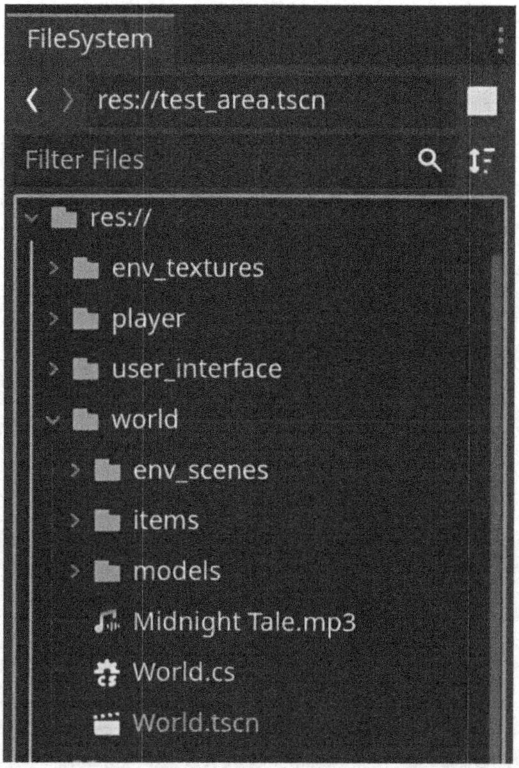

Figure 7.9: The FileSystem dock after importing a music track

Note

If the license for the music requires attribution, create a **Credits** button in your `MainMenu.tscn` scene and link it to a newly created **Credits** page, where you provide the attribution information.

Once done, close the `MainMenu.tscn` scene and open our `World.tscn` scene. Click the + icon on the scene dock, add another **AudioStreamPlayer** node, and rename it to `WorldMusic`. Even though we are working in a 3D space, we want the music to be heard throughout the scene and regardless of position, so we won't be using the 2D or 3D positional audio nodes.

Select the **WorldMusic** node and drag the audio file into the **Stream** property just as we did for the sound effect. Then, be sure to set the **Bus** property to **Music**. The properties for the **WorldMusic** node should look like those in *Figure 7.10*:

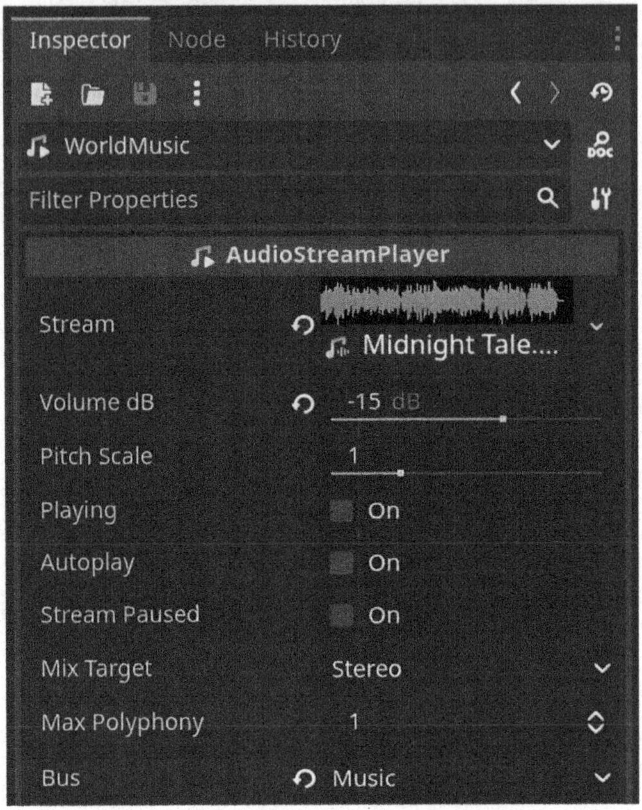

Figure 7.10: The WorldMusic node properties

Now, let's test the scene out, making sure we did not break anything by adding these new components. As expected, the game runs normally but does not play our new music. Let's open our `World.cs` file and create the variables and functions needed to run our music.

Under the class definition, let's add a new variable of the type `AudioStreamPlayer` for the audio node within the `World.tscn` scene, like so:

```
private AudioStreamPlayer worldMusic;
```

Then, at the bottom of the class, create a new function called `TriggerWorldMusic()`:

```
public void TriggerWorldMusic() { }
```

Within this function, add the call within the **AudioStreamPlayer** node's class to play the music by writing the following:

```
worldMusic.Play();
```

In *Chapter 6*, we nested our main menu scene into the `World.tscn` scene with its own camera, setting it up so that when we clicked play, the camera changed, and our player could move. Now, we could set these triggers up in the `_Process` function of our world, and although it works, it's not the best solution we can implement. So, we're going to go ahead and migrate some of the code to the new function we created and improve upon the work we did in *Chapter 6*.

The following lines of code should be moved to the `TriggerWorldMusic()` function after the `worldMusic.Play();` line:

```
menuCamera.Current = false;
player.ProcessMode = ProcessModeEnum.Always;
Input.MouseMode = Input.MouseModeEnum.Captured;
```

The `if` statement that these lines were in can be deleted, so now, our `_Process` function should be empty.

Now, the `World.cs` scene will have only two functions, `_Ready()` and `TriggerWorldMusic()`, alongside the variables that have been declared at the top. The `_Ready()` function should look like this:

```
public override void _Ready()
{
    menuCamera = GetNode<Camera3D>("MenuCamera");
    player = GetNode<CharacterBody3D>("Player");
    worldMusic = GetNode<AudioStreamPlayer>("WorldMusic");

    if (menuCamera.Current)
    {
        Input.MouseMode = Input.MouseModeEnum.Visible;
        player.ProcessMode = ProcessModeEnum.Disabled;
    }
}
```

The `TriggerWorldMusic()` function should look like this:

```
public void TriggerWorldMusic()
{
    worldMusic.Play();
    menuCamera.Current = false;
    player.ProcessMode = ProcessModeEnum.Always;
    Input.MouseMode = Input.MouseModeEnum.Captured;
}
```

The last thing to do to get our music playing is to call the new function. We want to call it in the `HideMenu()` function in our `MainMenu.cs` file because we want the music to play after the menu is hidden. Godot has a convenient function to do this called `GetOwner`, which allows us to get any valid parent from the node we're calling from.

Since `MainMenu.tscn` is nested in our `World.tscn` scene, the root of the scene is our **World** node. The `World` node has the `World.cs` script attached to it. We'll create a local `World` variable to access the node and its properties by typing this in our `HideMenu()` function after the `this.Visible = false;` line.

```
World root = GetOwner<World>();
```

Here, we've created a `World` variable called `root` and set it equal to what `GetOwner` is returning. The type we have `GetOwner` retrieve is of `World`, just like our variable.

Now, we can call any functions that are part of `World`, using `root` like this:

```
root.TriggerWorldMusic();
```

To ensure this only runs once, let's put a `print` statement to the Godot console by typing the following inside the `TriggerWorldMusic()` function:

```
GD.Print("About to start music.");
```

Typing `GD` is one way to access Godot's global functions, and `print` is one such function. This will print whatever you put in parenthesis out to the Godot console. We can pass either messages such as "Hello world!" or other useful things such as logging game states or tracking variables.

> Note
>
> You can read more about Godot's global functions here: `https://docs.godotengine.org/en/latest/tutorials/scripting/c_sharp/c_sharp_differences.html`.

Finally, save both our `MainMenu.cs` and `World.cs` files and test the game. When we hit play and are dropped into our world, music should begin playing. We should also see a print statement in Godot's output console like in *Figure 7.11*:

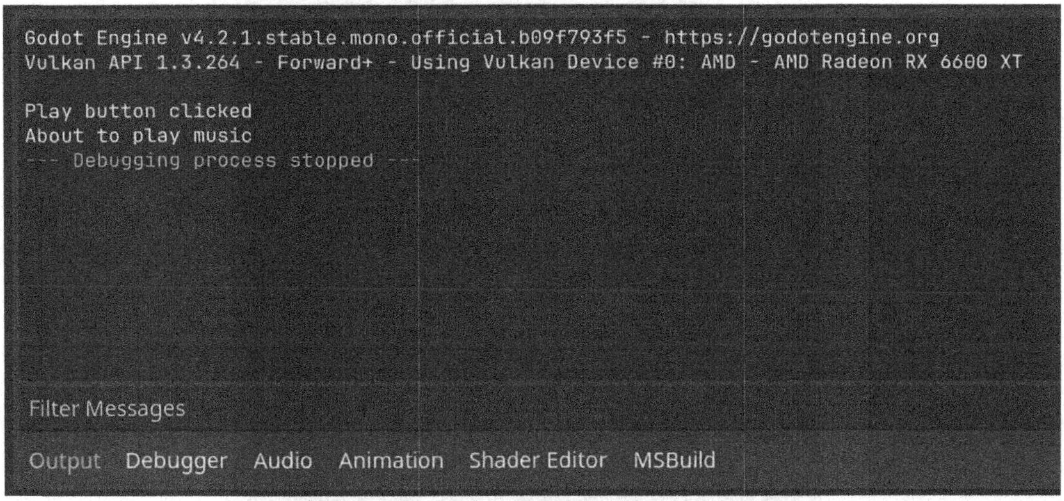

Figure 7.11: The Godot Output console after clicking the play button or hitting F5.

With both sound effects and music being added to our game, let's look at how to combine everything we've covered so far in this chapter by adding volume sliders to our settings page.

Making our settings page functional

In *Chapter 6*, we designed and laid out how the settings page looks. Now, it's time to make the volume sliders functional. We'll create signals to trigger the sliders to update as we change their value.

Tying Music to our MusicSlider

Open our `Settings.tscn` scene, select the node named **MusicSlider**, and look at the **Inspector** dock. As seen in *Figure 7.12*, there are lots of properties, however, we will just be adjusting four:

- **Tick Count**: This property determines the number of ticks shown on the slider that the slider can move through. This is a visual property only. We will set this to `1`.
- **Max Value**: As the name describes, this is the max value the slider can be set to. We'll also set this to `1`.
- **Step**: This property determines the value changes each time the slider is moved. We'll set this to `0.05`.

- **Value**: This property sets the starting value of the slider. We'll set this to 1 because we want the music to be set to max volume by default.

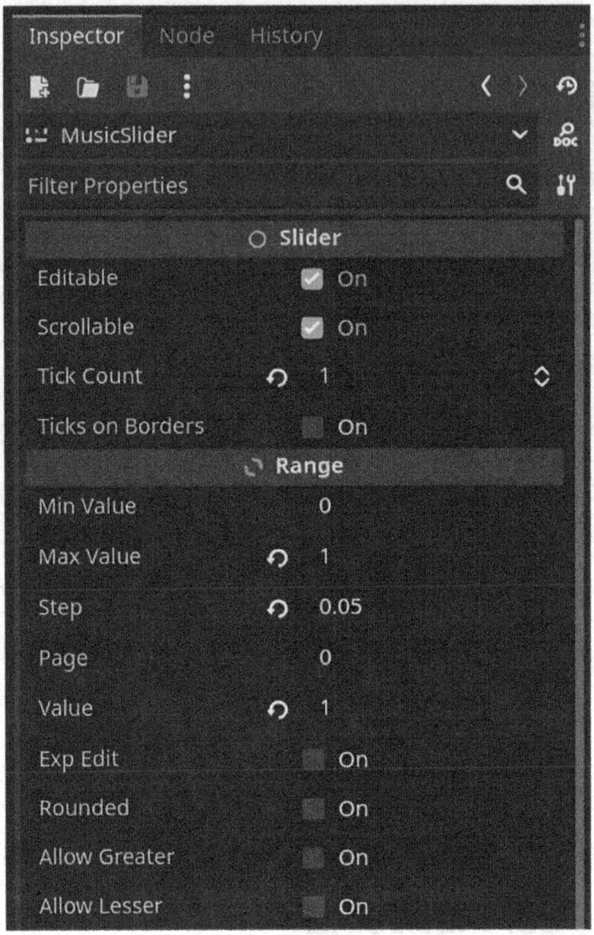

Figure 7.12: The MusicSlider node properties set correctly

Now, save the scene and run the game. Select the **Settings** button and test **MusicSlider** out by dragging the slider handle from left to right.

Now, we want to mimic what we did for the **MusicSlider** with the **SFXSlider**. The only difference here will be the audio bus that we connect the slider to, which will be the SFX bus. We can connect the SFX music bus to the Music SFX slider (**MusicSlider**) in our **Settings** scene. Select **SFXSlider** in the scene dock and consider its properties in the **Inspector** dock. We are going to take a moment to match the properties of both the Music and SFX sliders since they function at a UI level in the same way.

We're going to set the **Tick Count**, **Max Value**, **Step**, and **Value** properties to the same values that we did for **MusicSlider**. This is because we want the way our player interacts with both sliders to be the same.

With the properties of each slider set, go back to **MusicSlider** and connect the Godot signal to a function in our `Settings.cs` script. This is how we'll tell Godot when to fire the music. To get started, we'll keep the **MusicSlider** node selected in the scene dock. From there, click the **Node** tab at the top of the **Inspector** dock to access our list of signals. Once again, we're going to utilize the `value_changed(value: float)` signal. Double-click it and a popup menu will appear. We've seen this popup before but as a reminder, it will look like *Figure 7.13*:

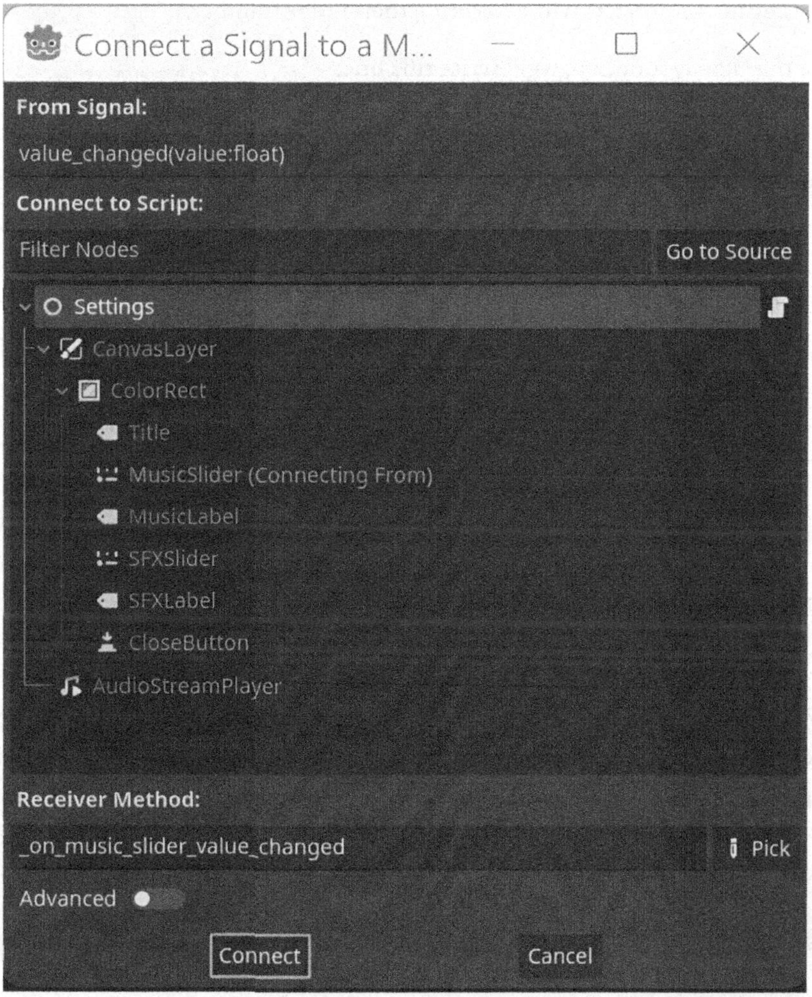

Figure 7.13: Popup menu for connecting a signal to our script

Notice that, in the **Receiver Method** box, it says `_on_music_slider_value_changed`. We're going to change that to `ChangeMusicVolume` and click **Connect**.

Now, if we open our `Settings.cs` file, we'll add the variables and functions we need. To access the audio bus for music, we need to declare a variable. Above our `_Ready` function, add the following line:

```
private int musicBus;
```

Each audio bus not only has a string (aka name) to identify it, but we also have a number. As we add audio buses, the order in which they're placed in the **AudioBusLayout** resource (`main_bus.tres` in our project) will determine their index number.

Now, inside the `_Ready` function, we'll write this line:

```
musicBus = AudioServer.GetBusIndex("Music");
```

This line uses the `GetBusIndex` function from the `AudioServer` class to find the right index based on the name we set in the `main_bus.tres` resource. Recall in *Figure 7.4* how we renamed the audio buses `Music` and `SFX`, respectively. To confirm the variable is set correctly, we can add a line after this one that prints out the value of `musicBus`, like so:

```
GD.Print(musicBus);
```

Now, when we run our program, when we navigate to the **Settings** screen, we should get a printout of `1` for the `musicBus` variable.

With our variable set, we can move on to adding the function we need to adjust the volume of the music bus. Inside our `Settings.cs` file, right after the `OnSettingsClose` function, we'll declare a new function with the following line:

```
private void ChangeMusicVolume(float value) { }
```

The `ChangeMusicVolume` function, much like the signal, takes in a `double`. What will happen is when **MusicSlider** changes its value (i.e., the player moves the slider), then the `value_changed(value: float)` signal will fire, passing the float variable to our `ChangeMusicVolume` function. With this float variable, we'll use it to change the volume on the audio bus. Therefore, our next line inside the function looks like this:

```
AudioServer.SetBusVolumeDb(musicBus, Mathf.LinearToDb(value));
```

Here, we access a function in the `AudioServer` class of Godot called `SetBusVolumeDb`, which takes two parameters:

- The first parameter is the audio bus that we're adjusting the volume for via its index number, which we set in the `_Ready` function. For **MusicSlider**, we're naturally adjusting the music bus.
- The second parameter that `SetBusVolumeDb` takes is the value the volume level should be for the chosen audio bus. Notice that the float variable we talked about earlier is being converted by a `Mathf` library function. The variable is converted from a linear number to one in decibels. This allows the slider values to make sense in decibels.

> Note
>
> `Mathf` is a C# library that's available in any C# script with a set of built-in mathematical operations.

Now, save the scene, and let's test it out. To test it, we need to do a little bit of work. First, we need to import an audio file and set it up in our **MainMenu** scene. Go ahead and find a piece of music that you've either created or have the rights to use in your project. Then, drag the file into the **FileSystem** dock to import it into the project, ensuring it's placed in the correct folder. I've placed mine in the `user_interface` folder for now.

Next, open the `MainMenu.tscn` scene and click the + sign at the top of the scene dock. Add an **AudioStreamPlayer** node to the scene and rename it `MainMenuMusic`. It should sit right under the **MainMenuTransition** node.

With the **MainMenuMusic** node selected, look at the **Inspector** dock where our list of node properties appears. In the **Stream** property, click the down arrow and select the **Load** option, as shown in *Figure 7.14*:

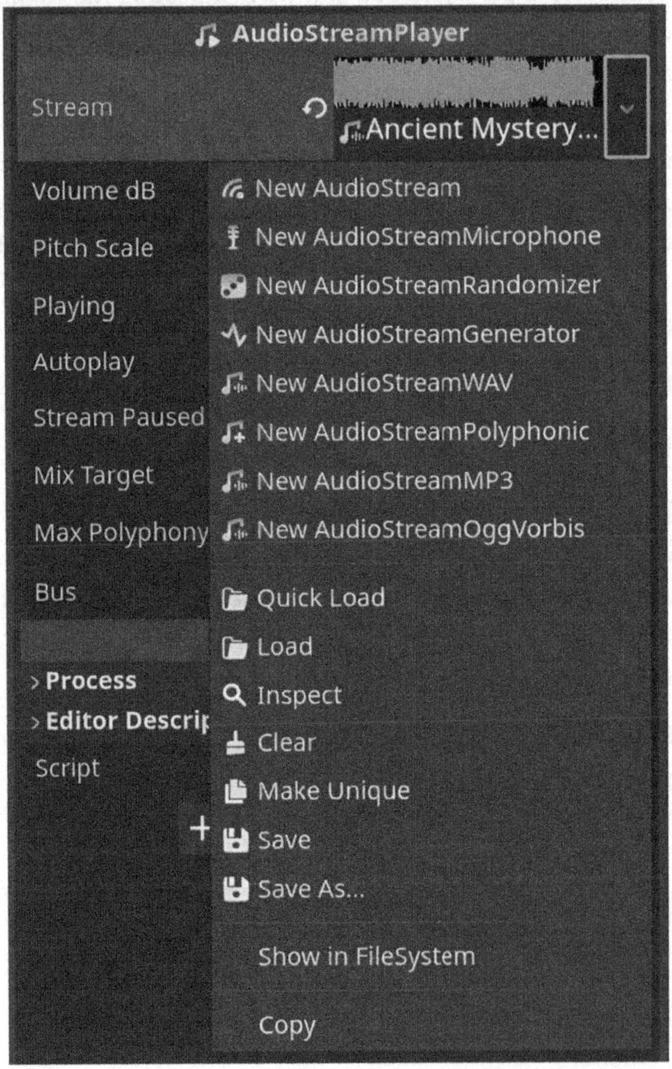

Figure 7.14: Adding an audio file to an AudioStreamPlayer node

Once **Load** is selected, browse to your audio file and select it. Enable the **Autoplay** checkbox and, most importantly, set the **Bus** property to **Music**. Save the scene. Now, you should be able to test **MusicSlider** by navigating to the **Settings** screen and adjusting **MusicSlider**. It should update as the slider moves without any other input.

Nice! Now, we'll just need to repeat almost all these steps for **SFXSlider**.

Tying sound effects to SFXSlider

First, connect a signal to our slider so that it fires when we adjust the slider. Open the `Settings.tscn` scene and select the **SFXSlider** node. Click the **Node** tab next to the top of the **Inspector** dock. Then, double-click the `value_changed(value: float)` signal. A popup menu will appear just like in *Figure 7.13*. Change the name of the **Receiver Method** box to `ChangeSFXVolume` and click **Connect**.

Save the scene and open the `Settings.cs` file. We'll declare a variable above the `_Ready` function for our SFX bus like this:

```
private int sfxBus;
```

Then, within the `_Ready` function, we'll set our `sfxBus` variable to the correct bus by writing the following:

```
sfxBus = AudioServer.GetBusIndex("SFX");
```

Next, we'll create a new function after `ChangeMusicVolume` and write the following function declaration:

```
private void ChangeSFXVolume(float value) { }
```

Within our function, we'll set the volume in decibels to the correct audio bus by writing the following:

```
AudioServer.SetBusVolumeDb(sfxBus, Mathf.LinearToDb(value));
```

Save the script and navigate to our `MainMenu.tscn` scene. Make sure the **MainMenuTransition** node is set to the correct audio bus. Select it and look at its properties in the **Inspector** dock. The **Bus** property should be set to **SFX**.

With that confirmed, go ahead and test **SFXSlider**. To test it, launch the game, navigate to the **Settings** page, and drag **SFXSlider** all the way to the left-hand side, which should mute any SFX that plays. Confirm this by exiting the **Settings** page and clicking the play button. With **SFXSlider** set to `0`, you should not hear the **MainMenuTransition** node after clicking the play button.

Summary

This chapter was all about adding audio to our game. We looked at what audio buses were and how to create them. We created an audio bus layout resource to hold our different audio buses. Then, we looked at how to fire off sound effects at the end of the main menu animation we created in *Chapter 6*. While adding our sound effects, we spent time looking at how to utilize `Task` from a C# library to make sure our sound effects fired in time with our animation. We also added functionality to the volume sliders we created in *Chapter 6* for both our music and sound effect audio buses, then we added logic to make those sliders functional.

In the next chapter, we're going to break down how navigation and pathfinding works. Specifically, we'll create a navigation mesh and add a series of markers to create a wandering **non-player character** (**NPC**) in our game. This will give our NPC a specific route where each point of the route will be chosen at random.

8

Adding Navigation and Pathfinding

Currently, we have a small, cozy game where we can collect mushrooms and run around our world. We also have a UI to navigate through the different menus, and in the previous chapter, we added audio to boost the ambiance of our game.

Now, we're going to look at filling our game with **non-playable characters (NPCs)** and utilizing the navigation nodes within Godot to make those NPCs wander about our forest land. Pathfinding and general navigation can be a huge component of your game, depending on the setting. If you're looking to populate a town with people and make it feel alive, then wandering NPCs could be extremely valuable. You could be creating a multiplayer game that uses escort missions. Then, the escort would need to know the path to get there.

In this chapter, we'll learn about the nodes Godot provides to create pathfinding, and then we'll use some of those nodes to create wandering NPCs in our world. To do that, we'll create a navigation mesh and see how to program a pre-determined path for an object. After understanding Godot's navigation nodes, we'll program our NPC to move from point to point, chosen randomly. When an NPC arrives at a point on the path, we'll create a timer to delay them moving to the next point to make our NPC feel more life-like and smoother.

Our goals for this chapter are the following:

- Understanding navigation nodes
- Creating a navigation mesh

- Creating an NPC
- Adding autonomous movement

Technical requirements

For this chapter, the technical requirements are the same as in *Chapter 1*.

All the code from this chapter is available in the GitHub repository here: `https://github.com/PacktPublishing/Game-Development-with-Godot-and-C-`.

Understanding navigation nodes

Much like the audio nodes we spent time learning about in the previous chapter, navigation nodes in Godot also feature a 2D and 3D set, as seen in *Figure 8.1*. The only difference between the 2D and 3D sets is whether they're used on a 2D or 3D plane. The usage and logic for both are relatively similar.

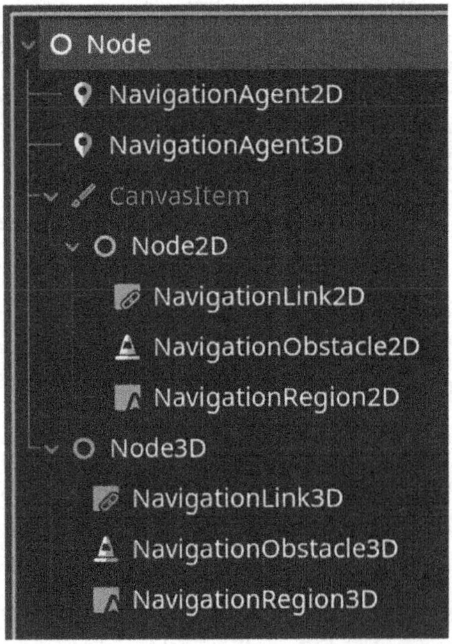

Figure 8.1: The navigation scene nodes available in Godot

Let's break down what some of these nodes do and briefly discuss how we'll utilize them (each of these nodes has many properties within them, but don't worry, we'll only be adjusting a few as needed):

- **NavigationMesh**: A navigation mesh is a resource for an area defined as navigable by navigation agents. While it is not a node in *Figure 8.1*, it is a critical resource that we will be interfacing with when using the navigation modes. So, if a navigation mesh, or NavMesh for short, doesn't cover a part of our level, then the NPC, our navigation agent, won't be able to traverse there.
- **NavigationAgent**: This node is used in conjunction with **NavigationRegion** and **NavigationMesh** to ensure a path is viable and to avoid obstacles. They are the actors that look for a viable path to navigate. For example, our NPC will be the navigation agent in this chapter.
- **NavigationLink**: This node connects two points on a navigation mesh.
- **NavigationObstacle**: This node allows the placement of obstacles to augment the path a navigation agent would take on a navigation mesh.
- **NavigationRegion**: This node will hold our navigation mesh resource, which will be a defined area for our NPC to traverse on.

A few objects that aren't listed as scene nodes but can be extremely useful are the **Astar3D** and **NavigationServer** objects – the **Astar3D** object will allow us to implement the A* pathfinding algorithm for our NPCs, and the **NavigationServer** object is a server API that finds the shortest path between two points of a navigation mesh. For a more detailed look at any of these nodes, you can check out the documentation here: `https://docs.godotengine.org/en/stable/tutorials/navigation/index.html`.

> Note
>
> From here on out, **navigation mesh** will be shortened to **NavMesh**, which is how it is often referred to.

With a better understanding of the nodes available to use, let's create our NavMesh for our navigation agent to move around on. Remember, the NavMesh defines the region that the navigation agent can move through.

Creating a navigation mesh

To create a NavMesh, open our `World.tscn` scene and click the + sign to add a new node. Search for **NavigationRegion3D**, then select it and add it to our scene tree. Once done, keep it highlighted in the **Scene** dock and look at its properties in the **Inspector** dock.

The first property listed will be **Navigation Mesh**, but currently, there is no NavMesh – the property should be empty. So, click on the word **<empty>** and select **New NavigationMesh**, as shown in *Figure 8.2*:

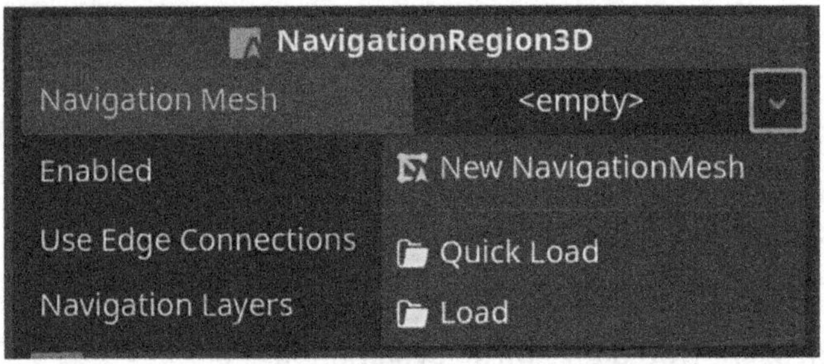

Figure 8.2: Creating a new NavigationMesh resource

Now, if we look at the Viewport, it doesn't look like anything has changed since creating the NavMesh. There are two reasons for this. They are the following:

- The first reason is how our scene is structured. Every object that will have a NavMesh on it for our NPC to traverse must be a child node of the **NavigationRegion3D** node.
- The second reason is that we need to bake the NavMesh for it to render viable pathing in our scene.

Let's step through and resolve each of these issues.

Within our **World** scene, we've structured the **Scene** dock in a way that's categorical. All the trees, ground, and terrain are parented under their own **Node3D** objects, as shown in *Figure 8.3*. This kept my **World** scene clean and now makes it extremely easy to apply my NavMesh to my world. Depending on how you designed your level, it could look different, but the objects I'm placing under my **NavigationRegion3D** can be seen in *Figure 8.3*. Make sure that whatever objects you want your NPC to both navigate on and avoid are included as a child of the **NavigationRegion3D** node.

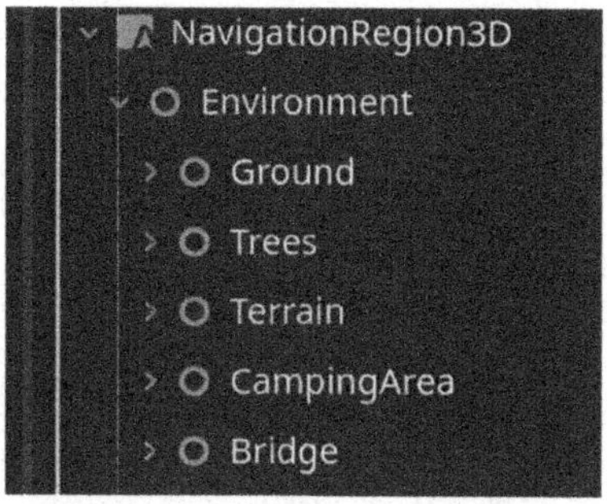

Figure 8.3: Every object in our level with a NavMesh

Notice that in *Figure 8.3* each of these **Node3D** objects has multiple children under them. All of these will be considered when creating our NavMesh. The purpose of adding our NavMesh to all these objects is to prevent our NPC from running into them as they wander throughout our level.

Now onto the second reason why our Viewport appears unchanged. Even though we have parented the correct objects underneath our **NavigationRegion3D**, there is no difference in the Viewport. This is because we need to bake our **NavigationMesh** into the world.

In game development, the term **baking** has a variety of uses. In general, it means creating and storing data that does not require any live calculations during gameplay. The most common examples of baking refer to lighting and textures, but it's also applicable to navigation and pathfinding. Let's go ahead and bake our NavMesh now to create a pathable area for our NPC.

> Note
>
> Every time you add or remove objects from the **NavigationRegion3D** node, you must re-bake your NavMesh for it to update.

Select the **NavigationRegion3D** node in the **Scene** dock, and there will be a new option directly above the Viewport, **Bake NavigationMesh**, as shown in *Figure 8.4*:

Figure 8.4: The NavigionationRegion3D node options for our NavMesh

Go ahead and select **Bake NavigationMesh**. Now, you should see a change in the Viewport. Everywhere our NPC can traverse will be highlighted with a mesh, illustrated in *Figure 8.5*.

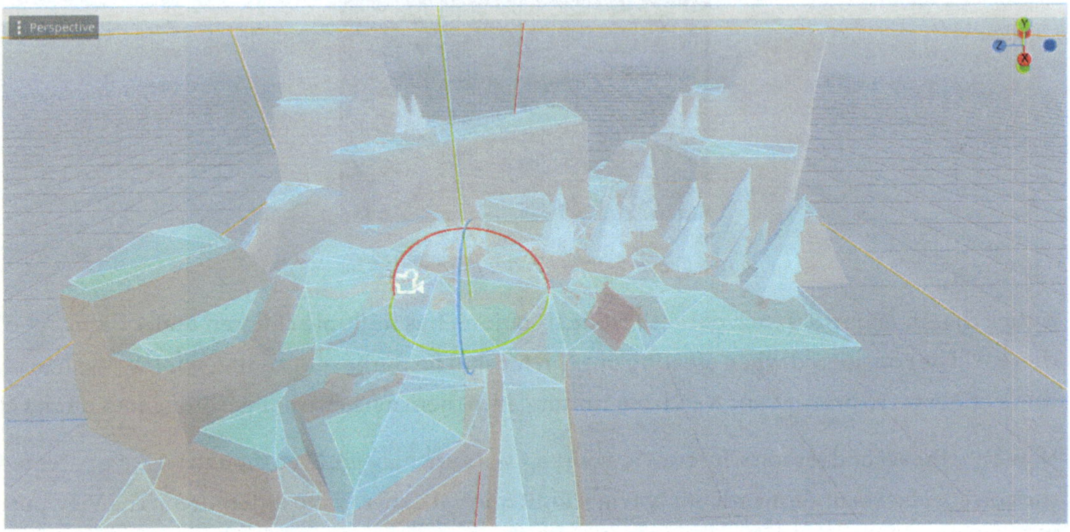

Figure 8.5: The NavMesh baked and generated in our world

> Note
>
> I've toggled off the rain particles for better visibility in *Figure 8.5*. You can do the same by selecting the eyeball icon in the **Scene** dock next to any node.

Excellent, we now have a functional NavMesh in our **World** scene. Next, we're going to create an NPC that will wander around our level based on specific points within our NavMesh.

Creating an NPC

To create our NPC, create a new scene by clicking the + sign above the Viewport. Then, select **Other Node** and search for `CharacterBody3D`.

We'll go through a very similar process to what we've already done, where we add collision and a mesh to an object, creating our NPC. Much like with our **Player** scene, we need both a collision and a mesh node for physics and collision. Click the + sign in the **Scene** dock and search for a **CollisionShape3D** node.

With the **CollisionShape3D** node highlighted, look at its properties in the **Inspector** dock. The first property, **Shape**, currently says **<empty>**, and we need to create a shape resource to create collisions. Click **<empty>** and select **New CapsuleShape3D**.

Once our **CollisionShape3D** node is added and has a shape, there should be blue lines in the shape of a capsule at the origin of our scene. It will look like *Figure 8.6*:

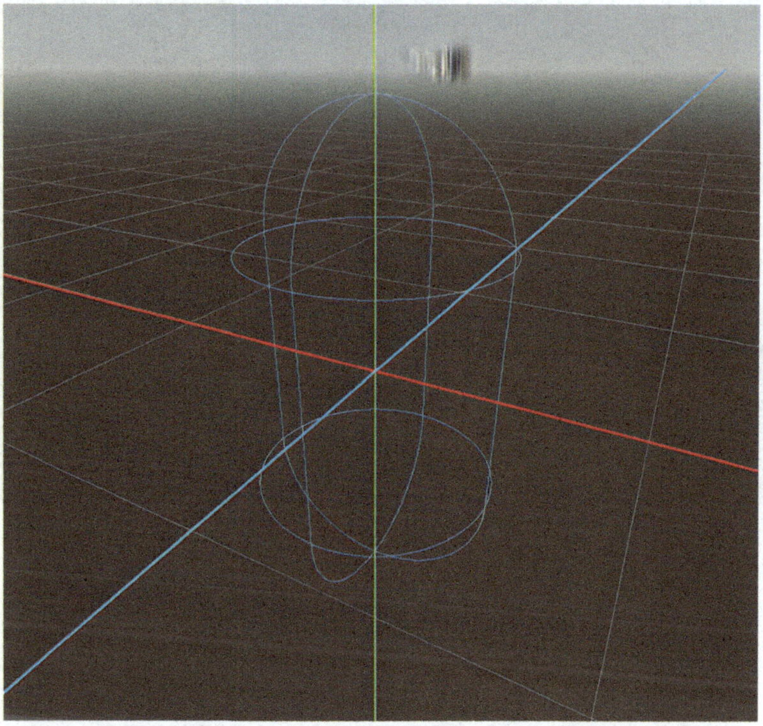

Figure 8.6: The capsule-based collision shape for our NPC

Next, we're going to add a mesh as a child node of our **CollisionShape3D**. As before, click the + sign in the **Scene** dock and search for `MeshInstance3D`. Select it and drag it underneath the **CollisionShape3D** node. The scene tree should look like *Figure 8.7*:

Figure 8.7: The current node tree for our NPC

After adding the **MeshInstance3D** node, highlight it and look at its properties in the **Inspector** dock. The **Mesh** property will be set to **<empty>** by default. Click **<empty>** and select **New CapsuleMesh**. A small gray capsule should appear in the Viewport of our NPC scene, as shown in *Figure 8.8*:

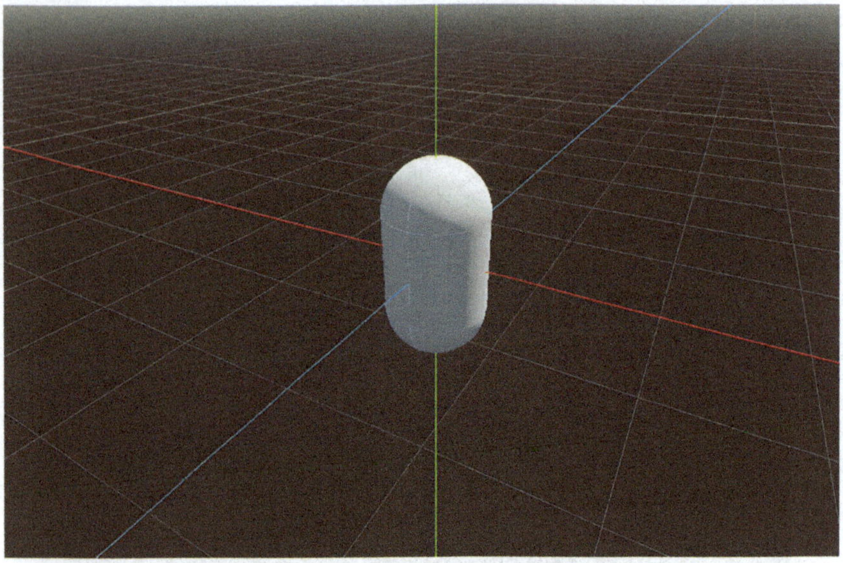

Figure 8.8: The NPC collision body in the shape of a capsule

> Note
>
> Using capsules for both collision shapes and mesh instances is an excellent way to prototype when you don't have animations or are using a first-person view to test other systems. Since players will not see the capsule in a first-person Viewport, it matters a lot less what the shape and feel of the player is. You can still test interaction systems and how a level feels to navigate in first person without a fully polished player controller.

The last thing we'll add to our scene is a **NavigationAgent3D** node. Click the + sign, search for **NavigationAgent3D**, and select it. This node has a target position it uses to determine a path forward. It checks for a new navigation path and allows our NPC to go from point A to point B and so on in our scene.

Once this node is added to our scene, let's make sure the agent knows to avoid objects in our scene. You'll notice there are three property headings: **Pathfinding**, **Avoidance**, and **Debug**. Let's expand the **Avoidance** heading, and you will see a set of properties like *Figure 8.9*:

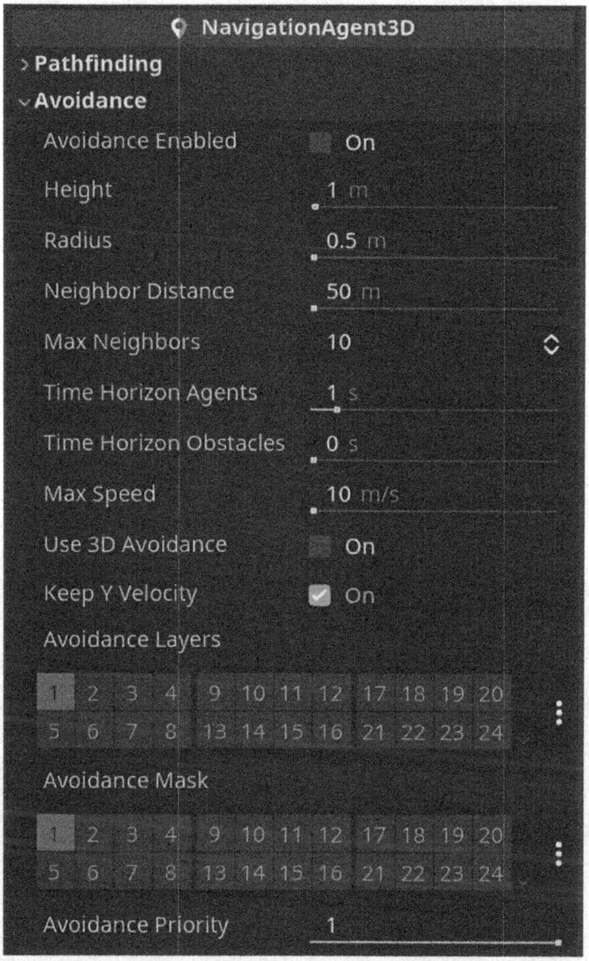

Figure 8.9: The Avoidance properties of our NavigationAgent3D node

The first property listed, **Avoidance Enabled**, is turned off by default. Let's go ahead and turn this on. As its name suggests, this means the agent will navigate the NavMesh in a way that avoids obstacles.

Click back to the **CharcterBody3D** node in our scene tree and rename it to `ForestDweller`. We're going to update the **Collision** property, so it can interact with our world correctly. Remember, we have a collision layer for our world, player, and collectibles so far.

We'll create a new layer for our NPC by clicking the three vertical dots to the right of the block of **Layer** numbers. You can find the **Layer** block under the **Collision** property, as pictured in *Figure 8.10*:

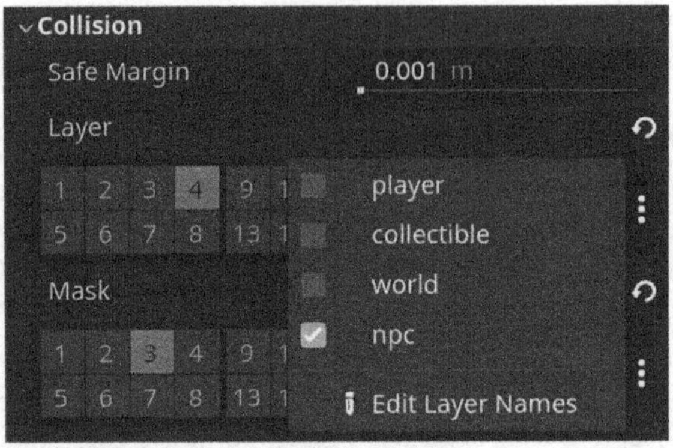

Figure 8.10: Adding a new collision layer for our NPC

Then, we'll click **Edit Layer Names**. This will give us a new pop-up window that lists the currently created layers and their names. You can see it in *Figure 8.11*. The rest of the properties we'll leave alone for now:

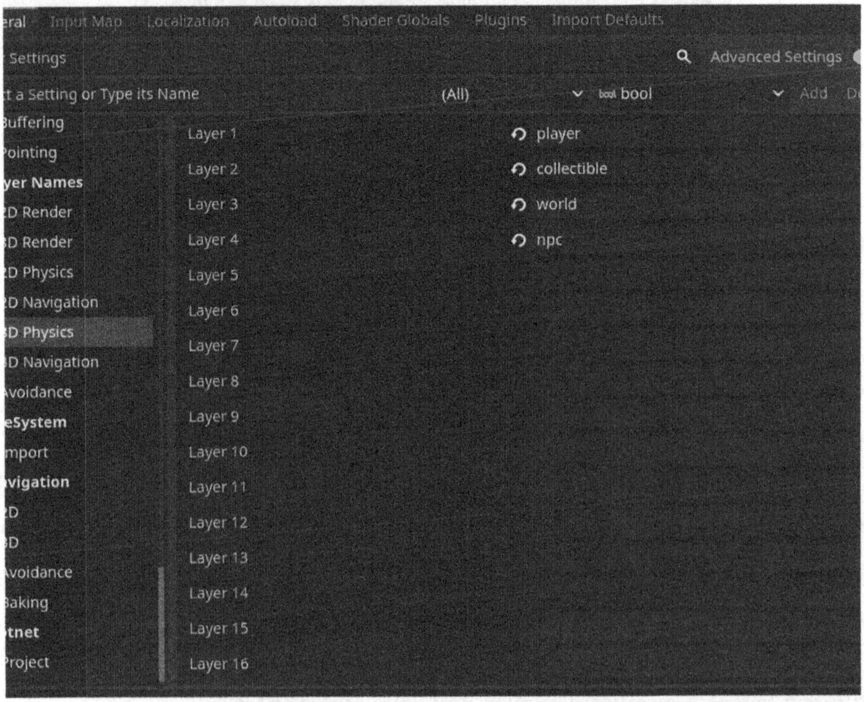

Figure 8.11: The collision layer names in our project

On **Layer 4** of the pop-up window, type `npc` into the box, which you can also see in *Figure 8.11*. Once that's done, click the **Close** button.

Now, be sure to set the **Layer** property for **Collision** for **ForestDweller** to **4**. If you hover over it, a tooltip appears that shows how Layer 4 is the **npc** layer we just named, as shown in *Figure 8.12*.

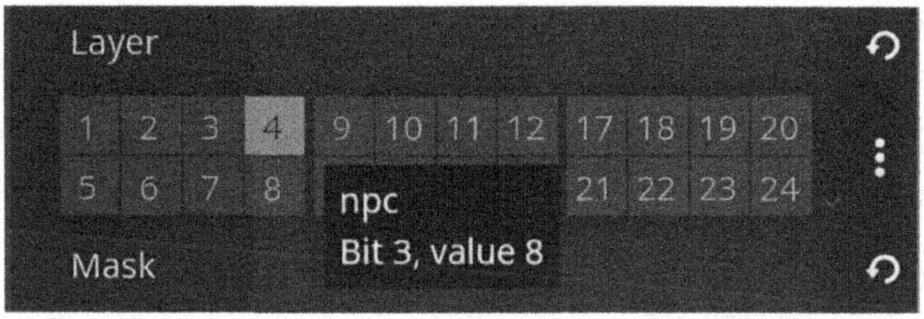

Figure 8.12: Hovering over the layer on the Collision property

Remember, for the **Collision** property, the layer is the collision for that object, while the mask is what that object collides with. For **Mask**, we'll set it to **3**, because we want our NPC to collide with any of our world objects.

Now, save this scene. The scene is currently named **NPC.tscn**; however, that is rather vague, so I decided to name my NPC scene `ForestDweller.tscn` instead.

With our NPC created and our NavMesh baked, we can start to look at how to create a patrol for our NPC to utilize in our **World** scene.

Adding autonomous movement

Creating a patrol for an NPC is a common feature of games, especially open-world ones. Once we've finished creating one patrolling NPC, it's easy to add multiple, as we'll instantiate the `ForestDweller.tscn` scene as needed. Before that, though, we'll need to provide logic for our NPC to move autonomously. We'll create a set of pre-selected points on our NavMesh. After choosing the points, we'll write code to have our NPC randomly choose one to move toward. Let's go ahead and implement NPC wandering now.

We'll start by opening the `World.tscn` scene and then dragging our `ForestDweller.tscn` scene from the **FileSystem** dock into the scene tree of our **World** scene. Feel free to place your NPC anywhere in the world; however, just make sure it's on the ground and not colliding with our player, any collectibles, or any other object in the scene (e.g., it's not overlapping with trees).

To adjust the position of `ForestDweller.tscn` in the **World** scene, click the **ForestDweller** node in the **Scene** dock and find the **Position** sub-property under **Transform** in the **Inspector** dock. There, you can directly enter the position coordinates. I've placed mine at the following points: **x**: `0`, **y**: `0.8`, and **z**: `-4.8`. You can see the placement of the NPC in the game in *Figure 8.13*:

Figure 8.13: ForestDweller.tscn placed in our world as seen in the Viewport

Great! Now, we're going to add a set of marker points in the level that our NPC can choose from. Then, we'll use those marker points to write code to have our NPC randomly choose a new point to path toward.

Adding marker nodes

To add our marker points, select the **ForestDweller** node in the scene tree, then click the + sign at the top of the **Scene** dock. In the pop-up menu, type `marker` and the results should look like *Figure 8.14*:

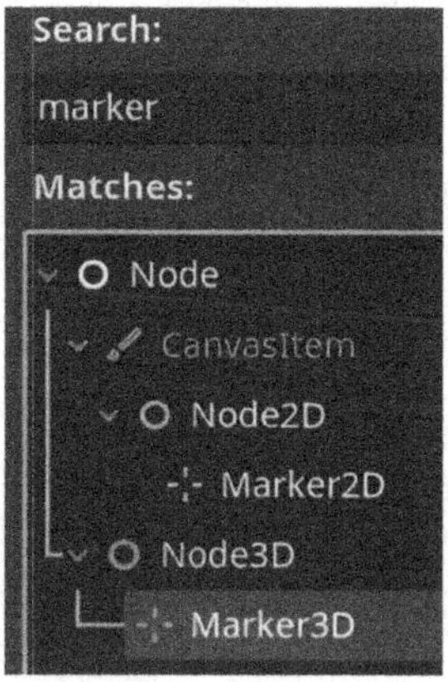

Figure 8.14: Searching for marker nodes

As with many nodes in Godot, we have both 2D and 3D options. We are going to select the **Marker3D** option. Once we click **Create**, the **Marker3D** node will be added as a child to our **ForestDweller** node. Rename **Marker3D** to `Patrol1`.

Repeat this process three more times until we have four patrol points. Just as we did with placing our NPC in the **World** scene, we'll move the patrol points to various places on the NavMesh. I've set the **Position** property for each marker to the following places in the level:

- **Patrol1**: x: `4.2`, y: `0`, and z: `0.186`
- **Patrol2**: x: `11.5`, y: `0`, and z: `-5`
- **Patrol3**: x: `11.5`, y: `0`, and z: `1.5`
- **Patrol4**: x: `8.42`, y: `0`, and z: `7.29`

The patrol points should be placed similarly to how they are laid out in *Figure 8.15*.

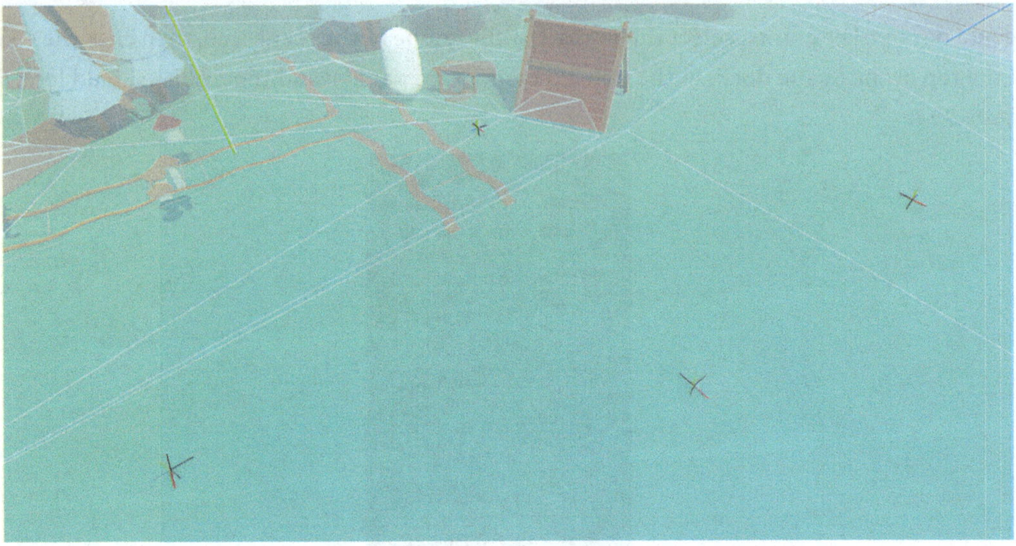

Figure 8.15: The patrol points placed in the level

I've toggled off the rain particles for clarity in the image. Notice how the marker nodes only have two black lines extending out from their origin. This is a gizmo in the editor to show where the points are in the Viewport. These can be made larger by making the **Gizmo Extents** property of the **Marker3D** nodes larger. The default is **0.25**, which is what I've left mine at as well.

> Note
>
> You can toggle the visibility of any node in a scene by clicking the eyeball icon that's to the right of the node in the **Scene** dock.

Excellent! Now that we have our NPC in the **World** scene and our markers have been placed, we can turn to programming the NPC to move through a set of points as marked on the NavMesh.

Adding code to World.cs

Start by clicking on the script icon next to the **World** node in the `World.tscn` scene to open the **Word.cs** file. This file will hold all the code and logic relating to the patrol points and the patrol itself.

Once open, we're going to create four different variables for our patrolling NPC above our `_Ready` function. The variables will be the following:

```
private Vector3 currPatrolPoint;
private List<Vector3> patrolPoints = new();
puiblic bool moveNPC = true;
private int patrolNum = 0;
```

Let's look at each one:

- The first variable is as follows:

  ```
  private Vector3 currPatrolPoint;
  ```

  The `Vector3` variable holds the current patrol point that our NPC is on. Since we're choosing a random point from our set of patrol points, we need to make sure we don't choose the one we're already at. Otherwise, our NPC would not move.

- Next, we'll create a list of the patrol points that we've created in the `World.tscn` scene by creating a second variable called `patrolPoints`:

  ```
  private List<Vector3> patrolPoints = new();
  ```

  This list, just like the patrol points, is of the `Vector3` type, since we're working in a 3D space.

- The next variable to create is a Boolean:

  ```
  public bool moveNPC = true;
  ```

  This Boolean allows us to pause our NPC. This is useful for a couple of different reasons. The first is we want our NPC to not be moving while our player is on the main menu screen. The second is when our NPC moves to one point, we want it to stay there for a few seconds before choosing another patrol point. The Boolean provides a simple and easy toggle to control this.

- Our final variable to add is an integer, which will track which of the patrol points from our list we're on. It will also be a number we randomly choose and then pull from the list at that index:

  ```
  private int patrolNum = 0;
  ```

Now, let's add some functionality to the variables we just created. We'll start by creating a function that will get a random patrol point for our NPC. Below our `PlayerStart` function, declare a new one by typing the following:

```
public void ChooseRandomPatrolPoint() { }
```

This function won't take any variables, and it won't return any either. All it will do is manipulate the variables that exist in this class.

Then, inside this function, add a line of code that will randomly select a number between 0 and 3, which are the possible indexes of our patrol point list. We're creating a random number by leveraging the `Random` class that's part of C#. To access the `Random` class, must write `using System;` at the top of the `World.cs` script. Now, we'll create a new random object inside this function:

```
Random rInt = new();
```

Here, we're creating a new integer variable called `prevPatrolNum` and assigning it to whatever our current patrol point is in the `patrolNum` variable. We do this because we're going to randomly select a number until we get a number that's not `patrolNum`:

```
int prevPatrolNum = patrolNum;
```

Next, we'll create a `while` loop to hold the code for randomly selecting a number like this:

```
while(prevPatrolNum != patrolNum) { }
```

For example, if our NPC moved to point 2, and our `Random` variable selected the number 2, we'd have `patrolNum` select another random number until it's something other than 2. This guarantees that our NPC will always move from point A to point B rather than staying in the same spot.

Now, within our `while` loop, we're going to add one line of code:

```
patrolNum = rInt.Next(0,3);
```

This is taking our `patrolNum` variable and setting it equal to a number between 0 and 3. We're using the `Random` variable, `rInt`, that we created at the beginning of this function and using one of the `Random` class functions called `Next`. You can learn more about the `Random` class here: `https://learn.microsoft.com/en-us/dotnet/api/system.random?view=net-8.0`.

Before we switch to our `ForestDweller.cs` scene, we have one more thing to do. Inside our `_Ready()` function, we need to add the position of these **Marker3D** nodes to the list of `patrolPoints`. Otherwise, the list will be empty. To do this, we write the following:

```
patrolPoints.Add(GetNode<Marker3D>("NPC/Patrol1").GlobalPosition);
patrolPoints.Add(GetNode<Marker3D>("NPC/Patrol2").GlobalPosition);
patrolPoints.Add(GetNode<Marker3D>("NPC/Patrol3").GlobalPosition);
patrolPoints.Add(GetNode<Marker3D>("NPC/Patrol4").GlobalPosition);
```

Now, let's pivot to the `ForestDweller.cs` file to finish writing the code needed for our wandering NPC.

Adding code to ForestDweller.cs

The ForestDweller.cs script is going to hold the bulk of the logic when it comes to our wandering NPC.

Let's start by creating two variables:

- The first is a speed variable, which looks like this:

  ```
  private float speed = 1.5f;
  ```

  You could export this variable to change it in the scene, but I've left it private as I like the speed I've set.

- The second is a variable to use the **NavigationAgent3D** node, which looks like this:

  ```
  private NavigationAgent3D navAgent;
  ```

  This will hold a reference to the node in the ForestDweller.tscn scene.

  After having created our variable, navAgent, we'll assign our scene node to it when the script is first called. Let's go ahead and assign the navAgent variable in the _Ready function by typing this:

  ```
  navAgent = GetNode<NavigationAgent3D>("NavigationAgent3D");
  ```

> Note
>
> Remember, the GetNode function must have both the type of node and how it's named in the scene. The syntax is this: GetNode<NodeType>("NameInScene");.

Now, we're done with the _Ready function and will move on to the _PhysicsProcess function. Here, we'll be getting the location of the NPC and then updating its location and velocity for each frame. The first line is going to be creating and declaring a Vector3 variable that will hold the current location of the NPC:

```
Vector3 currLocation = GlobalTransform.Origin;
```

We want to capture the current location, because we'll be using it in another line of code when determining the velocity between the current point and the point our NPC will be moving toward. Therefore, our next line will be creating and declaring the location of the next point along the path:

```
Vector3 nextLocation = navAgent.GetNextPathPosition();
```

This new variable, `nextLocation`, uses our **NavigationAgent3D** variable, `navAgent`, and utilizes a function within the **NavigationAgent3D** class called `GetNextPathPosition`. This function makes sure that there are no objects in the path and must be housed in the physics frame to update the path logic of the navigation agent.

Great, now we have both the current location and the next location the NPC will move to. To make sure the movement is fluid, we'll be normalizing these two vectors to calculate the NPC's new velocity. The code will look like this:

```
Vector3 newVelocity = (nextLocation - currLocation).Normalized() * speed;
```

To calculate the new velocity, we're normalizing the current location and the next location. After that, we multiply the normalized vector by the speed we created and assign that result to `newVelocity`.

Even though we have calculated the new velocity, we need to assign it to the velocity of our NPC. The node that the `ForestDweller.cs` script extends from is **CharacterBody3D**, and within the **CharacterBody3D** node class, there's a variable called `Velocity` – that's the one we need to update. It will look like this:

```
this.Velocity = newVelocity;
```

The last line of code to add to our `_PhysicsProcess` function is a function call to move the NPC:

```
MoveAndSlide();
```

Just like in our Player script, `MoveAndSlide` is called at the very end of the `_PhysicsProcess` function after new velocities have been calculated.

Awesome! That wraps up the code needed for our `_PhysicsProcess` function.

Now, we'll create two more functions within the `ForestDweller.cs` script and then we'll be super close to testing out our NPC. On a new line after the `_PhysicsProcess` function, declare a new function that looks like this:

```
public void SetTarget(Vector3 targetPosition) { }
```

This new function, `SetTarget`, will take in a `Vector3` and then pass that `Vector3` to the navigation agent, which will then pass it to the navigation server.

Inside the function, we'll write the following:

```
navAgent.TargetPosition = targetPosition;
```

This line takes our `navAgent` variable and uses a property that's part of the **NavigationAgent3D** class, `TargetPosition`, to update our NPC's path based on its current location. We set the `TargetPosition` property to the `targetPosition` that we pass into the function as a parameter.

The last function we'll be creating is one that will fire off when the navigation agent emits one of its built-in signals. Let's connect that real quick before adding the code for the function. If we switch back to Godot and open our `ForestDweller.tscn` scene, we have the **NavigationAgent** node at the bottom of the scene tree. Select the navigation agent, then the **Node** tab at the top of the **Inspector** dock, and you'll see a list of built-in signals as part of the **NavigationAgent3D** node. Double-click the **target_reached()** one and under **Receiver Method**, name our function `OnNavAgentTargetReached`, as shown in *Figure 8.16*:

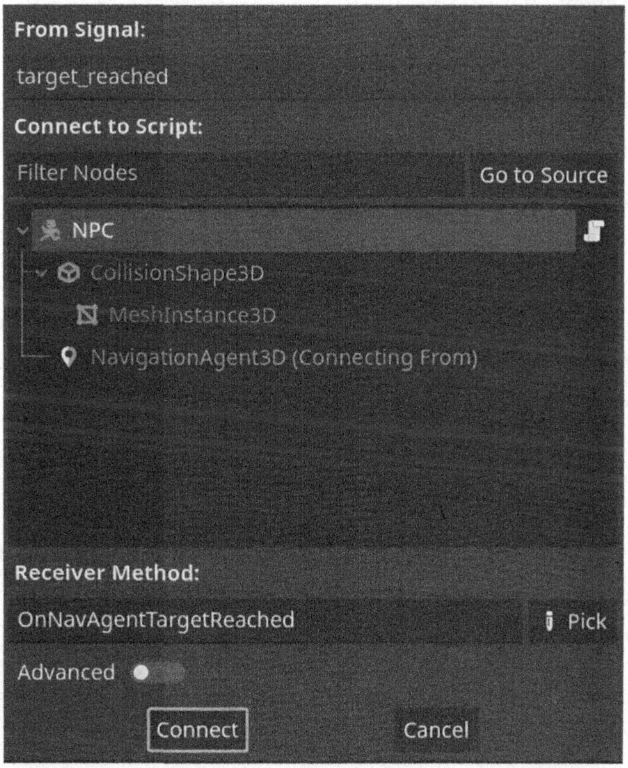

Figure 8.16: Connecting a signal to target_reached for our NPC

Once we click **Connect**, we can return to the `ForestDweller.cs` script and start writing our `OnNavAgentTargetReached` function. The function declaration will look like this:

```
public async void OnNavAgentTargetReach() { }
```

Notice we have the word `async` in the declaration there. We'll need it since we'll be using a timer inside the function to make the NPC wait a few seconds before moving on to its next position.

The first line we'll write inside this function is the following:

```
GD.Print("Position reached!");
```

This is more useful logging to ensure the order of our function calls is correct and that our NPC is behaving correctly.

The next line will be the following:

```
var root = GetOwner<World>();
```

While there are any number of different methods for acquiring the top of the scene tree, this will work fine for prototyping. `GetOwner` is a function that will get the owner of the current scene, which here will be the root node of the **World** scene. Another way is to utilize signals again.

After setting our variable root to get the root node of the **World** scene, we can call the function that we need to force the NPC to choose its next patrol point. But before doing that, we'll add a timer to delay our NPC from choosing the next location in its list of path options. This will create a `Timer` node in the code and add it to our **World** scene. After its elapsed time (we'll set it to three seconds), the timer will be dereferenced, and the next line of code will execute. To do this, we'll write the following:

```
await ToSignal(GetTree().CreateTimer(3f), SceneTreeTimer.SignalName.
Timeout);
```

This line is forcing our program to wait three seconds before continuing. We want the delayed timer, because we want our NPC to wait at its current position before moving on to the next one. It does this by following these steps:

- We use the `await` keyword to make our program wait until it finishes executing the line of code after the word `await` before moving on.
- Then, we create a signal in code, using the `ToSignal` syntax. This function takes two parameters:

    - The first argument in the call is the `Timer` we're creating in the scene tree where we set the duration to be three seconds.
    - The second argument is the signal that should be emitted, which is the `Timeout` signal that's built-in and part of the `Timer` node.
- Next, we create a timer on the scene tree by using `GetTree` to access the scene tree and use the `CreateTimer` function.

Now, after our NPC waits for three seconds, we want to call the function in our `World.cs` script to start the process all over again by choosing a new random patrol point. We'll do this by writing the following:

```
root.ChooseRandomPatrolPoint();
```

The variable, `root`, that we assigned to the **World** node in our scene tree also has the `World.cs` file attached to it. This gives us access to the public functions within it, such as `ChooseRandomPatrolPoint`.

With that, save this script and we'll go back to the editor for the final piece to programming our NPC, which is understanding how groups work in Godot.

Creating groups in Godot

When working on a project, we tend to categorize objects by what they do and how often they're in a scene. While we have a way to organize our project and keep our naming conventions the same, sometimes having that extra tag on a set of objects is useful, especially in code. The way we do that in Godot is by creating a group.

A good example of groups would be NPCs. Say we have a group of NPCs scattered about a woodland area. As time in the game progresses, the NPCs would wander from point A to point B. We can also pass in what those points are when we call on the group, which, ideally, would be different points in the level for different NPCs. We wouldn't want two NPCs to overlap with each other.

Let's create a group of NPCs and see how we can leverage this in our project. Make sure our NPC is selected in the **World** scene, then look at the **Inspector** dock. You will see three tabs across the top – **Inspector**, **Node**, and **History**. We've used **Inspector** countless times to access the properties of nodes and materials, but this time we'll click the **Node** tab.

By default, we see the **Signals** page, which has a list of functions we can connect to, but here we want to click the word **Groups** (I know, it doesn't look like a button), and the tab should switch to look something like *Figure 8.17*:

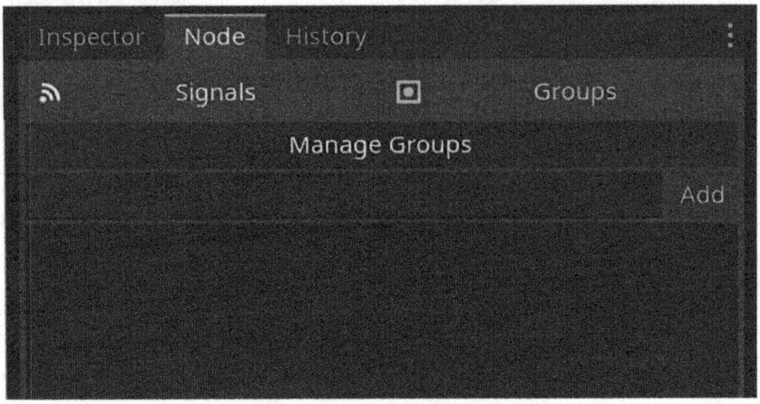

Figure 8.17: Accessing the Groups tab in the editor

Under **Manage Groups**, type npc in the box, then click **Add**. We've now created a group for our NPC. Doing this allows us to add instances of our NPC object and keep them all together. Having them be part of the same group means we can fire signals to all NPCs at once without needing to iterate through each one individually in code. Godot will do this automatically for us. An object in any group will have a list of the groups they're in. For now, our NPC is in the **npc** group, and it will look like *Figure 8.18*:

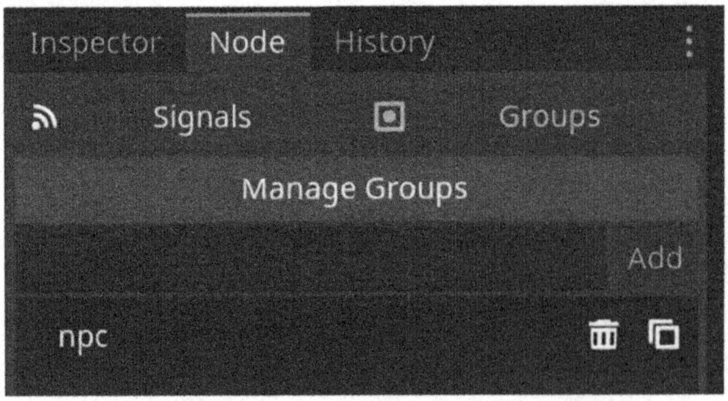

Figure 8.18: Creating a new group called npc

You'll also notice a new icon next to the NPC's **CharacterBody3D** node in the **Scene** dock. This icon, which looks like a square with a dot inside it, as in *Figure 8.19*, indicates the node is part of a group.

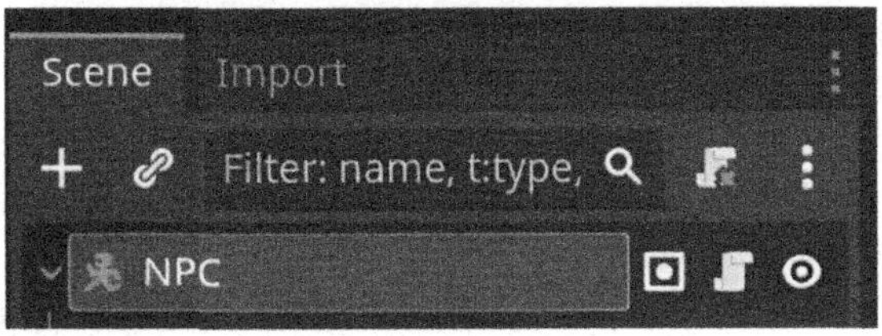

Figure 8.19: The group icon in the Scene dock for our NPC

Cool, we created a group. OK, so now what? We're going to create a new function in `World.cs`.

The function declaration will look like this:

```
public void CreatePatrolPath() { }
```

Then, inside this function, we're going to call the group we just created, like this:

```
GetTree().CallGroup("npc", "SetTarget", patrolPoints[patrolNum]);
```

Here, we're using a Godot function that's part of groups, `CallGroup`, and this will fire logic to any member of that group based on what we're passing in. The `CallGroup` function can be broken down like this:

- `npc`: This is the name of the group that we're calling on.
- `SetTarget`: This is the function that we're having every member of the group call.
- `patrolPoints[patrolNum]`: This is the value we're passing into the `SetTarget` function. Here, it would be the new point on the NavMesh that we selected from `ChooseRandomPatrolPoint`.

With groups, if we had five wandering NPCs instead of one, it would tell all five NPCs to fire the `SetTarget` function with the specific `patrolPoint` that was passed in. When extending this beyond one NPC, we want to add logic that didn't choose the same point for all five NPCs to move to (or maybe we would be depending on the game). The point is that creating and maintaining groups is an easy and flexible way to program logic for multiple entities that behave similarly.

Now that we have this new function that calls on groups, we need to call this function somewhere in our code. We're going to place it in the last line, after our `while` loop, of `ChooseRandomPatrolPoint`. This means that once our NPC reaches its destination, it will choose a new point to move to and then it'll start to move toward that point with `CreatePatrolPath`.

Lastly, we'll call this function at the end of the `PlayerStart()` function to ensure the NPC triggers after the player clicks the **Play** button.

The full function should look like the following:

```
public void CreatePatrolPath()
{
    GD.Print("Setting new target position.");
    GetTree().CallGroup("npc", "SetTarget", patrolPoints[patrolNum]);
}
```

We're ready to test out the scene and make sure everything is working as intended. To see the path the NPC will be moving along, we can set up some gizmos in Godot's editor. Return to the `ForestDweller.tscn` scene and select the **NavigationAgent** node. Look at the **Inspector** dock on the right and scroll down until you see a property called **Debug**. It should look something like *Figure 8.20*.

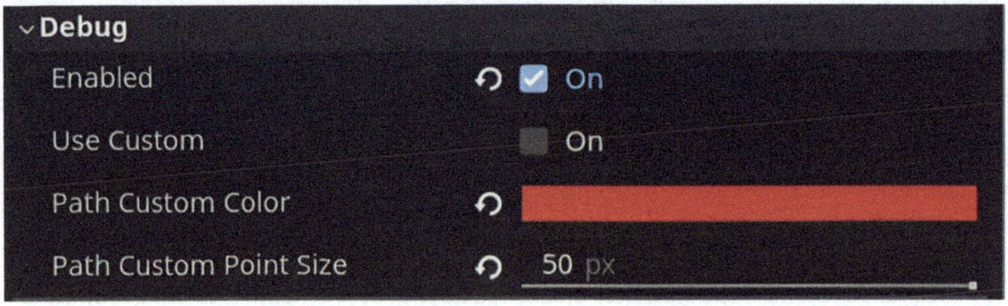

Figure 8.20: The Debug property on the NavigationAgent3D node

Make sure to check the **Enable** property. We'll also set the path to a custom color – I've chosen to use the color #CD0243 as it shows up very well against the backdrop of the level. The last thing to change is the size of the path points. I've set mine to `50` pixels, but you may need to change yours as needed.

Now, when you save the scene and run the game, you should see something like *Figure 8.21* in the Viewport:

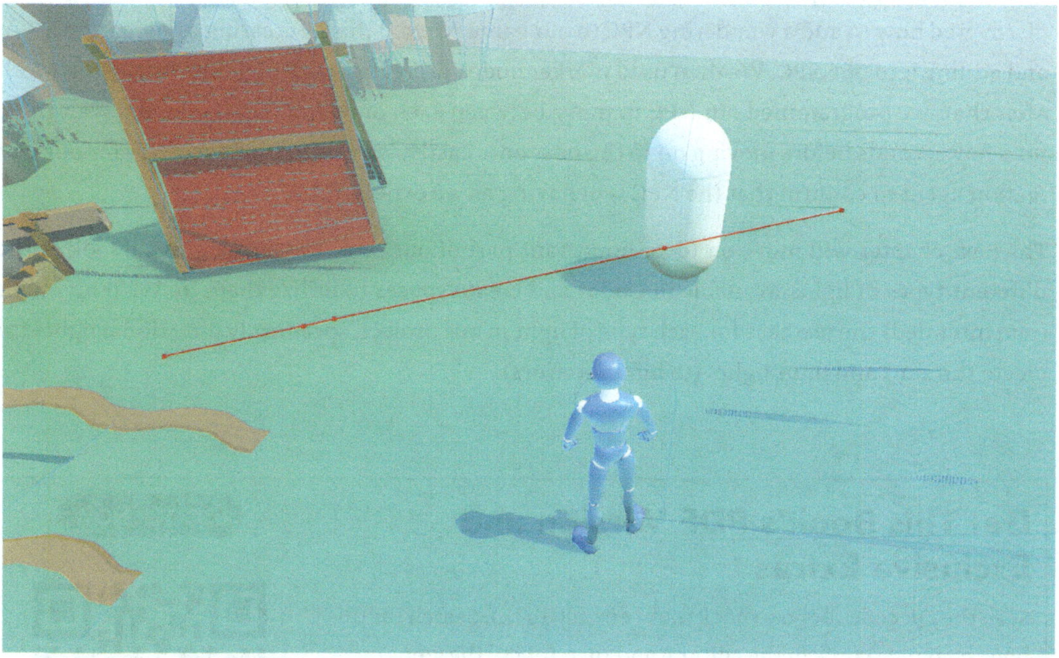

Figure 8.21: The Debug properties on the NPC in the Viewport

Notice the larger dots along the path. These are the path points, and then the line is simply the path the NPC is taking from its old position to the new one.

This kind of logic and setup provides many opportunities for implementing different game mechanics. This could be added to provide depth, via wandering NPCs. It could also be the basis for an escort mission in a first-person shooter game. The possibilities are endless and it is up to you, the game designer, on how best to leverage these concepts.

Summary

In this chapter, we spent time learning what NavMeshes are and how they function. We also discovered how to add a wandering NPC to our game. We did this by creating a navigation agent and adding it to our NPC. We then used marker nodes to create a path of points on the NavMesh. After that, we programmed our NPC to move between each of the marker nodes and wait there for a few seconds before moving on to the next one. Lastly, we utilized some gizmos for our navigation agent to confirm that the NPC is behaving as we expected.

The next chapter will move on to an important part of our project – lighting. We'll look at the different types of lights available in Godot and create spaces to utilize them in. We'll highlight (pun intended) the use case for each type of light in our project, specifically directional lights (to create the sun) and omnilights (to light interiors).

Part 3

Expanding Our 3D Action Game and Additional Resources

In this part, we'll dive into areas that aren't required to have a functioning project but add polish. These areas include lighting, ways to incorporate accessibility measures, and seeking other sources in the larger Godot community through Godot's asset library. We'll explore how to report bugs in the Godot Engine to the Godot Engine team and ways for you, as a developer, to contribute to improving Godot. We'll end the part by walking through the steps to export our project to the `itch.io` platform and other supportive communities to further your education about Godot. By the end of this part, you will have a firm grasp on the process for exporting projects, methods for flagging issues in Godot, and other resources to further your own development through both communities and third-party assets.

This part of the book includes the following chapters:

9

Setting Up Lighting in Godot

The previous chapter brought life to our game via pathfinding – this is where we created dynamic movement by adding wandering NPCs to our **World** scene and learned how to utilize both the **NavigationServer** and **NavigationAgent** nodes in Godot.

In this chapter, we'll discover how Godot uses lighting and explore its lighting nodes. We'll spend some time creating two different types of lighting in our scene: directional and **omnidirectional** (**omni**) lighting. Light, of course, cannot exist without darkness, so we'll be exploring some of the shadow (occluding) nodes that are available in Godot. We'll also create a day/night cycle for our **World** scene to show the passage of time in our game.

Lighting is an important component when it comes to developing games. It adds ambiance and sets the tone of a given space. It also adds details and depth to the environment and is often incorporated as a game mechanic. Whether by tracking sunlight through a day/night cycle or using lighting for a stealth game, light adds another dimension when it comes to game development.

In this chapter, we will cover the following topics:

- Discovering Godot's lighting nodes
- Adding a DirectionalLight node
- Utilizing OmniLight nodes
- Creating a day/night cycle

Technical requirements

For this chapter, the technical requirements will be the same as those in *Chapter 1*.

All the code for this chapter is available in this book's GitHub repository: `https://github.com/PacktPublishing/Game-Development-with-Godot-and-C-`.

Discovering Godot's lighting nodes

Before we dive into the different types of lighting nodes available in Godot, I wanted to spend a little time breaking down how lighting works in Godot. The options available for lighting will vary based on the renderer selected for the project, but for our project, we are using the **Forward+** renderer. The Forward+ renderer essentially allows machines with lower specifications to run your game.

> Important note
>
> For more information about Godot's internal rendering and how lighting is impacted by it, go to `https://docs.godotengine.org/en/stable/contributing/development/core_and_modules/internal_rendering_architecture.html`.

The following light nodes are available in Godot. Light can appear in a Godot scene in a variety of ways:

- **Materials**: Any material with the emission property can produce light.
- **Light nodes**: The built-in nodes (**DirectionalLight**, **OmniLight**, and **SpotLight**), all of which we'll cover in detail later in this section, have their own function in Godot. We'll utilize **DirectionalLight** nodes to add illumination to dark spaces in our level, as well as for our day/night cycle. We can use the **OmniLight** node for interior spaces; we'll create a small room in our test scene for this purpose. The last light, **SpotLight**, is used for more concentrated types of light. While we won't have an example of it in our project, we'll discuss it briefly.
- **Global and ambient light**: We briefly worked with global and ambient lighting when we created our **World Environment** resource back in *Chapter 5*, when we created our **Sky** resource and enabled **signed distance field global illumination** (**SDFGI**).

Depending on the renderer selected, the number of lights that can be in any given scene is limited. Since we're using the **Forward+** renderer, we can have up to 512. This is plenty for our scene, but for larger projects, it may not be. This number can be changed in the **Project Settings** area. However, if you are working in a different renderer or targeting older hardware, there are better alternatives that should be used, such as baked lightmaps. We'll explain this in greater detail later by creating one.

With a better understanding of how light can exist in Godot, let's look at the available lighting nodes. *Figure 9.1* provides a list of all the built-in nodes related to lighting.

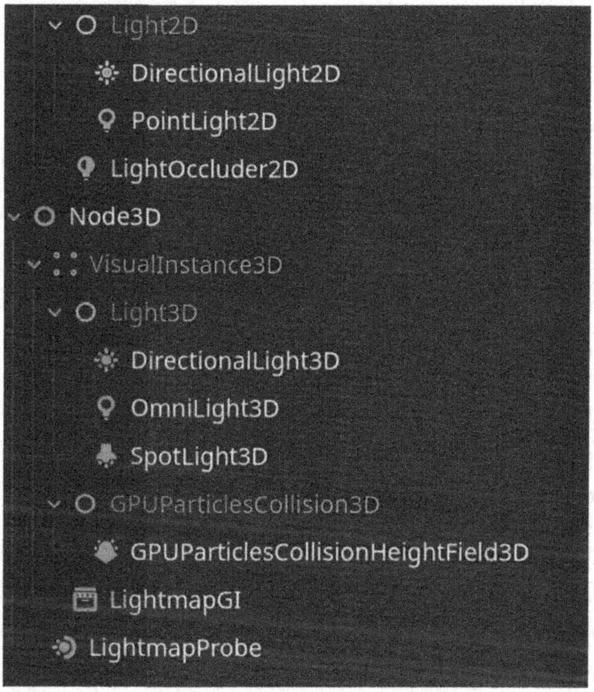

Figure 9.1: The available light nodes in Godot

We won't be using all the light nodes listed in *Figure 9.1*, but here are the most frequently used light nodes available:

- **DirectionalLight**: This is a light node that is used to project light that's from far away distances. A good example of this is using a directional light for the sun in your game, something we'll be doing shortly.
- **OmniLight**: This type of light emits in all directions based on a radius and other built-in properties. It's good for interior rooms, lanterns, or streetlights.
- **SpotLight**: These light nodes form a cone of light and are ideal for things such as a player's flashlight or car lights. They are like **OmniLight** nodes in terms of their properties (range, attenuation, size), but that's it.

Notice that these three nodes each derive from the **Light3D** node, as shown in *Figure 9.1*, meaning they share several common properties such as light, color, energy (intensity), and shadow settings. In this chapter, we will cover an example that uses each of these types of lights and explore their use cases. With this foundation in place, let's dive into how to implement each type in your scene, starting with adding a **DirectionalLight** node and discussing how it changes the scene.

Adding a DirectionalLight node

Now that we have a basic overview of the light nodes available in Godot, we're going to create a few examples highlighting how each works in Godot. By doing this, you can decide which of the examples you want to include in your project.

Let's start by opening our `World.tscn` scene. Click the + sign at the top of the Scene dock and type `light` in the search box. We'll find the same options that appeared in *Figure 9.1*. Select **DirectionalLight3D** and click **OK** to add it to our Scene tree. Once you've done this, it should be added to our scene. At this point, you will see the properties for it in the **Inspector** dock, as shown in *Figure 9.2*:

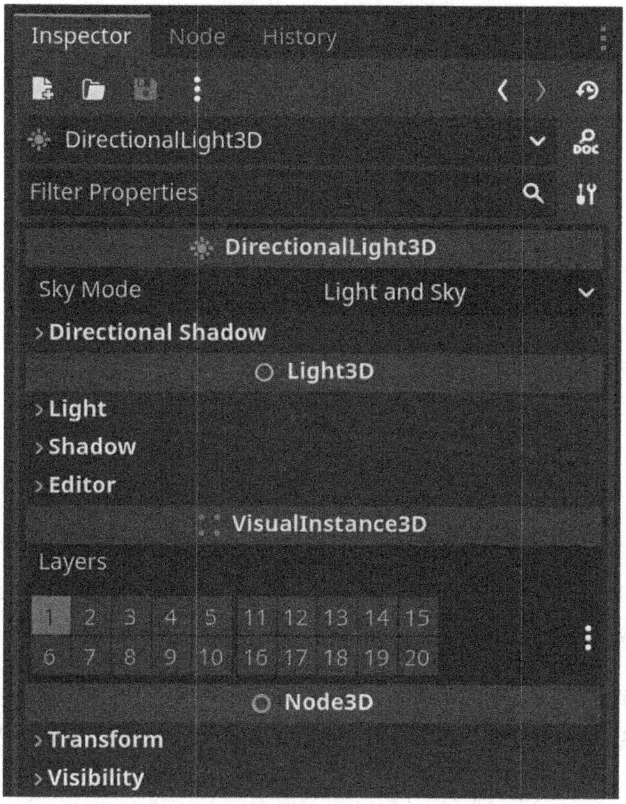

Figure 9.2: The properties of a DirectionalLight3D node

The first property, **Sky Mode**, determines how the directional light is rendered in the scene. There are three options for this property:

- **Light and Sky**: When this mode is set, the light is visible in both the scene lighting and the sky rendering
- **Light Only**: When this mode is set, the light is only rendered in the scene lighting
- **Sky Only**: When this mode is set, the light is only visible in the sky rendering

We'll leave **Sky Mode** as-is with its default setting of **Light and Sky**.

The next property is **Directional Shadow**. Upon expanding it, you should see **Directional Shadow** and its options, as shown in *Figure 9.3*. We're going to leave everything at the default settings except for **Mode**.

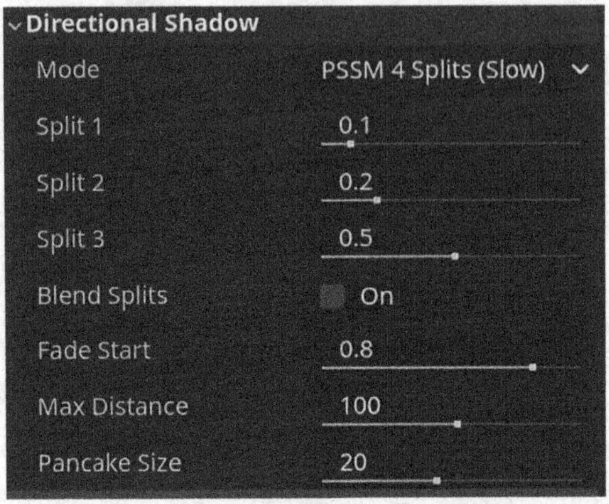

Figure 9.3: The Directional Shadow properties for a DirectionalLight3D node

The **Mode** property determines the algorithm used to render the lighting. The default is **PSSM 4**, which stands for **Parallel Split Shadow Mapping**. Here, **4** means the shadows are split into four regions, and each region gets its own shadow map. You can read more about this option here: `https://docs.godotengine.org/en/stable/tutorials/3d/lights_and_shadows.html`.

Before we adjust the **Mode** property, we're going to jump down the **DirectionalLight3D** list to the **Shadow** properties, shown in *Figure 9.4*. The first property in this list involves enabling shadows, which you should go ahead and do.

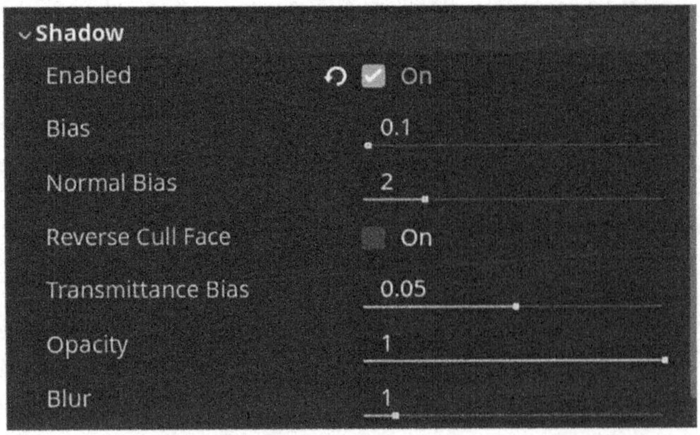

Figure 9.4: The Shadow properties of the DirectionalLight3D node

Shadows should appear on all the objects in the **World** scene. You can see them in the Viewport area. Position your view in the Viewport area over a region that includes some trees to watch the shadows change as we adjust the other properties of this light node. I've positioned my camera so that I can see the trees, player, NPC, and collectibles in the world. You can see what this looks like in *Figure 9.5*:

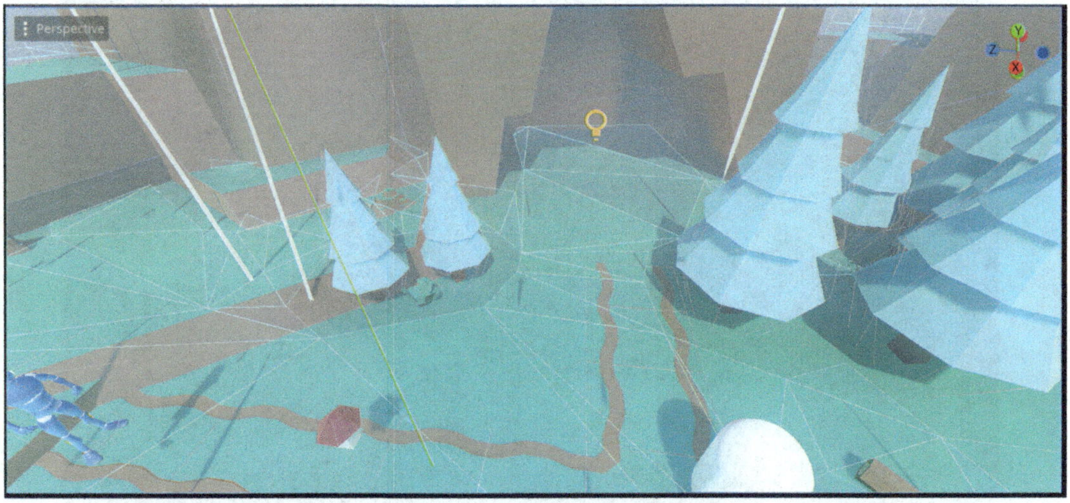

Figure 9.5: Positioning our view in the Viewport area with Mode set to PSSM 4

Now, going back to the **Mode** property, let's change it from the default of **PSSM 4** to **PSSM 2**. The shadows should now look slightly blurrier. This is because, rather than using four regions for shadow mapping, Godot will use two. While this uses fewer resources and is faster, it will also look a bit fuzzier. Let's change the **Mode** property to **Orthogonal** and notice how they're even blurrier.

The next set of properties for the **DirectionalLight3D** node can be found under the **Light** heading, as shown in *Figure 9.6*.

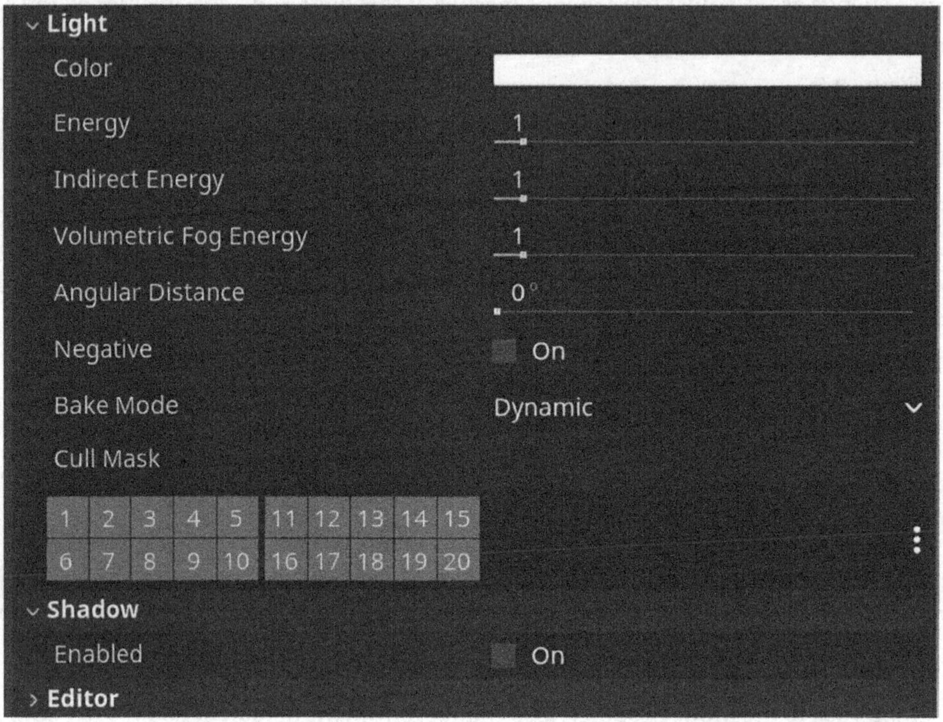

Figure 9.6: The Light properties for a DirectionalLight3D node

Notice that the default color is white, which makes the lighting and shadows very harsh. Let's click into this and change it to a softer yellow that's more akin to the sun to create a more natural environment. The hexadecimal color for this is `#FFFFC4`. Once you set the color of the light, there should be an immediate change in our scene. We'll learn more about this and how these lights look when we create our day/night cycle later in this chapter.

You can play with the choice of color if it's difficult to see the change. You could go for something more orange-based to mimic a sunset, or you could go for a stormy purple. This is one of the best things about creating a game – you are ultimately the creator of it.

Playing around and testing things out to see or feel what is the best fit for a mechanic, design, or anything else can lead to pleasant surprises in development. So, don't forget to have fun and play the game too!

With the key properties of the **DirectionalLight** node explored, we have a strong understanding of natural lighting and how it can be set in our scene. Now, let's explore **OmniLight** nodes.

Utilizing OmniLight nodes

With directional lighting in place for our outdoor scene and a beautiful sun shining in our world, we can turn our attention to **OmniLight** nodes. These nodes are better suited for interiors since the light expands spherically.

Our `World.tscn` scene doesn't have a great place to add an omni light because there are no interior spaces. So, let's open our **TestArea.tscn** scene, the test environment we created back in *Chapter 4*, to experiment with our player controller.

With the test scene open, let's add some more **CSGBox3D** nodes to make an enclosed room. As always, we can do that by clicking the + icon and adding the **CSGBox3D** nodes manually, or by selecting our floor and using *Ctrl + D*. Either way, we'll be adding five of these nodes to make three walls and a ceiling. The last one will be a wall with an open entry. It should look something like *Figure 9.7*.

Figure 9.7: A CSGBox3D building for testing OmniLight nodes

Now, drag the **Player.tscn** scene from the filesystem into the Scene dock, and position **Player** on the floor. If we run the scene now, **Player** will fall through the floor, even though collision is enabled on the **CSGBox3D** nodes. This is because the collision mask we set in the **World** scene to collide with **Player** isn't present here on these **CSGBox3D** nodes. Those settings have persisted on **Player**, so we need to update the collisions on the **CSGBox3D** nodes. Be sure to select **3** for **Collision Layer** for each node, as shown in *Figure 9.8*. The first layer will be selected by default, which is fine.

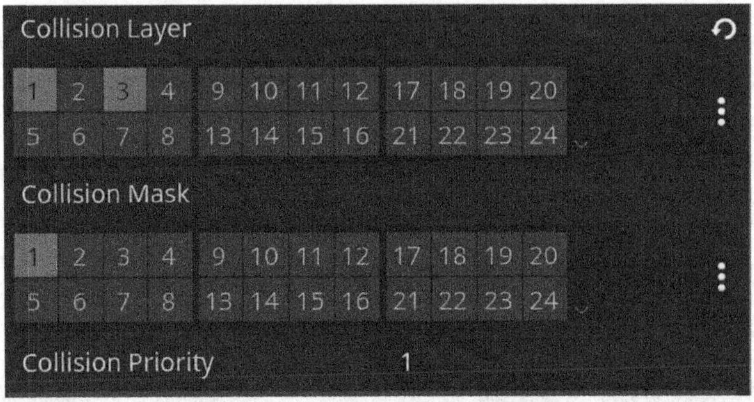

Figure 9.8: The collision layers for the CSGBox3D nodes

Go ahead and select the **Play** button (the clapperboard icon). You can see it highlighted in *Figure 9.9*. Since `World.tscn` is set to be the first scene that will play, if you hit *F5* or the **Play** button, it will load the wrong scene. Rather than changing this constantly in the **Project Settings** area, we can use the clapperboard **Play** button instead. This button means only the currently open scene, rather than the scene that's set to play in the project, will play. Using this button allows us to easily test new scenes without needing to change anything in **Project Settings**.

Figure 9.9: The Play button (clapperboard)

Test the scene out and run into the interior room. Notice that there's no lighting in our scene whatsoever. There's no sky, no sun, or any ambient light. So, click the + sign on the Scene dock and search for an **OmniLight3D** node. Once the **OmniLight3D** node has been added to the scene, position it inside the interior of the building we created. After placing it, you can adjust the range of the light by expanding it using the small white dot that's on the edge of the sphere. You can see this dot in *Figure 9.10*.

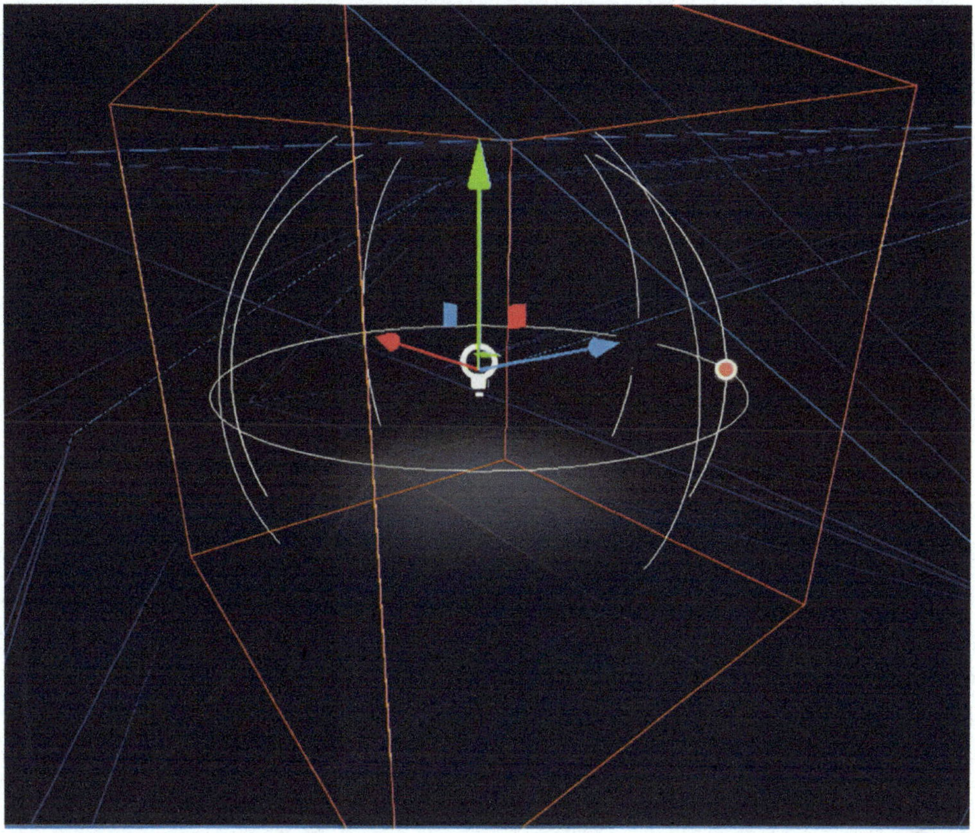

Figure 9.10: The OmniLight3D node highlighted in the Viewport area and placed in our building

In *Figure 9.10*, the light is very weak. With it selected and positioned where we want, let's look at the **Inspector** dock and examine some of its properties. For the **OmniLight3D** node properties, we have the following options:

- **Range:** This is the radius of the light node. The light may not cover the full radius, depending on how the **Attenuation** property is set.
- **Attenuation:** This is the brightness of the light node's actual light based on the distance set in the property.
- **Shadow Mode:** This sets how shadows should be rendered.

As we've demonstrated, **OmniLight** nodes are an excellent option for interior lighting. They can be used for specific, standalone lighting, such as candles or street lamps.

Creating a day/night cycle

Now that we've looked at a couple of different examples of how light nodes function in Godot, let's pivot to creating a day/night cycle in our **World** scene.

We'll start by opening our `World.tscn` scene. Notice the **WorldEnvironment** node in our Scene dock, as shown in *Figure 9.11*:

Figure 9.11: The WorldEnvironment node in the World.tscn scene

We created this in *Chapter 5*, when we were first setting up the **World** scene for our player. Right-click the **WorldEnvironment** node, click **Add Child Node...**, and look for **DirectionalLight3D**. Once you've selected the **DirectionalLight3D** node, click **Create**. Now, the Scene tree should look like *Figure 9.12*.

Note

Rather than adding a new **DirectionalLight3D** node, you can drag the **Sun** node we created earlier in this chapter and update its properties accordingly.

Figure 9.12: The DirectionalLight3D node added to the World.tscn scene

Once it's been added to the scene, you will see white light appear on one half of the **World** scene in the Viewport area, as shown on the right-hand side of *Figure 9.13*. The left-hand side shows how the **World** scene looked before the light was added.

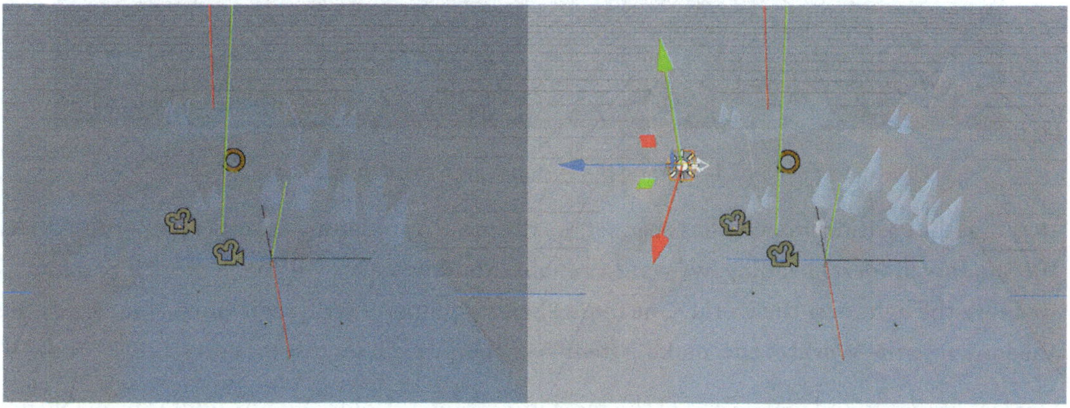

Figure 9.13: The World scene with no DirectionalLight3D node (left) and one with it (right) in the Viewport area

> Note
>
> For an easier time seeing the light and how it interacts with the **World** scene, I've toggled off the rain. You can do this by clicking the eyeball icon next to the node we named **Rain** in the Scene dock.

Before augmenting the light's properties, let's rename this **DirectionalLight3D** node to **Sun**. We can do this by double-clicking the node or by right-clicking and selecting the **Rename** option. With the node renamed, make sure it's selected in the **Scene** dock, then look at the **Inspector** dock for its list of properties.

The first property we'll set is **Position**. This can be found under the **Transform** heading. Once expanded, you can set it to the following:

- **x**: `7 m`
- **y**: `26 m`
- **z**: `7 m`

You can use *Figure 9.14* as a reference for setting the **Position** property.

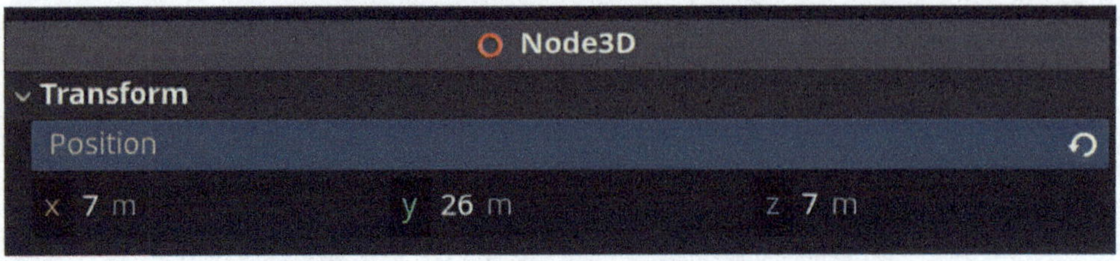

Figure 9.14: Setting the Position property of the Sun node

Now that the **Position** property has been set, we can move on to setting the other properties. Under the **Shadow** property heading, we want to enable **Shadows**. This will add a nice bit of detail as we move the light over the world. One more **Shadow** property we'll set is **Blur**. This blends the shadows into the **World** scene, making them less sharp. We'll set this property to 2.

Our last property, and maybe one of the most important, is **Color**. A white light is probably not the best color for our **Sun** node. Under the **Light** property heading, we'll find a property called **Color**. Clicking into the white bar, we'll see a color wheel appear that provides multiple ways for setting the color. You can see this in *Figure 9.15*:

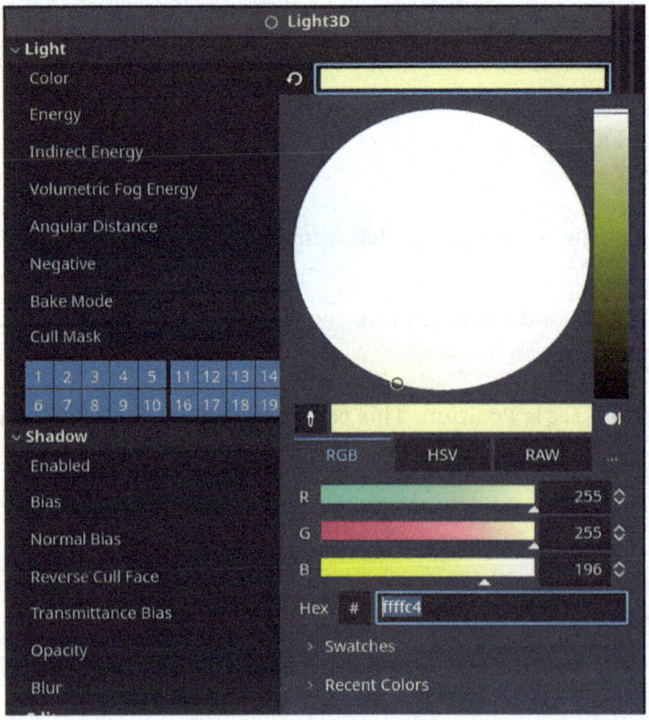

Figure 9.15: Setting the Color property of our Sun node in the World scene

I'm going to set my **Sun** node to a soft yellow by setting the **Hex** color to `ffffC4`. Feel free to play around with how the color looks in your **World** scene and toggle the **Rain** node on and off as needed. If you're still not sure about the color, don't forget that volumetric fog is enabled, and the light will look different with that turned off as well.

With the **Color** property set, we still only see the color on one half of the Viewport area. The **Sun** node should still be highlighted in the Scene dock, since we're adjusting its properties. This also means it's highlighted in the Viewport area, with each of the axes coming out from the center of the node, as shown on the right-hand side of *Figure 9.16*. By default, **Select Mode** is set in the Viewport area. We can put the Viewport area in **Rotate Mode** by selecting it in the Viewport tab, as shown in *Figure 9.16*, or by hitting *E* while in the Viewport area:

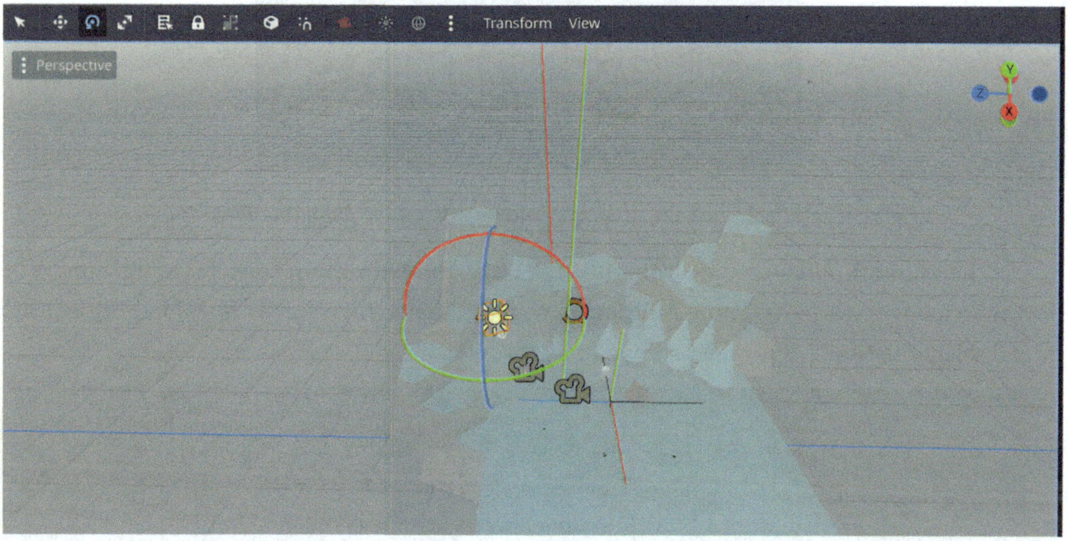

Figure 9.16: Rotating the Sun node in the Viewport area

With the **Sun** node in **Rotate Mode** and selected, drag the *X*-axis (the red curve) left or right. You'll notice the light moves across our **World** scene. Also, notice how the shadows change on the trees. Instead of doing this by hand, we'll be rotating the **Sun** node with an **AnimationPlayer** node and then playing that animation in script. Let's go ahead and right-click the **Sun** node and click **Add Child Node....** We want to look for the **AnimationPlayer** node and click **Create**. This will make our **AnimationPlayer** node a child of the **Sun** node. Our scene tree should look like *Figure 9.17*:

Figure 9.17: The Scene tree of World.tscn after adding the AnimationPlayer node

Select the **AnimationPlayer** node from the Scene tree; the **Animation** console should appear below the Viewport area. Inside the **Animation** console, there will be an **Animation** button. Click it and select the **New...** option, as shown in *Figure 9.18*:

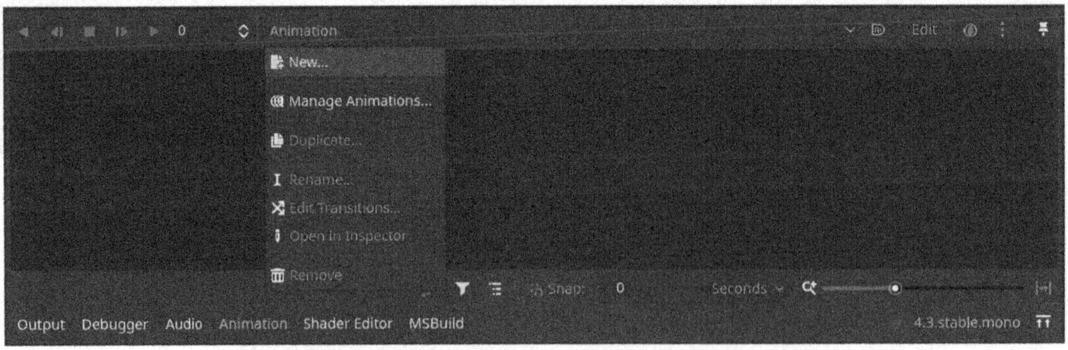

Figure 9.18: Creating a new animation for our Sun node

Once you click **New...**, a pop-up window called **Create New Animation** will appear, asking you to name the new animation. We'll name it `day_time` and click **OK**, as shown in *Figure 9.19*:

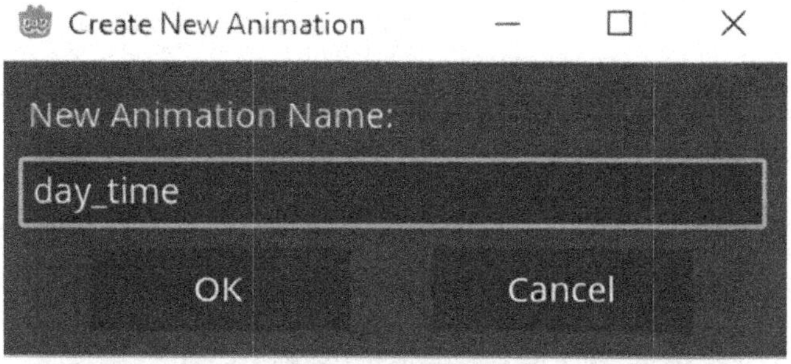

Figure 9.19: The Create New Animation popup

After clicking **OK**, an animation track will appear inside the console, below the **Animation** button. Next to the **Animation** button, the chosen animation, `day_time`, will be selected. This should be familiar since we did this with the imported model we used for our **Player** in *Chapter 4*.

Now that we have a new animation and a track, we can add properties to the animation. Click the **+ Add Track** button. A list of properties we can add will appear, as shown in *Figure 9.20*:

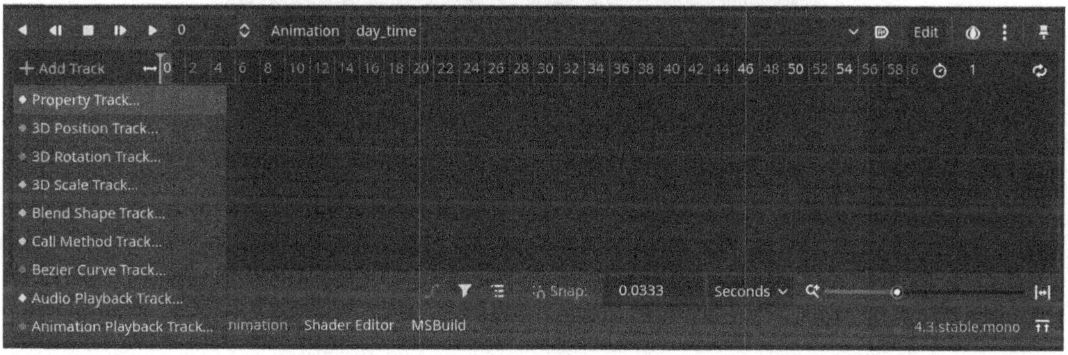

Figure 9.20: Adding a property to the day_time animation

Go ahead and click **Property Track....** A new pop-up window will appear, listing all the nodes from our **World** scene tree. We want to select the **Sun** node, since we're animating it around the level. Go ahead and click **OK**, as shown in *Figure 9.21*:

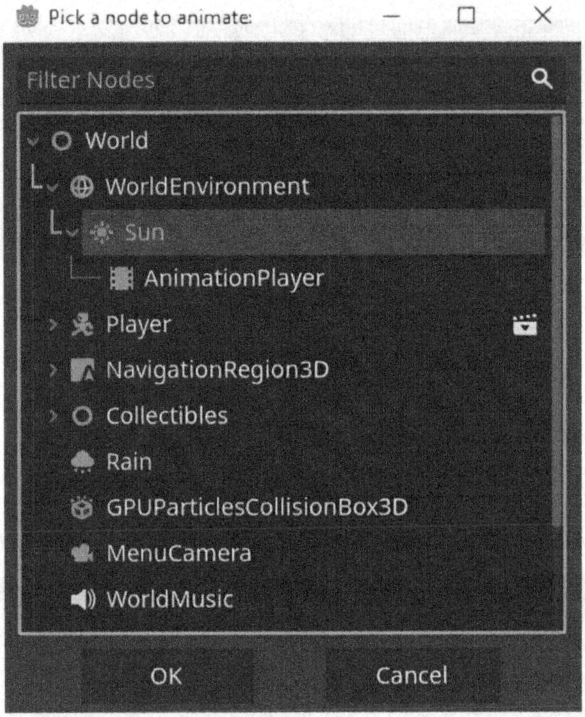

Figure 9.21: Choosing a node to animate

Immediately after selecting **OK**, the pop-up will change to a list of every property for the **Sun** node (see *Figure 9.22*). We want to find the **Rotation** property and select **Open**:

Figure 9.22: Selecting a property on the Sun node to animate

Clicking **Open** adds the **Rotation** property of the **Sun** node to the **Animation** console, below the Viewport area. Make sure the Editor area has the following set for each of its docks:

1. The **Sun** node is selected in the Scene tree.
2. The **Inspector** tab is selected.
3. The **Animation** console is open.

Now that our Editor area has been set up correctly, we can add the keyframes. Within the **Animation** console, set the length of the animation by typing 12 in the box next to the stopwatch icon, as shown in *Figure 9.23*. This will be the length of our in-game day. We also want to click the blue looping icon to the right of the animation's length.

Figure 9.23: Setting the animation's length

Once the duration and looping have been set, look at the **Inspector** dock and go to the **Rotation** property for the **Sun** node. Set the *X*-axis to `-90` degrees and then click the key icon that's next to the name of the property, as shown in *Figure 9.24*:

Figure 9.24: Adding a keyframe based on the Rotation property of the Sun node

Clicking the key will add a little diamond to the animation track. This is shown in *Figure 9.25*. This is the rotation the **Sun** node will start at when the animation begins.

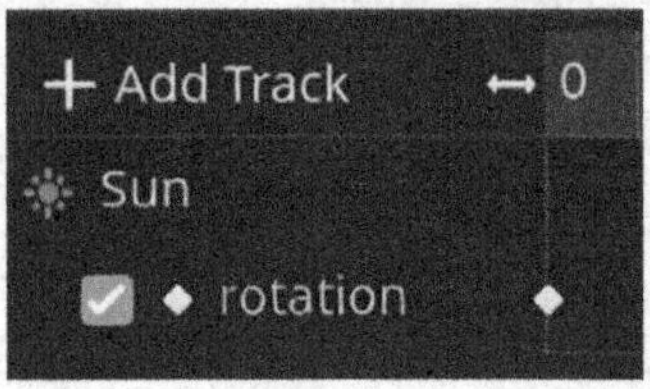

Figure 9.25: The keyframe added at the start of the day_time animation

Now, let's set the final keyframe of the `day_time` animation by going to the end of the animation. We can do this by typing 12 into the box above the animation track, as shown in *Figure 9.26*. This will move the animation track's blue bar to the end of the animation.

> Note
>
> There should be a blue bar on the animation track. It should be at the start of the animation, but I have moved it along the track to make the keyframe more visible in *Figure 9.26*. You can click and drag the blue bar throughout the animation to see how it will look in the Viewport area. It can also be useful for setting keyframes.

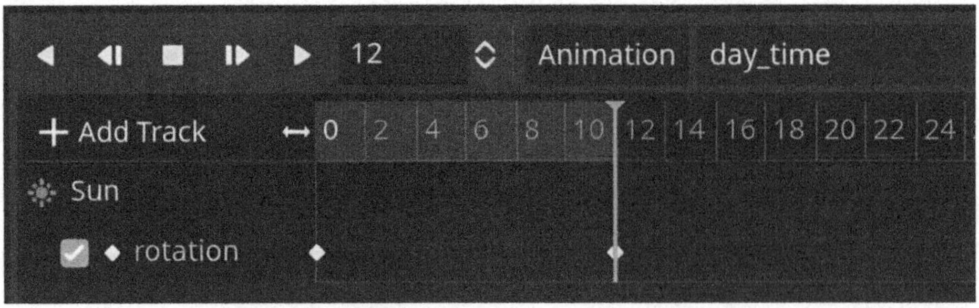

Figure 9.26: Seeking the end of the animation to set a keyframe

Back in the **Inspector** dock, let's set the **Sun** node's rotation to `270` degrees and then click the key icon again. A second diamond will appear on the animation track, as shown in *Figure 9.26*. We can now click the **Player** button in the **Animation** console (again, shown in *Figure 9.26*) to see the animation run.

There's one more step we need to take to complete our animation, and that's triggering the animation so that it starts in the script once the player clicks the **Play** button from our main menu. Let's go ahead and do that now by opening our `World.cs` script.

At the top of our `World.cs` script, where we declare our variables, we're going to create a new variable and write the following:

```
[Export] public AnimationPlayer sun;
```

The `[Export]` attribute creates a property in the Editor area, so we can drag and drop our **AnimationPlayer** node from the scene tree into the **Inspector** dock. This is a convenient way to access nodes and their properties without using the `GetNode` syntax that we have been using in the `_Ready()` functions of our script. Another reason it's convenient is that we don't have to rely on the node's path in the Scene tree. Rather, we can drag and drop the node and have direct access.

Go ahead and save the `World.cs` script, go back to the Editor area, and rebuild the project. You can do this by clicking the hammer icon next to the **Play** button, as shown in *Figure 9.27*:

Figure 9.27: The build button in the top-right corner of the Editor area

> Note
>
> You must rebuild the C# project each time you export variables to update the **Inspector** dock. For a full list of possible properties you can export, go to `https://docs.godotengine.org/en/stable/tutorials/scripting/c_sharp/c_sharp_exports.html`.

Once the project has been rebuilt, you can drag the **AnimationPlayer** node from the Scene tree directly into the **Inspector** dock, as shown in *Figure 9.28*:

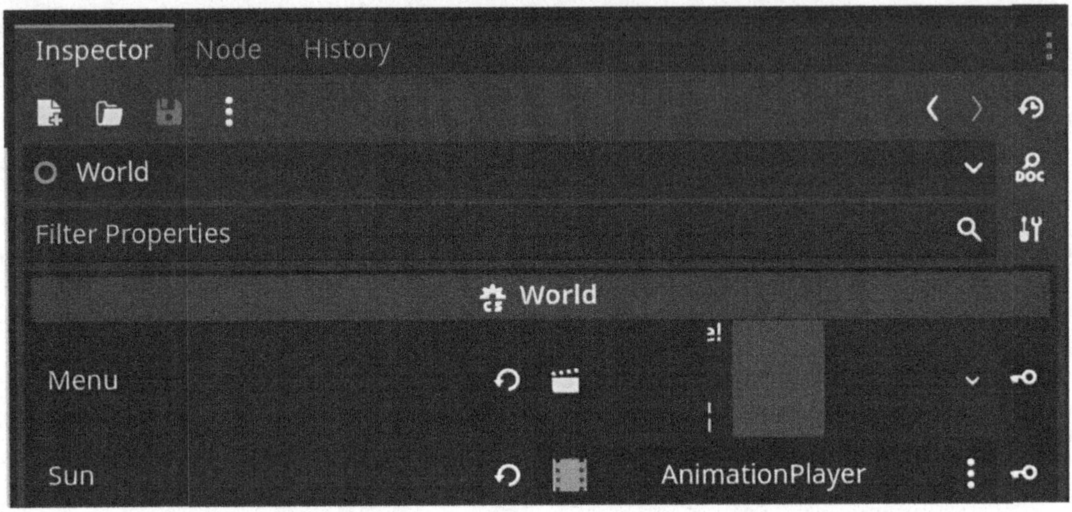

Figure 9.28: Adding the AnimationPlayer node to an exported property

We now have access to the **AnimationPlayer** node and can reference it in the script. Back inside our `World.cs` script, we'll find the `PlayerStart()` function we created in a previous chapter and trigger our sun animation so that it plays. We want it in the `PlayerStart()` function because we only want daytime to start after the player clicks the **Play** button on our main menu. So, write the following inside `PlayerStart()`:

```
sun.play();
```

And that's it! If we save our game and run it, we can test this by clicking the **Play** button, after which we can watch the light change over the **World** scene in the span of a few seconds. This can be seen in *Figure 9.29*.

Figure 9.29: The sun rotating in the World scene

Keep in mind that this is a very simple day cycle and can be expanded upon in a bunch of different ways. Rather than relying on the **AnimationPlayer** node to specify the length of our day, we could script it in our `World.cs` script and have an exported variable for the length to figure out what feels best for the game and our player. Another thing we could do is add another **DirectionalLight3D** node that's much softer and would only appear once the **Sun** node had "set," figuratively speaking, and simulate the idea of having a moon. Or, if it's a fantasy world, you could have more than one moon! The ideas are endless, but this was a jumping-off point to help you discover how directional lighting can be utilized in your project.

Summary

In this chapter, we learned how lighting works in Godot and how best to leverage it for our project. We discovered the various lighting nodes available to us and used the directional, omni, and point nodes. We also briefly discussed baking lightmaps and the benefits of doing so. With our newfound knowledge, we created a day/night cycle for our game while providing examples of interior lighting. The importance of lighting cannot be overstated. It adds the depth and realism that some games, such as colony simulator or survival games, need, and can even be included when it comes to designing the core gameplay.

In the next chapter, we'll consider accessibility in games and update and test all the pieces we've created so far. This will include tasks such as expanding our UI in-game, creating tweens, and making other small adjustments to enhance our game so that we can dive a little deeper into a variety of areas.

10

Understanding Accessibility and Additional Features

So far in this book, we've covered a variety of components within Godot and C#. We've created a player controller, programmed animations, and added different controls for our player. We've created a level that feels dynamic and lived in through particle effects, an item spawner, shaders, lighting, and NPC wandering. To bring it all together, we created some basic UI and added music and sound effects to give feedback and ambiance to our player. Take a moment to celebrate getting here and be proud of what you have created! I hope you've learned enough about Godot and using C# to extend this project and create your own.

However, while we have completed the basics of our project, there are still some important steps to take that this chapter will cover. This chapter is all about cleaning up and improving our project.

First, we'll look at understanding accessibility in video games. This is an extremely important topic that should not be overlooked, as the consideration and inclusion of different types of players is inviting and shows a level of inclusion and polish. While we won't make our game accessible in every way possible, as it's different for each game, we'll implement a couple of ways to make our game accessible in motor and visual ways.

Lastly, we'll discover different ways to save and load data in Godot, discussing the benefits and drawbacks of each.

Our goals for this chapter are the following:

- Understanding accessibility
- Discovering Save systems
- Adding additional features

Technical requirements

For this chapter, the technical requirements will be the same as *Chapter 1*.

All the code from this chapter will be available in the GitHub repository here: `https://github.com/PacktPublishing/Game-Development-with-Godot-and-C-`.

Understanding accessibility

Accessibility is a critical component of game development as it allows more people to play your game. While it hasn't always been at the forefront of development, it's rapidly getting there. With more and more game studios incorporating a wide array of accessible options and game jams such as Global Game Jam and the Godot Wild Jam, which encourage inclusive design, accessibility is a requirement for any aspiring or active game developer. In this section, we'll spend some time discussing ways to make our current project a little bit more accessible.

It can be difficult to provide concrete rules when it comes to accessibility, because there are a multitude of ways that a game could be inaccessible to different types of folks, whether it's related to visual, motor, or cognitive abilities. It also depends heavily on the type of game you're creating, such as a bullet-hell game that requires a lot of dexterity or a visual novel where the options on the font and text displayed in-game matter, but there are a handful of common implementations that can be implemented in a project, no matter the type of game you're creating, as follows:

- **Colorblind settings**: This is a filter that is applied to your UI and game world that allows anyone with any type of colorblindness to still experience your game in a way that is comfortable and accessible to them. A great tool for incorporating this option in your game can be found here, thanks to user Paulloz: `https://github.com/paulloz/godot-colorblindness`.
- **Rebindable keys**: Allowing players to rebind keys is a quick and easy way to give players agency in how they play your game. Rather than keeping them to one control scheme, you can give the player agency over what controls work best for them.

- **Subtitles**: It's important to provide both a visual and auditory way of engaging with a game and its story. Subtitles should not only be included by default, but the user should also be able to customize their size and color, particularly for those who are colorblind. Lastly, an optional textbox for the text to sit on makes the text contrast against the environment for easier reading.
- **Scalable UI**: As mentioned, when discussing bullet points, scalable UI is an important addition to making your game accessible. The option for adjusting the sizing of a UI component or HUD screen is important. With so many devices in the world, it's proactive to provide this type of customization to the player, so they can create an enjoyable way for them to interface with your game.

While this is by no means a comprehensive list for providing accessibility to your game, this is a solid foundation to start. For more information about including accessibility measures in your game, you can check out *Can I Play That?* (`https://caniplaythat.com/`). You can also explore the *Game Accessibility Guidelines* website, which has multiple tiers and is broken down by category in various ways to make sure your game can be played by everyone: `https://gameaccessibilityguidelines.com/`

> Note
>
> As of this writing, the Godot 4 Editor is not readable for OS screen readers. However, there is an open issue on the Engine's GitHub page for this problem, which you can find here: `https://github.com/godotengine/godot/pull/76829`.

With a brief overview of ways to make games accessible, let's look at how we can implement one of those ways. We're going to choose rebindable keys.

Revamping our Settings UI

Providing the option to rebind any controls is always a sure sign of a thoughtful and polished game. It gives players the opportunity to play the game in the way they want. We'll create the ability to rebind controls for our project by adding a page to our UI through the **Settings** menu first.

Right now, our **Settings** screen only has the **Music** and **SFX** sliders on it. We'll be revamping this page to have tabs along the top for **Controls** and **Audio**, as most settings pages do. It's a significant overhaul, but it will make the scene much cleaner and far more expandable in the long run. Let's go ahead and get started by opening our `Settings.tscn` screen.

With our `Settings.tscn` scene open, click the + sign at the top of the scene dock and search for a **TabBar** node. As mentioned, we're going to create two tabs: **Audio** and **Controls**. Then, we'll have these tabs run across the top of our **Settings** page. Make **TabBar** a child of **ColorRect**, as shown in *Figure 10.1*, by dragging the **TabBar** node underneath the **ColorRect** node. Let's see what that looks like here:

Figure 10.1: Placing the TabBar node in our scene tree

Now select the **TabBar** node and look at the **Inspector** dock to see its properties available. The first one is called **Tabs**. Here, we can create the tabs we'll have. Click the **Add Element** button, and a new box of sub-properties will appear, as shown in *Figure 10.2*:

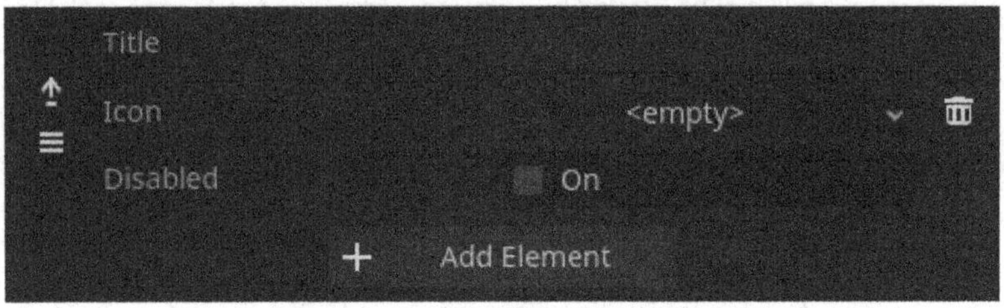

Figure 10.2: Creating tabs in the TabBar node

These sub-properties correlate to each of the tabs. For **Title**, type `Audio`. We won't use the **Icon** property here, as text is enough. We will also leave the **Disabled** property unchecked. The **Disabled** property means the tab is not interactable, but we want both tabs in **TabBar** to be accessible from the start of the game.

Repeat this process once more, naming the new tab `Controls` instead.

> Note
>
> The up arrow and hamburger menu on the left-hand side of *Figure 10.2* allow for quickly rearranging the order of tabs without needing to re-create them.

With our new nodes added, we can begin customizing the **TabBar** node. As a new node, the **TabBar** node was added to the scene at the origin and is very tiny. Let's resize and position it to where we'd like it. Under the **TabBar** properties, find the **Transform** property and use these values:

- **Size**: x: **399**, y: **85**
- **Position**: x: **90**, y: **55**

Great! If you used the same values as me, the **TabBar** node should be sitting on top of the **ColorRect** node towards the top-left of the scene with plenty of room on each side.

Next, we'll quickly change the style of the tabs using our **Theme** resource once more. Click the root node of our `Settings.tscn` scene from the scene dock, labeled **Settings**. The **Theme Editor** should pop-up below the Viewport. With this open, we can create a new theme type by clicking the + sign next to the currently selected theme type, as shown in *Figure 10.3*:

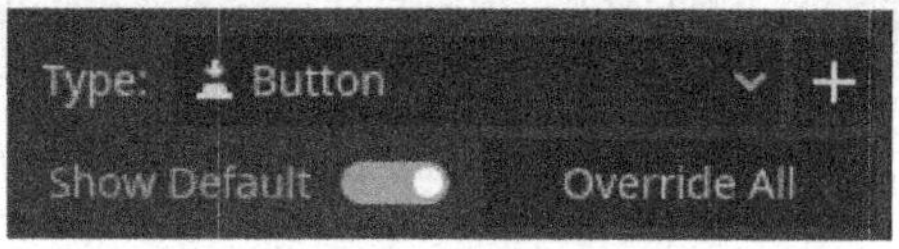

Figure 10.3: The theme type menu within the Theme Editor

A new pop-up will appear, asking what **Control** node we want to have a new theme type for. Search for **TabBar** and find it in the list of nodes, then click **Add Type**. Once added, be sure it's the selected type in the **Type** dropdown, as shown in *Figure 10.4*:

Figure 10.4: The TabBar theme type selected

Now we'll briefly style it so that it matches our page. We'll move through the property tabs from left to right, as we did with previous theme types, such as our buttons. You can see the property tabs in *Figure 10.4* as well.

We'll start with the left-most one, which relates to the color of the font. Once that tab is selected, notice how the listed properties are grayed out. We're going to change all but one of these, so click the **Override All** button above the property tabs, as shown in both *Figure 10.3* and *Figure 10.4*.

After that, every property listed should change from gray to white and have two icons to the right – a **pencil** and a **trash** can. We'll now change the colors to match what's shown in *Figure 10.5*:

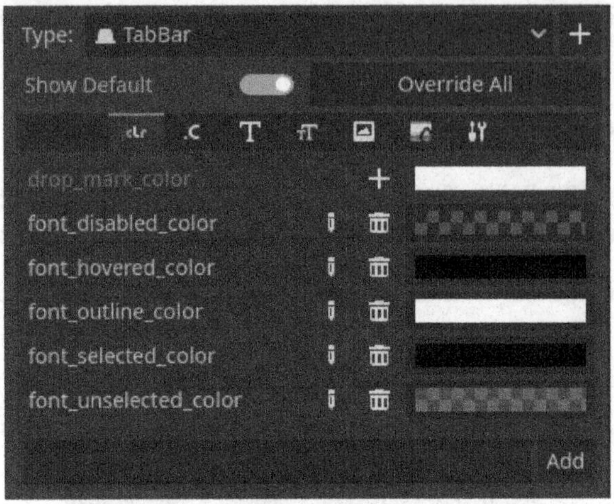

Figure 10.5: The font colors for various font states

To do so, click on each color box, and you should see a **Hex** box, along with a place to set the **Alpha** value (the box to the right of the up and down arrows), as in *Figure 10.6*:

Figure 10.6: Setting the Alpha and Hex color for font_disabled_color

So, to make sure the font colors match *Figure 10.5*, click each color property and enter these values:

- `font_disabled_color`: **Hex: 000000, Alpha: 168**
- `font_hovered_color`: **Hex: 000000, Alpha: 255**
- `font_outline_color`: **Hex: FFFFFF, Alpha: 255**
- `font_selected_color`: **Hex: 000000, Alpha: 255**
- `font_unselected_color`: **Hex: 484848, Alpha: 198**

As we make these changes, we should start to see the **TabBar** node change, since it inherits our theme resource from the **Settings** node.

Next, we'll move on to the fourth tab (see *Figure 10.4*), which only has the `font_size` property listed. Click the + sign next to the `font_size` property and set it to **40**.

The final property tab to adjust is our StyleBoxes. These can be found in the sixth tab from the left in *Figure 10.4*. It also has a **rainbow** icon with a droplet in the bottom-right corner of it. If we scroll down, we'll see the tab properties as shown in *Figure 10.7*:

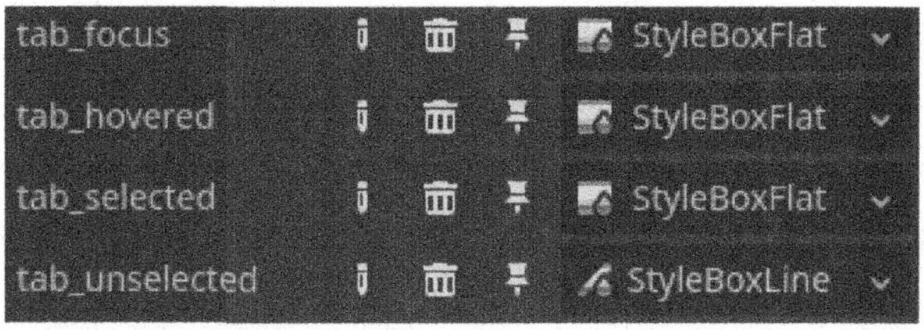

Figure 10.7: The StyleBoxes we're creating for TabBar

We'll be creating StyleBoxes (either flat boxes or lines) based on the state the tab is in (e.g., hover, selected, and so on). To do so, follow these instructions:

1. Click the + sign next to the `tab_focus` property.
2. Open the **<empty>** dropdown and select **StyleBoxFlat**. The selected **StyleBoxFlat** will be highlighted as shown in *Figure 10.8*:

Figure 10.8: Selecting StyleBoxFlat for tab_focus

3. Next, click **StyleBoxFlat** and the **Inspector** dock will change to show a list of properties for **StyleBoxFlat**. All we're going to change here is to set **Alpha** for **BG Color** to be 0 (leaving it at its default gives us some unwanted behavior). Now, let's repeat steps 1-3 for `tab_hovered`. Once we're inside the **StyleBoxFlat** properties, change the following options:
   - **BG Color**: Set the color to **#E86A17** and **Alpha** to **68**.
   - **Corner Detail**: Set this to **8** pixels.
   - **Border Width**: Set **Top** to **12** pixels.
   - **Border**: Make sure **Blend** is enabled, and **Color** is set to **#CCCCCC**.
   - **Corner Radius**: Set **Bottom Right** and **Bottom Left** to **7** pixels each.
   - **Expand Margins**: Set **Bottom** to **5** pixels.
   - **Content Margins**: Set **Left** and **Right** to **5** pixels, **Top** to **6** pixels, and **Bottom** to **-1**.

> Note
>
> We are moving quickly through these properties with little explanation, as we thoroughly covered them in *Chapter 6*, so if you're unsure of how a property behaves, review that chapter, which is all about UI and working with the theme editor.

Once more, repeat *steps 1-3* for `tab_selected`. We're going to move through the same properties with minor tweaks to what they are. We'll step through each of these properties for all the tabs, so they match and have cohesion throughout all states of the tabs. Unless noted, the properties should match those of `tab_hovered`.

- **BG Color**: Set the color to **#7B7B7B** and **Alpha** to **109**.
- **Border**: Make sure **Blend** is enabled, and **Color** is set to **#E86A17**.
- **Expanded Margins**: Set **Left** and **Right** to **5** pixels and **Bottom** to **3** pixels.
- **Content Margins**: Set **Left**, **Top**, and **Right** to **6** pixels while **Bottom** is set to **-1**.

The final tab property we're going to augment is the `tab_unselected` one. Repeat steps 1-3 as we have been, but this time, instead of **StyleBoxFlat**, select **StyleBoxLine**. Then, in the **Inspector** dock, we'll change the following properties:

- **Color**: The color will be black, which is **#000000**, and **Alpha** will be **255**.
- **Grow End**: Set to **5** pixels.
- **Thickness**: Set to **5** pixels.
- **Content Margins**: Set all to **12** pixels.

Now our **TabBar** node in the **Settings** scene should look like *Figure 10.9*:

Figure 10.9: TabBar styled and in our Settings scene

Excellent! Now that the styling of our tabs is complete, let's look at rearranging the **Settings** scene tree to toggle between the tabs.

Updating our Settings scene

When rearranging the scene tree, we'll use *Figure 10.10* and reference it as needed:

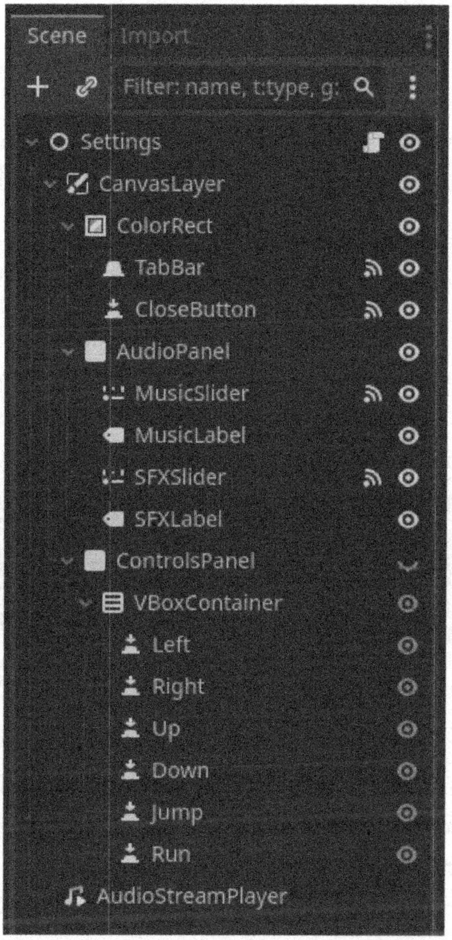

Figure 10.10: The scene tree structure for our Settings screen

We've already added the **TabBar** node to be a child of **ColorRect**. Now we're going to add two additional panels – one for the **Audio** page and the other for **Controls**. Click the + sign above the scene tree, search for **Panel**, and name it `AudioPanel`. Repeat this process and name the panel `ControlsPanel`. Then make them children of **CanvasLayer** by dragging them under **CanvasLayer**, as shown in *Figure 10.10*.

Now, let's position the two newly created panels, and then we'll reparent the correct nodes under each. The **Position** and **Size** properties of each panel will be the same and are as follows:

- **Size**: x: **1053** px, y: **482** px
- **Position**: x: **55** px, y: **133** px

Now, the panels will have a semi-transparent black background because we've added the **Panel** node as a theme type to the theme editor. Remember, we styled the panel for our main menu. Here, we're going to override the theme resource, so we can have a clear background on these panels only.

Before we can do that, however, we need to add our theme resource to the panel. Select **AudioPanel** and in the **Inspector**, find the **Theme** property. Expand it and let's load our `UI_Theme.tres` resource.

Next, expand the **Theme Overrides** property, and you should see another property called **Styles**. Check the **Panel** box under **Styles** and then load **StyleBoxEmpty** to override what we designed for the `UI_Theme.tres` resource. The option will look like *Figure 10.11* in the **Inspector** dock.

Figure 10.11: Overriding the Panel style in AudioPanel

Repeat the step of adding the theme resource for **ControlsPanel** in overriding the theme and adding the `UI_Theme.tres` resource. We want to select the **AudioPanel** node in the scene tree, view the **Inspector**, and then find the **Theme Overrides** property, as shown in *Figure 10.11*. We'll make sure the panel is enabled and then load **StyleBoxEmpty**. Again, we want to override the existing theme resource with a different design for the background of both the audio and control panels.

Once our theme resource is overridden, we'll also want to click the eyeball icon next to **ControlsPanel** in the scene dock, as we want it hidden on start and will only make it visible when the player clicks the **Controls** tab. Later in this chapter, we'll toggle the correct panel on and off based on clicking the right tab. For now, we want it hidden. Lastly, be sure to parent **MusicSlider**, **MusicLabel**, **SFXSlider**, and **SFXLabel** underneath **AudioPanel**.

For **ControlsPanel**, create **VBoxContainer** and then create six **Button** nodes. Name each **Button** node **Left**, **Right**, **Up**, **Down**, **Jump**, and **Run**, respectively. Again, you can see the scene tree in *Figure 10.10* if you're unsure what type of node needs to be added and how it's parented in the scene tree.

We'll also delete the **Title** label node we created previously that said **Settings** in the top middle of the screen. Our **Settings** screen should now look like *Figure 10.12*:

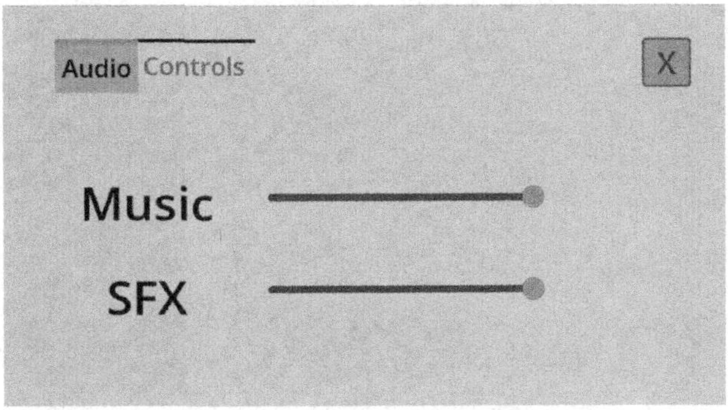

Figure 10.12: The Settings screen revamped

Awesome! Our **Settings** screen is looking polished now. Next, we're going to add a function to the `Settings.cs` file to alternate between the **Audio** and **Controls** tabs.

Programming our tabs

Adding functionality to our tabs is the last step before getting into rebinding our keys. Let's go ahead and select the **TabBar** node in the scene tree. Then, in the **Inspector** dock, we'll click the **Node** tab at the top. We're going to create a signal and add the function for it in our `Settings.cs` file. The built-in signal we're using is the `tab_selected(tab: int)` one. Find the `tab_selected(tab:int)` signal in the list of signals. Once highlighted, the **Connect...** button at the bottom of the list will be clickable, as shown in *Figure 10.13*:

Figure 10.13: The Connect... button at the bottom of the signal list

After clicking **Connect...**, a new pop-up will appear, as shown in *Figure 10.14*. Remember, the signal function must be tied to an existing script. In this case, our signal will be tied to the `Settings.cs` script.

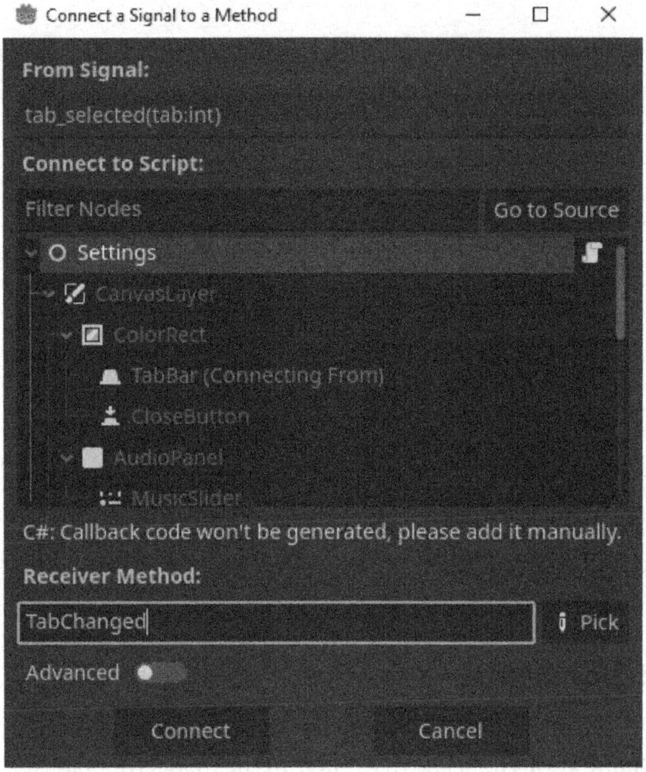

Figure 10.14: The pop-up window for adding a signal

Underneath the **Receiver Method** box, we'll change the auto-generated function name to `TabChanged`, as shown in *Figure 10.14*. Then, we'll click the **Connect** button. The pop-up will disappear, and we can see the function added in green text under the signal name, as shown in *Figure 10.15*:

> Note
>
> Notice the *yellow* text that states the callback code won't be generated and must be added manually. This means, as we've been doing, that a new function won't be created automatically in the script we're attaching the signal to. However, if we add the function call with the same name and parameters, it will be called correctly.

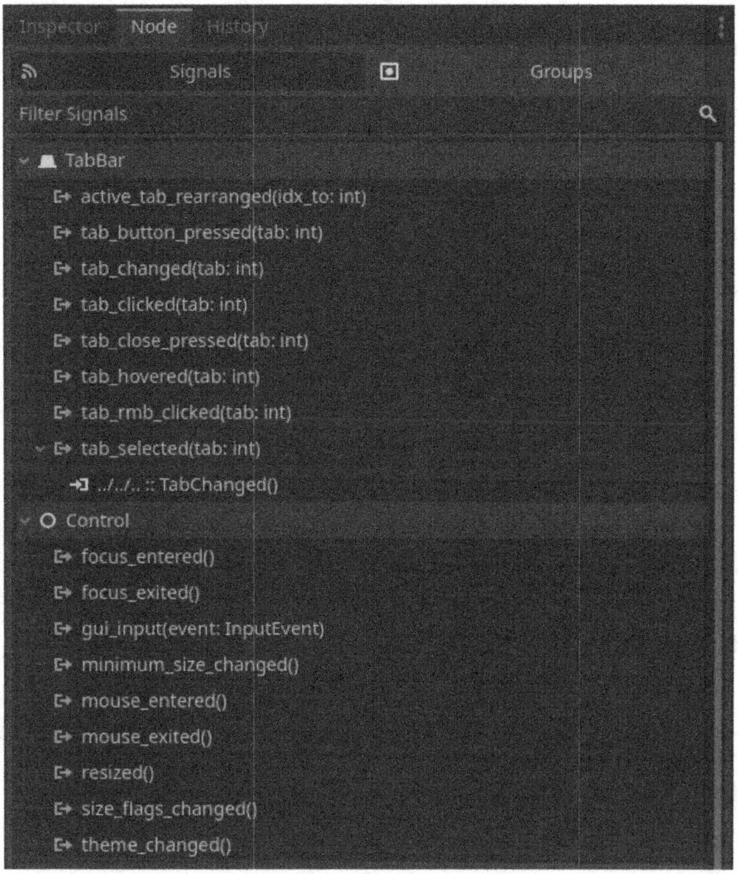

Figure 10.15: The list of signals on the TabBar node

With the signal created and connected to a function, let's create the function inside our `Settings.cs` script to finalize this functionality. To do this, we'll open the `Settings.cs` script and scroll to the bottom of the class. We want to create a new function that matches what we put in the **Receiver Method** box when connecting the signal. This means we will write the following:

```
private void TabChanged(int tab) {}
```

The function will take in a single parameter called `tab`, and this will determine which set of control nodes to show or hide. Within the function, let's create a switch/case statement to toggle the right control nodes on and off. We'll write the following:

```
switch (tab) {
    case 0:
        break;
```

```
    case 1:
        break;
}
```

We'll only have two cases, because we'll either be on the **Audio** tab or the **Controls** one. Let's go ahead and set the first case with the 0 to show the **Audio** tab, and the second case with the 1 to show the **Controls** tab.

Within the case 0 and before the line that says `break`, let's write the following code:

```
audioMenu.visible = true;
controlsMenu.visible = false;
```

The `audioMenu` and `controlsMenu` variables have a reference to the **Panel** nodes in our scene tree, and since all of their children have the information for each tab, we can simply hide one or the other. Remember that, by default, the state of the parent node will impact the state of all its children unless otherwise marked in the node.

Discovering Save systems

While there is not much to save in the way of data in our game, we'll briefly discuss how you can save data and the use cases for each. We'll be looking at the following ways to save data:

- Using JSON files
- Binary serialization
- Config files

Saving with JSON

The first one we'll discuss is using JSON files. **JSON** stands for **JavaScript Object Notation.** JSON files are formatted into human-readable text. If we wanted to create and save data about the player in a JSON file, it might look like the following:

```
{
  "player_name": "Kati",
  "mushrooms_collected": {
    "blue": 1,
```

```
        "red": 3
    }
}
```

In this example, we have two types of data being saved, which are `player_name` and `mushrooms_collected`. We can be more specific in the kinds of data we're seeking by nesting the JSON name-value pair and marking whether a mushroom we collected is blue or red.

> Note
>
> When exporting your project, which we'll discuss in the next chapter, it's important to mark JSON files, so they aren't exported as if they were a resource, scene, and so on.

While JSON files are easy to read, they can become quite cumbersome when there is a lot of data. They are also not necessarily the safest format to use. However, it's a perfect solution when it comes to creating game jam games or even working on a game with limited player data. For more information about JSON and how to use it in Godot, you can read about it here: `https://docs.godotengine.org/en/stable/classes/class_json.html#class-json`.

Let's look at some other ways we can save player data, such as through binary serialization.

Saving with binary serialization

Binary serialization is a way to take existing data and convert it to an array of bytes (that is made up of binary) for saving. Godot has a built-in API for doing this based on the `Variant` data type. The biggest reason to use binary serialization is how much space it saves, since it's machine-readable only. It's also a big downside, because you can't easily read it like when saving with JSON. Godot provides functions for converting the saved data and provides how much space each data type takes up when converted. You can read more about that here: `https://docs.godotengine.org/en/stable/tutorials/io/binary_serialization_api.html`.

Saving with ConfigFile

The final way to save data that we'll discuss is by using `ConfigFile`. With this, we write specific data to a new `ConfigFile` object and use the `ConfigFile`'s `save()` function when updating the data. `ConfigFile` is a great blend of the JSON and binary serialization methods for two reasons. The first reason is that it's human-readable, but it's also serializable. This means it won't take up as much space on the disk. It can also be encrypted, providing some security. You can find more information on creating and using a ConfigFile here: `https://docs.godotengine.org/en/stable/classes/class_configfile.html`.

Adding additional features

In this section, we're going to add some small quality-of-life improvements to our game in two specific areas. Both will be implemented in a script, but will have a wide array of impacts on the project, depending on how you want to further develop it. The list of features is as follows:

- Discovering and using tweens
- Switching scenes

Let's start by discussing what tweens are and how to use them.

Using tweens

Tweens are a convenient way to animate objects in Godot, especially when you don't know the expected value of the object. They allow us to interpolate an object between two points. We'll be using tweens to make our collectible mushrooms randomly rotate on either the *X*, *Y*, or *Z* axis. They are more lightweight than `AnimationPlayer` and are great when wanting some light animation or juice to add to an object or UI.

To do this, let's go ahead and open the `Collectible.cs` file. We'll be adding a tween object to the collectible and then augmenting tween properties to get a random set of rotations on the collectible. Adding a tween object requires one line of code and will be above the `_Ready()` function.

```
private Tween _itemTween;
```

Here, we've only declared a tween variable, but still need to create it and attach a tween object. After that, we can start to access the tween properties within the class, using our `_itemTween` object.

> Note
>
> A good guideline when using tweens is not to use more than one tween to modify the same property of an object, which is why it is good to assign a tween to a variable and track it.

Inside our `_Ready()` function, we'll create the tween and assign it to our `_itemTween` variable by writing the following line of code.

```
_itemTween = CreateTween().SetLoops();
```

The `CreateTween()` function creates a tween for us, and we immediately call `SetLoops()`. `SetLoops()` with no arguments passed into the function will ensure the tween runs infinitely. Now our tween has been created and assigned to our variable. Next, let's access the tween properties and have our collectible rotate around the *X* axis. Right below the line we just wrote, we'll write the following:

```
_itemTween.TweenProperty(this, "position:y", .25f, 1f).AsRelative();
```

Here, we're calling a tween function called `TweenProperty()`, which creates `PropertyTweener` and passes four arguments into the function. Let's break down each of these arguments:

- `this`: The object we want to be tweened, which is the collectible, so we self-reference it by typing `this`
- `"position:y"`: This is the property on the object we want to tween, and we provide a string to the property's path in quotes
- `.25f`: This is the final value the tween will modify the property over the duration. A second, initial value can be listed to keep the change bound, but we did not do that here.
- `1f`: This is the duration of the tween in seconds.

Once the arguments are passed to the created `PropertyTweener`, we call one final function, named `AsRelative()`. This takes the final value and will be used as a relative value instead.

Now let's rotate the collectible on the *X* axis by choosing a degree to rotate at random. Again, we'll use tweens for this by doing the following:

```
_itemTween.TweenProperty(this, "rotation:x", ChooseRandomDegree(), 1f).
AsRelative();
```

We're calling `TweenProperty()` to access the tween properties within, and the arguments are as follows:

- `this`: The object we want to tween, the collectible
- `"rotation:x"` The property we're tweening, which is the rotation of the collectible on the *X* axis
- `ChooseRandomDegree()`: This is a function we'll create that returns a float to select a degree at random for our *X* axis to rotate on
- `1f`: This is the duration of the tween in seconds

Lastly, we have the `AsRelative()` function again, to ensure the values are relative to our collectible object.

The last line of code we need is to add a small pause before the tween loops through and starts again. This line will look like the following:

```
_itemTween.TweenInterval(.5f);
```

The `TweenInterval` function creates a delay based on the float passed into it. Here, we're delaying the tween animation by half a second, and then it will start the tween over again, since we have `SetLoops()` to be true.

With our tween created and properties augmented, we need to also create the function we referenced in those lines of preceding code, `ChooseRandomDegree()`. We can do that inside the `Collectible.cs` script, since we're only calling that function in relation to the tween and its properties, which also live in `Collectible.cs`. At the top of the file, we need to add the `Random` class that's in the `System` library of C#. At the top of the `Collectible.cs` script, we'll write the following under the `using Godot;` line:

```
using System;
```

Next, we'll write the following:

```
public float ChooseRandomDegree()
{
    Random rDegree = new();
    float randomDegree = rDegree.Next(0, 30);
    return randomDegree;
}
```

The declaration of the `public float ChooseRandomDegree()` function returns a float. Then, the first line inside the function creates a random object, called `rDegree`. After that, we create a float variable, `randomDegree`, and use the `Next()` function from the `Random` class to generate a number between 0 and 30 and assign it to `randomDegree`. This is the value we return at the end of the function.

Save the script, and let's go back to Godot to test out our tween. If we hit play, we should see the collectible floating in the air and rotating around the world.

> Note
>
> If you don't have a collectible item in your **World** scene, you can drag the `.tscn` file from the **File** dock and into the **World** scene.

With tweens covered and implemented, let's move on to the last feature in this chapter, switching scenes. It's a common feature and necessary when it comes to keeping scenes contained, clean, and usable.

Switching scenes

Switching scenes is easy and encouraged in Godot. Having every piece of your game in one scene would quickly become too much to manage. We've already been using multiple scenes and having them loaded into scenes as objects. With that, there are a couple of different ways to switch scenes in Godot. Either way, we'll instantiate a new scene in our current scene, but after that, we'll have two options for how to handle our old scene root. They are the following:

- Option 1: Additively instantiate another scene on top of the current one
- Option 2: Manually remove the old root scene and switch to the new scene

Let's start with the first option and bind a key to instantiate and add a new scene on top of our existing one. We've already been doing this with scenes such as our player controller and our collectible item. This time, we'll do it with the test area scene we used in the lighting chapter. To start, let's open the `World.cs` file.

At the top of the script, where the variables are, let's add the following:

```
public node testScene;
```

This variable will hold the new scene we're loading in. Next, in the `_PhysicsProcess` function, let's create an `if` statement to change our scene based on keyboard input. We'll add the following lines of code:

```
if(Input.IsActionJustPressed("SwitchScene")) { }
```

Inside this `if` statement, let's assign our variable to the `ResourceLoader` class and call its load function with the following:

```
testScene = ResourceLoader.Load<PackedScene> ("res://test_area.tscn").
Instantiate();
```

Here, we take our variable and assign a packed scene, `test_area.tscn`, to `testScene`. At the end of this line of code, we call the `Instantiate` function, which is what adds `test_area.tscn` to the scene tree. Next, we'll write this:

```
GetTree().Root.AddChild(testScene);
```

This line finds the root of our current scene tree and adds the instantiated scene as a child. The last thing we need to do is bind a key to the input `SwitchScene`. Go to **Project Settings** in the top-left corner, add a new action called `SwitchScene`, and then click the small **plus sign** icon next to the new action. A new window will appear, asking you for input. Hit a key that has not been assigned, such as the number *1*, as shown in *Figure 10.16*:

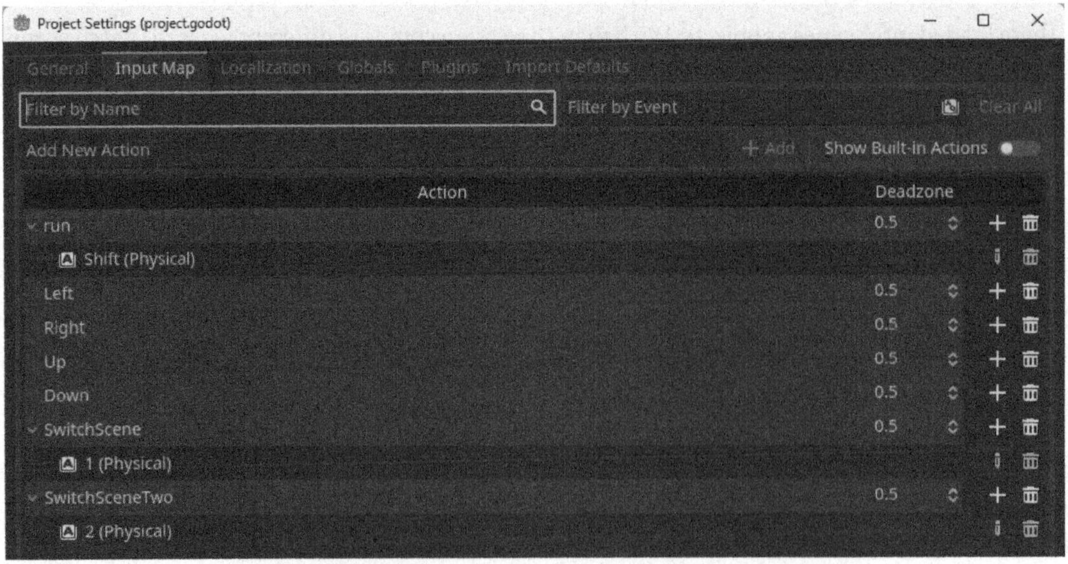

Figure 10.16: Binding key inputs for switching scenes in project settings

Now, run the game and click the **Play** button from the main menu. Once on the main level of the game, hit the number *1* key on your keyboard, or whatever key you've bound the `SwitchScene` input to, and you should see `test_area.tscn` added to the level. Notice how it sits on top of the `World.tscn` scene, because our root scene is still there. Sometimes this is useful, but in this instance, with levels, it's not quite as convenient as it was when we added our player or collectible. Let's consider a different way.

Before we start the second option, let's go ahead and create the new keybind for it, since we were just inside **Project Settings**. Go ahead and type, in the **Add New Action** space, the words `SwitchSceneTwo`, and bind it to something such as number 2, as shown in *Figure 10.16*.

Back in our `World.cs` file, let's add another `If` statement inside the `_PhysicsProcess` function. The `If` statement will start with the following:

```
If(Input.IsActionJustPressed("SwitchSceneTwo") { }
```

Here, we're tying the player input to the new keybind we did for `SwitchSceneTwo`. Next, we'll add this line:

```
GetTree().ChangeSceneToFile("res://test_area.tscn");
```

This line calls the scene tree and then utilizes a built-in function in the `GetTree` object called `ChangeSceneToFile`. Save the file and go ahead and test it out by running the game and selecting the number 2. Immediately, the level scene is gone, the music stops, and the lighting is much darker. This is because the new root of the scene is `test_area.tscn`, and all the nodes from `World.tscn` have been removed. The built-in `ChangeSceneToFile` function ensures that both scenes aren't running at the same time, but be warned that any data from `World.tscn` we may have wanted to access is no longer accessible now.

For more information on the pros and cons of each option we discussed, you can read more about them here: `https://docs.godotengine.org/en/stable/tutorials/scripting/change_scenes_manually.html`.

We've now covered a couple of different ways to change scenes in Godot to better equip you for managing resources and memory when it comes to adding and changing scenes.

Summary

This chapter highlighted how many different types of resources are available in the Godot community. Many developers freely share both their code and expertise to better support Godot and its community. Therefore, in this chapter, we spent a lot of time discussing the needs of accessibility and implementing features that added another layer of polish and depth to our project. When it comes to accessibility, there is no catch-all that works for every game, but we did discuss a few standard features, such as rebindable keys, subtitles, and a wide range of options for catering your game's UI to best suit the largest range of players. At the end of this discussion, we updated our **Settings** scene to have a page for rebindable keys.

After we looked at accessibility, we spent time analyzing the multiple ways you can save data in your project. While our project has little to no data that requires saving now, it was an important topic to cover as it's a foundational piece of every game created and played. Finally, we implemented two more features. The first was creating rebindable keys. The second was switching scenes. Both tweens and scene switching are common and easy features to include.

Now, we'll get into the details of exporting our project and uploading it to itch.io. In the next chapter, we'll look at exporting to Windows, Linux, and iOS. We'll discuss the current state of exporting in C# and its limitations. The last thing we'll do is create an account on itch.io and upload a project to make our game accessible to the world.

11

Exporting Your Game

By this point of the book, we've completed all the programming and settings for our project. Yay! Give yourself a huge round of applause for making it this far. I hope you are happy with your project and find it to be a good jumping-off point to continue developing games in Godot with C#.

However, we're not quite done, because we need to share our project with the world. To do this, we need to export our project and test out our exported version of the game.

In this chapter, we'll cover a variety of concepts relating to exports. We'll discuss what exporting your game means and what happens to your game in the process. We'll specifically look at how to export our project for Linux, Windows, and iOS. Briefly, we'll touch on exporting to HTML5, but given the current state of C# and web exports in Godot 4 as of this writing, we won't be able to do it.

Unfortunately, you cannot export a C# project to HTML. However, this will be added and supported once the Godot team is able. This is something they have stated repeatedly. The last thing we'll cover is how to upload our executables to itch.io to allow anyone in the world to play your game. It's important to know how to export your project, so you can share it with the world regardless of the system your players are on. While we'll primarily focus on exporting for Windows, we will briefly be discussing exporting to Linux and macOS.

So, in this chapter, we will cover the following topics:

- Understanding what exporting is
- Downloading export templates
- Exporting our game to Windows
- Uploading our game to itch.io

Technical requirements

For this chapter, the technical requirements will be the same as *Chapter 1*.

All the code from this chapter will be available in the GitHub repository here: `https://github.com/PacktPublishing/Game-Development-with-Godot-and-C-`.

Understanding what exporting is

If we were to browse to the disk location of our Godot project, we would find a file called `project.godot`. This file, along with the assets and C# solution of your game, allows people to play the game in engine. However, this also opens up the game's entire code base, which means people can modify it for better or for worse by easily importing the `project.godot` file and tinkering around.

Perhaps the biggest reason to export your project, especially when launching on platforms such as Steam and GOG, or even on a console, is to be able to deploy updates to your game as needed. This ranges from patches to fix bugs to added downloadable content.

The process of **exporting** means we can package our `project.godot` file along with all our scenes and resources to be an executable that's easy for our players to interact with in a way that's familiar to them and safe for developers.

Downloading export templates

Export templates are executables designed to work for specific platforms, not limited to just your standard operating systems. Export templates take the code and assets and convert them into executables for specific platforms. These platforms include options for mobile and web, as well as an option to create your own export templates – this option is particularly useful when you are using a specific or private **software development kit (SDK)**.

> Note
>
> As of this writing, you cannot export C# projects to HTML5. The Godot community is working on a fix, and many improvements have been made to web exports since Godot 4's release, such as Android support and an upgrade to .NET 8.

Accessing the export templates is easy. Start by clicking **Project** and selecting **Export**. A new window will appear that looks like *Figure 11.1*:

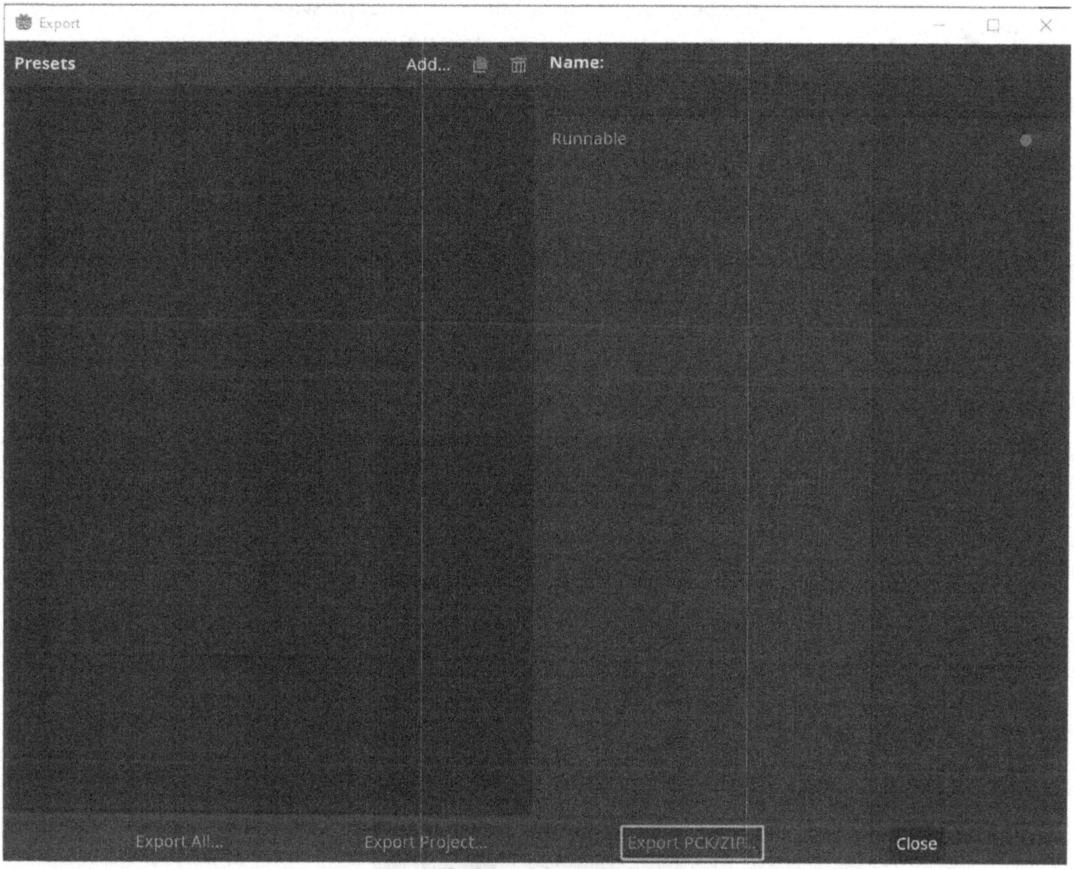

Figure 11.1: The Export menu in Godot

Currently, it's blank. This is because we have no export templates downloaded for exporting a project, but we'll be adding one for each operating system.

Note

It is possible to export to Windows, Linux, and macOS without owning a machine that has all three operating systems on it. With the correct export template downloaded, Godot will serialize the project correctly. However, if you want to test the exported project on a different operating system, you can ask a friend or set up a secondary environment for yourself.

Before we get into any one specific operating system, let's download the export templates for Windows, Linux, and macOS.

Click the **Add...** button at the top of the **Export** menu as shown in *Figure 11.1*. You should see a new drop-down menu, as shown in *Figure 11.2*:

Figure 11.2: The available export templates in Godot

Here, we'll select the **Windows Desktop** option. Once we do, it will be added under the **Presets** side of the **Export** menu, as shown in *Figure 11.3*:

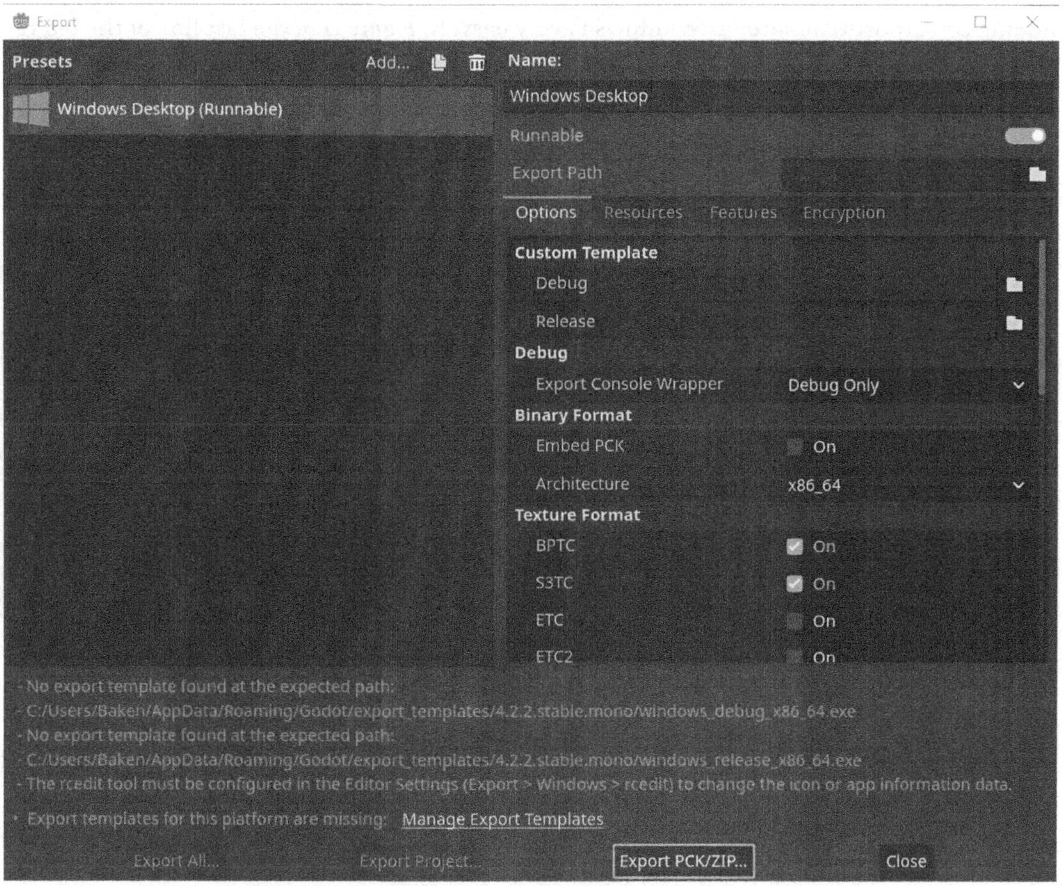

Figure 11.3: Adding the Windows preset to our export menu

You will also see that we have some red text at the bottom of the menu. This provides the default options for exporting on that platform. Oftentimes, we will need to add an export template, especially when more tools like SDKs are needed to properly export. By default, export templates are required when creating packages, which is what we'll be doing with our project.

Adding the export template for Windows is very easy. In *Figure 11.3*, the last line of the red text says, **Export templates for this platform are missing: Manage Export Templates.** As you can see, **Manage Export Templates** is a button. Click on it. The **Export** menu will briefly disappear and be replaced by the menu shown in *Figure 11.4*:

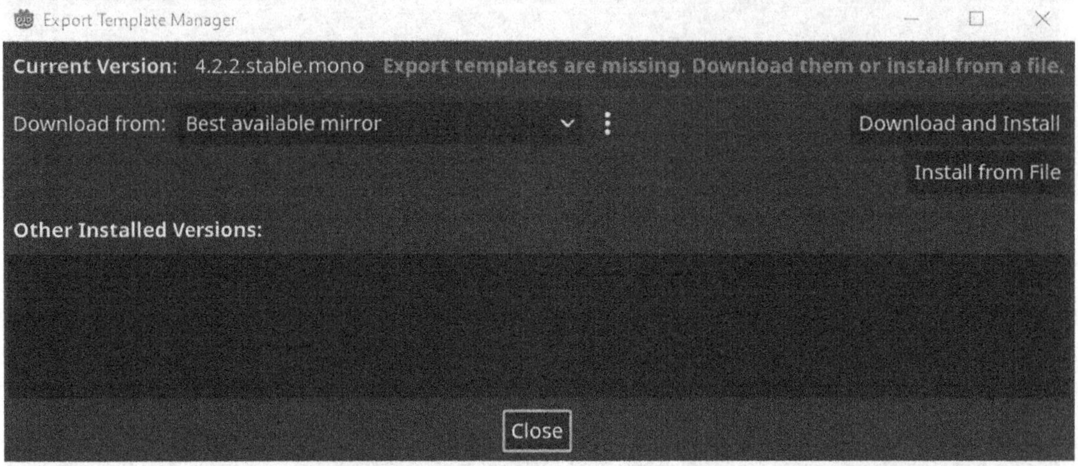

Figure 11.4: Downloading an export template

The new menu that appears is **Export Template Manager**. It gives you some options as to where to download the export template from, or if you have a custom one, you can browse to its location and install it. Simply click **Download and Install** and a progress bar will replace the **Download from** drop-down menu. Once it's complete, click the **Close** button.

> Note
>
> Make sure you are downloading the export templates for the correct version of Godot. Otherwise, they will not work, and Godot will have an error message in red text notifying you that you are missing export templates. If you're using an older version of Godot, you can find the export templates here by clicking the version you're using and then selecting the **.NET** button next to **Export Templates**: `https://godotengine.org/download/archive/`.

Now, let's click **Project**, then **Export** again to return to the **Export** menu. This time, the red text that was giving us an error should be gone, and we have a note in yellow text about changing the icon or app information data, as shown in *Figure 11.5*.

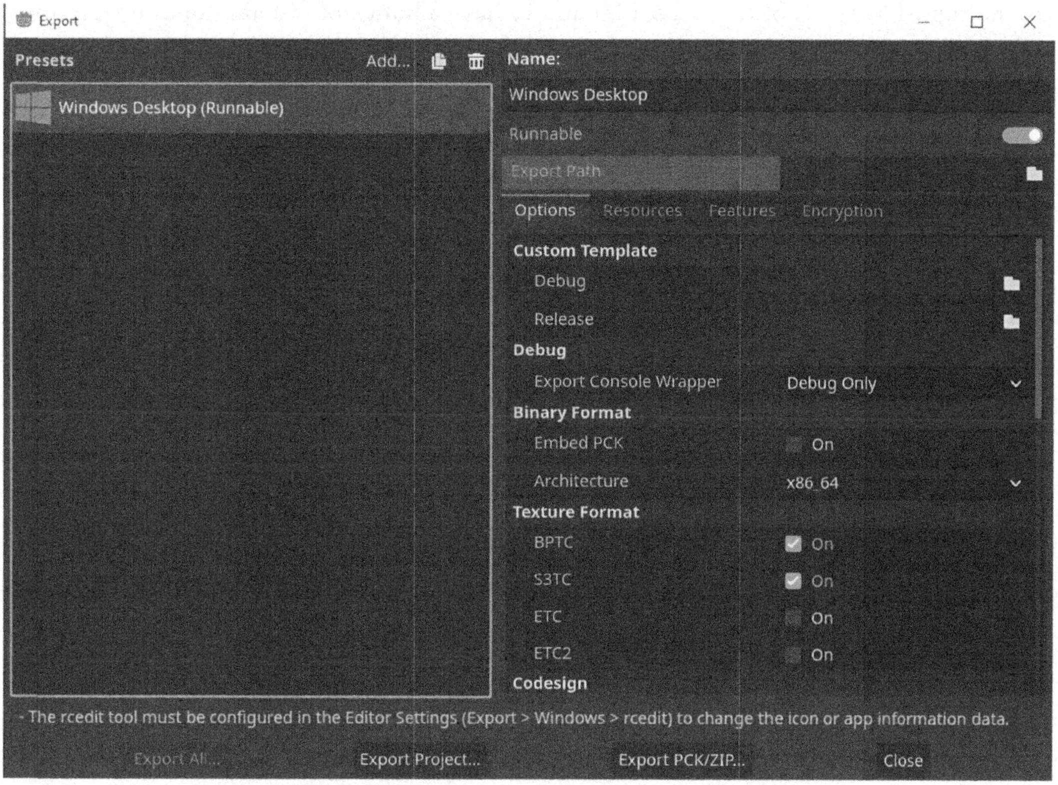

Figure 11.5: Export menu after adding the Windows export template

With one of our export templates installed, let's now talk about some of the **Export** menu settings. We'll start with the row of buttons along the bottom of the window, as shown in *Figure 11.5*:

- **Export All**: This option will export the project for all added presets. For example, once we add the Linux preset, if we click this button, it will export for both Windows and Linux.
- **Export Project**: Rather than exporting for all added presets, this option only exports for the platform that's been selected.
- **Export PCK/ZIP**: This exports the package as either a PCK or ZIP package. It's important to note that this does not make the game a playable build and is often used when uploading for HTML5 games.
- **Close**: This simply closes the **Export** menu window.

On the right-hand side of the **Export** menu, we have a bunch of different options for how to export our project:

- **Name**: This will be the name of the executable as users see it. At its default, it takes the name of the preset platform that's selected. It's important to rename this to your project.
- **Runnable**: This means the executable is a one-click deploy option for platforms where it may be applicable, such as mobile. You can read more about one-click deploy here: `https://docs.godotengine.org/en/stable/tutorials/export/one-click_deploy.html`.
- **Export Path**: This is where the project executable will be on your machine. Be sure to browse to a path that's outside of the project and somewhere you'll remember.

Underneath the **Export Path** option, we have a series of tabs: **Options**, **Resources**, **Features**, and **Encryption**. Let's break down the first tab, **Options**, and briefly discuss what's inside it (all options will be left in their default state):

- **Custom Template**: This has two properties, **Debug** and **Release**. These are both for browsing custom export templates, but since we're using the default ones from Godot, we don't have to worry about this.
- **Debug**: This option does some behind-the-scenes error guarding and should be selected when creating builds for games that are being tested. It also provides a debug log, which is useful for diagnosing crashes and other existing bugs in your game.
- **Release**: This option has some optimizations that ensure it runs a bit smoother and should be used when you're creating a final build for release.
- **Debug**: This is a great, useful option when sending a project to a friend and/or testing your exported project. The options allow the project to be packaged with additional output, if necessary.
- **Export Console Wrapper**: The drop-down menu has three options, **No**, **Debug Only**, and **Debug and Release**. The default is **Debug Only**, and this means we'll have console output go to a debug console with our executable. We don't want this option for a complete project, so select **No** if that's the case for you. Otherwise, a window console will be launched when the executable is run.

- **Binary Format**: Here, we have **Embed PCK** and **Architecture**:
    - **Embed PCK**: We want to enable **Embed PCK**. This means when Godot exports our project, it will bundle the PCK file that it generates into the binary of our project. It's one less file that you and your player need to keep track of. Some benefits of embedding the PCK are that the game is easier to hot patch, you can offer mod support, and you can keep the code base hidden. You can read more about the benefits of embedding the PCK or not here: `https://docs.godotengine.org/en/stable/tutorials/export/exporting_pcks.html`.
    - **Architecture**: The architecture will be based on what platform you want players to be able to access your game on.
- **Texture Format**: This is how textures are exported in the project. The first two options listed, **BPTC** and **S3TC**, are the default options. **S3TC** stands for **S3 Texture Compression**. The next options, **ETC2** and **ASTC**, stand for **Ericsson Texture Compression** and **Adaptable Scalable Texture Compression**. The default is primarily **ETC2** and **ASTC**. All of these are different algorithms for lossy texture compression, which you can read more about here: `https://docs.godotengine.org/en/stable/tutorials/assets_pipeline/importing_images.html`.
- **Codesign**: This is specific to Windows and macOS exports. Both operating systems will warn users about running your game, an executable, since it doesn't have a certificate that validates it as a safe program to run. Naturally, this can be alarming to players. For more information on how to sign an executable for the operating system you're exporting to, you can read about it here, as it differs for each OS: `https://docs.godotengine.org/en/stable/tutorials/export/index.html`.
- **Application**: This is information about your program and how it should present itself to users. Most of these options are only visible when **Modify Resources** is toggled on.
- **Modify Resources**: When toggled on, this allows the icon and metadata of the executable to be altered.
    - **Icon**: Browse to an image and change the icon that's seen with your executable. The default is the Godot icon image.
    - **Console Wrapper Icon**: This can be left empty by default and will use the preceding **Icon** property.

- **Icon Interpolation**: This is the interpolation method used to resize the application icon.
- **File Version**: This is to determine what version your files are. There are various formats for tracking software versions. The most common one follows the format of major, minor, and patch. For example, this would be version 1.0.0 for us.
- **Product Version**: This is the same as **File Version** except for the application itself. It would also be 1.0.0.
- **Company Name**: The company, or group, that created the application. It's required, and its default is **Company Name**.
- **Product Name**: This is the name of the project.
- **File Description**: This is the file description that will appear to users, or players, of the project.
- **Copyright**: This is for what kind of licensing the project is under.
- **Trademarks**: This is a space for trademarks and registered trademarks relating to the files.

Most of these options will be the same for each executable. The biggest differences will be how the export is packaged for each operating system. The same is true for web exports. We will look at this in more detail later in the chapter.

> Note
>
> With the **Modify Resources** option enabled, there will be a yellow warning message at the bottom of the **Export** window, telling the user that they must have the `rcedit` tool configured in **Editor Settings** for this option to work. You can follow the steps for that here: `https://docs.godotengine.org/en/stable/tutorials/export/changing_application_icon_for_windows.html`.

For now, let's move on to the **Resources** tab and review how resources are differentiated in the export process. Non-resources such as text files and JSON files need to be marked in the export settings, so Godot does not try to serialize them into an executable. Within this tab, there's only one option, and that's **Export Mode**. The other two are blank lines where we can specify the resources by file type to not include in the export process, as shown in *Figure 11.6*:

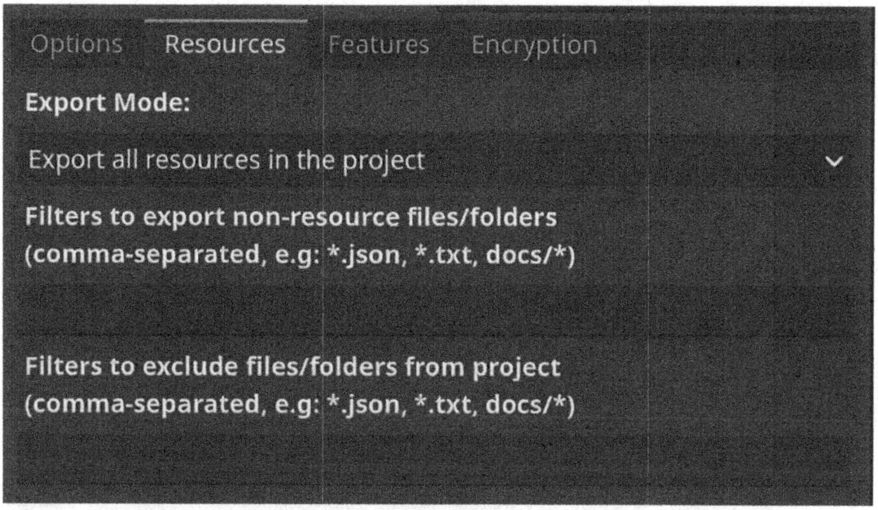

Figure 11.6: The Resources tab within the Export menu

If we click the drop-down menu, we'll get a set of options that look like *Figure 11.7*:

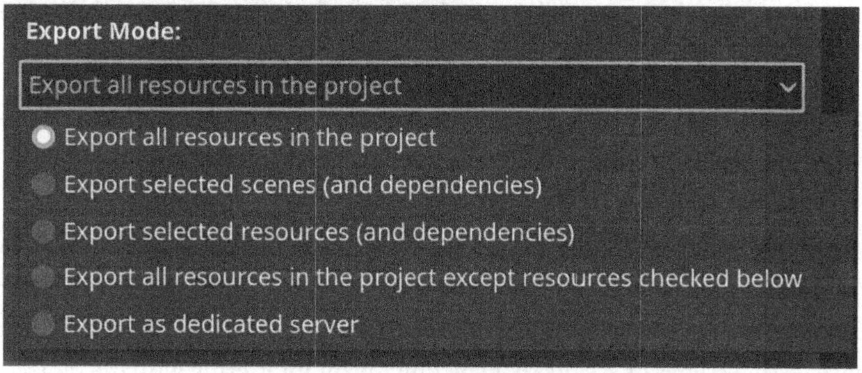

Figure 11.7: The Export Mode options for resources in Godot

Let's see what each of these options means and how they impact our project:

- **Export all resources in the project**: This exports everything in the project and does not stop to consider any special files or resources that may require a different process when being exported.

- **Export selected scenes (and dependencies)**: Selecting this option allows you to pick and choose which scenes and resources to export. This is useful when you don't want to include test or debugging components. You can see an example of this in *Figure 11.8*:

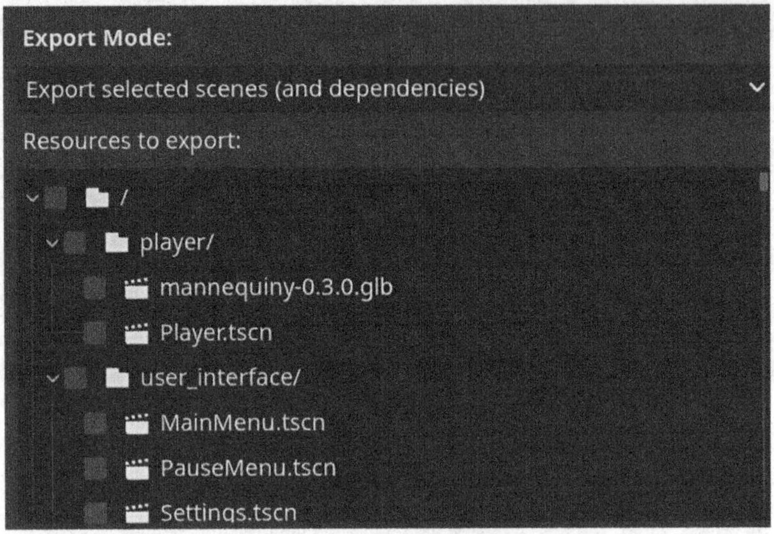

Figure 11.8: Exporting specific scenes in Godot

- **Export selected resources (and dependencies)**: This is the same as exporting specific scenes, but applies to resources instead. When selected, a window somewhat like *Figure 11.8* will appear.
- **Export all resources in the project except resources checked below**: This option does the same as **Export all resources in the project**, except for the ones you specifically mark that you do not want to be included in the exporting process. This is good for when you have testing scenes or scripts that you don't want interfering with the project.
- **Export as dedicated server**: This option will remove all visuals from the project and replace them with placeholders. For more information on which visuals are removed, you can read about it here: `https://docs.godotengine.org/en/stable/tutorials/export/exporting_projects.html`.

Most of the time, we'll select **Export all resources in the project** or **Export selected scenes (and dependencies)** when exporting a project. For this project, we'll select **Export all resources in the project**. We have no resources that need to be excluded from the exporting process, so it's fine to go with the default option here.

Moving on, we have a few more options to fill out in the **Export** menu. After selecting the scenes and resources we want exported, it's important to tell Godot if there are any files or folders that aren't resources. In *Figure 11.9*, we can see the two additional options. They're fill-in-the-blank style options where you input the file type and separate each with a comma.

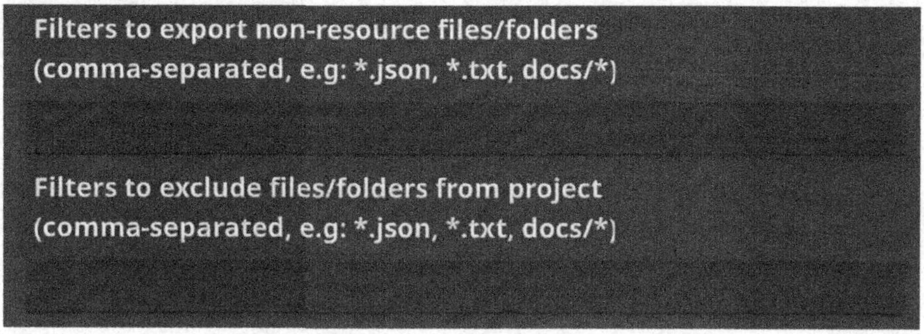

Figure 11.9: Excluding files from being exported in Godot

The most common example of when you will use this space is if you have dialogue that's in the `.json` format, or you have data that's loaded into the game from a `.csv` file or something similar. This is how we tell Godot that these are files that should not be packaged and exported along with Godot files, even though they're inside the project. Again, we have no non-resource files to include in the project, so we will leave it blank.

Now that we are familiar with export templates and the options available in Godot's **Export** menu, we can export the project and upload it to itch.io.

Exporting our game to Windows

Now that we've covered how to acquire export templates and the options that come with them, let's look at filling out that information and exporting the project to be executable. We'll specifically look at exporting for Windows, but the steps for Linux and macOS are similar.

To get started, let's return to the **Export** menu by clicking **Project** in the top-left corner of our editor and then selecting **Export...** if you closed the window. When the **Export** window appears, we'll select the operating system (Windows in this case) and notice the **Export Path** option above all the other information we filled out. Click the folder icon next to **Export Path**, and we'll browse to a place where all our executables and ZIP files will be created, as shown in *Figure 11.10*:

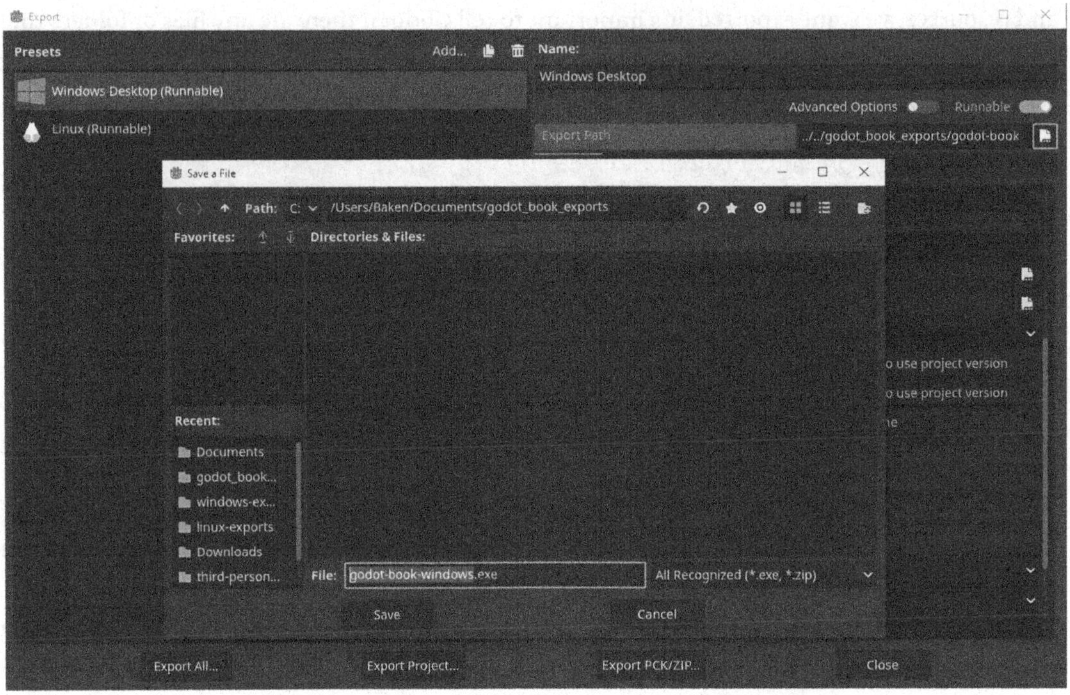

Figure 11.10: The Export Path window for the Windows export

Browse to somewhere you'll remember – I've chosen somewhere in my `Documents` folder – and create a new folder called `godot_book_exports`. This folder will hold all the exports you create for this project. In the **File** property at the bottom of this second window, name the executable `godot-book-windows`, so we know that it's the Windows export. Then click the **Save** button. Now, when we select the **Export** option in the **Export** window, the folder we created and the name we gave the executable are what will be created.

Looking at the **Export** window in *Figure 11.10*, we have three different ways to export. For now, we'll select the **Export Project...** option as it will export the project for the selected platform, which is Windows in this case. Once we select **Export Project...**, a new window will appear that looks almost identical to the **Export Path** one, but it is not! Once we click **Save** in this window, the project will be exported, and we'll see a small window with progress bars, as shown in *Figure 11.11*:

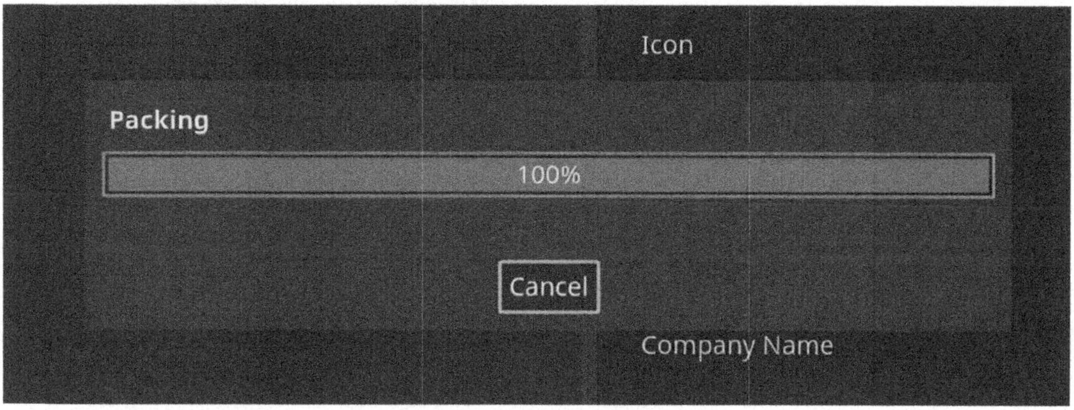

Figure 11.11: The project exporting

When Godot is finished exporting, *Figure 11.11* will disappear. You can then browse to the `godot_book_exports` folder, where you'll find a Windows executable called `godot-book-windows`, and it should have the Godot Engine icon as its icon. It's easy to rinse and repeat these steps for other platforms. For platform-specific questions, you can read more about exporting on those platforms here: `https://docs.godotengine.org/en/stable/tutorials/export/index.html`.

Now that we've successfully exported to one platform, let's look at uploading this executable to itch.io to share with the world!

Uploading our game to itch.io

Finding a home for your project once it's ready is a difficult decision. Of course, there's Steam and GOG.com, but both of those require an investment of time and money, whereas itch.io doesn't. **itch.io** has become the go-to website for hosting game jams and uploading games. It's an independently owned platform that has become a pillar in the indie game dev scene, especially when it comes to creating prototypes and participating in game jams. Both video games and tabletop roleplaying games are projects primarily hosted on the site.

Go ahead and navigate to itch.io now by using this link: `https://itch.io/`. In the top-right corner, click the **Register** button, and you'll be brought to a new screen that looks like *Figure 11.12*:

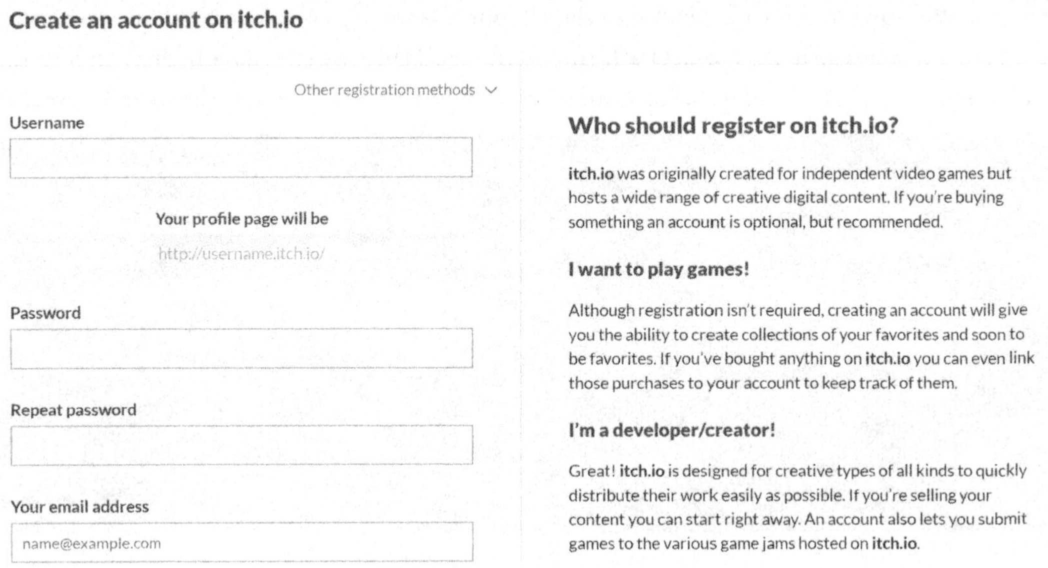

Figure 11.12: Creating an itch.io account

While filling out the form on the left-hand side, you can see on the right-hand side the type of platform that itch.io is. At the bottom of the page, as seen in *Figure 11.13*, you can also find some options for joining their newsletter as well as why you're signing up for itch.io (to enjoy free games or share them, or both).

Once you've completed creating your account, select the options you want, accept the terms of service, and click the **Create account** button.

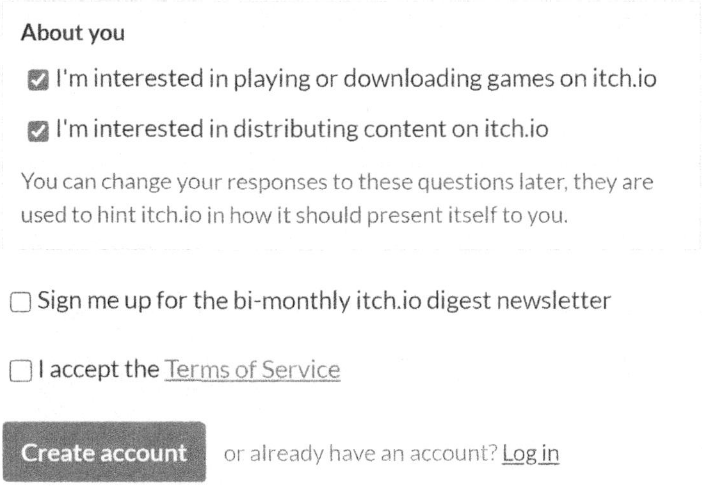

Figure 11.13: Finishing account creation on itch.io

Once your account is created, you should see it on your dashboard. It should look like *Figure 11.14*. This page is where you'll see your projects and analytics for those projects.

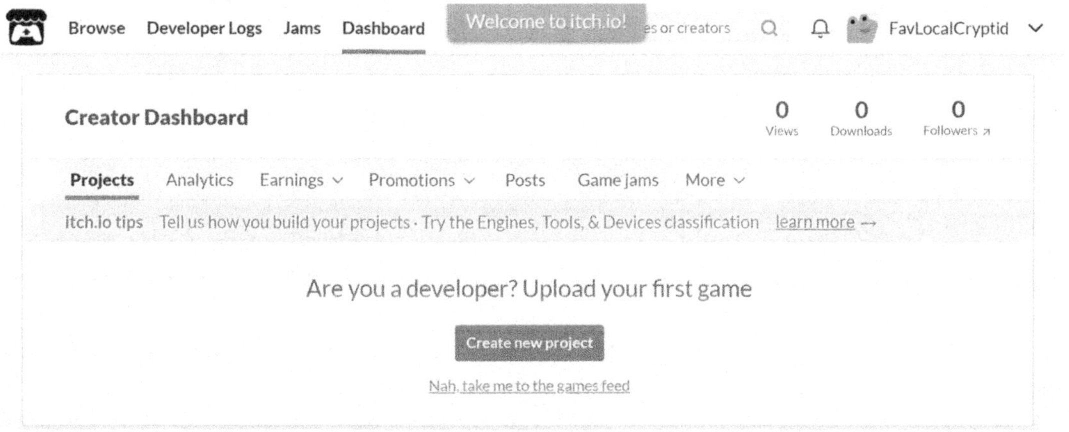

Figure 11.4: The itch.io dashboard after creating your account

The next step is to click the large **Create new project** button in the center of the screen. We'll fill out some information about our project and the best way for people to interface with it. Once that button is clicked, we'll get a new page, as shown in *Figure 11.15*:

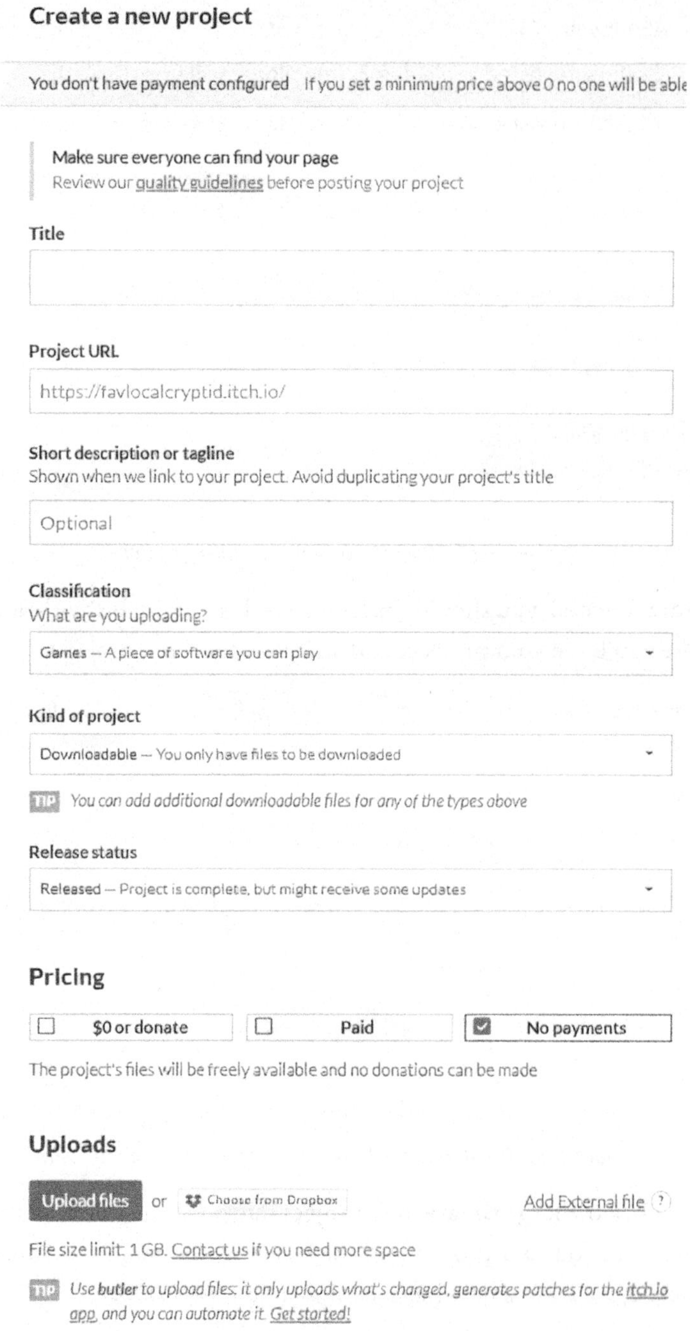

Figure 11.15: Creating a new project on itch.io

Most of the information on this page is self-explanatory, but let's walk through it to make sure we don't miss anything:

- **Title**: The name of the project and how it will appear on itch.io.
- **Project URL**: This is the URL you will give to people, so they can access your game page and download your project. A URL is auto-generated based on the title you choose, but you can change this before creating the project.
- **Short description or tagline**: Exactly as described. This is a small blurb that will appear when your project is shown to people who are browsing the site, so you want it to be a one- or two-line elevator pitch of what the project is.
- **Classification**: This option is used to classify how your game is categorized on itch.io. People can browse by category and tags, so it's useful in that regard. We'll make sure this is set to **Games**.
- **Kind of project**: This option asks what type of files are being used in the project. We'll leave this as **Downloadable**, since the project is a downloadable executable for people to try out.
- **Release status**: This option is to let people know where your project's at in development. We can set this to **Prototype** or **In Development**, as it's a project for educational purposes.
- **Pricing**: The next couple of options relate to pricing. You can sell and promote your game through itch.io, but since this is an unfinished prototype, select **No payments** when it comes to the price model.
- **Uploads**: Here, we'll click the **Upload files** button. It's best to upload a ZIP file as the file size limit is 1 gigabyte.

Below the section for uploading the project files, under the **Details** heading, this information is how people visiting your game page (the URL that's created once this project is created on itch.io) will interact with it, as shown in *Figure 11.16*:

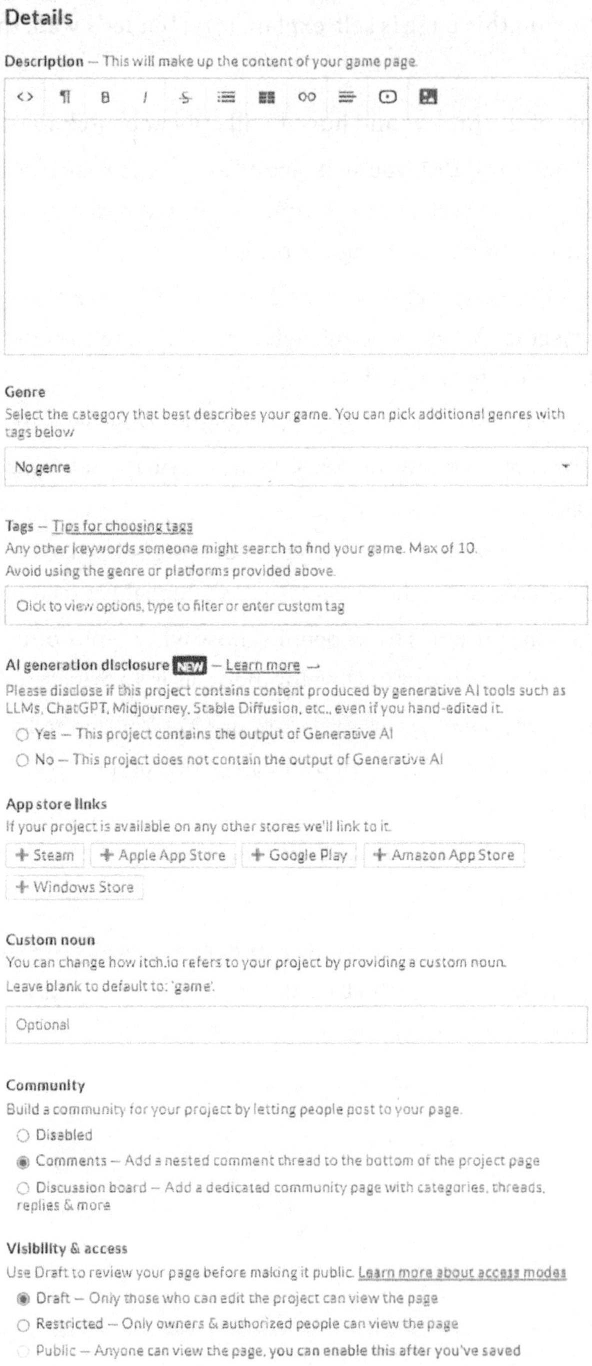

Figure 11.16: The Details options for creating a project on itch.io

Let's break down what each option entails. This includes the following information:

- **Description**: This is where you can put the pitch for your project, as well as credits and other information you want to relay to the player.
- **Genre**: Here, you select what genre the project falls under. It can only be one, so choose the one that fits best!
- **Tags**: Tags will help your project be shown based on the filtering and search a user on itch.io uses. Use common and concise ones that fit the project.
- **AI generation disclosure**: With AI on the rise, it's important for all creators to notify their players how they are utilizing it. This is a simple yes or no option.
- **App store links**: If there are other ways to play your game, such as on Steam or an app store, you can include those links here.
- **Custom noun**: If your project is something other than a game, you can specify that here.
- **Community**: This determines how people can interact with your game page – whether they can leave comments or not and provide feedback.
- **Visibility & access**: This option determines whether the game page is in draft form, restricted, or public. Each option is explained next to the listed options. For projects that you are still working on and don't want feedback on, a draft or restricted page is good.

Once all the information has been filled out, there are still a few more things that can be done to polish the project's page. If we scroll back to the top, there is a second column with options to upload a cover photo and provide screenshots along with a gameplay trailer link from somewhere such as YouTube. These aren't required for creating a project, but they help in the visibility of the project and add a level of polish that is nice to see. When you feel there is enough information about your project, we want to make sure we're uploading the correct files in the correct way for people to play. Scroll to the bottom of this page and click **Create new project**. This ensures all the information is saved before we move on to uploading the exported pieces.

After clicking the **Create new project** button, let's go back to **Upload files**, as shown in *Figure 11.17*:

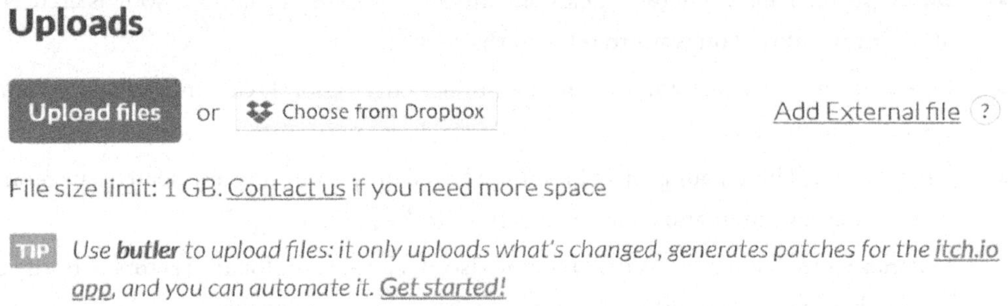

Figure 11.17: The Uploads section when creating a new project on itch.io

Click the **Upload files** button and a new window will appear to browse to the folder of exports we created earlier in the chapter. Select the Windows executable we created called `godot-book-windows.exe` and click **Open**.

> Note
>
> Do not navigate away from the itch.io project page while uploads are being done.

Once the upload is completed, there are some options for how the files should behave on the itch.io website. We want to select the box next to the Windows icon to tell itch.io that this is a Windows executable. Then, we want to uncheck the **Hide this file and prevent it from being downloaded** option. All of this is shown in *Figure 11.18*:

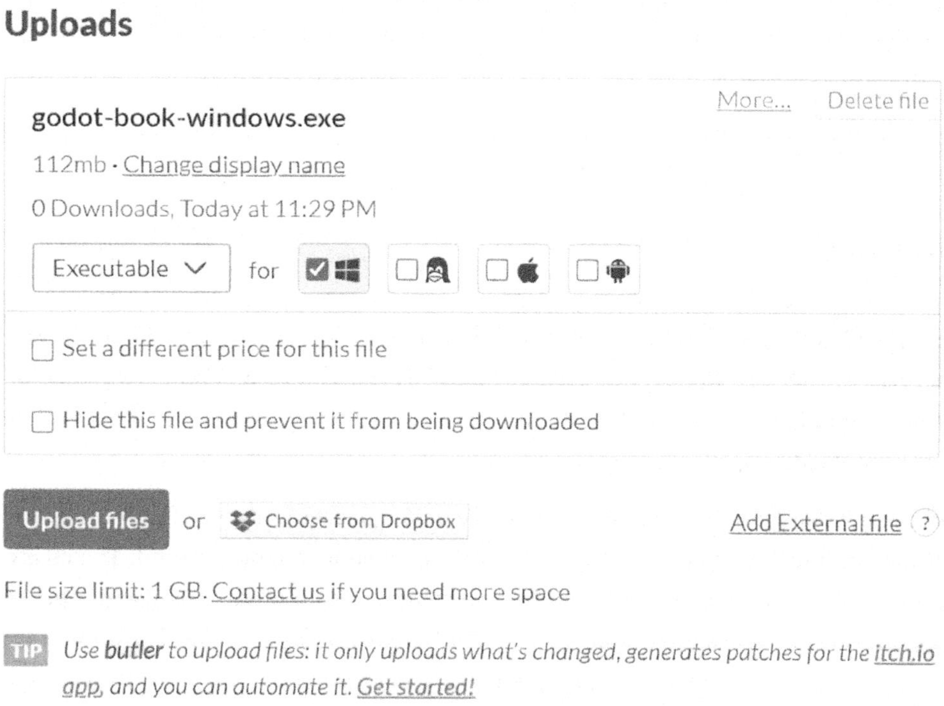

Figure 11.18: Uploading the Windows executable to itch.io

Once the options have been set, go ahead and scroll to the bottom of the project page and click **Save**. Next to the **Save** button, there is a button called **View Page**. After clicking **Save**, we'll click **View Page**, and you'll see something like *Figure 11.19* on your screen.

Figure 11.19: The project page on itch.io with the Windows executable

Great! We've now successfully uploaded our Windows executable to itch.io. Now, we can upload the rest of our exports and customise our game page to be more thematically tied to the project we've created.

Next, we'll take our attention beyond our project by looking at the Godot community and other available resources in it.

Summary

In this chapter, we explored the requirements and necessary components of exporting our project, such as downloading export templates in Godot. Next, we discussed how to configure our project for exporting to any operating system, with a focus on exporting from a Windows machine. Then, we created an itch.io account and learned how to upload and present that project on itch.io, a website renowned for games.

Knowing how to export your game means you can share it with friends, family, and the world. It's also a required step if you want to participate in a game jam of any kind. The chapter also explained how Godot creates and handles executables, as well as providing a glimpse into the world of how executables are managed across different platforms. Now, it's time to test your project, garner feedback, and iterate on it to make a game you're proud of having created.

With a project ready to be shown to the world, we'll turn our attention to other resources within the Godot community. We'll also spend time looking at the Godot Engine project on GitHub and the process involved in reporting bugs, issues, and other ways to interact with the Godot Engine community at large.

12

Contributing to Godot and Additional Resources

The project we've spent the last 11 chapters creating is now complete. We have created a C# project in Godot and then exported it to itch.io to share with others.

As we followed this journey, we learned about many different components within Godot, such as the UI, audio, and navigation. But beyond what Godot provides out of the box, there are also many more resources available. One of the great benefits of Godot being open source is that creators around the world can improve its usability and provide quality-of-life improvements that may be beyond the scope of what even the Godot team can accomplish.

In this chapter, we'll step through installing plugins and accessing Godot's Asset Library. We'll discuss how they're useful and allow developers to easily integrate tools and assets into their projects. Besides that, we'll spend time looking beyond the project and more at the Godot community. Specifically, we'll look at how to navigate Godot Engine's repository and how to contribute to the engine. Lastly, we'll discuss what other available resources there are and highlight some prominent creators in the Godot community.

In this chapter, we'll cover the following:

- Navigating the Godot Engine repository
- Contributing to Godot
- Reviewing useful plugins
- Highlighting Godot communities and creators

Technical requirements

For this chapter, the technical requirements are the same as in *Chapter 1*.

All the code from this chapter is available in the GitHub repository here: `https://github.com/PacktPublishing/Game-Development-with-Godot-and-C-`.

Navigating the Godot Engine repository

While we briefly covered creating our own GitHub account and repository in *Chapter 11*, accessing and understanding one not maintained by yourself can be a little overwhelming. Let's start by navigating to the Godot Engine GitHub page, which you can find here: `https://github.com/godotengine`.

In the middle of this page, you should see six pinned projects, as shown in *Figure 12.1*. Each of these projects is critical to the support and maintenance of Godot Engine. Outside of the first project, `godot`, which is all the C++ code for Godot, we also have the documentation, demons, bindings, proposals, and learning resources:

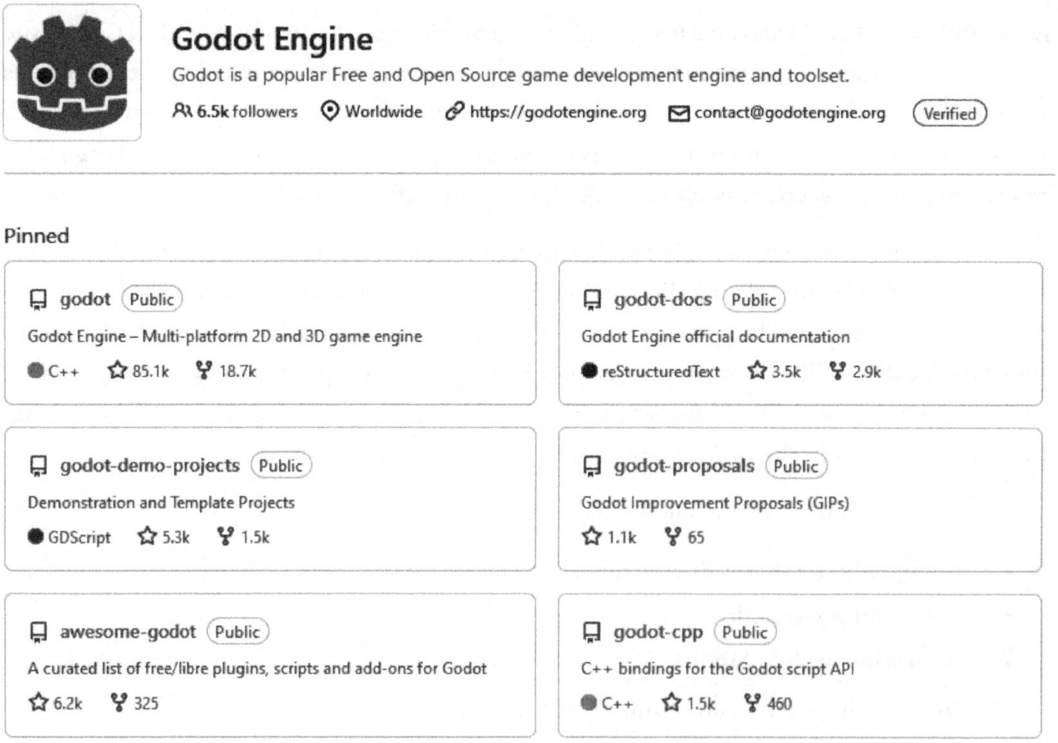

Figure 12.1: The Godot Engine GitHub page

While we won't step through every project on this page, we will look through a few, specifically `godot`, `godot-docs`, and `godot-proposals`. Each one serves a different purpose relating to Godot. The first one, godot, is the game engine's code, and the one you'll most likely become familiar with. You can access it by following this link: `https://github.com/godotengine/godot`.

At the top of the page, you'll see a bunch of folders and files with various options, such as **Code**, **Issues**, and **Pull Requests**. But first, let's scroll down to the `README`. This is a document that's included in every GitHub repository and is full of good information for users trying to interface with their work. The `README` will look something like *Figure 12.2*:

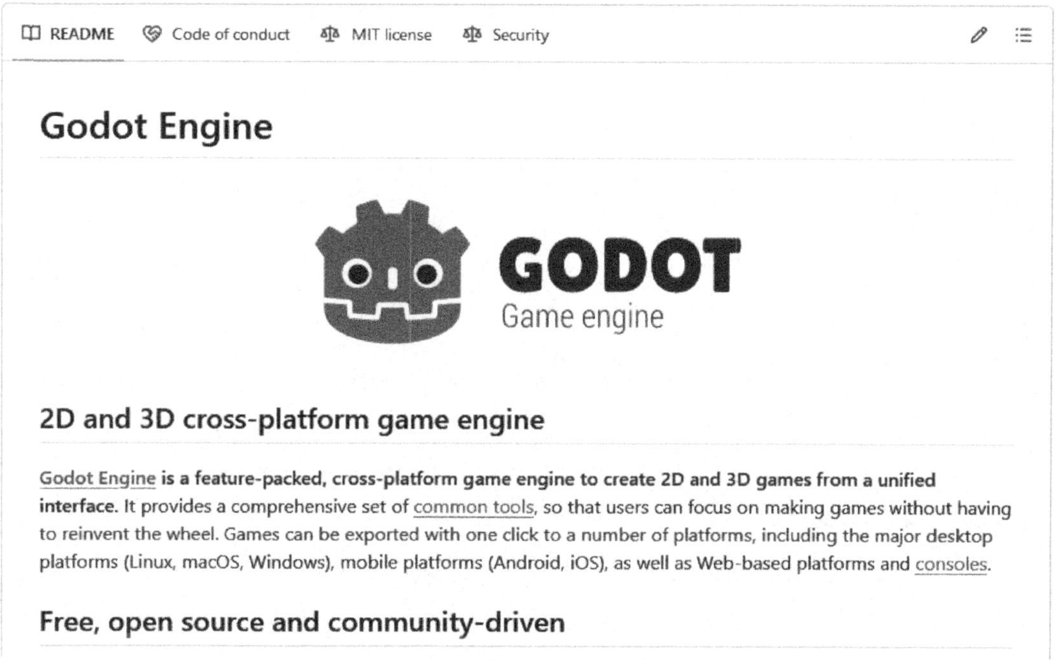

Figure 12.2: The README for the Godot Engine repository

The `README` file starts off by explaining what Godot is and what's included in this space. Notice at the top of *Figure 12.2* that it has some additional tabs – here you can find the code of conduct, as well as the license that Godot is under. Be sure to familiarize yourself with the code of conduct before engaging with the community to make sure you're doing so in a respectful manner.

If we continue scrolling through the `README`, we'll get to a section called **Community and Contributing**. This has a lot of useful links that we'll be referring to later regarding filing an issue found in the engine, as well as creating our own pull requests to submit fixes.

The last section, **Highlighting Godot Communities and Creators**, provides helpful documentation, demos, and various learning resources. We've referenced some of these throughout the book and will be highlighting more of them throughout this chapter.

Now, let's go back to where we saw the tabs for **Code, Issues**, and **Pull Requests. Code** is simply the source code for Godot, so if you ever wanted to look under the hood and see how something in the engine works, you can. This is the beauty of an open source game engine. **Pull Requests** contains existing pull requests from community members that either add or fix features of the engine. Finally, **Issues** covers existing bugs within the engine. This is what we'll be focusing on first. Click on the **Issues** tab, and you'll see a screen that looks like *Figure 12.3*:

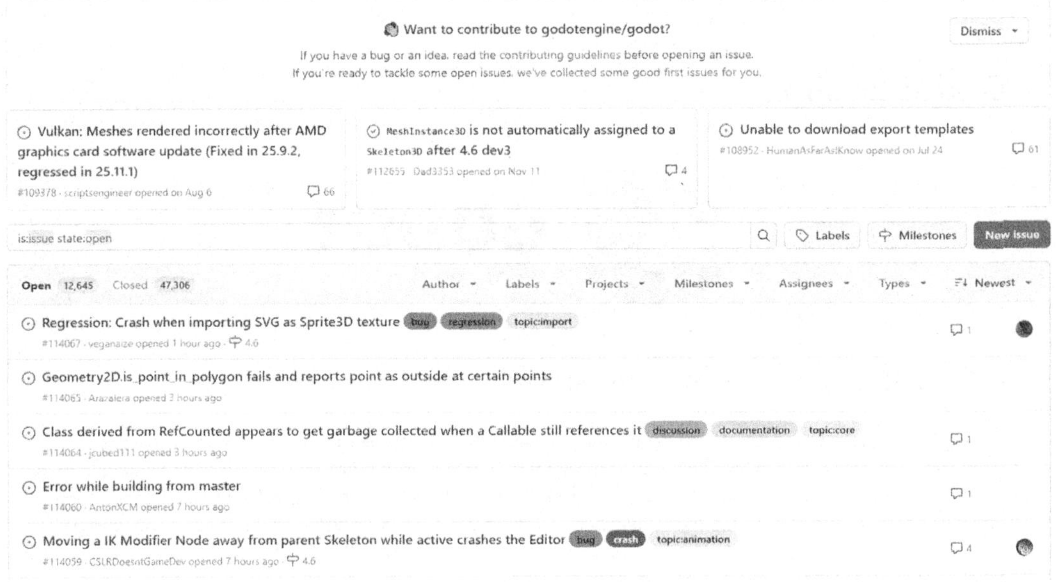

Figure 12.3: The Issues page of the Godot Engine repository

On the **Issues** page, we can see a list of existing issues that have been opened by anyone accessing the repository. Most of them are properly labeled (as they should be), which allows contributors to prioritize issues based on their time and skillset. Issues are existing bugs, incorrect behavior in the editor, or some other problem regarding functionality in Godot.

At the very top of this page, there's a call to action that provides a link to the contributor guidelines, as well as a list of good first issues for new contributors to work on. You can also find the good first issues by filtering on the **good first issue** label, which you can find by clicking the **Labels** button, shown in *Figure 12.4*:

Figure 12.4: The Labels and Milestones buttons on the Issues page

Clicking the **Labels** button takes us to a new page where we can see a list of every label in the repository. We can also see how many issues there are for each label. For example, there are currently **11** issues with the **good first issue** label, as shown in *Figure 12.5*:

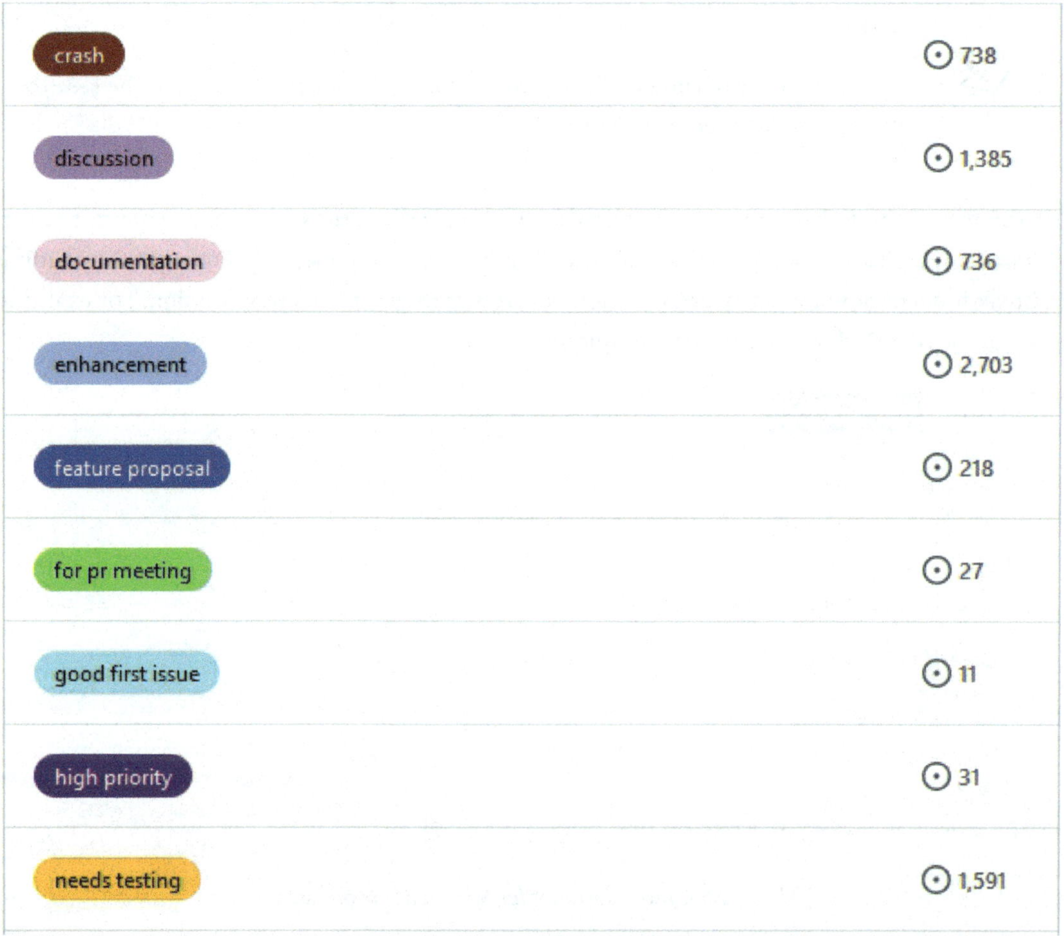

Figure 12.5: The list of labels in the Godot Engine repository

Keep in mind that every issue in the repository includes every version of Godot, including the LTS 3.6 version and any future ones. **LTS** here means **long-term support**. Even though Godot 4 is the recommended version, 3.6 is a stable one that continues to receive bug fixes and feature integration from Godot 4. This page is an excellent place to check if you're having an issue in the engine that is lacking clarity in the documentation, especially if you're using the latest version of the engine, which may not be a stable release.

> Note
>
> To report security vulnerabilities, the Godot team requests that emails be sent to `security@godotengine.org`.

At the top of the **Labels** page, there should also be a **Milestones** button, as shown back in *Figure 12.4*. Let's go ahead and click that. It will show us a new page, as in *Figure 12.6*, providing a breakdown of how far along each version is before it moves to the next version. For example, we can see that Godot 4.3 is at 80% completion.

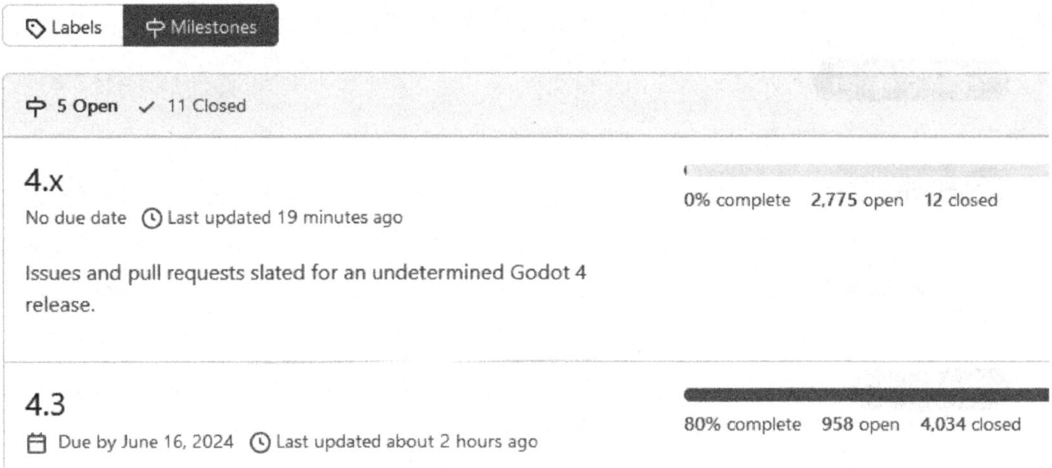

Figure 12.6: The milestones for Godot Engine on GitHub

Milestones are a great way to look at the big picture of how Godot is being developed and which versions are in the works. We can even click **958 open** and see the full list of each issue that needs to be fixed before 4.3 can be released. You can also browse the closed issues to see what new features and fixes are coming to the latest version of Godot. These are usually aggregated and shared in the Godot blog, which often provides only high-level updates for each area within the engine. You can read the Godot Engine blog here: `https://godotengine.org/blog/`.

As we continue through the chapter, we'll cover a couple of other areas that will be beneficial to you as a developer, such as pull requests and creating your own issue tickets.

For now, though, we've spent a decent amount of time exploring the GitHub repository for Godot. Let's spend some time interacting with and contributing our expertise to the Godot community.

Contributing to Godot

Now that we're familiar with the GitHub repository for Godot, let's look at how we can contribute to the community. We'll look at four primary ways that anyone can contribute – the first two will be developer-based ways, and the last two will relate to documentation.

As we saw earlier in the chapter, the `README` for Godot provides a link to contributing guidelines, which you can also find here: `https://github.com/godotengine/godot/blob/705b7a0b0bd535c95e4e8fb439f3d84b3fb4f427/CONTRIBUTING.md`.

Developer contributions

As mentioned, there are two different ways as a developer to contribute to Godot. The first is by finding and reporting bugs in the engine, while the second is fixing those same issues and submitting a pull request. While we won't go through every step of the process for each, we'll provide a great launching point for both.

Reporting bugs

Reporting bugs is a crucial and necessary step in improving Godot. If we navigate back to the **Issues** page on the Godot repository, we will see a green button called **New issue**, as shown in *Figure 12.4*. Once we click this, we'll see a new page that shows a big green **Get Started** button for reporting bugs. Click that and you will be taken to a new screen, as shown in *Figure 12.7*. This new screen is the form you fill out to create and submit an issue.

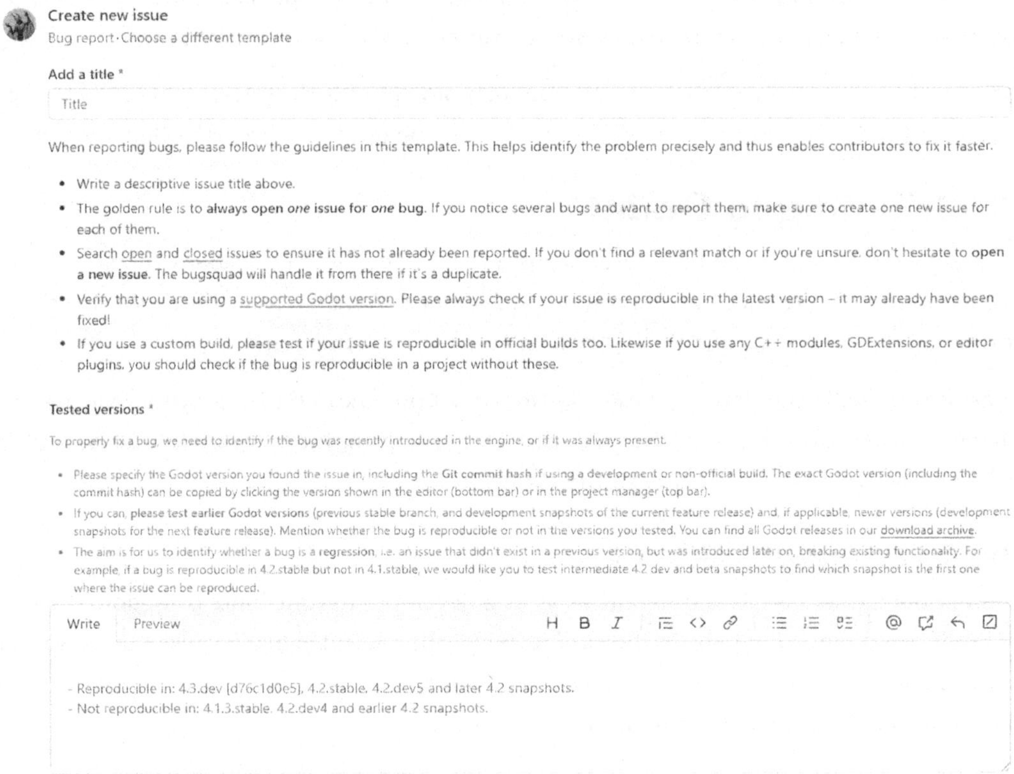

Figure 12.7: Creating a new issue on the Godot Engine repository for bugs

While there's a lot of text here, all of it is important to keep the issues created in the repository clear and clean so that any other user can easily and quickly replicate and work to resolve them. Let's briefly discuss each part of the form:

- **Title**: This is the name of the issue, which should clearly identify a single bug.
- **Tested versions**: As with any piece of software, there are multiple versions with varying levels of support, and this should be specified in your ticket. Since Godot can be built from source and modified to user needs, it's important to differentiate between whether the bug is in the official version or a custom-built one.
- **System Information**: This is general hardware information that allows the community to determine whether it's a driver issue or something else.
- **Steps to Reproduce**: This is a numbered list of the steps anyone could take in the version of the engine listed to encounter the same bug.
- **Minimal Reproduction Project**: This is a small, zipped-up project that has the bug present. This is extremely useful for members to try and reproduce the bug.

> Note
>
> Before creating any bug tickets, make sure you search for existing issues, so you aren't creating a duplicate ticket.

After all fields have been filled out, scroll down and click the **Submit new issue** button.

Understanding open issues

Let's use a closed issue as an example, specifically an issue with the **good first issue** label on it. I'm going to use the issue called **OpenGL: Environment fog does not affect sky rendering**. Here is the link for it: `https://github.com/godotengine/godot/issues/66456`. You can also see the beginning of the issue page in *Figure 12.8*:

Figure 12.8. An existing issue in Godot to use as an example

Notice how the title is very clear, and the issue post follows the same format as we just discussed. Scrolling through the rest of the page, you can find the steps to reproduce the bug as well as a link to a minimal reproduction project. Past the initial post, we can see where this issue has been, who has been involved, and its current state. *Figure 12.9* provides a snapshot of the issue's timeline:

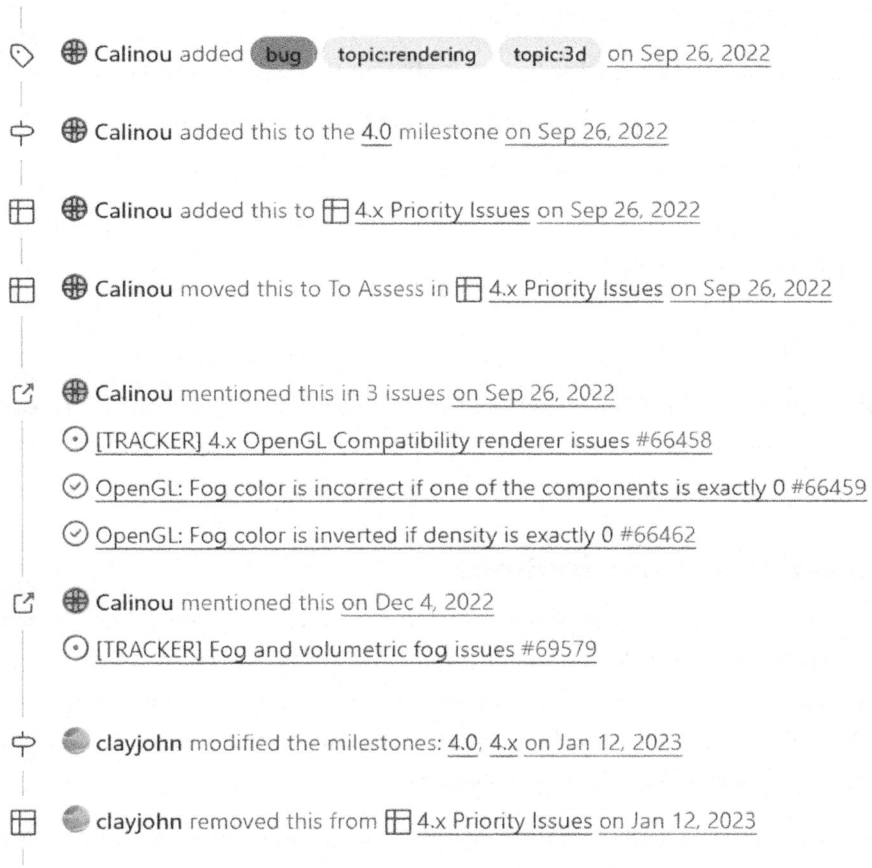

Figure 12.9: The timeline of the issue in the GitHub repository

Throughout this timeline, there are also comments about the state of the issue. For instance, we can see that this issue was confirmed to be a bug by the Godot team on September 26, 2022. It's also been added to Godot 4's milestone. Scrolling further down the page, we can see community members commenting and brainstorming together on a solution. It's important when considering an issue to fix to get all the information you can on the current state of the issue, as well as whether anyone is already working on a fix. Of course, commenting on it does not mean it's "yours" to fix.

Once you've found an issue you want to fix, like the one we're referencing here, your next step is to read some contributor guidelines and then fork the repository. Again, the guidelines for contributing to the engine can be found here: `https://github.com/godotengine/godot/blob/master/CONTRIBUTING.md`. It's important that you thoroughly read the community expectations and how to format the issue ticket when creating it as we highlighted previously.

Some of the important things to know are the following:

- Read the entirety of the contributing web page that's been linked here
- Consider readability in both your commit messages and pull requests
- Be sure to write unit tests to confirm the issue is fixed or proof that the issue exists

Once the ticket is created and the files uploaded to showcase an issue being solved (if it's to fix an existing issue), then you're done.

> Note
>
> Calinou, the author of this issue, is a member of the Godot team. If you're ever wondering which member is working on what part of the engine, you can always check the Godot Engine **Teams** page here: `https://godotengine.org/teams/`.

Documentation contributions

The Godot documentation is one of the best that I've ever encountered when it comes to software. It's easy to navigate, search, and understand. One of the big reasons for it being so good, I believe, is that anyone in the world can contribute to the documentation and then it's collectively reviewed to ensure accuracy. It can be found by navigating to the `godot-docs` repository, found here: `https://github.com/godotengine/godot-docs`.

There are two ways to contribute to the Godot documentation. They are the following:

- Contributing to class references and tutorials
- Translations of tutorials and engine documentation

Contributing to the class reference means adding documentation to the classes and functions that are part of Godot's API. These are the same documents we've linked to throughout the book when it comes to discussing new nodes. Something important to be aware of is that the process for updating the documentation is different when you're changing the online manual versus the offline version that's available in the editor. The biggest difference between the two is that the online manual requires changes to the `.rst` files, while the offline version in the editor requires changes to the `.xml` files. We can see the XML in the editor in *Figure 12.10*. This documentation can also be downloaded and accessed offline for developer convenience!

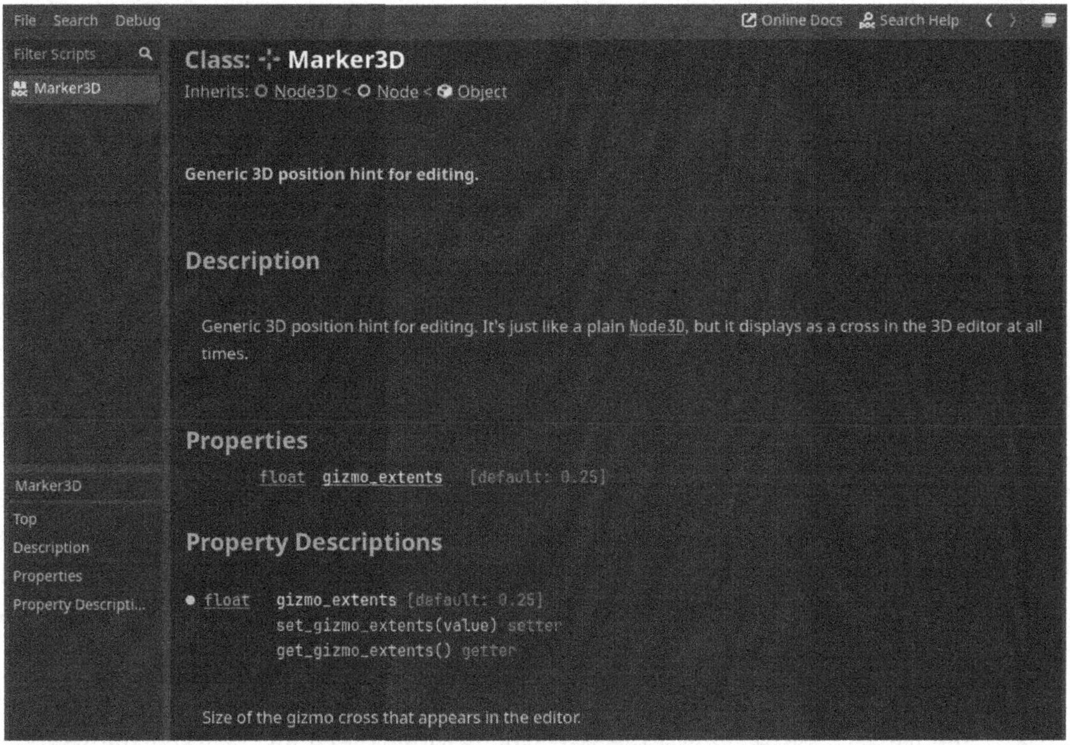

Figure 12.10: The Godot documentation in the editor

> Note
>
> To see what's missing from the class references, you can use this website, which is maintained by Godot: `https://godotengine.github.io/doc-status/`.

The second way to contribute to the Godot documentation is through translations. This is done through Weblate, which you can find a complete breakdown of here: `https://docs.godotengine.org/en/latest/contributing/documentation/editor_and_docs_localization.html`.

Here, you can help translate the editor, class references, and the online documentation. Weblate also provides a nice overview of what languages are currently supported and how far along they are. It's another way that Godot strives to support and include its community.

With the different ways to contribute to the Godot documentation covered, let's now pivot to some other resources in the Godot community, such as plugins.

Reviewing useful plugins

This section will cover a handful of plugins to aid you in your development process. While this is not an exhaustive list, the few I've chosen to include are ones that I've both used in my own project and had recommended to me by others. Some of these plugins augment the editor while others make our C# workflow a bit easier.

But before we start discussing plugins, let's first look at how we access the Asset Library and install plugins.

Installing plugins

There are two ways to install plugins in Godot. Let's quickly step through both methods:

- The first is to download the `.zip` file of the plugin, extract it, and copy it to an `addons` folder in our project. This is the same way you would install a plugin that's hosted on other sites, such as GitHub. Sometimes you may need to clone the repository instead, but either way, it will give you a copy of the plugin to add to your project. To see all the plugins available, you can browse Godot's Asset Library here: `https://godotengine.org/asset-library/asset`.
- Alternatively, you can browse the Asset Library within the editor by clicking the **AssetLib** button above the Viewport, as shown in *Figure 12.11*. From here, search for the one you want, select it, and click **Download**. This method will automatically create the `addons` folder and include the plugin information.

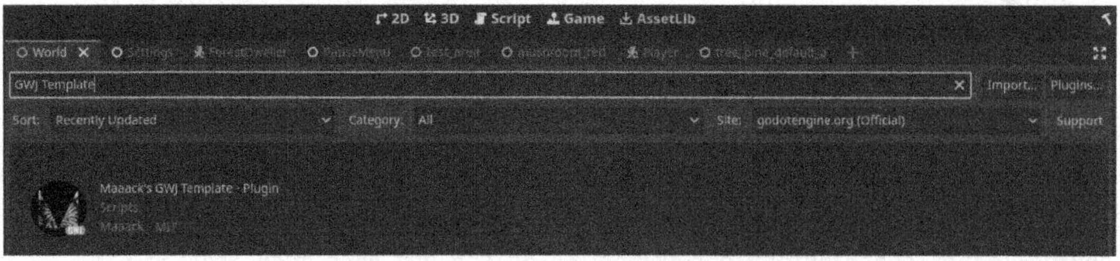

Figure 12.11: The Asset Library in the Godot editor

Here, we are looking at the **Maaack's GWJ Template - Plugin** plugin, which is the first plugin we'll look at in a moment. Let's briefly discuss what the rest of the information next to the plugin icon means:

- **Maaack's GWJ Template - Plugin**: This is, of course, the name of the plugin.
- **Scripts**: This is the type of plugin that it is which is Script. Every plugin is either an asset, tool, or script.
- **Maaack**: This is the username, or the creator's name, and also the owner of the plugin. This can either be a company or individual.
- **MIT**: This is the type of license that the plugin uses. It's important to note this as some plugins require a specific way to credit them based on their license.

> Note
>
> **GWJ** here stands for **Godot Wild Jam.**

The last thing to be mindful of when installing plugins is that it's important that you make sure they are viable for the version of Godot you're on. When we look at **Maaack's GWJ Template - Plugin** on the Asset Library's website, we can see the version of Godot that it's compatible with, as shown in *Figure 12.12*. If we're able to install it in the version of our editor, then it's compatible. Otherwise, the search result won't be rendered.

Figure 12.12: The Maaack's GWJ Template - Plugin information on the Godot Asset Library web page

Click on the plugin in the editor and a new page will appear, providing details about the plugins as well as options to download it, as shown in *Figure 12.13*:

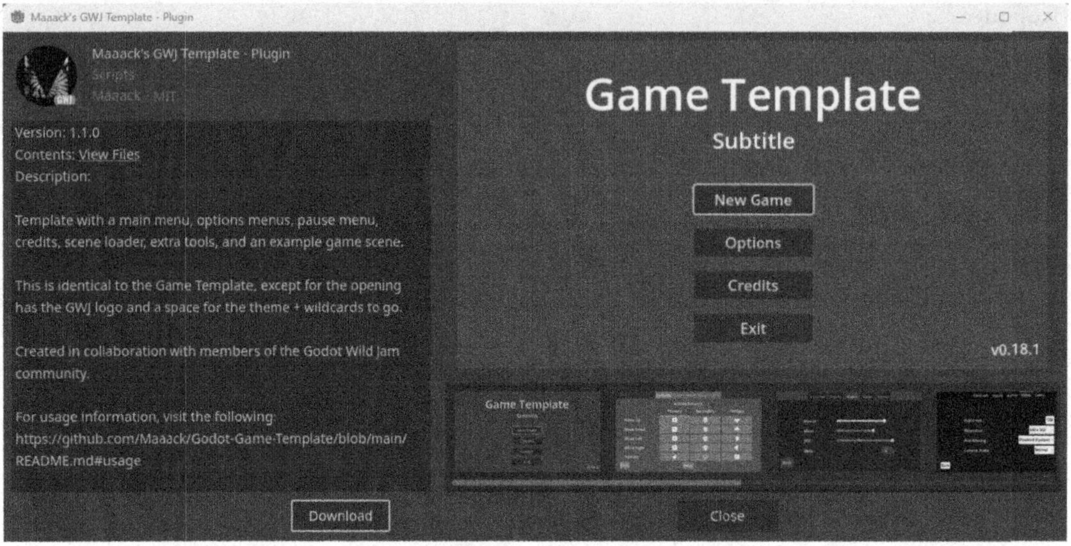

Figure 12.13: The details page for the Maaack's GWJ Template – Plugin page

With a plugin installed, it needs to be enabled. In Godot, click the **Project** button in the top-left corner. Then, in the dropdown, click **Project Settings**. A new pop-up menu will appear. Navigate to the **Plugin** tab at the top of the **Project Settings** menu. Then, enable the plugin by checking the **Enable** option, as shown in *Figure 12.14*:

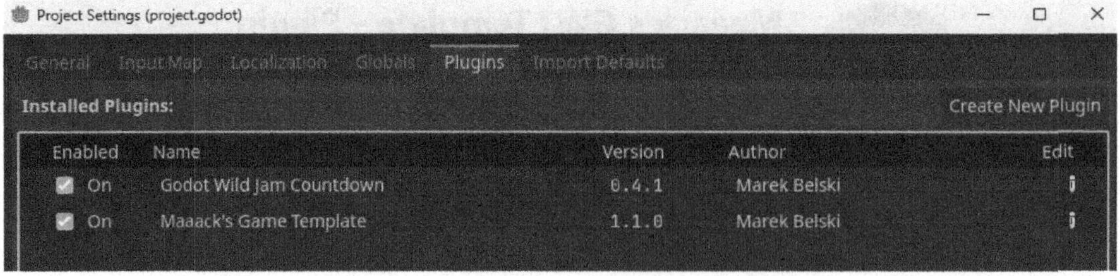

Figure 12.14: Enabling installed plugins in Godot

For more information about installing and enabling plugins, you can read about them here: `https://docs.godotengine.org/en/stable/tutorials/plugins/editor/installing_plugins.html`.

Now that we've discussed installing and enabling plugins, let's take look at some awesome plugins.

Camera Shake for C#

The **Camera Shake for C#** plugin, created by **DawrfSoftworks** (`https://godotengine.org/asset-library/asset/2488`), is a plugin that gives your camera some juice. Regardless of the perspective you're choosing for your game, there's an opportunity to utilize a camera shake, such as adding a camera shake in response to the environment, such as an earthquake, causing the player camera to jostle. Another example would be a bullet hell type game with a 2D camera shaking. There are plenty of ways to use this plugin.

GodotSharpExtras

The **GodotSharpExtras** plugin, created by user **eumario** (`https://github.com/eumario/GodotSharpExtras`), extends the core GodotSharp library to make writing C# in Godot easier and faster. For example, two C# attributes are added to reduce the amount of code needed. One of these attributes is `[NodePath]`, which removes the requirement of typing `GetNode<NodeType>()` every time you need access to a node in a scene. The second attribute is `[ResolveNodePath]`, which helps in fixing node paths. You can see an example of this in *Figure 12.15*:

Scene Tree:

Code:

```
using Godot;
using Godot.Sharp.Extras;

public partial class MyNode : Control {
    [NodePath] Control _mySpecialControl = null;
    [NodePath] Control MyNestedControl = null;
    [NodePath] Timer Countdown = null;

    public override void _Ready() {
      this.OnReady();
    }
}
```

Figure 12.15: An example of using the NodePath attribute with GodotSharpExtras

There are more useful functions like this in this plugin, especially regarding creating signals and utilizing the Singleton pattern.

Godot Ink

Ink is a powerful and awesome narrative scripting language. With **Godot Ink**, created by user **Paulloz** (`https://godotengine.org/asset-library/asset/1891`), you can integrate Ink into Godot. The plugin is designed to work with C# projects, but as Paulloz states, it is interoperable with GDScript. *Figure 12.16* provides a screenshot of an example of Ink. This shows the syntax for declaring variables, which is useful when it comes to tracking both inventory items and branching dialogue choices.

```
// Character variables. We track just two, using a +/- scale
VAR forceful = 0
VAR evasive = 0


// Inventory Items
VAR teacup = false
VAR gotcomponent = false


// Story states: these can be done using read counts of knots; or functions that collect up more complex logic; or variables
VAR drugged = false
VAR hooper_mentioned = false

VAR losttemper = false
VAR admitblackmail = false

// what kind of clue did we pass to Hooper?
CONST NONE = 0
CONST STRAIGHT = 1
CONST CHESS = 2
CONST CROSSWORD = 3
VAR hooperClueType = NONE

VAR hooperConfessed = false

CONST SHOE = 1
CONST BUCKET = 2
VAR smashingWindowItem = NONE

VAR notraitor = false
VAR revealedhooperasculprit = false
VAR smashedglass = false
VAR muddyshoes = false

VAR framedhooper = false
```

Figure 12.16: An example of Ink's syntax included in the plugin

While there are tons of excellent dialogue plugins out there, this one is specifically designed to work with C# projects.

Godot Firebase

The **Godot Firebase** plugin (`https://godotengine.org/asset-library/asset/1645`) brings Google's Firebase to Godot. If you're unfamiliar with Firebase, it's a serverless approach to a backend service that allows you to set up databases, authentication, and integration into other services. This plugin also makes mobile development a bit easier, since the plugin is integrated into Godot and does not require mobile-specific code to run Firebase applications.

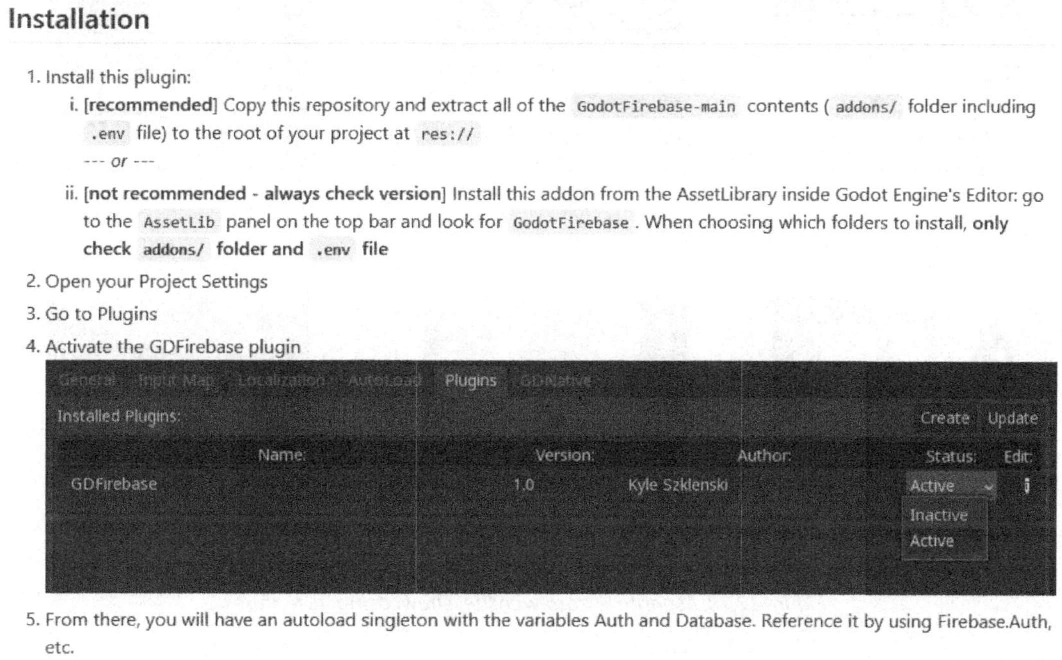

Installation

1. Install this plugin:
   i. **[recommended]** Copy this repository and extract all of the `GodotFirebase-main` contents (`addons/` folder including `.env` file) to the root of your project at `res://`
   --- or ---
   ii. **[not recommended - always check version]** Install this addon from the AssetLibrary inside Godot Engine's Editor: go to the `AssetLib` panel on the top bar and look for `GodotFirebase` . When choosing which folders to install, **only check `addons/` folder and `.env` file**
2. Open your Project Settings
3. Go to Plugins
4. Activate the GDFirebase plugin

5. From there, you will have an autoload singleton with the variables Auth and Database. Reference it by using Firebase.Auth, etc.

Figure 12.17: Installation screen for Godot Firebase

Aseprite Wizard

This plugin doesn't apply much to our 3D project, but for 2D developers, it's extremely useful. **Aseprite Wizard** (`https://www.aseprite.org/`) was originally created by David Capelloand and is now maintained by Igara Studio. This is an excellent tool for creating animated sprites. It allows users to export sprite sheets and create and manage sprite frames. It also has many tools to support pixel artists. **Aseprite Wizard** is not a free plugin; it requires a one-time purchase.

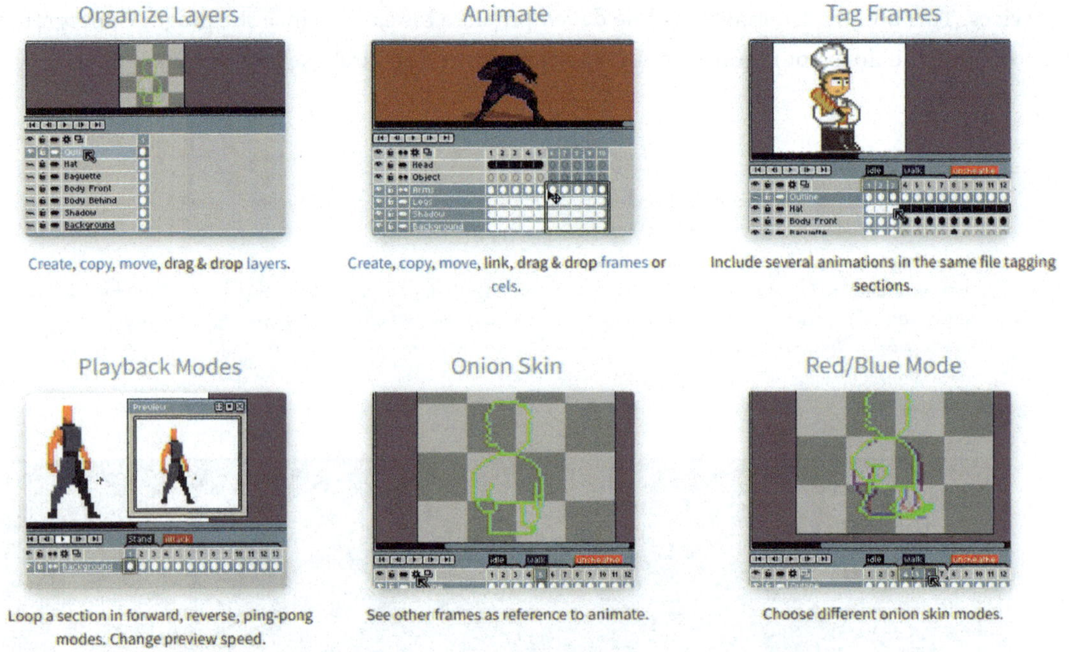

Figure 12.18: Asperite Wizard website, showcasing its features

Piskel

If you want to try out pixel art, you can use **Piskel** for free in the browser. It's a convenient tool for creating animated sprites and pixel art. It is very similar to **Aseprite Wizard**, with different features and options. It includes a nice list of examples that you can explore out of the gate for free.

Figure 12.19: Exploring one of Piskel's provided examples in the browser

This is a starting list of available plugins for Godot and will hopefully serve as a jumping off point to further explore plugins. There are many different types of plugins, such as scripts or tools. If you can't find what you're looking for, consider creating a plugin yourself!

Now, we'll turn our attention to existing Godot communities and their creators. Again, this won't be a comprehensive list but rather a good starting point to collaborate.

Highlighting Godot communities and creators

With Godot rising in popularity, so too are the number of creators. While this isn't an exhaustive list by any means, these are creators who have been involved with Godot for a long time or come highly recommended from other Godot communities I'm involved in. Just like with the plugins listed, I'll provide a link to each creator's work for you to check out the space and see whether it's something you might enjoy. Please note that not all of these listed creators work in Godot and C#, but all of them have something valuable to add to your Godot toolbelt.

Godot Wild Jam

Godot Wild Jam (`https://godotwildjam.com/`) is Godot's largest monthly game jam. It runs every month for nine full days of jamming, which includes two weekends, to give participants the opportunity to relax while being involved in a game jam.

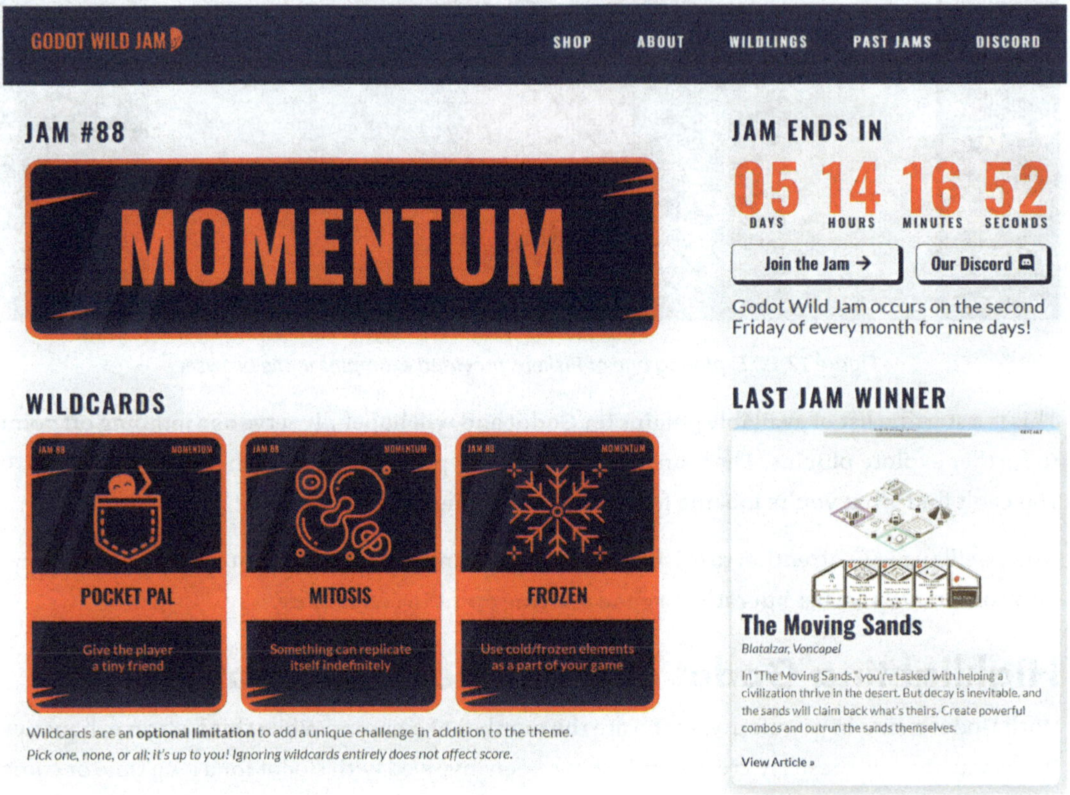

Figure 12.20: The Godot Wild Jam website with a countdown timer and the previous winner

If you're unfamiliar with the term game jam, it's when people get together and create a game in *X* amount of time around a theme or using specific tools. I'm the creator and organizer of the Wild Jam, and it's something I take a lot of pride in. Our jam has been running for six years now and has propelled many successful developers into professional spaces, such as Paradox Interactive, Crytek, and Ubisoft. The most exciting achievement is that a previous winner of ours is now on the Godot development team full time.

Chickensoft

Chickensoft (`https://chickensoft.games/`) is an excellent resource for people who want to do a deeper dive into the C# side of Godot than we've done in this book. While this book is a great primer, Chickensoft provides a variety of packages for C# development in Godot. They have an excellent tutorial for getting your C# environment set up. On top of that, the Chickensoft Discord is very active, and users enjoy discussing everything from C# libraries to architecture.

The community is another supportive and helpful place to showcase your C# work in Godot or get some help in troubleshooting a problem. Lastly, the creator of Chickensoft, Joanna, has an excellent third-person demo in Godot that utilizes all the Chickensoft packages as an example of how to leverage them in your own project.

Figure 12.21: The ChickenSoft landing page

GDQuest

We spoke at length about GDQuest (`https://www.gdquest.com`) at the beginning of this book, but here we're going to go into a bit more detail about what exactly GDQuest is and what they provide. They have multiple courses on Godot 4, although they are primarily in GDScript. Still, they have useful tutorials on engine-specific processes, such as understanding raycasts and using the TileMap editor. All of their courses and tutorials include videos and step-by-step written instructions. Not all of their content is free, but they do provide many free resources that are great for learning, such as the 3D mannequin we've been using in our project.

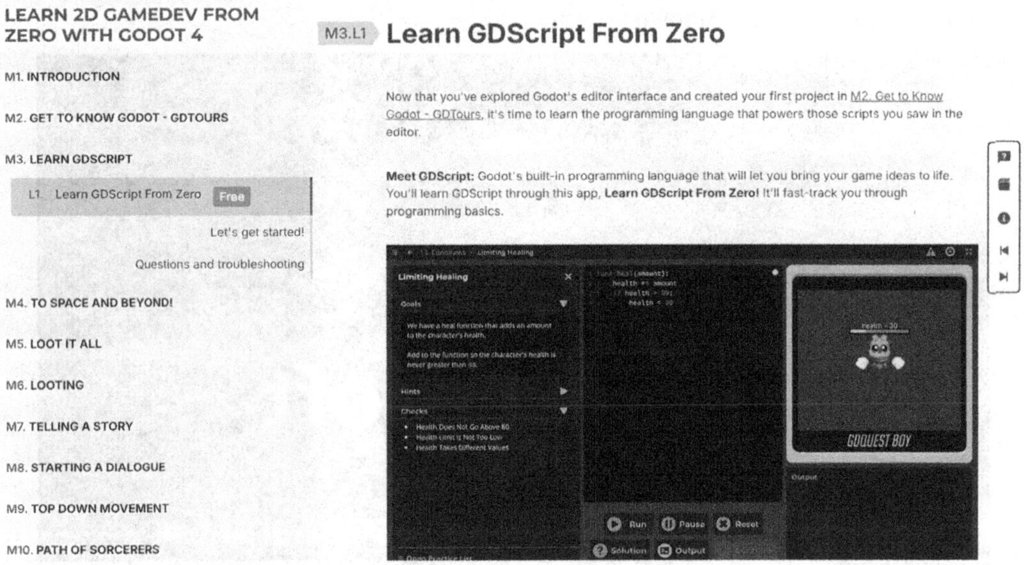

Figure 12.22: A screenshot of one of GDQuest's tutorials from their website

I know there are countless more out there, and I hope the ones listed here provide a good pathway into the Godot community. It can be scary sharing your work with others, but it is oftentimes worth it. The feedback and motivation you can get from sharing something is much more valuable than the fear or insecurity that may be keeping you from sharing your work. So, go and explore these Godot communities and be sure to share whatever you make in the end!

Summary

In this chapter, we spent time looking at the Godot community and learning what's available to us beyond the engine and this book. We explored the list of projects on the Godot Engine's profile page on GitHub. Specifically, we explored the Godot Engine repository. We also stepped through the main steps when contributing to the engine as either a developer or regarding documentation. After that, we highlighted some excellent plugins and content creators in the Godot community, including teachers, YouTubers, and general community spaces.

Our final chapter will focus on ways to push the project we've created here even further. This will be done by providing a list of challenges for you to complete and incorporate into your project. The challenge list will be a perfect opportunity to dig deeper into areas we've worked on in the project but also a chance to explore parts we didn't interact with at all. These challenges will be outlined in a way that provides clear goals and expectations. They'll also have a starting point with general directions on how to progress.

13

Next Steps as a Godot Developer

Our final chapter is an extensive challenge list that offers you the opportunity to expand the project we've developed or use it as a jumping-off point for creating your own. This book cannot cover everything that's needed to create any video game, but it is a solid foundation for implementing any ideas you may have. These exercises can also be a great resource and challenge in game jams. Feel free to randomly pull a handful of exercises from the list and use them in an upcoming Godot Wild Jam.

Now that we've created our project, explored Godot, and learned how to submit bug fixes and pull requests, we'll go through a curated challenge list broken down by category. The categories may be areas we've briefly mentioned or dive deeper into components we've already covered. You can jump around the challenge list and complete them in any order you like.

This chapter will cover the following topics:

- Participating in game jams
- Exploring the challenge list

Technical requirements

For this chapter, the technical requirements will be the same as *Chapter 1*.

All the code from this chapter will be available in the GitHub repository here: `https://github.com/PacktPublishing/Game-Development-with-Godot-and-C-`.

Participating in game jams

In previous chapters, we've mentioned game jams. We will talk briefly about what they are and how to get involved in them. To start, what is a game jam? Well, it's a set time, often a weekend, week, or longer, where people get together and create a game based around a theme. Anyone can create and host game jams. Often, schools or communities will host them. The best place to find a list of upcoming or current game jams is on a website called **itch.io**. You can access the website by following this link: `https://itch.io/`. We've already discussed itch.io and posting our projects there in *Chapter 11*. Now, we'll look at some other features it offers, such as finding and joining a game jam.

We will navigate to the website where we can see a menu bar at the top left, as shown in *Figure 13.1*.

Click the **Jams** button on the bar, and it will take us to a new page with a calendar view of the current and upcoming jams. We can also see a row of tiles above this calendar view with some of the featured jams available, as shown in *Figure 13.1*:

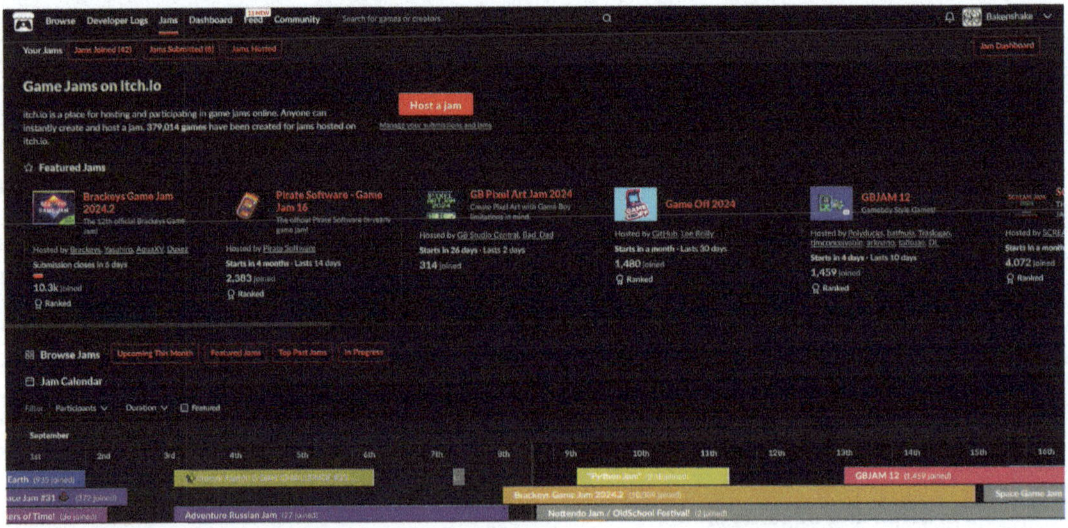

Figure 13.1: The Jams page of itch.io

Clicking any of the jams will take you to the jam page. Every jam varies in its structure. Some offer prizes, others have no ratings or rankings.

Let's walk through the Godot Wild Jam as an example. You will find the Godot Wild Jam in the calendar. It starts on the second Friday of every month. I'll link one here as an example and will use the screenshots from it for the remainder of this section. You can find the jam page here: `https://itch.io/jam/godot-wild-jam-74`.

The first thing you'll see is the header of the jam page, as shown in *Figure 13.2*. Below the jam page's logo, there's the following information:

- *Name of the jam*: The name of this jam is **Godot Wild Jam #73**.
- *Hosts of the jam*: Below the name of the jam, there's a line that shows who the hosts are of this jam, which is the **Godot Wild Jam** itch.io account.
- *Participant number*: To the right of the name of the jam, you'll see a number, and this is the number of people who have joined this jam. In *Figure 13.2*, we can see it's **682**. This number fluctuates throughout a jam as people join and leave as things happen in real life. It's expected, so if you join a jam, do not feel that you have to complete an entry for the jam. Taking care of yourself is first and foremost the most important thing to do.
- *Jam sub-pages*: Below the host names, there are two tabs. One is **Overview** – the page we're on – while the other one is a **Community** page. We'll look more closely at the **Community** page after reviewing the one we're on.
- *Jam/voting times*: Further down the page, there's a block denoting the remaining time in the jam. In this example, there's 1 day, 13 hours, and 33 minutes left to complete an entry for the jam.
- *Join the jam*: Outside of when the jam time is, the second most important thing is clicking the **Join jam** button that sits within the box where jam and voting times are listed.

Figure 13.2: The top of the Godot Wild Jam page for their 73rd jam

Scrolling further down the page, we see a lot of information. The Godot Wild Jam breaks the information down into the following categories:

- **Theme**: This is a very common thing in game jams. A large majority of game jams reveal a theme when the jam starts that's either picked by the community or the organizers themselves.
- **Wildcards**: Wildcards are a unique thing to the Godot Wild Jam. They are optional challenges that push developers to try new systems or mechanics.
- **Rules**: A common section of any game jam, outlining what is and isn't allowed. This can include the type of content in your game and the tools that are allowed.
- **Frequently Asked Questions (FAQ)**: This section covers common questions, such as when the jam is and the expectations of participating in the jam.
- **Links**: These are useful resources to help folks who are using Godot for the first time, specifically when it comes to exporting their project.
- **Judging**: The Godot Wild Jam is a ranked jam, which means there is a winner at the end of it.

Not every game jam will have these categories. Some have more, some have less. It's very dependent on who the hosts are and what their goal with the jam is. Godot Wild Jam is very focused on continual learning and community, which is why there are no monetary prizes.

Now that we've understood the rules and expectations of this jam, we'll look at how to submit our game to the jam next.

Submitting a game

To be able to submit a game to the jam, you must click **Join jam**. Then, at any point before the jam ends, you must submit a project to the jam. Let's look at how to submit an entry to the next Godot Wild Jam as an example. If the game jam hasn't started yet and you click **Join jam**, you'll see the following on your screen:

Figure 13.3: The screen you see when joining a jam that hasn't started yet

When you submit to a jam on itch.io, you're submitting the game link that has the build of your game attached to it, which we created in *Chapter 11*. When the jam has begun and you have your game page created, you can click the **Submit** button that will appear on the jam page. It will take you to a submission page and will ask for some information about your entry. The Godot Wild Jam has a short questionnaire that's used to track open source projects as well as gauge the average experience of participants. The submission page will look something like *Figure 13.4*:

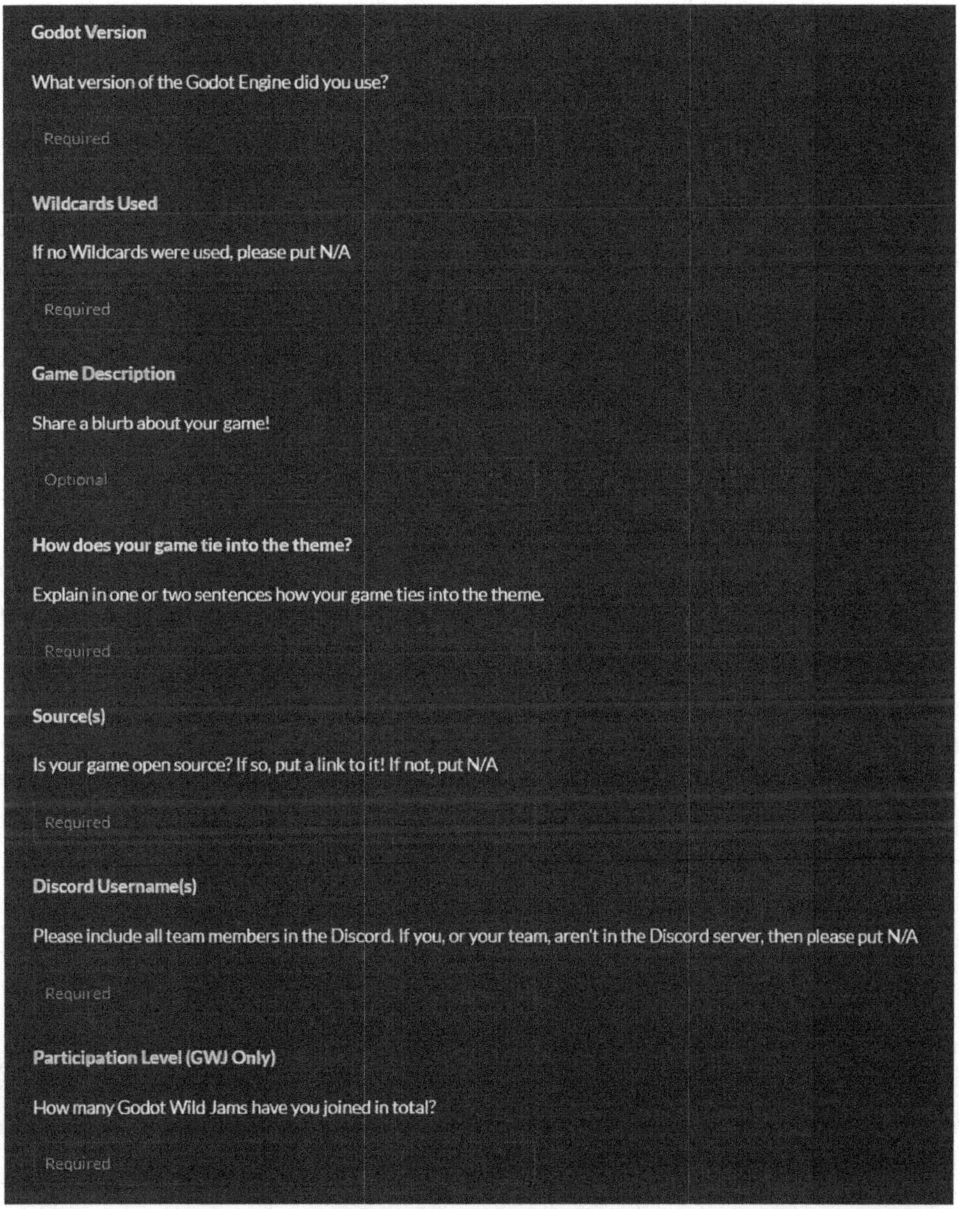

Figure 13.4: The submission page on itch.io for Godot Wild Jam

Again, not all jams will require this much information, but due to the size and frequency of Godot Wild Jam, the team likes to have data to track its impact and make improvements. Let's explain what each part of the submission page entails.

- **Godot Version**: This question pertains to the version of the engine you created your project in. While the jam page suggests using version 4 for a stable experience, technically, anyone can use any version of Godot to participate in the jam. The specification here is a good marker of which version is most frequently used.
- **Wildcards Used**: Wildcards are an optional challenge in Godot Wild Jam. There are always three cards that are voted on by the community. Occasionally, there is a fourth card for special events. The challenges can cover any field of game development. They could be narrative, artistic, programming, and so on. Participants can use 0, 1, 2, or 3 wildcards. It doesn't impact an entry at all. It's a fun challenge for participants who want a specific challenge.
- **Game Description**: This box is for a very brief – think one to two sentences – description of the game.
- **Theme tie-in**: This is another box for a brief explanation of how your entry ties into the theme for the current Godot Wild Jam.
- **Source(s)**: This is a simple question on whether your entry is an open source project or not. It's not a requirement for participation in the jam, but in the spirit of Godot Engine being open source, the organizers of GWJ want to encourage more open source projects to be created.
- **Discord Username(s)**: If participants are in the Godot Wild Jam Discord server, they should list each team member's Discord handle in case they are the winners of the next jam. Even though there are no prizes in GWJ, the winners are given the *Wildling* role until the next jam winners are announced.
- **Participation Level (GWJ Only)**: This only requires a number to be entered into the box. If this is your first time participating in GWJ, you'll enter 1. Otherwise, provide the correct number of times you've participated in GWJ.

After filling out the submission page, there is a **Submit** button at the bottom of the page. Once this is clicked, the game page on itch.io is added as an entry to that specific jam. This process is the same for any game jam on itch.io. The only differences between jams are the rules and requirements of each jam.

Now that you know how to create a project on itch.io and submit it to a game jam, let's talk about ways to expand your game project and discover more exciting ways to interact with the Godot Engine.

Exploring the challenge list

In exploring the challenge list, the challenge will include some test use cases for how to utilize the challenge. The use cases are meant to be a springboard for further creativity. Implementation will be on your own, but some challenges may include a *Getting started* section for how to begin, as well as a *Why implement this?* section. I'm not placing difficulty levels on the challenges because everyone comes into game development with varying levels of experience. Therefore, what might be difficult for one person might be easy for someone else. Above all, if you need help, reference the extensive list of helpful communities that were mentioned in *Chapter 13* and the Godot documentation!

Some of these challenges will be extremely open-ended, while others will be clear-cut tasks to add polish or a new mechanic to the project. At the end of this list, there will be a table with all the listed challenges by category that you can check off as you go along. Yes, mark up the book, or print out that single page if you're reading digitally. I hope you bookmark the pages and make notes in the margins as you progress through the challenges. Circle the ones you're interested in, so you know which ones to come back to. There is no right or wrong way to approach this.

Understanding juice

Juice is a term that's often thrown around when working on a video game project. It can be difficult to define, as it's not one specific thing but rather the cumulative polish effect you see in a game. This can range from anything from a screen shake when the player takes damage to a series of detailed animations and particle effects showcasing a player's move. It could also be something where the UI pops at the right moment during a sequence of attacks. This is why it's hard to define what juice is for one game, as that may not be something that adds juice to another. It comes down to what components of the game you want to highlight to provide players with a sense of awe and satisfaction when interfacing with your game.

We'll be referring to this term throughout the challenge list, so now you should have a better idea of what it means when we say that a challenge adds juice.

User interface

The challenges listed in this section will all relate to the **user interface** (**UI**) in one way or another. This can be more than just visual updates and changes. Some will include auditory enhancements to add depth to a game.

Now, let's look at what those challenges are. Feel free to jump around the list and explore ones that interest you or your project:

1. **Challenge: Create a radial menu to select objects:**
    - *Possible use cases*:
        - Selecting weapons for a player
        - Switching ammo types
        - Changing player outfits
        - Expressing an emote
    - *Getting started*: Create a UI container that holds two or more buttons that can be cycled through.
    - *Why implement this?* UIs are so much more than blocky buttons or static menu pages. Discovering ways to better utilize space in the UI is a critical component of any UI/UX designer. Radial menus are also commonly used when it comes to console games, as the joystick allows quick and easy navigation through options. Radial buttons also allow for the mouse to be at a certain angle, which may sometimes be more navigable than clicking a specific key on the keyboard.
2. **Challenge: Add audio sounds when entering different button states (e.g., hover, click):**
    - *Possible use cases*:
        - Increase accessibility of your game
        - Provide player feedback when interacting with the UI
    - *Getting started*: Extend the `Button` class within Godot, as this function is not natively included.

- *Why implement this?* Adding audio to different button states is a great way to add both player feedback and accessibility. It immediately notifies the player when they interact with a specific piece of the UI. This, in combination with a visual change, adds a lot of clarity when navigating the UI. Small things like this give any project a very polished feeling, specifically in what players can and should do in a game at any given point.

3. **Challenge: Create a heads-up display (HUD) that can be toggled on and off:**

    - *Possible use cases*:
        - Provide useful information to the player
        - Allows the game to be more accessible
        - Can be used to incorporate gameplay mechanics
    - *Getting started*: Use a `CanvasLayer` to add a UI to the player's screen and keep it in place.
    - *Why implement this?* An HUD is a common way for developers to give immediate player feedback. They can also provide information for players that allows them to make more informed decisions. Some games with an HUD also allow a setting for it to be toggled off completely. This can be to make the game more challenging, or perhaps to allow players to enjoy the scenery and game more. Either way, it adds a level of immersion that's customizable for the player.

4. **Challenge: Use tweens to add juice, or game feel, to your game, specifically in the UI:**

    - *Possible use cases*:
        - Responsive feedback
        - Confirm gameplay mechanics
        - Relay important information without detracting from other game events
    - *Getting started*: Animate a button on your *START* screen by making it bounce with tweens.

- *Why implement this?* Juice in a game is defined by how it looks and feels. It can relate to the way a game's UI responds and how the transitions between menus behave. Short pauses before destroying an enemy or adding an exciting kill animation are other ways to add juice. Juice is not limited to only the UI, but adding it to the UI is an easier start. Utilizing tweens to complete this task is a natural and surefire way of creating an awesome UI without having to hardcode it in.

5. **Challenge: Animate a piece of the UI, such as the HUD, buttons, or something else**:
   - *Possible use cases*:
     - Add juice and polish to your game
     - Give players feedback about something in the world through the UI
   - *Getting started*: Choose a panel or set of UI elements to animate when being called on.
   - *Why implement this?* Clicking through menus and navigating sub-menus is almost always required when playing a game. Making sure those interactions are fast, responsive, and clean is vital to a game's success. Even with innovative gameplay mechanics and interesting stories, it can be challenging to overlook a UI that is frustrating to navigate.

Player-based

The challenges listed in this section will all relate to ways to improve the player controller, whether that's in expanding the animations, adding more abilities, or something else:

1. **Challenge: Add a particle effect when your player lands on the ground after a jump**:
   - *Possible use cases*:
     - Adding juice to your game
     - Throwing items on the ground
     - Player landing on the ground
   - *Getting started*: Trigger a particle effect by using a key, then tie it to the player landing on the ground.
   - *Why implement this?* Creating impact particles adds immersion and depth to your game. When adding something like this, it takes the project to that next level of polish, which is what many of these challenges strive to do.

2. **Challenge: Create a dash ability for the player and use the animations built into the model for it:**
   - *Possible use cases:*
     - Providing an ability for players to unlock
     - Allowing players to traverse levels faster
     - An ability required for completing puzzles
   - *Getting started:* Increase the velocity of the player and map it to a key, like running but faster.
   - *Why implement this?* Adding more player abilities gives the player a new and interesting way to explore the world you've created. It can also add depth to the world by creating areas that are only accessible by utilizing certain abilities to access them. There is also a player satisfaction in allowing them to dash around the world rather than simply walking or running, especially if the player is backtracking in any way in games such as metroidvanias and platformers.
3. **Challenge: Add a double jump to your player:**
   - *Possible use cases:*
     - To solve environmental puzzles
     - To defeat enemies
     - To find hidden areas in a world
   - *Getting started:* Poll for the player's *JUMP* key, and if the player is already in the air, have them jump again. Be sure to limit how many times they can jump in the air.
   - *Why implement this?* A player having a double jump allows them to explore more of the world with some depth. It's a great way to stagger access to other areas of a level by making the ability unlockable at a later point.
4. **Challenge: Create a finite-state machine for your player:**
   - *Possible use cases:*
     - Easy extension of the `Player` class
     - Cleaner code when reviewing or expanding different states
     - Decouples the `Player` class into smaller scripts per state

- *Getting started*: Create two additional scripts, one called `Idle` and one called `Walk`, and write code to alternate between the two. Create a function that takes in a state and switches to the correct one based on input from the player.
- *Why implement this?* This makes the player controller very robust and allows the creation of new types of player states very easily. Each state having its own script also makes for cleaner code and makes it easier to add and adjust logic for each state.

Expanding our world

This section of challenges focuses on expanding the world and the level we've created:

1. **Challenge: Expand our day/night cycle in the world**:
   - *Possible use cases*:
     - To create a planet system
     - To trigger events based on the time of day
     - To add depth and immersion with lighting
   - *Getting started*: Create a directional light and rotate it with a moon-like color that's softer than the Sun in our game.
   - *Why implement this?* A day/night cycle is an excellent addition to games that relate to time passing or need time to pass to trigger specific events. Using lighting in this way also adds realism to your game and can show off the visual effects you've worked hard to include in your game.
2. **Challenge: Add a door/portal to move the player to another level or room**:
   - *Possible use cases*:
     - When an area needs to be broken into chunks
     - When you want to switch environments
     - When you want the player to discover a secret area
   - *Getting started*: Add an object to our world and attach a script that loads a new scene.
   - *Why implement this?* Changing scenes is a common technique for loading levels or moving players to another scene for a conversation or a cutscene. It's a foundational skill that's useful in any project. The important thing when doing it is making sure you don't lose any data in the process. It also allows for less resource loading.

3. **Challenge: Add an interactive system to start a conversation with the NPC in the world:**
    - *Possible use cases*:
        - Triggering objects in a level
        - Starting a conversation
        - Triggering cutscenes
        - Picking up objects for the player
    - *Getting started*: Add a trigger when the player comes within a certain range of the NPC.
    - *Why implement this?* Interacting with the world, level, or NPCs is a fundamental way to give players the agency of setting their own pace in a game. It also sets up nice break points for triggering cutscenes or other in-game mechanics as needed. Of course, NPCs are often the way in which the game communicates with the player outside the UI.
4. **Challenge: Use the New Inherited Scene button in the Scene menu to create a variety of mushroom collectibles in the world:**
    - *Possible use case*: Creating multiple copies of an object that inherits the same properties
    - *Getting started*: Click the **New Inherited Scene** button and create a mushroom that's a variant of the one we created earlier.
    - *Why implement this?* Most likely, you'll have items in your game that are similar but not quite identical. Being able to group together some of their resources without needing to recreate them every time is a huge time saver.
5. **Challenge: Create or find a dialogue plugin and have a conversation with an NPC:**
    - *Possible use cases*:
        - Sharing a story
        - Adding flavor text to items or in-game moments
    - *Getting started*: Consider checking out plugins such as Dialogic or Mad Parrot Studios for implementing a dialogue system. Tie an action key when in range of the NPC and trigger the conversation. You can also create your own, but there are many different ways to go about it, so do some research first or try one of the mentioned plugins.

- *Why implement this?* Many games have players or characters that speak, whether it's through text or audio, so adding a dialogue system will be a boon to delivering all that information, whether it's narrative or tutorial.

6. **Challenge: Add visual effects (VFX) to the mushrooms that float in the world:**

- *Possible use cases:*
  - Conveying a narrative or gameplay mechanic
  - Adding flair to character animations
- *Getting started:* Add a 2D particle system to the collectible mushroom scene and explore the different settings for it.
- *Why implement this?* VFX can add polish and make a game feel dynamic and responsive. Whether the VFX is from an item in the world meant to draw the player's attention or the result of a cool move the player performs, VFX.

Cameras

Creating and managing cameras adds a lot to the immersion of games. Beyond them being the only way we see into the game world, they're also pivotal in cutscenes and

1. **Challenge: Add a camera shake to juice up your game without using a plugin:**

- *Possible use cases:*
  - When an in-game environment change occurs
  - When activating a specific item
  - When something happens to the player
- *Getting started:* Map a key to move the camera in one direction and then back to its starting point.
- *Why implement this?* Camera shake is a simple way to add immersion and feedback to your game at a very low cost of time and assets. It requires only some knowledge about the world space of your game and how cameras behave in Godot. Not only is this a useful feature for player feedback, but it can also be integral to cutscenes or gameplay.

2. **Challenge: Pan the first level of your game like an introductory cutscene:**

    - *Possible use cases*:

        - Showing player goals
        - Creating dynamic cutscenes
        - Showing different points of view in games
        - Switching player views by toggling between two characters

    - *Getting started*: Create a script to lerp a camera between two points.
    - *Why implement this?* This can be a great way to introduce goals that exist in levels for players. It can be used to highlight points on a map or in a world for onboarding or as points of interest. Being able to move cameras fluidly makes it much easier to highlight what players need to know about to be successful in the game.

3. **Challenge: Add the ability to zoom in on your player character:**

    - *Possible use cases*:

        - Show off cosmetics in-game
        - For photo mode with characters
        - Useful tools in strategy games when examining maps

    - *Getting started*:
    - *Why implement this?* Regardless of the type of game you're creating, there is a benefit to allowing the player to zoom in on various objects. Whether it's a map for a strategy game or to showcase cosmetics in a third-person action game, players love looking at the details and artwork the game and world create.

4. **Challenge: Add a toggle for switching from third-person to first-person view:**

    - *Possible use cases*:

        - Appreciate the character art on the player's body
        - For a photo mode
        - Get a different, or better, view of the world
        - Solve environmental puzzles

    - *Getting started*: Create another camera and have a key bind to toggle between which camera is the current camera in the scene.

- *Why implement this?* Adding the option between first and third person views can allow players to see their player character in the game world through a different lens.

5. **Challenge: Create a split-screen for local cooperative play**:

    - *Possible use cases*:

        - Allowing local co-op
        - Mechanics involving multiple cameras

    - *Getting started*: Create a second player controller and a set of player controls to control an additional player.
    - *Why implement this?* Local cooperative games are an excellent way to step into creating multiplayer games, even if the multiplayer is local. There is also an audience for local co-op games, as people want to play games together, such as successful titles including *It Takes Two* and *Castle Crashers*.

Shaders

1. **Challenge: Create a shader effect for a piece of the UI**:

    - *Possible use cases*:

        - Adding a burn/dissolve effect to items
        - Shift the tone of a piece of the UI to convey something different narratively/mechanically

    - *Getting started*: Check out *Godot Shaders* to get more practice with shader code.
    - *Why implement this?* The feedback provided to players' input can incentivize players to continue playing. For example, when opening a booster pack in *Balatro*, the burn effect of the booster pack fading is very satisfying. Similar moments can be achieved when adding that little bit of polish to your UI and through shaders, much more easily than you think.

2. **Challenge: Create a shader to stylize the sky or add clouds to your existing sky**:

    - *Possible use cases*:

        - Create a realistic-looking sky
        - Add clouds to your sky to give it character and depth

- *Getting started*: Explore how to create a custom shader script to apply to the **Sky** material in your world environment.
- *Why implement this?* There will probably be clouds and other effects you'll want to have included in your sky rather than a generic blank, blue sky. It's also an opportunity to explore more of the shader code we touched on briefly earlier.

Miscellaneous

If you're looking to push your skills further, these miscellaneous challenges provide creative ways to experiment with Godot's more advanced systems:

1. **Challenge: Make your game multiplayer by creating a networked lobby and allowing one player to join your level**:
   - *Possible use cases*:
     - Allow the creation of multiplayer games
     - Create lobbies for a multiplayer game with different modes
   - *Getting started*: Go through Godot's documentation relating to networking, specifically the first tutorial in it, to create a lobby.
   - *Why implement this?* Understanding how networking works in Godot opens the possibility of creating our own multiplayer games. Creating a simple lobby is a good introduction to the topic.
2. **Challenge: Have your NPC navigate in your level by choosing random points rather than predetermined ones**:
   - *Possible use cases*:
     - Makes the world or NPCs feel more life-like and adds depth
     - Can confine an NPC to an area rather than a set of points
     - Could be used for other creatures or objects in a game, not just NPCs
   - *Getting started*: Look through the A* Star algorithm of pathfinding and understand how it's performed in the engine.
   - *Why implement this?* Implementing this adds a level of realism that makes the world feel lived in. It's also a great way to learn an algorithm that's seen in a lot of different components of game development. Whether it's making an NPC feel more alive or creating an escort mission where the player must follow an NPC, the usage of pathfinding is high!

3. **Challenge: Use noise textures to create a heightmap for terrain:**
    - *Possible use cases:*
        - Create a variable terrain for a world
        - Create multiple maps of terrain quickly per level
        - Add biomes to your world
    - *Getting started:* Explore the **HeightMap3D** node and understand how noise textures create heightmaps.
    - *Why implement this?* This is a great opportunity to create a dynamic world for the player to explore without having to hand-craft each piece of the land. Once you have it in place for generating the height of each piece of ground, you can extend it to generate biomes and then specific objects in those biomes. It's a good space to start with terrain generation if that's something that interests you.

While this challenge list is not exhaustive, it's a deeper dive into all the topics we've discussed in this book. Ideally, these challenges will lead you to discover more ways to leverage the usage of Godot in your projects.

Summary

If you're reading this, then you've made it to the end of both the chapter and the book. Thank you for being on this journey with me as we explored Godot, C#, and the relationship between the two. While we didn't cover everything around these three topics, we did cover a substantial amount, such as writing C# scripts for Godot, understanding Godot's node system and how it uses resources, and how both Godot and C# interface with each other. Let's take a moment and review what you've accomplished in depth.

In this first part of this book, we spent time getting our ducks in a row. We spent time downloading the tools we'd need to develop with Godot in C# and configured our environment in a way suitable for us. After that, we dabbled briefly in computer science theory, discussing project structure and how best to organize our own.

The second part of the book is where we began creating our player controller and developing our level. At this point, the project came alive, and we were able to create a player to run around our world. We expanded that world by creating a UI and adding audio. We went further with our world and created an NPC to roam it and lighting to reflect all that we created before. Having multiple systems in place, we spent time refining them and discussing the importance of accessibility in game development.

With our project in a good place to pause and reflect, we explored the Godot community and the myriad of resources available through game jams, plugins, and other Godot content creators. The last piece of this project provided you with a challenge list for you to continue your Godot journey in a way that's best for you.

Good luck, and please share your projects with the Godot community at large!

14

Unlock Your Exclusive Benefits

Your copy of this book includes the following exclusive benefits:

- Next-gen Packt Reader
- DRM-free PDF/ePub downloads

Follow the guide below to unlock them. The process takes only a few minutes and needs to be completed once.

Unlock this Book's Free Benefits in 3 Easy Steps

Step 1

Keep your purchase invoice ready for *Step 3*. If you have a physical copy, scan it using your phone and save it as a PDF, JPG, or PNG.

For more help on finding your invoice, visit `https://www.packtpub.com/unlock-benefits/help`.

> **Note:** If you bought this book directly from Packt, no invoice is required. After *Step 2*, you can access your exclusive content right away.

Step 2

Scan the QR code or go to `packtpub.com/unlock`.

On the page that opens (similar to *Figure 14.1* on desktop), search for this book by name and select the correct edition.

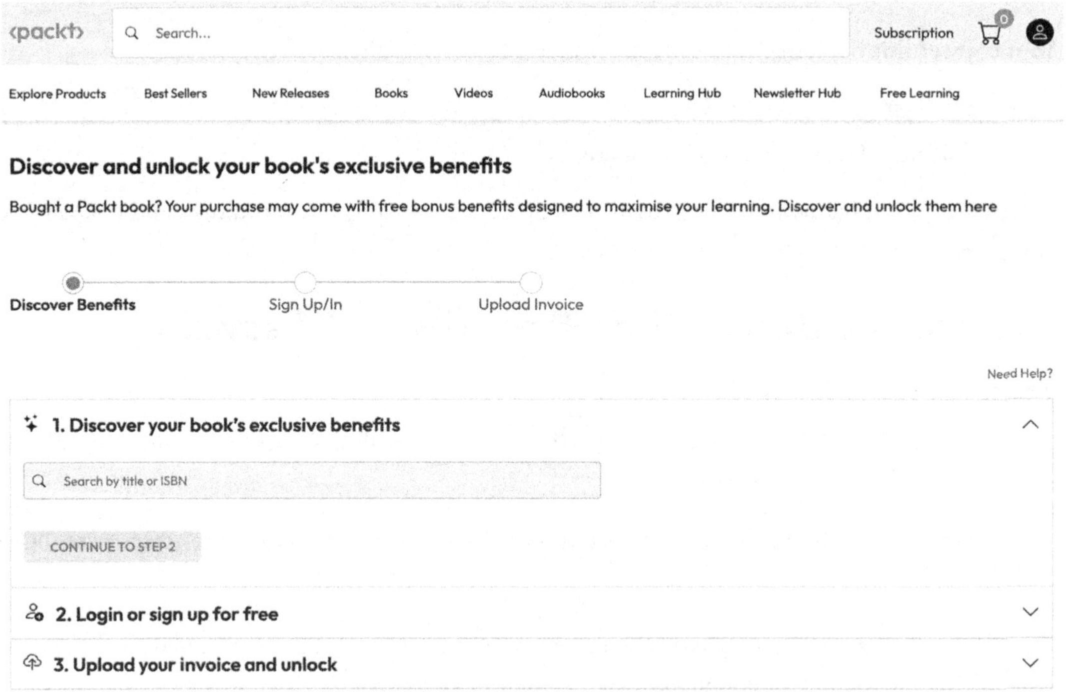

Figure 14.1: Packt unlock landing page on desktop

Step 3

After selecting your book, sign in to your Packt account or create one for free. Then upload your invoice (PDF, PNG, or JPG, up to 10 MB). Follow the on-screen instructions to finish the process.

Need help?

If you get stuck and need help, visit `https://www.packtpub.com/unlock-benefits/help` for a detailed FAQ on how to find your invoices and more. This QR code will take you to the help page.

Note: If you are still facing issues, reach out to `customercare@packt.com`.

Appendix: Transitioning from Godot 3 to Godot 4

Upgrading any project to a newer version of a tool can be a daunting and difficult task. However, the Godot community has done an excellent job of providing documentation to help users navigate the upgrade process. Alongside this, they have kept excellent and transparent records of the changes implemented in the engine. In this chapter, we'll be talking about how to transition from Godot 3 to Godot 4.

In this process, it's a boon to us, as users, that the Godot Engine is open source. It's possible to follow along on GitHub and watch changes be approved in real time, as well as seeing what the community is interested in pushing forward with new versions of the engine. With that in mind, there are a multitude of improvements. Some will require new workflows, while others are quality-of-life improvements.

To better understand this, we'll be breaking down some differences between Godot 3 and Godot 4. The goal of this chapter is to be able to make a more informed decision on whether you should transition to the newer engine version. As we go through this chapter, we will assume that an upgrade is wanted or needed and provide the necessary steps and changes to do so.

Our goals for this chapter are as follows:

- Analyzing engine version changes
- Discovering what's in Godot 4
- Preparing for an upgrade
- Using the project upgrade tool

Technical requirements

For this chapter, the technical requirements are the same as in *Chapter 1*.

All the code from this chapter is available in the GitHub repository here: `https://github.com/PacktPublishing/Game-Development-with-Godot-and-C-`.

Analyzing engine version changes

While we won't cover everything that's changed from Godot 3 to Godot 4, we can look at the largest systems impacted. This will be a brief overview to highlight what is new, what's changed, and what is completely removed. Throughout this section, we'll be referencing the Godot documentation quite a bit. If you're ever in doubt about what's available in an engine version, refer to the documentation.

Much like how anyone can contribute to the source code of the Godot Engine, so too can folks contribute to the Godot documentation. If you discover something in the engine that's not covered in the documentation, you should consider adding it. The odds are pretty good that if you are looking for the information, someone else is too! To learn how to contribute to the documentation, you can go to the GitHub repository here: `https://github.com/godotengine/godot-docs`.

The Godot documentation is regularly updated by the community and is often a great starting point for almost anything relating to the engine, including upgrading from Godot 3 to Godot 4. Here, the Godot community highlights the changes from Godot 3 to Godot 4: `https://docs.godotengine.org/en/stable/tutorials/migrating/upgrading_to_godot_4.html`.

The two important notes that stand out to me are the following:

- Godot 3 is stable and has a **long-term support** (**LTS**) status. Godot 3 has a lower likelihood of crashing or having unexpected output. However, Godot 4 has all the new features and bug fixes that 3 doesn't. Note that Godot 4 will have a longer support period than 3 did, which means that getting familiar with this version right out of the gate is a huge benefit. There is also better error reporting from the engine to better troubleshoot issues that might be occurring.
- Godot 4 changed to utilize the .NET SDK, and currently, exporting C# projects to iOS, Android, and HTML5 is not possible. While initially this may seem like a huge drawback for C# developers, the Godot community has stated that support will be implemented in later 4.x versions of Godot. The .NET support means there is more access to newer C# implementations, which, long term, will outweigh the lack of platform support that's currently there. Note that exporting to iOS, Android, or HTML5 is still possible in the GDScript version, just not in the C# one. However, inclusions of this are planned in Godot 4's roadmap.

For a more detailed overview, let's look at the differences between each version of the engine by the various systems included in it:

System	Godot 3	Godot 4
Rendering	GLES2/3	Vulkan, FSR, OpenGL (future DirectX support)
Lighting	Lightmaps	Global Illumination, **VoxelGI** node
Occlusion	Occluder nodes had to be manually set	Occluder culling is performed automatically
Shaders/visual effects	N/A	Sky shaders, volumetric fog, decals, noise texture options, computer shaders
Scripting	GDScript, C#, VisualScript	GDScript, C#
Physics	KinematicBody, single threaded, no cylinders, no height maps, no soft bodies	Cylinders, height maps, and soft bodies; multithreading; CharacterBody
Performance	N/A	Visual Profiler
Engine plugin	GDNative	GDExtension
Editor UI	N/A	Multiple windows, bi-directional support for languages, History dock for redo/undo
Localization	N/A	Bi-directional text

Figure Appendix.1: Differences between Godot 3 and Godot 4

It cannot be overstated that upgrading from Godot 3 to Godot 4 will be an undertaking. The amount of time is dependent on the size and systems of the project. Since much of the engine was refactored, the way components are processed will be vastly different from 3 to 4.

Thankfully, Godot will do some of the work for you. For example, some of the nodes in Godot 3 are named differently in Godot 4. What's called a **Spatial** node in Godot 3 is called **Node3D** in Godot 4. This renaming affects many scenes and scripts, but Godot automatically updates older node names when opening the project in Godot 4.

For more information about the changes to Godot from version 3 to 4, see `https://godotengine.org/article/godot-4-0-sets-sail/`.

We can't tell you whether it's worth upgrading your project. What we can tell you is what it will take to upgrade the project. Consider the amount of technical debt you're willing to take on if you're working to tight deadlines. If it's a passion project or a game jam, then consider the merits of upgrading or even recreating the project in Godot 4.

If you don't want to upgrade to Godot 4, that's completely understandable. Support for Godot 3.x has continued since Godot 4's release, and the community has stated that they plan to backport many compatible features to their LTS release of Godot 3, which is Godot 3.6. Don't feel too pressured to upgrade if some systems are too different or removed, or if it doesn't fit your current project.

Looking ahead, we'll now take a little bit of a deeper dive into what's new in Godot 4. We'll look at what systems have been rewritten and will be more difficult to upgrade, as well as which systems have remained the same and which ones have been completely removed.

Discovering what's in Godot 4

I've mentioned that there have been significant changes from Godot 3 to Godot 4. There has been core engine refactoring, new renderers for graphics, different node names, and so on. Let's take a moment and dive into some of the biggest changes to make a better assessment of how long upgrading to Godot 4 may take and what systems might be most impacted.

2D and 3D rendering

One of the biggest and long-awaited improvements to Godot has been its renderer. Godot's renderer is now in **Vulkan**, having migrated from OpenGL, which provides better performance for things such as shading, lighting, and shadows, plus better utilization of your CPU and GPU.

On the 2D side of things, the Godot community has not forgotten mobile or low-end devices. They have written their own renderer that is based on OpenGL. It can be used in 3D environments but has limits.

There is also support for AMD's Fidelity **FX Super Resolution** (**FSR 1.0**) and plans for support for FSR 2.0. If you're unfamiliar with FSR, it allows games to be run at a lower resolution and then uses upscaling to fill in the details. Even though it's made by AMD, it can be utilized by both AMD and NVIDIA graphics cards.

Also noted in the release of 4.0 is the goal of creating a renderer for DirectX 12 for better Windows and Xbox support.

Overall, the options available when it comes to rendering in Godot 4 make it extremely viable for multiple platforms.

TileSet and Tilemap editors

If you're a 2D developer, then the complete overhaul to the tilemap and TileSet editor will be a huge change in your pipeline. The **tilemap** system is how tiles are painted in environments, while the **TileSet editor** is what allows marking various tiles for physics and layering the tiles to add depth and foreground. The system has been completely rewritten from scratch and is a great upgrade and addition to Godot 4. It allows faster 2D level design and requires less work in a myriad of ways.

Some of the changes include the following:

- Adding layers to distinguish between foreground and background pieces
- Randomized painting to allow decorative/environment pieces to be added
- Granular options for collision layers on tiles
- Select tool for creating stamps to paint larger pieces
- No tile gaps!

With an entirely new system for creating and designing 2D levels, it is exciting to think about the added support and fixes that may come along in a future version of Godot 4. This new system is an excellent addition and one I personally love when teaching or doing game jams.

Shaders and VFX

Something that will benefit both 2D and 3D developers is the improvement on the shaders and visual effects side of the engine. The two exciting improvements we'll talk about are the volumetric fog nodes and improved shader language.

Volumetric fog has been added, with its own node, **FogVolume**, for placing the fog in specific locations within your environment. Along with this, both the **Shader Editor** and **Extended Shader Language (ESL)** have received a lot of updates to make them more accessible. Within ESL, new syntax features have been included that we will explore later in the book.

Other interesting components that have been added or improved on the VFX side are the following:

- **Decals**: Stamping materials over other materials to make objects in your environment look more realistic or add depth to the world you're creating
- **Sky shaders**: These special types of shaders allow users to draw sky backgrounds and update them dynamically

- **GPU-based particles**: These particles appear more life-like in that they have trails and collisions and can interact with objects in the environment, such as bouncing off surfaces
- **Noise filters**: Additional noise filters have been added that aid in procedurally generating content and making spaces feel more dynamic

One last thing to note about shaders in Godot 4 is the fact that the way shader files are named and stored has been augmented. In Godot 3, two file extensions for shaders exist, while in Godot 4, there is only one that is now supported. This will be important when preparing to upgrade our project, which we will discuss later.

Editor UX

The **Godot editor** itself has had some major overhauls when it comes to navigating it and interacting with its various systems. One major change is that Godot now supports multiple windows. This may seem trivial at first, but when working on multiple monitors or having a large list of properties on an object, it is very convenient. To enable multiple-window support, we can click the three dots that are next to any dock and select the **Make Floating** button, as seen in *Figure Appendix.2*.

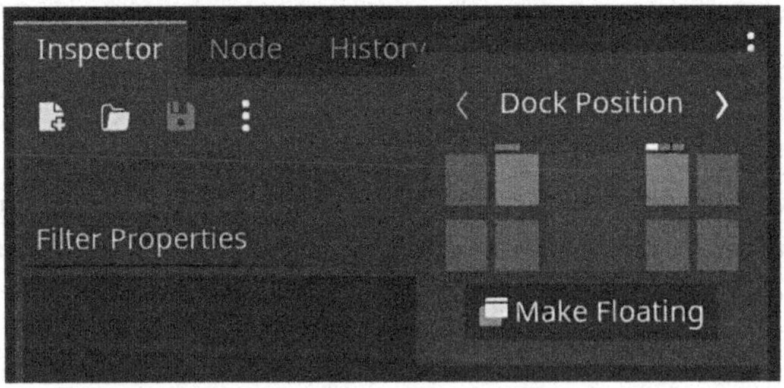

Figure Appendix.2: Creating multiple windows in Godot

It's exciting to see the changes from Godot 3 to Godot 4, especially since we'll be utilizing quite a few of them in the following chapters. Now that we're aware of some of these big system overhauls, let's step through what needs to happen to our project to prepare for upgrading to Godot 4.

Preparing for an upgrade

If you've gotten this far and have decided to upgrade your project, there are some important steps that you should take and know about beforehand. While you don't have to take these steps, it will make upgrading smoother and more enjoyable for you as a developer.

Creating a backup

The first thing is having a backup of the current project. If your project is housed in something such as a GitHub repository, make two new branches from it:

- The first would be a preserved Godot 3 version of the project as it is. This allows you to continue development on it if you choose to upgrade and don't like the changes or don't have the time to update your project to accommodate those changes.
- The second branch would be for upgrading, which you could then merge once you've thoroughly tested it.

In this way, you preserve the work you've done and allow yourself to see the time and effort it would take to upgrade to Godot 4.

Updating nodes

As we've mentioned in previous chapters, every object in a Godot scene is derived from a Node object. Earlier in this chapter, we also mentioned that some node names have been changed to better reflect the type of node that they are. There is one more area where nodes have changed, and this is related to tracking time and using tweens. Let's break down what this means and what has changed.

Tweens

Tweens are a useful tool when it comes to animating objects. Specifically, tweens animate objects dynamically and create smooth animations for when we don't know where an animation might end. In previous versions of Godot, tweens were housed under a separate node that had to be connected to the node you wanted to animate. However, the tweening system has been rewritten in Godot 4 to be easier to integrate with other nodes:

GDScript C#

```
Tween tween = GetTree().CreateTween();
tween.TweenProperty(GetNode("Sprite"), "modulate", Colors.Red, 1.0f);
tween.TweenProperty(GetNode("Sprite"), "scale", Vector2.Zero, 1.0f);
tween.TweenCallback(Callable.From(GetNode("Sprite").QueueFree));
```

Figure Appendix.3: The Godot documentation page for tweens

In *Figure Appendix.3*, function calls such as `TweenProperty` can be part of a script that's on the object you want to tween. Previously, you had to create separate nodes to create and trigger tweens. Now, tweens are created, managed, and destroyed in the script and are much more flexible when it comes to their usage. With this new system, tweening is extremely easy, and there are additional functions in the system to support things such as easing the tween and overlapping multiple tweens.

For more information on tweens and the `Tweener` object, you can find the documentation here: `https://docs.godotengine.org/en/stable/classes/class_tweener.html#class-tweener`.

Tracking time

Keeping track of time is often a critical component of game development. Whether it's tracking a time challenge or managing a day/night cycle, accessing time is a common and necessary feature.

In Godot 3, time functions were only accessible in OS functions, but now, in Godot 4, they have their own Time object.

When migrating from Godot 3 to Godot 4, it is important to make a note anywhere that functions relating to time are called, since they are now their own object in Godot. Noting this change in your project is a proactive step in upgrading so as not to further take away from development time.

More information on the Time class can be found in the documentation here: `https://docs.godotengine.org/en/stable/classes/class_time.html#class-time`.

Renaming shaders

In Godot 4, shaders have a different file extension. Previous versions of Godot supported both `.shader` and `.gdshader`. However, only support for `.gdshader` is carried into Godot 4. Reviewing the existing shaders in your project is another proactive step in ensuring a smooth transition from Godot 3 to Godot 4.

With these few steps taken to prepare for an upgrade to Godot 4, there is not much else left to do except one of two things:

- You can use Godot's project converter tool (which we will discuss in the next section)
- You can continue development in Godot 3.6 LTS

In the next section, we look at utilizing the project upgrade tool and note common errors you're likely to encounter when upgrading. These errors will most likely be from systems that have been completely rewritten and, therefore, there is no easy transition for changing them except manually.

Using the project upgrade tool

Along with the great documentation and videos from well-known Godot contributors, there is also the project upgrade tool. When Godot 4 was initially released, the tool was a standalone component that you had to use outside of the Godot Engine, but thanks to the wonderful community, it has now been merged into the engine.

Let's go through the steps, using an example game of mine. The source code for the game is included in the book's repository, which has been linked in the *Technical requirements* section.

I've left a game jam project folder in the project's repository called `convert-project`. If you aren't familiar with what game jams are, they are small prototypes created in X amount of time and centered around a theme or various challenges.

Importing the project

Once you've downloaded the ZIP file, you can open the Godot Engine and click the **Import** button that's on the right-hand side of **Project Manager**, as seen in *Figure Appendix.4*:

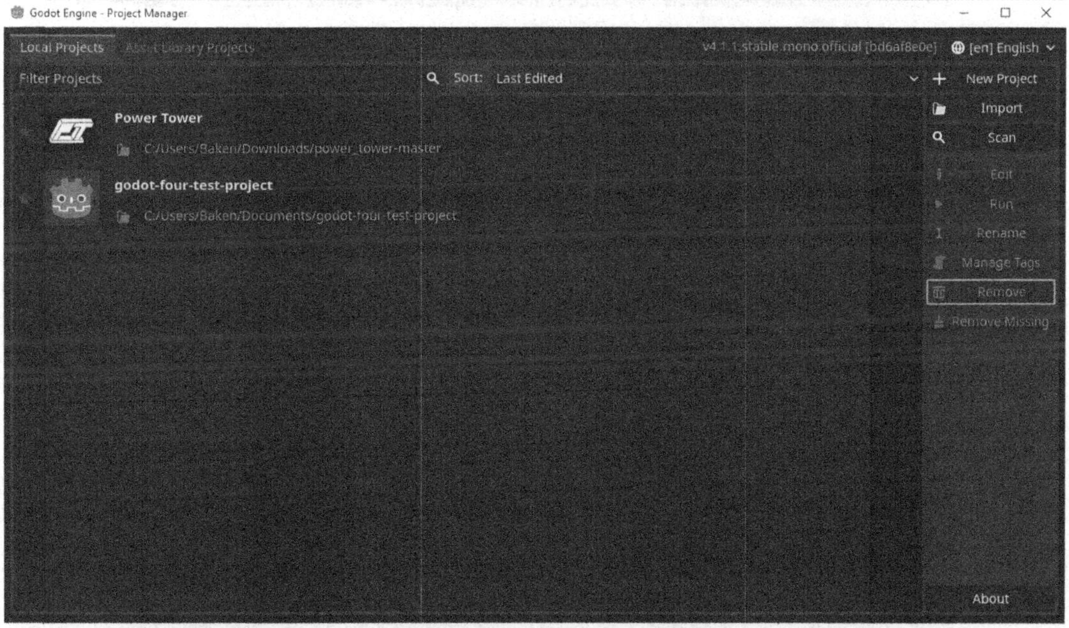

Figure Appendix.4: Available buttons in Godot 4 from the Project Manager

As soon as you click the **Import** button, a prompt will appear asking whether you'd like to convert the project to Godot 4. There are two buttons at the bottom – **Convert Full Project** and **Convert project.godot Only**. Click **Convert Full Project**.

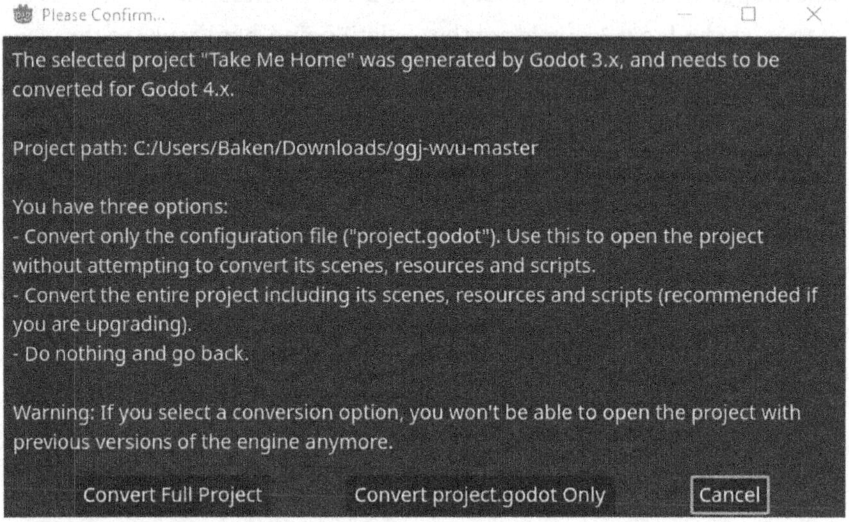

Figure Appendix.5: Project conversion tool prompt in Godot 4

Note

We would only suggest selecting the **Convert project.godot Only** button for specific use cases, such as the conversion tool failing.

Godot will then confirm that you want to upgrade the project with another prompt. Once we click **OK**, the project should now be in our project list, and we can open it up.

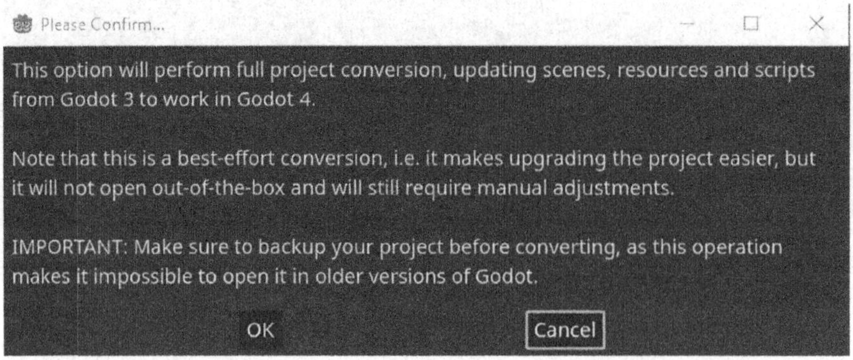

Figure Appendix.6: Confirmation on converting the project to Godot 4

Once the conversion is completed, you'll be able to review everything. Scenes and IDs for resources should be updated to the correct Godot 4 terminology. As *Figure Appendix.6* shows, it will still require you to go through the project piece by piece to make sure everything is functioning as it was in Godot 3. It's hard to say whether you should upgrade, depending on how far into the project you are, but either way, Godot is actively supporting both options until further notice.

Other Books You May Enjoy

If you enjoyed this book, you may be interested in these other books by Packt:

Godot 4 for Beginners

Robert Henning

ISBN: 978-1-83620-308-7

- Navigate and master the Godot 4 interface effectively
- Utilize nodes and scenes for structured game development
- Create dynamic 2D and immersive 3D game environments
- Manipulate lighting to enhance game visuals
- Script game mechanics using GDScript
- Implement key elements such as players, enemies, and collectibles
- Design engaging levels and manage game states

Learning GDScript by Developing a Game with Godot 4

Sander Vanhove

ISBN: 978-1-80461-698-7

- Develop your GDScript 2.0 programming skills from basic to advanced, emphasizing code cleanliness
- Harness Godot 4's integrated physics engine to control and manipulate in-game objects
- Design a vibrant and immersive game world by seamlessly integrating a diverse array of assets
- Master the art of processing input from various sources for enhanced interactivity
- Extend the reach of your game by learning how to export it to multiple platforms
- Incorporate simple multiplayer functionality for a dynamic gaming experience

Packt is searching for authors like you

If you're interested in becoming an author for Packt, please visit `authors.packt.com` and apply today. We have worked with thousands of developers and tech professionals, just like you, to help them share their insight with the global tech community. You can make a general application, apply for a specific hot topic that we are recruiting an author for, or submit your own idea.

Share your thoughts

Now you've finished *Game Development with Godot 4 and C#*, we'd love to hear your thoughts! Scan the QR code below to go straight to the Amazon review page for this book and share your feedback or leave a review on the site that you purchased it from.

`https://packt.link/r/1805124137`

Your review is important to us and the tech community and will help us make sure we're delivering excellent quality content.

Index

Symbols

A

B

C

D

E

F

G

W

Made in United States
Orlando, FL
04 November 2026

90201358R00243